A WINDFALL
OF MUSICIANS

A WINDFALL OF MUSICIANS

Hitler's Émigrés and Exiles in Southern California

Dorothy Lamb Crawford

Yale University Press / New Haven and London

Published with assistance from the Ann Loeb Bronfman Foundation and the foundation established in memory of Philip Hamilton McMillan of the Class of 1894, Yale College.

An earlier version of chapter 6, "Arnold Schoenberg," was first published as "Arnold Schoenberg in Los Angeles" in *Musical Quarterly* 86 (2002): 6–48. Reprinted by permission of Oxford University Press.

Set in Minion type by Integrated Publishing Solutions.
Printed in the United States of America.

The Library of Congress has cataloged the hardcover edition as follows:

Crawford, Dorothy L.
    A windfall of musicians : Hitler's émigrés and exiles in southern California / Dorothy Lamb Crawford.
        p. cm
    Includes bibliographical references and index.
    ISBN 978-0-300-12734-8 (hardcover : alk. paper)   1. Musicians—California, Southern.   2. California, Southern—Emigration and immigration.   3. Refugees, Jewish—California, Southern.   4. Jews, German—California, Southern.
    5. Exiles—United States.   I. Title.
ML200.7.C2C73 2009
780.9794'9—dc22

                                                                    2008051177

ISBN 978-0-300-17123-5 (pbk.)

A catalogue record for this book is available from the British Library.

10 9 8 7 6 5 4 3 2 1

This book is dedicated to the memories of

the late Leonard Stein

and

the late Herbert Zipper,

both of whom gave me invaluable encouragement

at the outset of this project;

and to the friends who saw me through it—

chief among them my beloved and steadfast daughter,

Susan.

CONTENTS

This book's subject arises from a historical coincidence: the rise of Adolf Hitler and the Nazi regime in 1930s Germany, and the simultaneous development of sound in the Hollywood film industry. The former caused many talented musicians (among, of course, thousands of other people) to flee Europe; the latter produced an unprecedented and far-reaching surge of musical development in Southern California. Inevitably, many European musicians found their way to California; together, they constituted Hitler's (unintentional) gift to American music.

Starting in early 1933, Hitler began banning, arresting, and curtailing the civil liberties of prominent musicians in Germany. His policies to exterminate Jews, socialists, homosexuals, and modernists became a wider threat as he invaded or assumed control of Austria, Czechoslovakia, Poland, France, and Hungary, formed an alliance with Italy, and exerted ideological pressure on Switzerland. Musicians from each of these countries also found their work banned or eliminated, their civil liberties denied, and their means of survival extinguished. An enormous exodus of highly trained musicians from Europe ensued. Some were prominent members of the Europe's intellectual and artistic elite; others were younger and not yet secure or well known.

These political refugees initially sought safety elsewhere in Europe. But because the global Great Depression created economic barriers to sustaining work in other nations, many emigrated to the United States. Conditions there were hardly better: insufficient opportunities in America's northeastern and midwestern cities, their own poverty, and the expenses of living in harsh climates led many to turn their hopes toward Los Angeles, which offered the possibility of work in film for performers and composers. Large studio orchestras were hiring masses of musicians who had been left without work when American vaudeville and burlesque theaters closed in the face of competition from the new talkies and musical films. The movie industry was hardly unknown to the émigrés: several important German producers and directors had been lured to Hollywood during the silent-film era, and Berlin was well aware of technical advancements there.

The émigrés were able, with some difficulty, to obtain citizenship. Unlike their European colleagues who were writers and visual artists, most of the musicians who migrated to Southern California remained there for the rest of their lives. A few who chose exile returned to Europe after the war. They all found anguish in resolving the conflicts of their double identities. The actual number of fleeing musicians who assembled in the area around Los Angeles has not been fully counted, but it may well constitute the greatest migration in Western musical history to one concentrated area, in one period, for one reason.

The emigration came in several waves: the first in 1933, at Hitler's assumption of power; another in 1938, following the Nazi occupation of Austria (the Anschluss) and Mussolini's enforcement of the Manifesto of Race in response to Hitler's initiative in the Rome-Berlin Axis Pact; and a third in 1940, with the Nazi occupation of France. Significantly, after the war's end the collective presence of European talent in and around Los Angeles became an attraction in itself, drawing additional émigré performers who had established careers elsewhere in the country to seek opportunities to perform and teach in Southern California. Many retired there.

Hitler's prejudices, displayed in a mocking exhibition of "Entarte (degenerate) Musik" in 1938, demanded the censorship of both concert programming and musical criticism, the replacement of opera and oratorio librettos written by or about Jews, the destruction of monuments to Jewish musicians, and elimination or revision of condemned compositions essential to the rich traditions of the "most German of all the arts." Meanwhile, ironically, the persecuted musicians who settled in Southern California brought a wealth of creativity to what had been musically a relatively sleepy region. A different irony lies in the fact that the Hollywood film studios themselves were quasi dictatorships. Their music departments created almost impossible conditions for newcomers eager to create film scores. For the European composers, Hollywood fully justified the title of Bertolt Brecht's 1941 poem about Los Angeles, "On Thinking about Hell."

Yet along with the White Russian refugees from the Bolshevik Revolution already established in and around Hollywood, the influx of European actors, directors, producers, and writers created culturally stimulating conditions in Los Angeles and the coastal communities of Pacific Palisades and Santa Monica. Émigré circles in these communities provided meeting places where new artistic collaborations and friendships were formed that might not have arisen in Europe. Over time, employment possibilities expanded beyond the film industry to academic institutions in Los Angeles and other nearby communities. Up and down the coast, émigré musicians found opportunities for fruitful leadership in new institutions such as the Music Academy of the West in Santa Barbara and the music department of the University of California, San Diego, in La Jolla.

Because it is clearly impossible to make this study all-inclusive, I have chosen to discuss composers and performers whose work in Southern California made a particular difference, and whose skills and nationalities represent the variety within the migration. My choice encompasses both the famous and the not-famous, both those who succeeded in their personal artistic goals in spite of emigration and those who experienced difficulties in doing so. I discuss their Californian compositions, many of which have been neglected. In approaching musicians who are well known and often written about, I sought untapped materials that might add new light or a different angle to the body of published work. Wherever possible, I have used written or recorded sources that enable the individuals to speak for themselves about the challenges posed to their art and attitudes by their ejection from Hitler's Europe. Stories of cultural disruption, tenacity and musical achievements in the face of limited comprehension, and influence on American music and musicians are the focus of this book. Because of the gathering of European talent, Southern California's music scene evolved from what was called a "cultural desert" in the 1930s to a "musical mecca" in the postwar years. Through the further legacy passed to subsequent generations by the Europeans' fortunate—and inevitably dispersed—American students, the influence of this musical migration continues to resound throughout America and beyond.

ACKNOWLEDGMENTS

First I wish to thank the Ann L. Bronfman Foundation for its bountiful support of the publication of this book, and for the enduring friendship and goodwill that accompanied the subvention. My gratitude for the initiation of this project belongs to Doris Kretschmer, at the time music editor of the University of California Press. The generosity of the Getty Research Institute for the History of Art and the Humanities in inviting me to participate in their Getty Scholars program for 1996–97, the topic of which was "Perspectives on Los Angeles: Narratives, Images, History," enabled me to carry out essential research in Los Angeles after I had moved from the area for family reasons. My Getty colleagues' discussions of their investigations into aspects of Los Angeles' buried past—difficult to uncover in such a habitually changing city—inspired me in my own excavations.

My work was further immeasurably helped by contributions from many individuals: Mirandi Babitz; Laurence Berman; Rosalind Bickel; Britta Marcus Björnsson; Kalman Bloch; Frans Boerlage; Sarah Bollinger; Garret Bowles; the late John Cage; Ann Caiger; Brendan Carroll; Lisbeth Castelnuovo-Tedesco; Anthony Christlieb; the late Don Christlieb; Pete Cotutsa; Paul Cummins; Aurelio de la Vega; Mark DeVoto; Jephta Piatigorsky Drachman; Timothy Edwards; Gail Eichenthal; Pia Gilbert; the late Jakob Gimpel; Peter Gimpel; Beverly Grigsby; Paul Guglietti; Bryan Harlan; Berndt Heller; Melodie Hollander; Marilyn Horne; Lucy Horwitz; Kathrin Korngold Hubbard for the estate of Erich Wolfgang Korngold; the late Louis Kaufman; Leon Kirchner; the late Gwendolyn Williams Koldofsky; the late Lotte Klemperer; Lisa Koch; Naomi Krasner; Gladys Nordenstrom Krenek; Steve LaCoste; Alan Lareau; Heidi Lesemann; Laurence Lesser; the late Natalie Limonick; Anthony Linick for the estate of the late Ingolf Dahl; William Malloch; David Martino; Carol Merrill-Mirsky; Annette Morreau; Virginia Newes; Marni Nixon; Nuria Schoenberg Nono; Deborah North for the estate of the late Leonard Stein; Vivian Perlis; Christopher Peter for Schott Music; Kathleen Powell for the estate of the late Mel Powell; the late David Raksin; Peter Redlich for the estate of the late Herta Glaz-Redlich; Ronald and Judith Rosen; Micha Schattner; Barbara

Zeisl Schoenberg; E. Randol Schoenberg; Lawrence and Anne Schoenberg; Alice Schoenfeld; Marje Schuetze-Coburn; David Seubert; the late Eudice Shapiro; Wayne Shoaf; Melvin Small for the estate of the late Hugo Stre-litzer; John L. Stewart; Elizabeth Surace; the family of the late Lorenzo Tedesco; Sheila Tepper; Michael Tilson Thomas; Gerald Turbow; John Waxman; Horst Weber; William Weber; Lawrence Weschler and the Weschler/ Toch family; the late Franzi Toch Weschler; James Westby; Lynne Withey; Peter B. Yates for his father, the late Peter Yates; Claude Zachary; Les T. Zador for the estate of his father, the late Eugene Zador; Maria Zahlten-Hall; and the late Herbert Zipper. I am deeply grateful for their help, and mourn the fact that so many have passed on.

MAIN CHARACTERS

	Birth Date	Country	Arrival in Area	Death Date	Place of Death
Composers					
Castelnuovo-Tedesco, Mario	1895	Italy	LA 1940	1968	LA
Dahl, Ingolf	1912	Germany	LA 1939	1970	Switzerland
Eisler, Hanns	1898	Germany	LA 1942–48	1962	East Berlin
Hollander, Frederick	1896	England	LA 1933–55	1976	Munich
Korngold, Erich W.	1897	Czechoslovakia	LA 1934	1957	LA
Krenek, Ernst	1900	Austria	LA 1947	1991	Palm Springs, CA
Schoenberg, Arnold	1874	Austria	LA 1934	1951	LA
Stravinsky, Igor	1882	Russia	LA 1940	1971	New York
Tansman, Alexandre	1897	Poland	LA 1941–46	1986	France
Toch, Ernst	1887	Austria	LA 1936	1964	Santa Monica, CA
Waxman, Franz	1906	Germany	LA 1934	1967	LA
Weill, Kurt	1900	Germany	LA 1937–38	1950	New York
Zador, Eugene	1894	Hungary	LA 1940	1977	LA
Zeisl, Eric	1905	Austria	LA 1941	1959	LA
Conductors					
Byrns, Harold	1903	Germany	LA 1948	1977	LA
Klemperer, Otto	1885	Germany	LA 1933	1973	Switzerland
Lert, Richard	1885	Austria	LA 1934	1980	LA
Popper, Jan	1908	Czechoslovakia	LA 1949	1987	Palo Alto, CA
Strelitzer, Hugo	1896	Germany	LA 1936	1981	LA
Walter, Bruno	1876	Germany	LA 1939	1962	Beverly Hills, CA
Zipper, Herbert	1904	Austria	LA 1972	1997	LA
Zweig, Fritz	1893	Czechoslovakia	LA 1947	1984	LA
Pianists					
Gimpel, Jakob	1906	Poland	LA 1938	1989	LA
Rubinstein, Artur	1887	Poland	LA 1941	1982	Switzerland

	Birth Date	Country	Arrival in Area	Death Date	Place of Death
Violinists					
Gimpel, Bronislav	1911	Poland	LA 1937	1979	LA
Szigeti, Joseph	1892	Hungary	LA 1940	1973	Switzerland
Cellists					
Feuermann, Emanuel	1902	Poland	LA 1941–42 (summers)	1942	New York
Piatigorsky, Gregor	1903	Russia	LA 1949	1976	LA
Harpsichordist					
Ehlers, Alice	1887	Austria	LA 1938	1981	LA
Singer					
Lehmann, Lotte	1880	Germany	Santa Barbara 1938	1976	Santa Barbara, CA
Stage Director					
Ebert, Carl	1887	Germany	LA 1948	1980	Santa Monica, CA
Dance Pedagogue					
Gilbert, Pia Wertheimer	1921	Germany	LA 1946–85		

Notes

LA = Los Angeles County, not necessarily the city; other cities within the county are named when known.
When a second date is shown in the "Arrival in Area" column, it indicates the date of departure. No attempt
is made to name the place of residence; the place of death may also be inaccurate.

1

Europe

A school dropout at age sixteen, Adolf Hitler based his life's ambition "to become the people's tribune" on the example he found in the arrogant, destructive hero of Wagner's early revolutionary opera, *Rienzi*. ("In that hour it began," he boasted to Winifred Wagner at the Bayreuth Festival in 1939.[1]) In 1908, rejected in his application to art school in Vienna at age nineteen, he set himself the ambitious project of attempting to complete the text, design the theater sets, and to compose the music for a mythic play that Wagner had outlined and rejected. "It was as though a demon had taken possession of him. Oblivious of his surroundings, he never tired, he never slept. He ate nothing, he hardly drank ... for he was too completely wrapped up in his work," remembered August Kubizek, a childhood friend who was studying music in Vienna at the time, while trying to help Hitler with the craft of composition. "Listening to Wagner ... transported [him] into the blissful regions of Germanic antiquity, that ideal world which was the lofty goal for all his endeavors." These preoccupations contributed at the time to Hitler's youthful conception of "the Reich of all the Germans," the ideal state in which he planned to realize social reforms through what he called the "Storm of the Revolution." His plans included ten "mobile Reich's orchestras," which would spread knowledge of classical works to all corners of the Reich. Hitler kept a pocket notebook in which he wrote the titles of the works he heard in Vienna concerts, their composers, and any conductors he thought well of, for future selection in programs for these orchestras.[2]

Between 1909 and 1914, his homeless but formative years in Vienna, Hitler assimilated the ideas of Houston Stewart Chamberlain, a Wagner expert and Cosima Wagner's favorite propagandist for her husband's work and theories. Chamberlain published widely the racial notion, spawned in Vienna following his own studies of Wagner, that true Germans derived from the Aryan group of Indo-European peoples; that Aryans were nobles or lords, the source of the best in "Germandom," which was being contaminated by the influence of Jews. "It is not a matter of whether we are Aryan but whether we *become* Aryan," Chamberlain wrote in 1915. He married Wagner's daughter Eva and moved from Vienna to Bayreuth. Immediately following his first meeting with Hitler at Bayreuth in 1923, the year of Hitler's imprisonment authorship of *Mein Kampf*, Chamberlain wrote to Hitler, "You are not a fanatic. A fanatic heats the head; you warm the heart," and proclaimed him the god-sent leader of the Germans.[3] With the strong support of the Wagner family, Hitler made Bayreuth his court as he grew in power.

By 1926 Berlin had become a "sinners' Tower of Babel," in Hitler's opinion.[4] The idealistic Weimar Republic had opened doors to Jewish leadership in both politics and culture. In contrast to musically conservative Vienna, Germany's capital was a hotbed for musical experiment: modernist compositions, boldly conceived modernist stagings of opera, and the new encroachment of American jazz into widely popular cabaret, all of which were attracting highly talented composers, playwrights, stage directors, conductors, and performers to Berlin from other nations. There were constant changes in musical language and style, reflecting the postwar political, economic, and moral turbulence in the Weimar period. Expressionism—resulting from artists' demands for psychological truth in their rebellion against the rigid mores of the late nineteenth century—had, beginning in the first decade of the twentieth century, forced drastic changes in both the languages and attitudes of new music. After World War I, a new generation of composers continued to employ the style, if not always the essence, of this subjective mode in the arts. However, the disillusionment produced by the chaos of Germany's 1923 hyperinflation contradicted the hyperemotionalism of expressionism, which gave way to a pragmatic look backward to cool objectivity and balance, the ideals of classicism. Artists embraced the psychologically distancing neoclassicism and—particularly in Germany—*Neue Sachlichkeit* (the New Objectivity), a reactionary turn to systems of order and attitudes of emotional reserve.[5] Functional, matter-of-fact, socially conscious applications such as community music, workers' choruses, mechanical music, radio and film music, miniature operas, music for children, and instructional music for amateurs were further extensions of the new aesthetic.

Between 1923 and 1933 the pace of change in the arts was overwhelming, particularly in Berlin. With the assimilation of new technologies, of jazz and other cabaret styles, there were so many crosscurrents merging in new composition that the city seemed a host to constant musical fads. The Austrian composer Ernst Krenek, who reflected many of the current stylistic changes in his own music, later recalled that "in Berlin, which had become the center of the European music industry, a new, epoch-making, and definite style was announced about every season. . . . At least a new composition had a real chance: after all, it was sure of being performed!"[6] Theaters and opera houses, following princely traditions of patronage, were subsidized in the Weimar Republic by the governments of the states. This presented an ideal situation for composers.

The chief of music in the Prussian Ministry of Culture, Leo Kestenberg, a concert pianist and passionate educator, was a Slovakian Jew who recognized extraordinary gifts and leadership in many of his recommendations for state positions in theaters and academic institutions. Kestenberg had studied with the pianist and composer Ferruccio Busoni, and after Busoni's death he appointed Arnold Schoenberg to take over Busoni's master class in composition at the Prussian Academy of the Arts in Berlin. The 1925 announcement of this prominent appointment was greeted with a strongly worded anti-Semitic article by a Berlin music critic, protesting Schoenberg's induction as "a provocation [intending] a contest of strength between Germandom and—and now we must also be quite frank—the specifically Jewish spirit in music. . . . What sort of Judaism Schoenberg belongs to and wishes to be part of he has not only demonstrated with great clarity but also stated in so many words. His appointment . . . represents . . . a stupidity of the first order. . . . The days of the current musical regime in Prussia are counted."[7]

Schoenberg had so frequently suffered anti-Semitic attacks in Vienna that by 1924 he had begun developing his own variant of Zionism, which was intended to rescue European Jews from impending doom in Europe and resettle them in a "new Palestine" located outside the Promised Land, so that "Mohammedan enemies" would not be a threat to them. The Berlin critic's 1925 attack spurred Schoenberg to begin a play, *Der biblische Weg* (1926–27), which, like his opera *Moses und Aron*, reflects the conflicts he foresaw in his quest to save European Jewry. These religiously based works, both to some extent autobiographical, reveal the depth of Schoenberg's commitment to spiritual striving. A text he wrote in 1925 for a short choral work indicates his inner struggle in this tumultuous period:

> *You must not honor small things!*
> *You must believe in the spirit!*
> *Immediate, without feeling*
> *And without self.*
> *You must, you Chosen One, you must,*
> *You must remain yourself.*[8]

In 1926 Hitler acted to strengthen the failing Nazi Party's focus on his goals. He named Josef Goebbels as Nazi Party leader (*Gauleiter*) of Berlin and took him to Bayreuth to meet the seventy-year-old Chamberlain, who, in this last year of his life, became one of Goebbels's chief influences. Who better should Hitler's chosen propagandist consult about the "most German of the arts" than the Wagner expert and senior theorist on the superiority of the Aryan race?[9] Crippled since childhood, Goebbels was a supreme opportunist, gifted but frustrated intellectually. He had joined the Nazi Party in 1924. He had written an expressionist novel in 1926 that had not been published; he had also called for the expulsion of Hitler from the Nazi Party that year, but easily switched his allegiance to become so masterful at carrying out orders to change cultural life in Berlin that in 1928 Hitler named him the party's propaganda leader.

Only a few days after arriving in Berlin in January 1926 to take up his prestigious and seemingly secure teaching position, Schoenberg completed the *Three Satires* for mixed chorus, op. 28, the texts of which—possibly written by his second wife, Gertrud Schoenberg—reflected negatively upon the latest fashions in modern music, most specifically upon Igor Stravinsky's neoclassicism. In a 1925 New York interview, Stravinsky had announced, "I despise all of modern music. I myself don't compose modern music at all nor do I write music of the future. I write for today. In this regard I don't want to quote names, but I could tell you about composers who spend all their time inventing a music of the future. Actually this is very presumptuous."[10] A German translation of Stravinsky's interview found its way to the hypersensitive Schoenberg, and, with the publication of his *Three Satires* immediately after their January 1926 completion, the battle lines were drawn between Stravinsky's return to eighteenth-century styles and Schoenberg's method of composition with twelve tones, which he had predicted in 1921 would be the music of the future. This open clash of ideas in 1925–26 grew gradually into an apostles' feud that would keep the two composers from speaking years later when they both lived in Los Angeles, and would divide both Europeans and Americans active in modern music into hostile ideological camps for more than a quarter of a century.

In the 1920s the Viennese composer Ernst Toch was rising to the forefront of musical modernism in Germany. A prodigy, self-taught amid a ghetto family that did not value his talent, Toch had earned his musical education by winning composition prizes. He had become an established professor of composition at the Mannheim Conservatory of Music and had earned a doctorate in music from the University of Heidelberg. His works were widely performed by the top concert artists of the day. B. Schott, the foremost German music publisher, gave him a contract that provided him considerable publicity and a steady income outside his teaching. In 1927 the successful Baden-Baden festival premiere of his one-act chamber opera, *The Princess and the Pea,* spawned Toch's passion for composing operas. Two years later he left his teaching career to compose in Berlin, secure in the expectation that performances and publications of his works would support him and his family. In the year 1930, Toch's orchestral works alone received an average of one major performance a week in Germany. Settled with his wife and baby daughter in a fashionable suburb of Berlin, he wrote to his sister that he was living in paradise.[11] His continuing preoccupation was to compose opera, the chief musical currency of the time for classical composers in Berlin.

An important stimulant to modern opera was the conductor Otto Klemperer, appointed in 1927 by Kestenberg to lead the Kroll Opera, which was conceived to serve a middle-class audience in Berlin and to encourage new forms of artistic expression fostered by the Weimar Republic. Over the four-year span of Klemperer's reign at the Kroll (1927–31), these two concepts came into profound contradiction: Kroll's middle-class audience was ripe to embrace Nazi ideology and to reject all forms of modernism. Nevertheless, Klemperer brought new operas to the Kroll and modernized the staging of established repertoire. He had been propelled in his meteoric early career by Gustav Mahler's recommendations and, like Mahler, had converted from Judaism to Catholicism. Called by a leading music critic "perhaps the best theater conductor in Germany," Klemperer took as his model Mahler's practice of involving himself in all aspects of operatic production.[12] Klemperer's experiments at the Kroll inspired opera houses in Dresden, Leipzig, and Frankfurt to adopt modernism. Opera became an open concept embracing musical theater. Stravinsky, Paul Hindemith, Leoš Janáček, Schoenberg, Krenek, Kurt Weill, and Toch were encouraged by performance opportunities to compose new works for the stage.

Stimulated by the new dramatic possibilities in opera, the Berlin-born actor and stage director Carl Ebert, trained by the renowned Austrian theater director Max Reinhardt, decided to turn his talents to opera and musical theater when he accepted a post as general director of the Darmstadt State Theater in 1927. That year, when Klemperer took over at the Kroll and Ebert at Darmstadt, forty-three new operas were premiered in Germany; a year later there were sixty premieres.[13]

At this time in his career, Klemperer rejected expressionist attitudes and adopted the New Objectivity. In 1928 Schoenberg commented in his diary on Klemperer's new approach: "He makes music in a way that is less laden with feeling than is usual here. . . . We are indeed living in an anti-romantic period."[14] Stravinsky's jazz-influenced *Histoire du soldat* exemplified the new attitude. Klemperer's 1928 performance of this work at the Kroll, with Ebert cast as the Narrator, met with vehement whistling, hissing, and shouting from the audience, which by this time was dominated by Nazi rowdies—Goebbels's street fighters, primed for battles and brawls—who objected to Klemperer's Jewish origin, were hostile to the ideals of the Weimar Republic, and resisted new works. Yet Klemperer regularly gave the first Berlin performance of each new work composed by Stravinsky, three times with the composer himself as soloist.

In his dominant position at the Kroll, Klemperer was a powerful advocate for the Weimar theory that art and society were now sweeping to a new synthesis; art would follow life as well as inevitable social and economic change.[15] The Austrian Jewish writer Stefan Zweig described this period, when "All values were changed, and not only material ones; the laws of the State were flouted, no tradition, no moral code was respected, Berlin was transformed into the Babylon of the world. . . . In the collapse of all values a kind of madness gained hold particularly in the bourgeois circles which until then had been unshakable in their probity."[16] The expression of widespread cynicism and licentiousness that characterized Berlin life in the 1920s allowed popular and classical music to be mixed with new ease and energy. The younger generation of composers took up these ideas; in the hectic musical ferment of Berlin they learned to become quick-change artists, readily adapting to new fashions in the arts.

Ernst Krenek, a Viennese of Czech descent, came to Berlin barely out of his teens in 1920, when his teacher, the Viennese composer Franz Schreker, was appointed by Kestenberg to direct the Berlin Conservatory of Music (Hochschule für Musik Berlin). As an expressionist in the mid-1920s, Krenek published polemics against Schoenberg's twelve-tone technique.[17] When the Viennese pianist and composer Artur Schnabel, also living in Berlin, introduced him to the American music of George Gershwin, Irving Berlin, and Vincent Youmans, Krenek decided to repudiate the atonal expressionism he had developed since 1922, in order to write a light opera that would "make quicker money than with the heavier type of music." He told Schnabel he would imitate popular music, "and probably do it better."[18] The result was *Jonny spielt auf* (*Johnny Strikes Up*). Its main character was derived from a jazz-influenced hit composed in 1920 by the successful Berlin cabaret composer Frederick Hollander (born Friedrich Hollaender), about a black barroom violinist whose music wins a new "bride" every night.[19] The sensational 1927 premiere of Krenek's opera in Leipzig eclipsed the premieres of other new German and Austrian operas, scandalized the public, and sent this work on to productions in a hundred cities—including at New York's Metropolitan Opera—and translation into eighteen languages. The fame and wealth he gained from *Jonny's* overwhelming success bewildered Krenek. He returned to Vienna to live, reverting for a while to a compositional style derived from Schubert. In 1930, worried that he was reaching a dead end, Krenek reversed himself again to become an intransigent adherent of Schoenberg's twelve-tone method. His first twelve-tone opera, *Karl V,* composed for the Vienna State Opera and scheduled for production in 1933, probed the morality of a dictator.

Back in Berlin, Kurt Weill, in his collaborations with the Communist poet and playwright Bertolt Brecht, was at the forefront of the new view of art in its relation to contemporary German life, beginning with the *Mahagonny Songspiel,* a small-scale musical composed for the 1927 Baden-Baden music festival. Weill's subsequent work with Brecht, *Die Dreigroschenoper* (*The Threepenny Opera,* an adaptation of John Gay's *The Beggar's Opera*), particularly defined the cynical "Weimar style." Written quickly in 1928, *The Threepenny Opera* was intended as an antithesis to sentimental operetta in its simplicity, its cabaret-like satirical numbers, its deliberate musical distortions, and its debt to jazz. It ran for a year in Berlin; within a week of its opening it had been booked for more than fifty theaters all over Germany, and it became an unexpected international success. Recordings and a film version made the tunes available everywhere. The Frankfurt critic and Marxist social theorist Theodor Wiesengrund Adorno called it "the most important event in musical theater since [Alban Berg's] *Wozzeck*."[20] Like Krenek, Weill became for the first time secure financially with this suc- . cess. In 1930, however, his partnership with Brecht was irreparably disrupted by a lawsuit over the filming of the work. Brecht turned to Hanns Eisler to compose the incidental music for his play, *Die Massnahme* (*The Measures Taken*), about the violent means necessary to political rebellion, and Weill abandoned his pseudojazz, Brecht-dominated style to compose his most ambitious opera, *Die Bürgschaft* (*The Guarantee*), 1930–31, on the topical subject of the tyranny of money and power.

Eisler, one of Schoenberg's favored students in Vienna and the 1924 winner of Vienna's Künstlerpreis (Artist's Prize), had become convinced in 1925 that the city's musical conservatism would be a dead end for him. He moved that year to Berlin, where his older siblings, Gerhard Eisler and Ruth Fischer (born Elfriede Eisler), were active Communists. In 1926 he applied for and formally registered his membership in the German Communist Party, but, lacking income, he neglected to pay his dues and was not a member in good standing. Imbued that year with his new mission to change the role of music in society, Eisler rebelled against Schoenberg's influence, announcing that he was "bored by modern music, it is of no interest to me; much of it I even hate and despise. If possible I avoid hearing or reading it."[21] In 1927 he met Brecht in Berlin and came under his lasting influence. While Eisler gained success composing music for leftist theater, agitprop groups, cabaret, and films, as well as marching songs, workers' songs, and choruses, he also wrote essays attacking modernism in music as "death rattles," and modern music festivals as "downright stock exchanges, where the value of the works is assessed and contracts for the coming season are settled." He saw the anarchic character of modern music as an obvious sign of crisis in bourgeois music, and took on the idea of "distancing" implied in Brecht's theory of alienation. Music, Eisler wrote, must be "constructed to avoid expressing anything pathetic, banal or magnanimous. Ideally it should be refrigerated, should not stir the inner emotions of the listeners." On the other hand, he also wrote that *Tendenzmusik* (didactic music) must stir the emotions of militant workers.[22] These contradictions were a natural outcome of the rapid pace of Eisler's musico-political career. His workers' songs became internationally known. He traveled to the Soviet

Union in 1930 and 1931, and in 1932 he became a committee member of the Soviets' International Music Bureau.

Berlin's satirical cabarets thrived in the Weimar atmosphere of cynicism, and they particularly welcomed jazz. Cabaret writers and composers were predominantly Jewish, and as anti-Semitism became more widespread, comic skits created by Jews—and satirizing Jews—became cynical in-house jokes between Jewish comedians and their audiences. They laughed at themselves, but they also laughed at Hitler. Frederick Hollander found his first artistic home in Berlin cabarets, where he could apply his multiple skills as pianist, composer, writer, and director. London-born and Berlin Conservatory–trained, Hollander had studied composition with Engelbert Humperdinck and came from a distinguished family of Berlin musicians, most of whom had worked in Germany with Max Reinhardt, as had Hollander himself.[23]

In 1927 Hollander became the pianist for a group of German Jewish jazz players, the Weintraub Syncopators, and directed them as they became widely popular. One member of the group was the twenty-one-year-old Berlin Conservatory student, Franz Waxman (born Wachsmann), whose talents as an arranger, composer, and conductor Hollander recognized and fostered. While Hollander was busy writing cabaret revues, operettas, and incidental music for plays, he also began composing scores for silent films produced by Berlin's Universum Film Aktiengesellschaft (Ufa), which dominated the growing German film industry.[24] Hollander's songs (among them, "Ich bin von Kopf bis Fuss auf Liebe eingestellt," or "Falling in Love Again") for the 1930 sound-film *The Blue Angel* propelled Marlene Dietrich to worldwide success. Hollander assigned Waxman, then twenty-four, the jobs of orchestrator and conductor for the film, which was directed by Erich Pommer, a powerful German film figure also well established in Hollywood.

In 1928 Goebbels was elected—as one of only ten Nazis—to the Reichstag. The government announced in September the sudden dismissal of the Berlin-born conductor Bruno Walter from his post as general music director of the Berlin Municipal Opera. Walter, perhaps the best known and most revered of Jewish musicians, learned about his dismissal through the newspapers.[25] By 1929 the right-wing press was calling Klemperer's Kroll Opera a "Jewish Opera," in which "what goes on has nothing to do with German artistic spirit," and making demands that the company be closed.[26]

Marlene Dietrich with Frederick Hollander, ca. 1930. Courtesy of Melodie Hollander.

After the October 1929 New York Stock Exchange crash reverberated in Europe, rising unemployment, poverty, and discontent darkened the German political atmosphere. In this situation, Goebbels's organizational and propaganda skills became so effective that in September 1930 Nazis were elected to 107 seats in the Reichstag. Listening to the election results with Walter, the Austrian cellist Emanuel Feuermann, at age twenty-eight then the youngest professor at the Berlin Conservatory, remarked, "It's all over with Germany; all over with Europe."[27] Hitler, in his hatred of both Jews and Communists, blamed "cultural Bolsheviks" for the freedoms of Weimar culture.

The Weimar government, pressed financially by the worldwide Depression, was unable to resist the newly strengthened Nazi Party. In 1931 the Kroll Opera was closed, and its staff—including Klemperer—was absorbed into the Berlin State Opera. As he lost the leadership post that had offered him so much creative freedom, Klemperer, who had suffered since he was twenty from bipolar disorder, went into a prolonged phase of depression and began doubting his abilities as a conductor.

The same year, Hollander founded his own political cabaret, which he called the *Tingel-Tangel-Theater*. In this venture, Hollander's parodies of Hitler and the Nazis' attitudes toward the Jews broke all attendance records. The *Film-Kurier* called Hollander "Friedrich the Great in this sort of cabaret."[28] Goebbels targeted Hollander for revenge; Nazi spies were planted in the audiences. By 1932 they no longer bothered to disguise themselves but sprang onto the stage to spit on Hollander's piano fingers. Hollander himself seemed fearless in his disrespect and in the liveliness of his ideas. His method was to grab the audience's attention through his use of rhythm, parodying, for example, the rabble-rousing speech technique Hitler used when he proclaimed the faults of the Jews.[29] But such parody became useless in 1932, as Hollander's mentor Max Reinhardt—who had discovered, trained, and fostered many of Berlin's finest theater and musical talents—lost his German theater empire to the Nazis and was forced to retreat to Austria. In the spring of 1933 Hollander and his wife returned to Berlin from a London film assignment (for Pommer) as their apartment was being searched by the Gestapo. Seeing their taxi arriving, Hollander's mother-in-law signaled to them from the apartment window not to enter. Hollander's blonde Aryan wife, Hedi, commandeered the taxi. With Hollander crushed under a coat to the floor of the automobile, they escaped through a cordon of Nazis back to the Berlin train station. They bought tickets on the first train leaving Berlin and made their way to Paris.[30] Hollander's protégé, Franz Waxman, beaten in the streets by Nazis, followed soon after.

Immediately after Hitler's January 30, 1933, appointment as chancellor, the press, radio, films, music, publishing, and the arts came under the authority of Goebbels, who laid out the Nazi rationale regarding music leadership in Germany: "Judaism and German music are opposing forces which by nature stand in glaring contradiction to each other. The war against Judaism in German music—for which Richard Wagner once assumed sole responsibility" was to be carried out by "a united people," and not by "outsiders," namely the Jews.[31] Stefan Zweig commented on the jolting new awareness Hitler brought: "The Jews of the twentieth century had for long not been a community. They had no common faith, they were conscious of their Judaism rather as a burden than as something to be proud of. . . . To dissolve themselves in the common life was the purpose for which they strove. . . . Only now, for the first time in hundreds of years, the Jews were forced into a community of interest . . . the ever-recurring—since Egypt— community of expulsion."[32] Jews, liberated in the Weimar Republic, were forced into a community of expulsion.

A Nazi campaign was intensified to force prominent musicians to emigrate. Walter was shut out of his own Leipzig Gewandhaus rehearsals by the Saxony government, on the pretense that the safety of the musicians could not be guaranteed if public demonstrations occurred. Four days later, Walter's request for police protection for his Berlin Philharmonic concert was turned down, and the government announced that an Aryan should conduct the concert. Richard Strauss stepped in, and Walter moved to Austria, where he had been associated with the Salzburg Festival since 1925.

In early February 1933, Klemperer's stylized production of *Tannhäuser* at the Berlin State Opera was assaulted in the press as a "presumptuous attack on Wagner and German culture" and had to be withdrawn. The general administrator of the Prussian state theaters, Heinz Tietjen, told Klemperer, "There will be no scandal. . . . This government knows when there is going to be a scandal." After the February 27 burning of the Reichstag, and the parliament's subsequent move into the abandoned Kroll Opera, Klemperer wrote to his thirteen-year-old son Werner, "Never talk about politics, get on quietly with your work, and live *privately*."[33] Klemperer's Berlin performance of Beethoven's Ninth Symphony on March 30 was canceled. On April 4 he took his son out of school and left Berlin for Switzerland. His wife baked money into a cake and followed with their daughter. In May notice of his dismissal from the Berlin State Opera was sent to Klemperer. He settled his wife and children in a rented apartment in the Schönbrunn Palace in Vienna. In Florence for the first Maggio Musicale, Klemperer met by chance a woman from Los Angeles, who suggested that he take the post of principal conductor of the Los Angeles Philharmonic. He continued to dismiss all thought of Los Angeles until he learned that a warrant had been issued for his arrest should he return to Germany.[34] In June 1933 the remaining four years of Klemperer's Berlin State Opera contract were canceled. With no other openings available to him in America, Klemperer set out in October to lead the Los Angeles Philharmonic, leaving his family in Vienna.

Others dismissed from Germany in the early months of 1933 included Carl Ebert, whose innovative opera successes in Darmstadt had brought him back to Berlin to succeed Bruno Walter as general director of the Municipal Opera. In his two years' tenure in that position, Ebert fused the Municipal Opera's company of stars into an ensemble and established a partnership with the conductor Fritz Busch that lasted until Busch's death in 1951. Although Ebert was not Jewish, his office was bugged; his socialist and modernist tendencies were ascertained. In March 1933 he and Busch were forced out of the Municipal Opera by a mob of storm troopers (members of the Nazi Sturmabteilung).[35] In the face of Goebbels's proposals that they continue their artistic careers under Nazi control, Busch and Ebert left Germany in protest.

In the spring of 1933 the Nazis undertook a "cleaning up" of the Berlin Conservatory. Hugo Strelitzer, a Berlin-born opera coach and choral conductor who had worked at opera houses in Freiburg, Cologne, and Berlin, was dismissed from the faculty and incarcerated in the SS fortress prison in Berlin. With the help of the conductor Wilhelm Furtwängler, he was released to work as an opera coach in the Jüdische Kulturbund, the cultural organization set up to ghettoize Jewish arts and artists.[36] Strelitzer remained in Berlin until the Nuremberg Laws of 1935 deprived him of any professional function. In 1936 Frances Cheney, a young woman from a prominent Southern Californian family, helped his emigration to the United States.

The cellist Feuermann was also ejected in the spring of 1933 from his post at the Berlin Conservatory. A prodigy who had made his debut at the age of eleven with the Vienna Symphony Orchestra under Felix Weingartner, he had gained successful teaching posts from the age of seventeen. Touring was the logical escape from Nazi persecution for solo performers, and in 1934–35 Feuermann set off on his first world tour; the following season another world tour included performances in Los Angeles with Klemperer.

In April 1933 the final three concerts of Artur Schnabel's Beethoven piano sonata cycle in Berlin's sold-out Philharmonic Hall were canceled. The May 1933 celebration of Johannes Brahms's centenary at the Berlin Singakademie, with announced appearances by Schnabel, the esteemed Polish violinist Bronislaw Huberman, and the Russian cellist Gregor Piatigorsky, was also canceled because the performers were Jewish. Instead, Goebbels chose Hungarian-born Josef Szigeti to broadcast the Brahms Violin Concerto. Out of respect for Huberman, who, as a thirteen-year-old, had played the Brahms concerto to the profound approval of its composer, Szigeti refused to substitute and never again played in Germany. He was not Jewish, but he was a performer of great integrity and intellect. He then toured worldwide, first appearing in Los Angeles for a recital in 1933. (The Polish-born concert pianist Jakob Gimpel, who had played up to eighty performances a year in Germany, also left Europe in 1933 for Palestine, where he became Huberman's touring accompanist.) Schnabel, Germany's foremost concert pianist at the time, sailed with the Klemperer family to New York and toured across the United States. Piatigorsky, principal cellist in the 1920s of the Berlin Philharmonic and a distinguished soloist, moved to France as the base from which he toured for several years. At his wife's insistence, he left Europe with his family in 1940 on the last ship to leave France before Hitler's invasion of that country.[37] After teaching at the Curtis Institute of Music in Philadelphia, Piatigorsky moved with his family to Los Angeles in 1949.

Nazi demonstrations against Jewish composers escalated in 1932–33. Productions of Weill's successful opera *Die Bürgschaft* and a satire on political tyranny, *Der Silbersee* (*The Silver Lake,* a play with music), were shut down. Informed that he was to be arrested, Weill left for Paris at the end of March 1933, leaving his newly acquired Berlin home.[38] In 1932 Toch was nearly run over in Berlin's Potsdammerplatz by youths who attempted to hit him with their car because he looked Jewish.[39] In the spring of 1933 his opera *Der Fächer* (*The Fan*) was being readied for a Cologne premiere when the Gestapo broke into a rehearsal and snatched the baton out of conductor Wilhelm Steinberg's hand. Toch's works were soon banned, and publisher Schott's printing plates of his recently premiered Second Piano Concerto were broken.[40] His German royalties ceased. He left the country in April for the Maggio Musicale in Florence, then went to Paris, where he sent his wife a prearranged message: "I have my pencil." She rented out their Berlin house and joined him with their four-year-old daughter.

The president of Berlin's Academy of Arts declared in March 1933 that Jewish influences must be ended at that institution. On May 17, warned by his brother-in-law Rudolf Kolisch's telegram that Berlin was unsafe for him, Schoenberg, with his young wife and baby daughter, left for Paris. There Schoenberg threw his considerable energy into plans to rescue Europe's Jews, setting aside his composing. In July he rejoined the Jewish religion in Paris, thirty-five years after leaving Judaism as a twenty-four-year-old in Vienna.

In Germany in the early 1930s, Stravinsky's works were the most often performed of all non-German composers. With his German publisher Schott's frequent advice, Stravinsky campaigned to maintain his status in the country that provided the greatest share of his income. In 1932, the year he conducted his ballet, *Petrushka,* at the Berlin State Opera, Stravinsky gave an interview for the German press in which he said, "Nowhere is the art of music so consciously cultivated as in Germany, and that is a sign of a love for music. In the southern countries, the concept of music is less serious, while in America it is treated as a sport."[41] After Hitler's assumption of power in April 1933, however, Stravinsky found himself named on a German list of Jewish composers; he was even rumored to be a Jewish Bolshevik. Angered and alarmed, he sent Willy Strecker at Schott genealogical details to prove that his father and mother were members of the hereditary Russian nobility. Strecker, whose older brother and business partner Louis is reported to have been a Nazi, sought to placate Stravinsky: "This movement has so much that is healthy and positive that one can regard the artistic and other consequences quite calmly. The battle is directed primarily against the communists and Jews, whose influence is being checked to a considerable degree. A welcome cleaning-up has been undertaken . . . in an attempt to restore decency and order." Strecker continued to counter harsh correspondence and negotiations about Stravinsky's "degenerate Bolshevik art," but Stravinsky's German performing engagements dwindled, and his royalties ceased. In November 1934, to counteract a boycott of Stravinsky's works, Strecker placed an article in the *Frankischer Kurier,* in which he stated that Stravinsky was reported by Richard Strauss to have been enthusiastic about the ideas of Hitler. Strecker then wrote Stravinsky, "One must remain quiet now and let the thing run its course."[42]

Stravinsky, virtually stateless since the October 1917 Russian Revolution, took French citizenship. According to Robert Craft, however, Stravinsky preferred the orderliness of Mussolini's fascism to British or French democracy. He presented Mussolini with birthday greetings and gifts and twice visited him in the spring of 1935. He said to reporters in Rome: "I told him that I felt like a fascist myself. Today, fascists are everywhere in Europe. . . . Mussolini did me the great honor of conversing with me for three-quarters of an hour. We talked about music, art, and politics."[43]

In 1935 and 1937 Stravinsky made his second and third concert tours to America, promoting himself and his music as pianist in violin recitals of his works with the Jewish violinist Samuel Dushkin and as a conductor of his own works. His study of English enhanced his appreciation of the United States, and in July 1937 he reported to a Belgrade newspaper: "I have become convinced that interest in . . . serious music, old and new, is steadily increasing among Americans. . . . The best orchestras in the world are now in America."[44]

Opening the May 1938 exhibition of "Degenerate Music" in Düsseldorf on the 125th birthday of Richard Wagner, Goebbels reported on the progress since 1933 of removal and systematic reform that would revive "the domain of an art that until [the years of the Weimar Republic] had been seen throughout the world as the most German of all. . . . [National Socialism] has produced change," he announced. "In a great burst it has swept away the pathological products of Jewish musical intellectualism." He claimed that the power of Jewry was now broken in the realm of German music.[45] "Aryanization" of all music in the Third Reich proceeded, with jazz gradually eliminated, new titles created for Handel's Old Testament operas, new translations fashioned for Da Ponte's librettos set by Mozart, the removal of Mendelssohn's statue from in front of the Leipzig Gewandhaus, and the elimination of Mendelssohn, Meyerbeer, Offenbach, and Mahler, as well as the modern composers, from the repertoire. In the Jüdische Kulturbund, the degrading ghettoization of not only Jewish performing artists but "Jewish music" lasted from 1933 to 1941.

In this exhibition, Stravinsky was proclaimed a foremost representative of the foreign influences "suffocating" German Romanticism; his racial purity was again questioned. Stravinsky was enraged and asked French officials in Berlin to demand an apology for this violation of his rights as a French citizen. The apology, when it came months later, was evasive, but it offered the hope that he would not suffer humiliation in the future.[46] He received no German performances for the duration of the war, and his recording royalties were not paid. His property was threatened in France, where he was still considered Jewish until April 1942.[47] The death of his elder daughter at the end of 1938, the illness and subsequent deaths of his wife and mother in 1939, and his own serious illness from tuberculosis forced Stravinsky to cancel his planned American tour as a performer in 1938–39. While recovering, he received an invitation from Harvard to deliver the prestigious Norton lectures in the fall of 1939. He was relieved to accept.[48]

During Hitler's invasions and occupations, expulsions of musical talent in other countries echoed those in Germany. Austria at first seemed a refuge for fleeing musicians. The day after Hitler was appointed chancellor, all

German performances of Krenek's music were summarily canceled, and his income from German royalties ceased. Krenek's name was not only associated in Nazi lists with jazz and "cultural Bolshevism" (because of the topic of *Jonny spielt auf*), but he was also identified as a Czech Jew. This experience was repeated in Austria, where Krenek had settled. When his opera *Karl V* came to the stage of the Vienna Opera in the spring of 1934, Clemens Krauss, the conductor who had requested the opera, withdrew his support; rehearsals were called off, and the production was canceled.

With no prospects in his homeland, Krenek undertook to adapt Monteverdi's opera *The Coronation of Poppea* for the Salzburg Opera Guild, a small group planning to tour the United States in 1937–38. At the suggestion of Sol Hurok, the tour's New York manager, Krenek accompanied the group (for a short while as its conductor) because he was recognizable to American audiences through the fame of *Jonny spielt auf.* Krenek wanted to explore the United States, and he was particularly drawn to California. His return to Europe coincided with the March 13, 1938, Anschluss in Austria, about which CBS radio correspondent Edward R. Murrow reported from Vienna, "Hitler is expected at about 10 a.m. There is a mood of jubilation. They raise the arm a little higher here in Vienna than in Berlin."[49] Krenek immediately retraced his steps, this time emigrating to the United States. The figure of his Jonny, pictured with a saxophone instead of a violin, was prominently used as the poster symbol of de-Germanized, jazz-oriented, Jewish cultural infiltration in the 1938 Düsseldorf exhibit, and Krenek was on the list of degenerate composers.

After Hitler's assumption of power, Eisler's music was forbidden in Germany, where it was life-threatening to own an Eisler recording or to sing his songs. Performances of his theater collaborations with Brecht were shut down. His Berlin apartment was searched by the Gestapo. Eisler fled to Austria, then moved constantly: to Czechoslovakia, to Paris, to Denmark— where Brecht had settled—and to London, where he scored a film satire on Hitler.[50] Earnings from film work became essential to his survival. His politically engaged documentaries brought him the approval of Soviet officials, and in 1935 he was made president of the Moscow-based International Music Bureau, an organization he had helped to establish.

The Viennese composer Erich Wolfgang Korngold—endorsed as a prodigy by Mahler and Richard Strauss—had been internationally acclaimed as an opera composer since the age of eighteen. In 1934 the thirty-seven-year-old composer was in the midst of composing his fifth opera, *Die Kathrin,* when Max Reinhardt, who was in Hollywood that year, asked him to undertake the arranging and direction of Mendelssohn's music for Shakespeare's *A Midsummer Night's Dream* in a Warner Brothers film of Reinhardt's recent Hollywood Bowl production. Korngold arrived in the United States at the end of October 1934, just as the Nazis banned performances of Mendelssohn's score in Germany because the nineteenth-century composer was Jewish. Given this news upon disembarking in New York, Korngold predicted to reporters that "Mendelssohn will survive Hitler."[51]

The Hungarian composer Eugene Zador had been established since 1921 at the New Vienna Conservatory as professor of composition and orchestration. He had trained in composition and musicology in Vienna and in Germany, where he had earned a doctorate at Münster University. Zador's Vienna career had developed rapidly, with performances of three operas and several orchestral works. On the day of the Anschluss he returned to his homeland for protection, but it was soon clear to him that Hitler's prohibitions against Jews were going to extend to Hungary. With the help of the New York College of Music, which invited him to teach and sponsored his entry to the United States in 1939, Zador sailed for America. On the voyage he composed an opera, *Christopher Columbus,* to a libretto by his private student the Archduke Josef Franz von Habsburg, a cousin of Emperor Franz Josef and a descendant of Isabella and Ferdinand, sponsors of Columbus's voyages.[52]

Bruno Walter served as director of the Vienna State Opera from 1936. Alma Mahler Werfel and Franz Werfel introduced him to Chancellor Kurt Schuschnigg, who shared with them a profound love of music. Walter optimistically believed in the Austrian government's ability to stand against Nazism. When Schuschnigg was bullied into powerlessness in February 1938 by Hitler, Viennese musical colleagues advised Walter to leave Europe. His performances were interrupted by Nazi stink bombs; he received several death threats and had to be protected by bodyguards; but his characteristic optimism blinded him as he continued performing. He was in Amsterdam conducting the Concertgebouw Orchestra during Hitler's takeover of Austria in March 1938. Walter wrote in anguish that the country's downfall was accompanied on the radio by music, "as if no historical tragedy were being enacted, the suffering and death of human beings were not involved, nor the victory of evil." Haydn's national anthem, Viennese waltzes, then Prussian military marches were played, while "there was no sign of resistance anywhere. Schuschnigg himself had ordered his inwardly torn country to submit to the aggressors." Walter immediately requested release from his Vienna State Opera and Salzburg Festival contracts. Perhaps because of his association with the fallen government, Walter's older daughter was arrested and detained for two weeks in Vienna. The family apartment and car were confiscated by the Nazis. Austria became "Ostmark," and the Walters' Austrian passports were invalidated. They managed to obtain French passports, and their two daughters rented a villa for the family at Lake Lugano in Switzerland. Here, between conducting engagements, Walter continued to hope "that a reasonable world would put a stop to Hitler's devilish plans."[53] In August 1939, as war was about to break out, the family's momentary tranquility was again cruelly shattered by the murder of their younger daughter by her husband, a film producer, who shot her and himself in a jealous rage over her five-year love affair with the famous bass Ezio Pinza. Walter had toured in America frequently since the inflation-ravaged winter of 1923. Conducting in the Hollywood Bowl in the summer of 1927, he had been moved by "the splendor of the California night, of the starry sky, . . . the touching silence of the immense throng."[54] At the end of October 1939, broken in spirit, he asked to have all his European contracts rescinded and sailed for New York; his goal was a vacation in Beverly Hills.

Like her close friend Walter, the Prussian-born soprano Lotte Lehmann had adopted Vienna as her home and thought of herself as Viennese at heart. Her early training at the Hamburg Opera in 1910, under the young Klemperer, set her on her path of intensely emotional immersion in her operatic roles. From 1916 she became a favorite at the Vienna Opera, where she personified Viennese emotional warmth and charm. Her lieder recitals with Walter became extraordinary events, particularly at the Salzburg festivals. In April 1934 Lehmann received a peremptory order from Hermann Göring, Hitler's second in command, to come to Berlin. Göring, who sent a private plane to bring her to Berlin, displayed a riding crop and a knife on the table between them. He announced that he wanted her to sing exclusively in Germany and promised her a villa, a pension for life, and a horse, presumably for her husband, Otto Krause, a Hungarian-born Viennese insurance executive and cavalry officer. When Lehmann returned to Vienna, she found the Berlin contract waiting for her signature, but none of Göring's promises were included. She complained; Hitler was informed; and she was forbidden to sing in Germany, possibly because the Nazis considered Krause and the four children of his first marriage to be Jewish.[55] Lehmann had sung in the United States since her 1930 debut with the Chicago Opera and had spent Christmas 1932 in Santa Barbara, California, with Krause. The encounter with Göring and increasing political pressures at the Vienna Opera made it clear to her that she and Krause should seek a new home. Lehmann took on responsibility for Krause's children after their mother's death in 1936 and emigrated with the family to the United States.

In Italy, from 1922 until the spring of 1938, Benito Mussolini did not interfere with the showcasing of new compositions, and Jews were not bothered—possibly because Mussolini's mistress was Jewish. Mario Castelnuovo-Tedesco, a wealthy Florentine, was able to devote himself entirely to composing and became well known in Italy as a composer of operas, ballets, and numerous overtures on Shakespeare's plays. His works were promoted by the pianist, composer, and modern music impresario Alfredo Casella, and performed by Walter Gieseking, Gregor Piatigorsky, Andrés Segovia, Arturo Toscanini, and Jascha Heifetz. Mussolini himself commissioned Castelnuovo-Tedesco to compose incidental music for a grandiose production of Rino Alessi's play *Savonarola* for the Maggio Musicale of 1935. No difficulties arose for Castelnuovo-Tedesco, whose family were Orthodox Jews of Spanish descent, until 1938, following the Rome-Berlin Axis Pact and Mussolini's subsequent enforcement of the Manifesto of Race. At that time radio performances of Castelnuovo-Tedesco's Second Violin Concerto (*I profeti,* the three movements of which he composed in 1931 for Heifetz on texts of the Jewish prophets Isaiah, Jeremiah, and Elijah) were abruptly banned. The composer, a former child prodigy whose music had been published in Munich when he was fifteen, was no longer allowed to concertize or to receive royalties. An intellectual aristocrat conversant in at least six languages, he suddenly found himself declared a noncitizen, unable to send his two children to school. He and his family escaped to the United States through Switzerland, with the help of Toscanini, Heifetz, and the violinist Albert Spalding.[56]

The policies against Jewish musicians spread as Hitler occupied Czechoslovakia and Poland in March and September 1939. Bohemian-born Jan Popper was working at the German Theater in Prague under conductors George Szell and Fritz Zweig in the late 1930s. As Czechoslovakia struggled under Nazi domination, Popper became a freedom fighter, serving as a parachutist in the Masaryk League. Both his parents were gassed in Nazi concentration camps. In 1939, with help from an uncle in charge of the

Czechoslovakia exhibit at the Golden Gate International Exposition in San Francisco, Popper escaped to California.[57]

France, and Paris in particular, was the choice for many of the earliest refugees from Hitler. But in 1933 the consequences of the worldwide Depression forced those who had initially found employment there to seek their livings elsewhere, for many French musicians were unemployed, and emergency funds for refugees were being exhausted. Toch, building a career in film composing, moved from Paris to London—where the same economic restrictions blocked him—and then on to the United States. Hollander, Waxman, and Weill, working in the same field, also moved to the United States. The fall of France in 1940 brought a further wave of escaping musical émigrés to the United States, including the Polish pianist Artur Rubinstein, the Piatigorsky family, the young Austrian composer Eric Zeisl, and conductor Fritz Zweig.

Switzerland had honored the status of "political refugee," which carried an automatic right to asylum under the Swiss constitution, in the early 1930s. Walther Ingolf Marcus, a German music student, sought this protection. He was the oldest child of a prosperous Hamburg lawyer and a Swedish-born mother (née Dahl). He had enjoyed prodigious early success as a pianist and conductor who began composing in his teens. He was deeply affected, however, when his thoroughly assimilated family was identified as Jewish; his father had rejected his own Jewish identity, and young Marcus and his siblings were raised "almost as unaware of what it was to be Jewish as Hindu," according to his sister.[58] As Ingolf Marcus, in 1931 he left Hamburg to study composition at the Cologne Conservatory for one academic year. In the summer of 1932 he left Germany for Zurich, where he remained for almost six and a half years, living with his uncle's Jewish family. He worked his way upward from an internship at the Municipal Opera to become an assistant conductor. This led to his direct participation as chorus master and opera coach in the world premieres of Berg's *Lulu* and Hindemith's *Mathis der Maler,* as well as productions of Dmitri Shostakovich's *Lady Macbeth of Mtsensk* and Arthur Honegger's ballet-melodrama *Amphion.*

In 1933 Switzerland suddenly denied Jews the status of "political refugee." Marcus suffered a nervous breakdown soon thereafter. The uncertainty of his political status would have been a likely cause; another could have been the growing Nazi campaign against homosexuality. By 1935 the SS was demanding death for homosexual activities.[59] In the midst of his personal crisis, Marcus met a Californian woman, Etta Gordon Linick, who became his confidante and his reason for emigrating to America in 1939. The 1936 Swiss imprisonment of a Jewish medical student, who had assassinated Hitler's personal representative to Switzerland, provided a strong warning that Jews should remain inconspicuous and not protest as the "neutral" country conformed to Nazi laws. After Hitler's annexation of Austria in 1938, as numberless Jews attempted to cross their border, Switzerland demanded that the passports of Jews be stamped with a "J." Marcus found himself deprived of conducting assignments at the opera and relegated to playing keyboard and percussion instruments in the orchestra pit. When, on February 15, 1939, at the age of twenty-six, he arrived in Los Angeles by bus from New York, he brought with him his European experience, his high ambition, and, to enhance his employment prospects, his new identity as Ingolf Dahl.[60]

For these musicians and others who will appear in this book, flight from Europe had become a matter of life or death. As refugees, they escaped the fate suffered by the relatives they left behind and were too often unable to rescue. Subsequent chapters will explore why and how they moved to the southwestern coast of the United States, rather than settling in the more culturally mature cities of the Northeast, where there were more established ties to European musical tradition; how they and their music fared in California; what kind of society they built for themselves; why they, rather than their compatriot writers or visual artists, became American citizens and raised families there; and how their presence influenced generations of America's musical talent.

2

Paradise?

It was a mass migration of a thrown-together elite unprecedented in history.

—Gottfried Reinhardt

The first impression was of the beauty of the area. The writer Vicki Baum, formerly a child harpist and youthful professor at the Vienna Academy of Music, remembered: "A gentian-blue sky above us, filled with glittering stars and the perfume of jasmine in the cold nights; hillsides and gardens sparkling with dew each morning, with all the colors of a wild Van Gogh palette as the sun rose, the air so clear you didn't want to breathe but drink it. I think I stayed drunk for weeks with this sun and air and the beauty of the hills."[1] Baum had left Austria for a temporary visit to Hollywood in 1931 to work as a writer, but after she saw what was happening politically in Austria, she established a Los Angeles home for her family and a new career there writing for films. Her husband, the Viennese conductor Richard Lert, who at that time was a conductor at the Berlin State Opera, was able to join his wife and children for summers in California, from 1932 conducting programs at the Hollywood Bowl. When his European conducting assignments dwindled and his Berlin contract was canceled because he was Jewish, he moved permanently to California.

Despite Baum's appreciation of the beauty of Southern California, it was not a logical destination for musicians. Those entering the United States in flight from Nazi Europe in the 1930s expected to work on the East Coast; few of them intended to settle in California when they first reached the haven of America. New York drew Hanns Eisler, Ernst Toch, Kurt Weill,

Eugene Zador, Eric Zeisl, Lotte Lehmann, Bruno Walter, and Hugo Stre-
litzer. Ernst Krenek, Arnold Schoenberg, and Igor Stravinsky went first to
Boston; Emanuel Feuermann and Gregor Piatigorsky to Philadelphia. (Lert,
Otto Klemperer, Frederick Hollander, Franz Waxman, and Ingolf Dahl
were among the very few who moved directly to the Los Angeles area from
Europe.)

The harsh economic realities of the Depression and insufficient potential for sustaining work in the East forced the composers to move west,
where they hoped to find lucrative opportunities composing for Hollywood films. Klemperer's appointment at the Los Angeles Philharmonic in
1933 proved magnetic to both performers and composers who had known
and worked with him in Europe. The climate, so attractive to Baum, also
appealed to others. Schoenberg and Stravinsky, sixty and fifty-eight when
they settled in California in 1934 and 1940, faced serious health concerns
and needed the warmth of the Southwest. From 1934 until 1938 Korngold
worked seasonally in Hollywood, returning to Austria each summer. He
brought his family to Hollywood during a film assignment in 1936 because
one of his sons had tuberculosis. For those who came as political refugees,
with virtually nothing, Southern California offered less expensive housing,
heating, clothing, and food than the East Coast cultural centers.

The U.S. immigration laws, which dated from 1921, gave precedence to
the highly talented among the refugees. Temporary visitor visas were based
on the immigration quotas of their various countries of application, but
these had to be extended every six months. The quota system could be bypassed by a "nonquota" visa if the refugee obtained employment in the
United States and was vouched for with affidavits from U.S. citizens willing
to assume responsibility for the applicant's financial welfare. A refugee who
aspired to more permanent status had to leave the United States and be
readmitted through consulates in bordering countries (Mexico, Cuba, or
Canada), at which point he or she could apply for citizenship, which might
be granted after several years. It was clear that an offer of employment from
the film studios, a performing organization, or a university was necessary.

From Klemperer's arrival in October 1933 until Stravinsky's departure in
1969 and Dahl's death in 1970, Los Angeles became host to "a greater concentration of musical talent than existed in any other city at that time," as
Klemperer's biographer, Peter Heyworth, put it. This windfall from Nazi
persecution developed the area's musical maturity dramatically and influenced an untold number of young performers, composers, teachers, and

music lovers. However, as Heyworth added, "Never was a city less prepared for the role it was about to fulfill." Klemperer's privately expressed opinion of 1933 Los Angeles included the exclamation, "My God, my God, I didn't know that such a lack of intellectuality [*Geistigkeit*] existed." To the locally adored Klemperer, America was "the wrong place."[2] Mark Brunswick, an American composer who had lived in Europe and knew many of the refugee musicians, agreed that "America was not ripe for a sudden musical renaissance through this immediate contact with the more intensive and in that sense higher musical culture of Europe. . . . We had to try to explain to [the European musicians] the unparalleled and destructive centralization of our music."[3] The centralizing influence was New York City, and Southern California was not yet on the cutting edge of the American cultural experience.

Surrounded by ocean, desert, and mountains, Los Angeles was called "an island on the land" by its early sociologist, Carey McWilliams. John Russell Taylor, describing the city's domination in the 1930s and '40s by the film industry, modified this image to call Hollywood "an island off the coast of the world" and noted that it was "an L.A. specialty to insulate oneself from the rest of the world."[4] Isolation and a natural anti-intellectualism encouraged by the climate were psychological aspects of life in Los Angeles the émigrés found difficult to accept. Dione Neutra, a cellist and widow of the Viennese architect Richard Neutra, described the "almost intellectual starvation" of arriving Europeans in the 1930s: "The first thing to be understood is that cultural life in Los Angeles was still fairly limited at that time, in spite of—or maybe even because of—the motion picture industry. Of course there was the Los Angeles Philharmonic and Klemperer, but there was no established operatic or instrumental concert life, and the same was true of theater. Everyone went to the films and that was that. . . . We [Europeans] clung together, for that gave us security and a feeling of continuity. At that time, there concentrated, within a few square miles, the greatest community of artistic talent ever assembled in one place. And yet, we were largely ignored by the Americans who did not know who we were, still less what we stood for."[5]

Earlier oil, agriculture, and real estate booms had made the area into a sprawling patchwork of separate municipalities with little central coherence. Politically and socially, Los Angeles was controlled by white Republican Protestants from the Midwest and rural South who were conservative in their attitudes and had little interest or background in the arts. In contrast to the East Coast cultural centers, where American wealth was proudly invested in European-influenced operas, orchestras, and conservatories, Los Angeles as yet had little to brag about in musical institutions or in civic support of the few that existed. Even greater were the contrasts with European centers, where the performing arts were often subsidized by the government. Whereas Berlin boasted three opera companies, several superb orchestras, forty theaters, and twenty music schools in 1930, Los Angeles had no opera and only one shakily established orchestra. The city lacked fine concert halls, and by the time weary visiting concert performers had toured the continent by train, they were apt to perform hackneyed repertoire. The Depression was undermining what advances had been made in the 1920s by the larger local educational institutions to develop musical training, which was still largely the province of small private conservatories founded by solo performers to instruct students in their particular art.

Although the isolated nature of the region allowed nonconformists creative individualism in the arts, ventures into new languages of art found stiff resistance from the general public. Visual artists who had left other cultural centers to come to Southern California were often nonconformists who needed isolation; they devoted themselves to their individual creativity, often without audience, patronage, or competition. A painter who broke this tradition of isolation from the larger world of art was Stanton Macdonald-Wright, who organized an exhibit of modern painting in Los Angeles in 1920 and, with "a miniature group" of such distinguished modernists as the Austrian architects Rudolph M. Schindler and Neutra, was said to be "pounding away at the conservatives" in 1929.[6] Schindler, trained by the Viennese architect Otto Wagner and inspired by the work of Adolf Loos and Frank Lloyd Wright, came to Los Angeles in 1920. In 1922 he built Los Angeles' first purely modern house on Kings Road in the bean fields of what later became West Hollywood. Neutra arrived in 1923; the Schindler and Neutra families shared the Kings Road house for a while. The International Style houses that both architects designed in Los Angeles and Newport Beach in the 1920s made modernism visible to all.

In the 1930s American modern dance was in its vibrant but relatively obscure youth in Southern California. Lester Horton's work with Native American dance, Martha Graham's new abstractions, the voluptuous costume experiments of Ruth St. Denis, and the pioneering all-male ensemble of Ted Shawn all created opportunities for young American dancers. European modern dance artists such as Mary Wigman and Harald Kreutzberg visited to perform in 1933 and 1934. At the time, however, music for dance offered no income for the newly arriving musical émigrés, who needed to establish themselves in more lucrative fields.

By 1933, when modern music's most outstanding European proponent, Klemperer, arrived, modern music was failing in Los Angeles. That year, young Canadian-born Peter Yates, a recent Princeton graduate who had settled in the area in 1931 hoping to stimulate interest in modernism, found the concertgoing public "open-mouthed for knowledge, breathing discussion, but unwilling to sacrifice one jot or tittle of their convictions or prejudice. Open ears, closed minds; hearts ajar, souls fisted."[7] By then, Henry Cowell had suspended his New Music Society of California after two seasons of presenting compositions by "ultra-moderns" in the ballroom of downtown Los Angeles' Biltmore Hotel. Sponsored by the oil heiress Arline Barnsdall from 1925 to 1927, these programs had offered to present "musical works embodying the most progressive tendencies of this age, and to disseminate the new musical ideals" in Los Angeles. Along with new works by the Americans Carl Ruggles, Leo Ornstein, and the French-born Dane Rudhyar, Cowell had presented selections by the Europeans Arnold Schoenberg, Edgard Varèse, and Darius Milhaud. Newspaper critics had dished up devastating opinions: to one, the first season's music "sounded like a traffic jam" and was definitely "left wing"; another was certain the musical pandemonium would "drive us back to a better appreciation of the old purists."[8] Financial support from Barnsdall withered, and Cowell took the New Music Society to San Francisco. From 1926 through 1929 the British conductor Eugene Goossens—a composer himself—consistently brought modern music to the Hollywood Bowl, performing works by Bartók, Honegger, Prokofiev, Schoenberg, and Stravinsky, who conducted his own works. But resistance to modernism was solidifying even among composers. In 1930 supporters of local conservative composers, led by the American Indianist Charles Wakefield Cadman, began developing a Society for the Advancement of American Music. Furthering this attitude in 1936, composers Cadman, Roy Harris, Mary Carr Moore, Homer Grunn, and Richard Drake Saunders would form the Society of Southern California Composers, joined by Rudhyar, Joseph Achron, William Grant Still, and others. Amalgamation of this society that year with the Federal Music Project Symphony Orchestra (organized for unemployed musicians in 1934 by the Works Progress Administration and familiarly known as the WPA Orchestra) would entice recently arrived Europeans—among them Schoenberg—and their students into membership. From 1939 to 1944, however, in order to avoid confrontation with the arriving foreign modernists, the Americanists would reorganize as the Society of Native American Composers, by which they meant to exclude composers not born in America.[9]

The area's lack of cultural coherence encouraged domination—even dictatorship—by individuals and militated against a true musical community. In the 1930s and early 1940s, presentation of solo artists' concert programs in Southern California was controlled by an entrepreneur with little musical knowledge. Lynden "Len" Ellsworth Behymer had risen from peanut vendor to publisher of event programs and then to his booking monopoly. Behymer's first musical venture had brought the Metropolitan Opera Company to Los Angeles in 1900; his chief interests were spectacles and touring virtuosos. In 1933 he merged his productions with NBC's and Columbia Concerts' artists' managements.[10] His instinct for the commercial aspect of performances prevailed over his interest in music as an art, and his choices informed the tastes of much of the Los Angeles concertgoing public in the period before the arrival of the émigrés.[11] Consequently, audiences were generally more interested in performers' personalities than in the music they played; newspaper reviews of concerts in the early 1930s show a prevailing fascination with child prodigies. José Rodriguez, a local music critic and musicologist who compiled a yearly publication of articles titled *Music and Dance in California,* commented in 1940 on the local selling of music by "high-pressure methods. . . . It was found that it was difficult if not impossible to sell music, but, under conditions of specialized bally-hoo it was possible to sell personalities. Thence the poisonous growth of the star system. . . . People went to see Paderewski, not to listen to Schumann. . . . No matter what drivel Tibbett sang or Menuhin played, people accepted it as one accepts the tricks of a trained seal. . . . This attitude spelled decadence and ruin."[12]

The first wave of European musical émigrés also faced the Anglo-Saxon notion that music was a social accomplishment, not a profession, and was therefore a field in which female energies flourished. There was a strongly positive component to this female dominance, however. Women had pioneered the development of the area's performing arts since the founding of the Los Angeles Conservatory in 1883 and the creation of the Women's Orchestra of Los Angeles in 1893 (it was conducted by men). Women had established music instruction in what later became the University of California, Los Angeles (UCLA), and in the University of Southern California (USC); were prominent in the teaching and supervising of music in the Los Angeles public schools; and were successful instrumental teachers and composers. Most of the female leaders of prominent performing organizations were trained musicians. All excelled in organizational skills and worked passionately to better the city's cultural environment. One of the most prominent local clubwomen, Bessie Bartlett Fraenkl, who had studied in Europe as a singer and a composer, was general chairman of the Philharmonic from its inception in 1919.[13] In her various activities she exercised enough power that Schoenberg would endeavor to gain her favor. Artie Mason Carter, a pianist trained in Vienna by the great Theodor Leschetizky, was the dynamic force behind the development of the "Symphonies under the Stars," initiated at the Hollywood Bowl in 1922 to gain essential summer income for the Los Angeles Philharmonic. The success of Carter's effort convinced Barnsdall to make important financial contributions to the Bowl, retiring the debt on its acreage and underwriting and promoting contemporary music programs. Elizabeth Sprague Coolidge, an amateur pianist internationally known by the 1930s for her important patronage of composers and chamber music ensembles, often spent winter months in Los Angeles. Her enlightened beneficence was important not only for the free chamber concerts she presented at the city's Central Library and in UCLA's Royce Hall but also for her commissions for the émigré composers Stravinsky, Schoenberg, and Toch. Beginning in 1931, her close friend Marian MacDowell, widow of the composer Edward MacDowell and sponsor of the important MacDowell Colony in New Hampshire, wintered in an apartment on Vine Street in Hollywood, and in the last years of her life she also gave essential support to Toch.

The city's newspapers at this time counted on part-time music critics—several of whom were women—to review concerts. Isabel Morse Jones, a former violin teacher, was a strong proponent on the *Los Angeles Times* staff for "an intellectual awakening in music" on the West Coast. She crusaded heroically, often fruitlessly and almost desperately, for greater financial support for music in what was then a philanthropically slothful environment. In 1933 she called Southern California "a comparatively new subdivision of America," and went so far as to champion a proposal to tax visiting virtuosos to aid city music, claiming that "if San Francisco and Los Angeles were to take a stand for the West, it might, and quite probably would, change the whole nation's attitude toward music." Jones also noted the dearth of opportunities for young musical artists: "Every mail brings news of Los Angeles' bright youngsters who have been forced to seek experience and practical encouragement elsewhere."[14]

Ironically, a factor in this exodus of young talent was the stifling effect the great number of women's social clubs were having upon striving local performers. Music critic and composer Richard Drake Saunders raged in print about this: "The musician must look to music clubs and musical organizations for his concert appearances. . . . Ninety percent of these expect the artist to donate his services for their entertainment. . . . [This is] nothing more or less than an organized 'racket' whose object is to prey upon musicians."[15] Severe frustration with this situation and the low quality of programming involved was one factor contributing in 1939 to Peter Yates's creation, with his pianist wife, Frances Mullen, of the adventurous and long-lasting chamber music series, "Evenings on the Roof," which became the steadiest performance forum for émigré composers in Los Angeles. These concerts took place in the roof studio designed for the purpose by Rudolf Schindler in the Yates's house. From 1942 on they expanded to more accessible venues.[16]

In contrast to the rest of the area, by the 1930s internationalism was a welcoming factor the musicians found well established in and around Hollywood. Not only were the studio moguls themselves Jewish European emigrants from a previous generation, but since the 1920s they had been importing film talent from Europe and England. Vicki Baum, whose novel *Grand Hotel* was made into an Oscar-winning film by MGM in 1931; scenarist Salka Viertel, who wrote exclusively for Greta Garbo; directors Berthold Viertel and William Dieterle; and the actress Luise Rainer were among many in Hollywood's German-speaking community who were generous in their help for many of the arriving émigrés. Erich Pommer, Ernst Lubitsch, and Marlene Dietrich, artists with whom the composers had worked in Europe, were also established in Hollywood. Lubitsch, the Viertels, and the Dieterles had been trained by Max Reinhardt, who worked in Hollywood in 1934 and settled there in 1937. Visiting film artists became instant émigrés themselves when their homelands were occupied by the Nazis. There were also Hungarians and a dominant group of White Russians, who had fled their country in the 1920s after the Russian Revolution. Prominent among them, the Russian-born violinist Jascha Heifetz had become a U.S. citizen in 1925, had married a silent-film actress, and in the 1930s was living in Beverly Hills. He would commission violin works from Alexandre Tansman, Toch, Waxman, Korngold, and Castelnuovo-Tedesco and would form ensembles with Rubinstein, Feuermann, and Piatigorsky. Peter Meremblum, Heifetz's classmate at St. Petersburg's Imperial Conservatory, would found the Southern California Junior Symphony, a superb training orchestra for legions of young instrumentalists.[17] Stravinsky's law-school friend from St. Petersburg, Alexis Kall, would arrive in 1935 to establish a piano studio in West Los Angeles. European and Russian musicians were already important members of the Los Angeles Philharmonic; they were also among the key performance teachers in the area, and were well established in the large pool of fine instrumentalists attracted to the film and radio broadcast studios during the Depression.

By the 1940s there had gathered in a few square miles between Hollywood and the Pacific what Max Reinhardt's son Gottfried, working for Lubitsch at Paramount, called "a mass migration of a thrown-together [artistic and intellectual] elite unprecedented in history." Beside the musicians, there were writers, actors, screen and stage directors, architects, sociologists, and philosophers, "the most extraordinary influx of knowledge and talent to another continent. Since the Jews in this community of exiles were, for once, not in the minority, it is, I believe, permissible to call it a ghetto . . . formed voluntarily, because its inhabitants were inclined to stick together in foreign lands." While the natives frequently did not know what to make of the émigrés, empathies formed among them quickly. Gottfried Reinhardt observed that "though most of [the Europeans] had not necessarily been good neighbors at home, often, except for insults, not even on speaking terms, they were now, at least geographically, close neighbors in exile and learned to speak with one another with silver-alloyed tongues."[18] He further remembered (in a 1991 lecture titled, "It Was No Paradise") that "there was nothing unusual in having one evening with Thomas Mann and the next with [the German writer Lion] Feuchtwanger and the next with [the Austrian writer] Franz Werfel, or in driving downtown to the Philharmonic to hear Klemperer or having lunch and playing ping-pong with Schoenberg, having coffee and cake with Korngold, or visiting Alma Mahler, [the famous Viennese operetta singer] Fritzi Massary, welcoming Gregor Piatigorsky, Arthur Rubinstein, etc."[19] In this "ghetto," the European custom of entertaining by open invitation on Sunday afternoons, or in more formal dinner evenings, offered opportunities for stimulating encounters and fruitful connections between artists of differing disciplines that probably would not have occurred in Europe. These led to important creative results, particularly during the Second World War, before those who considered themselves exiles returned to Europe. In itself, this extraordinary international gathering of talent of all kinds around Hollywood became an attraction to musical émigrés settled elsewhere in the United States.

Americans amongst filmdom's celebrities of the time—notably composers George Gershwin, the recently arrived George Antheil, and composer-actor Lionel Barrymore—also supported and welcomed the musicians fleeing Hitler's Europe. Barrymore and Mickey Rooney would both study composition with Mario Castelnuovo-Tedesco, and each would produce a symphony. British-born Charlie Chaplin became an important supporter of Alexandre Tansman, Frederick Hollander, and Hanns Eisler.

The musicians' first impressions of the United States as a new homeland were optimistic, and their principal emotion was gratitude. Upon arrival they were deeply moved by the freedoms granted in the U.S. Constitution. On October 9, 1934, Schoenberg introduced himself in Hollywood by contrasting himself to the snake driven out of the paradise of Adam and Eve: "I, on the contrary, came from one country into another . . . where I am allowed to go on my feet, where my head can be erect, where kindness and cheerfulness is dominating, and where to live is a joy and to be an expatriate of another country is the grace of God. I was driven into paradise!"[20] One of Schoenberg's Viennese students, the émigré composer, pianist, and musicologist Paul Pisk, who taught at the University of Redlands from 1936 to 1945 and returned to California for his retirement, stated that the first and lasting revelation about his new homeland was that American people could freely express their opinions in the 1936 Franklin Roosevelt–Alfred Landon campaign for the presidency. "I felt this kind of liberation. . . . I am one of those who felt *never* the slightest desire to go back." When Vienna honored Pisk with an invitation to return after the war, "It didn't take me half a day to say 'Thank you, no.'"[21] Hungarian composer Eugene Zador was amazed to hear harshly outspoken criticism of President Roosevelt, which signaled a democratic society that was entirely new and inspiring to him. The sense of political freedom and Roosevelt's promotion of the United Nations seem to have provoked Ernst Toch's fierce objection in March 1945 to the establishment of a Jewish Community Center in Santa Monica. He wrote that he would rather give wholehearted support to a "Human or World Community Center," for he advocated "the abolition of Religions and the replacement by Religion. . . . What we must do, all of us, is tear down the walls instead of erecting new ones." He desired "the Santa Monica Center for World Humanity, without a syllable hinting to Jewish origin or Jewish confinement."[22]

Roosevelt's death in April 1945 shocked and grieved the émigré community. Vera Stravinsky wrote, "Everyone is upset and Igor is ill."[23] Thomas

Mann, since 1940 the leading figure among the German-speaking circles in the area, expressed the feeling of émigré Europeans when he wrote about the beloved president in a letter, "This is no longer the country to which we came. One feels orphaned and abandoned."[24]

Many well-known German literary figures, including Thomas and Heinrich Mann, Bertolt Brecht, Alfred Döblin, Leonhard Frank, Bruno Frank, Emil Ludwig, Erich Maria Remarque, and Ludwig Marcuse, haunted by the loss of their language, left the Los Angeles area after the war—some for political reasons in the McCarthy era. For most of the writers, life in California proved to be an exile, described by Thomas Mann as "waiting room days," from which they hoped to return to Europe.[25] Because of the universality of their creative language, the émigré musicians had an advantage over writers whose languages were foreign to Americans. This difference played a large role in the musicians' choice to remain in their new homeland until the ends of their lives. In so doing, the European musicians helped bring Southern California's musical culture to maturity.

In turn, the émigré musicians were changed by this experience: Los Angeles became a place where Hugo Strelitzer could dream of, plan, and execute a new American approach to opera training; it was a place where Otto Klemperer, always the frustrated composer, could study composition with Schoenberg; where Schoenberg would return periodically to tonality in his desire to have his music more widely appreciated; where Stravinsky would transcend his antipathy toward Sergey Rachmaninoff and become so influenced by Schoenberg that Ingolf Dahl would find the Stravinskys' living room filled with the sounds of Schoenberg's *Verklärte Nacht*. It became a place where Stravinsky could hear Leadbelly (the folk and blues musician Huddie Ledbetter); where the youthful John Cage's enthusiasm could stimulate Toch's composition of a new work; where novels by Thomas Mann and Lion Feuchtwanger would inspire compositions by Toch and Zador; where Franz Waxman's film and television income would enable him to found and lead for twenty years a music festival of international scope. Up the coast, Lotte Lehmann could envision a music school to be established in Santa Barbara. Down the coast, Ernst Krenek would establish a revolutionary faculty of composers at the new University of California, San Diego.

Performance institutions such as the Pasadena Symphony, Yates's "Evenings on the Roof," and its successor, the "Monday Evening Concerts," would gather strength from and give steady support to the émigrés, while the more established institutions would variously notice, ignore, or exploit them. Despite this remarkable assembly of talent, Los Angeles itself continued to be a place of conservative—even reluctant—musical patronage. As a result, composers in particular felt a prolonged neglect. Geographic isolation, the lack of any established opera or dance company, and—after Klemperer's forced resignation in 1940 owing to illness—unsympathetic artistic direction of the Los Angeles Philharmonic made the creative situation particularly difficult. Jerome Moross wrote in his column "On the Hollywood Front" for *Modern Music* in the spring of 1941: "The concentration of important musical figures in America is at the moment very heavy in and around Hollywood." He noted that the composers Stravinsky, Schoenberg, Toch, Zador, Joseph Achron, and Castelnuovo-Tedesco were living in Southern California, "which probably has the smallest audience for new music to be found anywhere."[26] Aaron Copland, exploring Hollywood possibilities for himself in 1937, commented in a letter that "the conditions of [film] work are very unsatisfactory. . . . The only thing for sure is there's money here."[27] In 1948 Peter Yates, who had steadily promoted and performed the émigré composers and their work, became so outspoken in his criticism of the city's musical establishment for ignoring the Europeans that his "Roof" concert organization lost its annual grant from the Los Angeles County Music Commission. Undeterred, in 1949 Yates pronounced it "shameful that our own Philharmonic and Hollywood Bowl orchestras . . . did not commission a single work by a Los Angeles composer! What do we lack in civic pride, in vision, in professional leadership, in communal wisdom and musical perspective, that we allow these occasions, when we might honor our most famous citizen-composers and proudly proclaim our awareness of their reputation, to pass out of our grasp? . . . These are the voices of our city far more truly than the complaints, already lost in time, of those who refuse to recognize or understand them." Looking back twenty years later, Yates wrote that Los Angeles had never been aware that it had gradually become—because of the presence of the émigrés—"the creative center of the musical world."[28]

Taking into account performers as well as composers, teaching could be considered the European musicians' most immediately fruitful legacy. In a 1976 interview, conductor Richard Lert stated, "Teaching is the important thing; much more important here than in Europe. . . . Here the young musicians are thrown into the water; they have to swim. It is not that way in

Europe." Lert, who had grown up in a musical Viennese family and as a child had known Brahms, confessed that he loved to teach, finding it "more important than conducting," and he went on to inspire many young American conductors.[29] In 1940 Schoenberg noted the difference between his American and European teaching: "I myself, who would rather be teaching 'finishers' now have to teach beginners. But I passionately love teaching, and so I can by now feel quite satisfied with my situation."[30] (During the time Schoenberg taught there, UCLA was developing a graduate division and considering a Center for the Performing Arts, but it did not adopt his elaborately worked out plans for a music division.) Pisk, whose American career was devoted to teaching, stated that "American students are much more willing to learn."[31] Numbers of talented American youth found in Southern California the training and close exposure to artistic genius that prepared them for important subsequent careers.

The training was rigorous, and there was a constant need to bridge the cultural differences. From the European point of view, said Marta Feuchtwanger, the novelist's wife, "There are very great differences between the Americans and the Europeans. . . . When you come from Europe, the Germans are so individual, and every neighbor is an enemy; here people are so neighborly and helpful. . . . It's a kind of very easy relationship between people here—maybe not so very deep sometimes, but it is the only way to live together. There is a kind of solidarity of people. . . . I think it must have something to do with the mixture of the people here. They come from so many countries, so you have something in common with everybody." Émigrés from Germany were called *die Bei-unser:* "'By us', you know—where we came from. . . . Every thing was better in Europe than here."[32] Americans tended to feel insulted by émigré stories pointing out European cultural superiority and American lack of tradition. But for the young bent on reaching their potential as musicians, the great artists in their midst presented unimagined opportunities. The composer Leon Kirchner studied at UCLA with Schoenberg, had contact as well with Eisler, Toch, Stravinsky, and Aldous Huxley, attended readings by Lion Feuchtwanger and lectures at UCLA by the British philosopher Bertrand Russell, who had come to the States in 1939 as a pacifist and conscientious objector, like his countrymen Huxley, Christopher Isherwood, and others. Kirchner was one of many who took these daily encounters for granted. He later told an interviewer, "I realize now what escaped me then. That era had the magical and metaphorical thrust given it by these remarkable personalities. Perhaps its most

immediately apparent characteristic was energy . . . vast amounts of it, produced by these great human generators."[33]

Largely because of the investment of energy in and passion for their art
contributed by these displaced Europeans, the cultural isolation of the
area's musicians and adventurous music lovers was gradually eliminated, as
composers, conductors, singers, instrumentalists, music teachers, and even
critics took the opportunities for study and exposure that were uniquely
and easily available to them. Los Angeles, however, still lacked the performing institutions—a world-class music center, an opera company, a dedicated
symphony hall—to sustain them. After they had begun to absorb the disciplines and layers of tradition inherent in European musical training, young
Southern California musicians—particularly the performers—scattered
into the postwar world to develop experience and professionalism. Although Los Angeles is a city of perpetual and rapid change, it took until the
mid-1960s to begin to found and fund the institutions that the master musicians from Europe and their students had so sorely needed. After the end
of World War II, aspiring student singers and instrumentalists moved to
Europe for their apprenticeships, in a reverse migration. They often settled
there, making prominent careers. Thus, in its unsuspecting way, Southern
California contributed not only to America at large but also to the rest of
the world its precious asset of musical artists, many of whom became leaders and teachers themselves.

An alphabetical list of those who benefited directly from the European
migration follows (with my sincere apologies that it is probably not complete).

Composers

John Cage
Hugo Friedhofer
Lou Harrison
Earl Kim
Leon Kirchner
Peter Jona Korn
Oscar Levant
Henry Mancini
Douglas Moore
Alfred Newman
Alex North

Mel Powell
André Previn
David Raksin
Leonard Rosenman
John Williams

Conductors

Lawrence Foster
Charles Hirt
William Kraft
Michael Tilson Thomas
Roger Wagner

Singers

Jeannine Altmeyer
Lucine Amara
Judith Beckmann
Heinz Blankenburg
Grace Bumbry
Nadine Connor
Jean Fenn
Catherine Gayer
Marilyn Hall (professional name Maria Zahlten-Hall)
Marilyn Horne
Ella Lee
George London
Nan Merriman
Carol Neblett
Maralin Niska
Marni Nixon
Roderick Ristow
Brian Sullivan
Theodor Uppman
Benita Valente
Sam van Ducen

Pianists

Irving Beckman
Jeffrey Kahane

Natalie Limonick
Daniel Pollack
Leonard Stein

Harpsichordist

Malcolm Hamilton

Violist

Milton Thomas

Cellists

Steven Kates
Laurence Lesser
Kurt Reher
Nathaniel Rosen
Jeffrey Solow

Opera Stage Director

Lotfi Mansouri

Ethnomusicologist

Mantle Hood

Music Critic

Mildred Norton

3

Otto Klemperer and the
Los Angeles Philharmonic

My home is where I can work the best.

—Otto Klemperer

Otto Klemperer arrived in Los Angeles on October 14, 1933, with no plan to bring his family from their new home in Vienna. He was forty-eight and impressively handsome; he was also intellectually inclined and awkward in social situations. Much to his discomfort, he was greeted at the station with brass fanfares and tossed into a maelstrom of social gatherings, including a film-star-studded dinner at the Biltmore. On the 17th he was presented to the press, which reported his height variously at six feet seven and six feet five, his eyes as expressive and dark, and his face as that of a student or a dramatist. He said that he had been impressed with the number of nationalities in the Philharmonic personnel; he had used four different languages at rehearsal. He hoped to schedule a Mozart opera and to have a chorus for Beethoven's Ninth Symphony, and he hoped that Los Angeles would like him as well going away as arriving.[1] He had no comments for the press about Hollywood movies and film stars; the only film he admired was Russian, and the only film director he could name was French.

At first Klemperer presumed that his would be a temporary appointment to the Los Angeles Philharmonic, which was in a precarious condition because of the Depression. On June 10, 1933, only a week before Klemperer and the orchestra's founder contracted in Paris for his appointment, the *Los Angeles Times* had published an article headlined "Sound Rebuilding of

39

Music in Southland Held Urgent. Symphony Situation with Personal Interests in Conflict, Declared in Need of Complete Overhauling." The article's author, Isabel Morse Jones, echoed the newly elected President Roosevelt in asking that a "new deal" be proposed to save the orchestra. On June 15, just two days before the appointment of Klemperer was announced in Los Angeles, the Philharmonic as an entity refused to sign contracts for the Hollywood Bowl season because union wages were bypassed by the Bowl's management. Individual musicians with loyalty to the orchestra agreed to save the situation by playing the Bowl season at half salary.[2]

The Philharmonic's founder, William A. Clark Jr., heir to his "Copper King" father's enormous mining fortune, was an amateur who enjoyed playing in the second violin section—and conducting. He had financed the orchestra single-handedly since 1919, paying high salaries to such first-class principals as Alfred Brain of the English dynasty of horn players, and Frederick Moritz, a bassoonist from the Leipzig Gewandhaus Orchestra. The New York Stock Exchange's disastrous crash in 1929 had diminished Clark's wealth, and on January 12, 1933, he gave notice that he would withdraw his support at the end of the season. Two days later, the orchestra's conductor, Artur Rodzinski, announced that he had accepted an offer from the Cleveland Orchestra and would leave the Philharmonic owing to the uncertainty of its future. At the time, critic Jones reported that "Los Angeles is the fifth largest city in the United States, yet artistically far behind small cities such as Cincinnati, Cleveland, St. Louis, Minneapolis, Rochester, San Francisco, and Boston, where great symphony orchestras are supported and have splendid concert halls wherein to perform." The continuance of the Los Angeles Philharmonic would require $150,000 annually.[3] *Saturday Night's* music critic, Bertha McCord Knisely, challenged the Hollywood Bowl Association and motion picture studios to help in addressing the problem, as both enterprises depended on the musicians of the Philharmonic.[4] The Bowl Association was itself tottering financially, however, and the motion picture recording studios assumed that the Philharmonic's underpaid players would join the film orchestras for more lucrative year-round employment contracts.

Klemperer's first performance, a mere five days after his arrival, astonished the audience, which began to assume that he had brought the orchestra with him from Europe, so changed was the sound and musical approach.[5] The program consisted of an arrangement of Bach's Toccata in C Minor, Stravinsky's *Petrushka* suite, and Beethoven's Fifth Symphony. Jones reported in the *Times* that "[Klemperer] won by musicianship, authority, and well-nigh ideal control over the resources of the orchestra." Knisely found the change "nothing short of astounding. Strings, brasses, wood-winds and percussion appeared in a new relationship. . . . The season looms as . . . something so significant for the west that I boldly assert New York may envy us. My faith is revived, my hopes boundless." José Rodriguez, in *Script* magazine, exclaimed that it was the first time that he had heard the Philharmonic play "as a genuine ensemble." The *Beverly Hills Town Topics* critic agreed: "The orchestra has not performed with such balance and clar-ity for a long time."[6] The Berlin-trained Sven Reher, who soon joined the orchestra and was made principal violist in 1944, recalled that at the close of this first concert the conductor was greeted by an ovation such as Reher had not heard before or since.[7] Klemperer was disconcerted to hear whistling in the applause, as he was accustomed to this meaning disap-proval in Europe. Max Reinhardt's twenty-year-old son Gottfried, working at MGM as an assistant to Ernst Lubitsch, brought Charles Chaplin, Salka Viertel, and the film director King Vidor backstage to congratulate the con-ductor; young Reinhardt witnessed Klemperer receiving another jolt when, after the performance, he heard Clark conducting his orchestra in Sousa's *Stars and Stripes Forever,* in the empty hall. "Stop! Stop! Stop it at once!" Klemperer bellowed. "I always do this, it is my hobby," said his employer meekly, but he obeyed.[8]

In Berlin, Klemperer—primarily an opera conductor in government-subsidized houses—had never prepared an entire season of concerts, and his work had not been subjected to constant budgetary constraints. Now he had to present new programs every two weeks over a period of six months, with careful attention to box office appeal. His concert repertoire was lim-ited; he was a slow learner who insisted on memorizing and conducting without a score. In his first season there was no money for soloists. Re-quests for works that did not interest him could cause him stomach upset; he would storm out of rehearsal if players were missing; informality irri-tated him; a player chewing gum provoked his wrath. Another source of irritation was the Philharmonic Auditorium on Pershing Square. It was owned by an adjacent Baptist church whose choir practices could be heard during concerts. Although the acoustics in the hall were excellent, concerts were also disturbed by traffic noises, squeaking seats, uncarpeted stairs, and a primitive ventilation system.

As time wore on, Klemperer wrote to friends and family in Europe that Californian food tasted different, he found the heat a torment, and the remoteness was depressing. Something indefinable was lacking. The city seemed to him "an enormous village. Lots of small low houses. Distances such as we can hardly conceive of. It takes me twenty-five minutes by car to the concert hall."[9] (Like several of the emigrating Europeans, Klemperer never learned to drive.) English was difficult for him, and he turned to German-speaking acquaintances. At first young Gottfried Reinhardt showed him around. Salka Viertel, by then writing Greta Garbo's film scripts and hosting a salon for Hollywood's central Europeans, invited him to congenial gatherings at her Santa Monica home. One of the few Americans with whom Klemperer felt comfortable was Richard Buhlig, a concert pianist who had studied in Vienna, had concertized widely in Europe, and had known Klemperer's close friend and colleague Artur Schnabel since their early studies with Theodor Leschetizky. Buhlig was a broadly cultured intellectual, and he provided rare companionship for Klemperer, who found Los Angeles "an intellectual desert such as we don't know in our Europe."[10]

Although the conditions were not the best for his work in Los Angeles, after his initial discouragement Klemperer accepted the challenges he faced. He persevered wholeheartedly with the Philharmonic, expanding his repertoire, bringing the orchestra to extraordinary heights, and drawing enthusiastic and growing audiences, so that critic Rodriguez wrote, "It seems as if Klemperer has broken down the icy wall of . . . indifference which has hitherto spoiled the best efforts of the Philharmonic." Klemperer gradually accustomed himself to the audience's untutored applause between the movements of a symphony, remarking to the press that "when Beethoven conducted his Seventh Symphony in its first performance, in Vienna, the audience was so transported by the lovely *allegretto* that applause continued until the movement was played in repetition."[11] In what young musicians of the time came to think of as a "golden age," Klemperer offered Los Angeles' first full cycle of Beethoven symphonies, an extended Brahms cycle, its first performances of such works as Bach's Brandenburg Concerto No. 1, Haydn's "Clock" and "Farewell" symphonies, Bruckner's Fourth and Seventh Symphonies, Mahler's Second Symphony and *Das Lied von der Erde,* and recent works of Stravinsky, Hindemith, Kurt Weill, Ernst Toch, Ernest Bloch, Roger Sessions, Roy Harris, and William Grant Still. While he performed Arnold Schoenberg's tonal music, he tried to convince Schoenberg that the Los Angeles public was not yet ready for atonal or twelve-tone music.[12] He conducted young people's concerts, giving the introductory comments himself. He founded and occasionally conducted a Junior Philharmonic and conducted educational concerts at UCLA's Royce Hall. Starting in 1936 he even reluctantly agreed to conduct the Easter sunrise service at Los Angeles' famed Forest Lawn cemetery, a task that violated his artistic and religious attitudes because of its "showbiz religiosity."[13] To his greater satisfaction, he was awarded honorary doctorates by Occidental College in 1936 and UCLA in 1937.

The music critics responded with pressure on the public to support, not lose, their heroic new conductor. Jones wrote in February 1934 that "Klemperer not only makes Brahms sing through this glorious instrument he has made of the Los Angeles Philharmonic Orchestra, but he makes Brahms's music speak eloquently of his own life-experience and of the wisdom gained in years of conducting. . . . Surely if Los Angeles thinks it can do without the Philharmonic, it should hear the Brahms Third now and know better." The last program of Klemperer's first Philharmonic season was Beethoven's Ninth Symphony, with the Los Angeles Oratorio Society prepared by its conductor, John Smallman. Jones reported a "wildly enthusiastic demonstration" of twenty minutes for Klemperer, Clark, and Smallman. "Los Angeles music lovers have never expressed themselves so emphatically or so spontaneously as they did last night in their tribute to Klemperer."[14] Well might they pay tribute, for in June 1934, during this perilous yet promising time for the orchestra and its conductor, Clark died suddenly, at the age of fifty-seven, of a heart condition. Between 1919 and his death, Clark had spent three million dollars on the orchestra. At his death he willed nothing to it, although his fortune, considered vast at the time, was estimated at five million dollars. Shock at Clark's sudden demise was so great that the *Times*'s front page was devoted to it, with headlines of a size normally used for earthquakes and declarations of war.

In August 1934 Jones announced in the *Times* that a group of citizens was working to bring Klemperer back to the Philharmonic for the next season, claiming that "the desire for a hero around whom we can rally is strong in this town."[15] The new Southern California Symphony Association was a coalition of business and educational leaders headed by a wealthy engineer, Harvey S. Mudd, and the president of Occidental College, Remsen D. Bird. Klemperer had returned to his new home in increasingly anti-Semitic Austria for the summer. Pessimistic about the Los Angeles orchestra's survival, yet worried about the future for his family in Europe, he accepted fall and winter guest engagements with the New York Philharmonic, from which Arturo Toscanini was planning to retire, and the Philadelphia Orchestra, from which Leopold Stokowski was—temporarily, as it turned out—resigning as musical director. By October, Mudd and his associates were able to guarantee Klemperer's salary in Los Angeles for a six-week season between these East Coast engagements. Just before the concert season began in November, the Philharmonic players who had not deserted for film and radio recording studios were offered contracts. Klemperer, whose wife, Johanna, accompanied him to Los Angeles in the fall of 1934, insisted that he be given a three-year contract. Mudd agreed to personally guarantee his salary for that period, although such a guarantee for the orchestra personnel was not assured.

From Klemperer's first sold-out program in November 1934, it was clear that the Philharmonic's audiences were even larger and more enthusiastic. Jones wrote that Klemperer was attracting new young players for the orchestra. "He is here in Southern California permanently, if the people want him. . . . The men in the orchestra work harder for Klemperer. . . . They rave and tear their hair over the rehearsals sometimes but they all adore him, fear him, respect and esteem him. . . . It is a matter of Klemperer's enormous sincerity. . . . The man has a dignity that is overwhelming at times but never oppressive. Certain facetious intimates of the orchestra call him 'The Big Bad Wolf.'" As he departed for New York in December, Jones proclaimed again that "Klemperer is the musical hero of this city, beyond any shadow of a doubt." In the short 1934–35 season Klemperer conducted Bach's Brandenburg Concerto No. 1 from the keyboard; he also gave the first West Coast performances of Hindemith's *Mathis der Maler* symphony, and Stravinsky's *Pulcinella* suite. Honoring Schoenberg, who had arrived in Hollywood in October, Klemperer conducted his *Verklärte Nacht* in mid-December. Jones wrote of the response that "The large audience clapped and cheered after the momentous performance of Schoenberg's ardent tone-poem until Schoenberg and Klemperer had returned to the stage five times. A demonstration of this kind is unusual in any city, but, following the presentation of a little-known modern work, . . . it marked a new peak of enthusiasm for Los Angeles."[16]

Klemperer arranged for Schoenberg, Stravinsky (on his second American tour), and the recently arrived Viennese composer Erich Wolfgang Korngold to guest conduct programs with the Philharmonic in the spring of 1935. Klemperer had conducted Korngold's most celebrated opera, *Die tote Stadt*, in Cologne in 1920, at the time of its simultaneous world premiere with Hamburg. The composer, Max Reinhardt's favorite musical collaborator, was in Hollywood arranging Mendelssohn's music for the filming of Reinhardt's spectacular Hollywood Bowl production of *A Midsummer Night's Dream*. Klemperer ended the 1934–35 season with Mahler's gigantic Second Symphony ("Resurrection"), performed the last week of May in the enormous Shrine Auditorium. This work's special meaning to Klemperer derived from the fact that his preparation of the chorus for its 1905 Berlin premiere under Mahler had been the genesis of his own conducting career. (In December 1935 Klemperer's performance of the same work with the New York Philharmonic, while a triumph artistically, ended his hopes of a permanent position with that orchestra, for his manager, Arthur Judson, was angry at the substantial financial deficit the work incurred in three performances, making difficulties that enraged Klemperer.[17])

In February 1935 the Southern California Symphony Association appointed Florence Irish to be manager of the Los Angeles Philharmonic. She had training both as an organist and as a public speaker. She had worked under Artie Mason Carter and had successfully managed summer concerts at the Hollywood Bowl from 1926 to 1929. She was stout, overdressed, and exuberant. Klemperer initially considered her a vulgar busybody, but her energy and devotion to him and to her tasks of rescuing the Philharmonic won him over.[18] She managed to talk him into conducting during the Hollywood Bowl summer season. "It's not very dignified, and there is only one rehearsal for each concert," he complained, but the Philharmonic had assumed responsibility for the summer concerts, and as music director he could not refuse involvement.[19] The high standard of his programs at the Bowl, and the solo artists he worked with, set attendance records. The final concert of the 1935 Bowl season coupled Wagner's Prelude and Liebestod from *Tristan und Isolde* with Beethoven's Ninth Symphony this time with the Los Angeles Oratorio Society rehearsed by Klemperer's colleague from Berlin, Richard Lert, a regular guest conductor in the Hollywood Bowl who had emigrated in 1934.

Klemperer applied for American citizenship in May 1935, gave up his Vienna apartment, and settled with his wife and two children in a spacious rented home in the glamorous Bel Air section of Los Angeles. Perhaps in connection with the 1935 Bowl performance of Beethoven's Ninth Symphony, Klemperer gave a summer party at his new home that was attended by a distinguished international gathering of conductors, including Lert, Pierre Monteux, José Iturbi, Pietro Cimini, and Bernardino Molinari. Photographs of the occasion (including Schoenberg, looking tanned and convivial in a snappy white summer suit) reflect Klemperer's magnetic attraction for European musicians. He wrote in a letter at the time that he knew his task in Los Angeles was that of a pioneer, but also realized that "the people are endlessly grateful and really love me. . . . About the life (and everything that goes with it) I still often have doubts. . . . But how infinitely grateful I must be to the great America, which gives me bread and work— and, if God so wills, will also provide for our children."[20]

The dire political situation in Europe was producing an onrush of new arrivals. World-class soloists Klemperer had known well and worked with were moving to the United States, and in January 1936 he was able to announce a stunning list of soloists invited to perform with the Philharmonic, including the Hungarian violinist Joseph Szigeti, German soprano Lotte Lehmann, Polish violinist Bronislaw Huberman, Austrian pianist Artur Schnabel, Austrian cellist Emanuel Feuermann, and Russian cellist Gregor Piatigorsky. While Klemperer had previously been frustrated by the lack of funds to engage these artists for solo appearances with the orchestra, he had already drawn several of them to Los Angeles for recitals. Feuermann, still in his early thirties and making his first trip to the West Coast, played for his April 1936 Philharmonic program Schoenberg's virtuosic Cello Concerto, composed in 1933 for Pablo Casals after a keyboard concerto by Mattias Monn.[21] Feuermann had premiered this concerto the previous year in London. "It is involved in instrumentation, but has the Schoenberg luminosity and romanticism. The solo part shines through in unusual beauty," wrote critic Jones.[22] The month of this performance, Schoenberg sent a heartfelt testimonial to the *Los Angeles Herald Examiner* in response to the annual plea for funds to cover the Philharmonic's deficit: "As the materialism of our time seems to endanger the whole sphere of spiritual culture, I believe it is the duty of every man to fight for the existence of one of the most vital symbols of man's higher life."[23]

In spite of the considerable excitement generated by Klemperer, the Los Angeles public was not yet fully supporting the Philharmonic. In the summer of 1936, as it became clear that there was again no certainty about paying the orchestra members in the coming season and that there would be no decision until October, Klemperer called a meeting of the orchestra's board, to which he proposed a "voluntary music tax." He was told that there was not the widespread interest in music to permit such a tax.[24] In response, Jones pointed out in the *Times* that Los Angeles had collected the

Otto Klemperer, 1934. Photo Murillo Studio, Venice, California. UCLA Library, Philip Kahgan Collection of Concert Programs, Photographs and Papers.

largest public music library in the country and that the segment of its population with high incomes was abnormally large in comparison to that of other cities. "Is it possible," she asked, "that the world's richest market cannot afford to stock a symphony orchestra?"[25]

In the fall, Klemperer returned to Austria to open the season of the Vienna Philharmonic with Alban Berg's new Violin Concerto on October 25, 1936. The soloist was the American violinist Louis Krasner, who had commissioned the heartrending work. While composing it in the last exhausted months of his life, Berg had learned that his government no longer consid-

Richard Lert with Vicki Baum, 1932. UCLA Library, Philip Kahgan Collection of Concert Programs, Photographs and Papers.

ered him and his work to be genuinely Austrian. The concerto's premieres in Barcelona and London had aroused great anticipation among musical circles in Vienna, Berg's home. Nazi-dominated orchestra members threatened to boycott the Austrian premiere, but Klemperer refused to withdraw Berg's composition. The moment the last note ended at the performance, the entire orchestra membership rose as one and marched off the stage, leaving Klemperer and Krasner, both Jews, standing alone on the stage to face the audience, accompanied only by the revered concertmaster Arnold

Klemperer's Bel Air reception, 1935. From left to right: Conductor/pianist José Iturbi; conductors Otto Klemperer, Richard Lert, Henry Swedrofsky, Pietro Cimini, and Bernardino Molinari; composer Arnold Schoenberg; conductor Pierre Monteux; and cellist William (Willem) van den Burg. Otto Rothschild Collection, Music Center Archives, Los Angeles.

Rosé, who applauded them and gripped their hands in a signal of solidarity against such demonstrations.[26]

Back in Los Angeles, because of further attrition of Philharmonic players to the film studio orchestras, Klemperer made significant changes in the orchestra's personnel in 1937. He introduced a new concertmaster, the twenty-six-year-old Polish violinist Bronislaw Gimpel, in a concerto with the Philharmonic at the Hollywood Bowl. Klemperer was the first Philharmonic conductor to admit women to the orchestra; three women were among the fourteen replacements who had auditioned behind a screen, with first-chair players listening. The twenty-one-year-old clarinetist Kalman Bloch, who had prepared himself in four years' training with New York's National Orchestral Society, had just about decided to go into the field of dentistry when he was called to audition for principal clarinet, his first job. He won the position, later recalling with enthusiasm that "the orchestra was very good, mostly European-trained musicians. The woodwind section included famous players, who accepted me with kindness. Klemperer's musicianship and sense of rhythm impressed me very much. Despite his moments of temper, the men would play their hearts out for Klemperer. There was a magic about his conducting; he didn't talk much."[27]

In a 1960 interview, Klemperer's own laconic comment about conducting was, "Mostly one conducts with the eyes."[28] The Viennese mezzo-soprano Herta Glaz said that her American concert debut in the West Coast premiere of Mahler's *Das Lied von der Erde* in March 1937 was one of the high points in her career: "[Klemperer's] mental power was such that you really couldn't do anything else but what he wanted. . . . Like a magnet, he transferred his thoughts to me. I was also a little afraid of him. He could be very sarcastic. He could put you down in front of the whole orchestra. . . . His willpower was enormous. . . . [Yet, when Schoenberg] came to one rehearsal. . . . Klemperer went to him [and asked] 'Maestro,' (as if he was a child) 'Was it good? Please tell me.'"[29]

By 1938, when Klemperer signed another three-year contract, the orchestra's deficits were rising, no endowment had been established, and there was no pension fund for the players. Schnabel, Artur Rubinstein, and Piatigorsky, whom Klemperer called "the greatest string player in the world," appeared as notable soloists in 1938 and 1939. In March 1939 Klemperer invited Hindemith to play his Viola Concerto with the orchestra and to conduct a suite from his 1938 ballet, *Nobilissima visione*. Hindemith's music "left the audience, for the most part, either bewildered, resentful, bored, or militantly in favor of it," according to Jones, who found it "cerebral."[30] Hindemith wrote to his wife in Europe that he had been allotted eight hours of rehearsal with the Philharmonic, which had responded easily to his demands, giving his works the best success they had so far enjoyed. He also reported that Los Angeles was too provincial for him. He described with malice the lack of a musically educated society in this "gigantic" city. Florence Irish and the ladies of the Junior Women's Association of the Philharmonic made him queasy. In his opinion, the émigrés Schoenberg, Toch, and Lert had found themselves in lamentable situations.[31]

Klemperer created a special fund, announced February 2, 1938, by Jones in the *Times*, to enable the orchestra to pay royalties for new works. His willingness to explore new territory (beside the Sessions, Harris, and Still works mentioned earlier) included works by American composers John Alden Carpenter, Deems Taylor, Daniel Gregory Mason, Harl McDonald, Gerald Strang, Edward Burlingame Hill, Samuel Barber, Russian-born Louis Gruenberg, and Polish-born Joseph Achron. In 1939 Peter Yates, who was in correspondence with Charles Ives and had obtained some of his scores, wrote to Klemperer about Ives's music. The conductor wrote in response that he was very interested in what Yates had told him about the music of Charles Ives, but the music might be too difficult with his limited orchestral rehearsal time. Nevertheless, if Yates could help him obtain an orchestral score without a soloist, he would be glad to take a look at it. In any case, he was looking forward to hearing Yates's pianist wife, Frances, play Ives's *Concord* Sonata in a coming program. Klemperer attended this performance, on June 25, 1939, of the *Concord* Sonata at the recently inaugurated "Evenings on the Roof." Afterward, Yates explained to Klemperer that Ives was now too ill to compose. "With that, Otto grew very sad—he is not at all well himself," wrote Yates to a friend. Persuaded that *Three Places in New England* was the only suitable possibility amongst Yates's collection of Ives compositions, Klemperer borrowed Yates's score.[32]

At the end of April 1939 the *Times* reported that Klemperer had conducted one of his most strenuous seasons: sixty-four concerts, including nine out-of-town and four young people's concerts. This had included fifteen performances of works new to Philharmonic audiences, including one world premiere and several first American performances, and the *Times* article noted that he was about to take an extended vacation. In reality Klemperer was unwell. He was suffering from depression, but even worse were his growing problems of balance, difficulty with his right hand in playing the piano, and a noticeable decline in his usually enormous stamina. Unfortunately, he received the same misdiagnosis George Gershwin had been given two summers previously: hysteria, arising from depression. Klemperer tried swimming and massage at a resort at Lake Arrowhead; the depression lifted, but the balance problems increased. In the summer concerts at the Bowl it was difficult for him to walk across the stage.

Klemperer's Bowl concerts were always elevated intellectually as well as musically above the usual summer fare. On August 24, 1939, his *Lohengrin* Prelude "put the acoustic properties of the Bowl through severe tests with his pianissimo," but the beauty of the program, which featured Lotte Lehmann (whose career had begun with Klemperer in 1912), "rededicated [the Bowl] to music of lofty character," wrote Jones. On the eve of Germany's invasion of Poland, Klemperer conducted the final Bowl concert of the season. It included the overture to Mozart's *Abduction from the Seraglio,* the Sibelius Violin Concerto with Heifetz as soloist, and Tchaikovsky's Sixth Symphony ("Pathétique"), and ended with Schoenberg's orchestral arrangement of Brahms's Piano Quartet in G Minor. (Knowing Schoenberg's affinity for the music of Brahms, in the summer of 1937 Klemperer had suggested this assignment; Schoenberg liked to call it "Brahms's Fifth.") Again these programs attracted record attendance, and the orchestra ended the 1939 season with a healthy surplus of funds.

Two weeks later, Klemperer's brain tumor was belatedly diagnosed in Boston. He underwent two surgeries that left him partially paralyzed on the right side and exacerbated his bipolar illness. During and after recovery in New York, Klemperer entered the longest manic phase of his life. His behavior, both public and private, was destructive to his reputation, leading to his release from his Los Angeles contract. The dismissal angered and hurt him deeply. He still felt an emotional tie to the orchestra he had nurtured, and he sent a warm telegram to the Philharmonic for the opening concert of its 1939–40 season: "As ever my heart is with you all. May a glorious season start today."[33]

The first and most commanding presence among the astonishing array of musical talent driven to Southern California by Hitler, Klemperer was the charismatic leader Los Angeles needed. Although he returned to Los Angeles during and after his recovery and conducted the orchestra as a guest, the loss of Klemperer as music director of the Philharmonic created a lasting vacuum. The 1939–40 Philharmonic season was hastily put together with guest conductors: Bruno Walter was living in Beverly Hills; the British conductor Albert Coates was available; Leopold Stokowski was in Hollywood on an eighteen-month contract with Disney, filming *Fantasia.* Jones wrote that Walter's opening program, featuring Mozart's Symphony No. 40 in G Minor, "carried the listeners to another plane . . . lost to this world and safe with Mozart and Walter in a better one," dispelling some of the doubt and chaos following the loss of Klemperer's powerful leadership, and reflecting the fact that—although at first the conflict seemed very distant to Southern Californians—the Second World War had begun.[34]

The parade of guest conductors continued for four years, with no single artistic focus or goals for the Philharmonic. In 1940, to fill the dearth of new and unusual works in Los Angeles' orchestral programming, Werner Janssen, an American composer of film scores and Broadway musicals who had studied conducting in Europe with Felix Weingartner, founded the Janssen Symphony Orchestra. This enterprise endured until 1952, giving many important premieres of works by émigré composers. In 1947, with a similar desire to bring greater musical interest to the city, Franz Waxman, by then a successful Hollywood film composer, established the Los Angeles Festival. This annual series of musical events featured orchestral repertoire new to Los Angeles, including compositions and performances by eminent

Europeans. A third ensemble, gathered in 1949, was the Los Angeles Chamber Symphony Orchestra, founded by the German émigré Harold Byrns.

In the summer of 1943, at a time when wartime patriotism was a strong influence upon the country's arts, an American, Alfred Wallenstein, was appointed musical director of the Philharmonic. Wallenstein, a cellist, had grown up in Los Angeles and had played with the Philharmonic in its initial season, then as a principal with the Chicago Symphony and with the New York Philharmonic. His tenure as director of the Los Angeles Philharmonic from 1943 until 1956 proved to be a disillusioning process for the city's maturing musical community. Wallenstein was often absent, enjoying the social circles in Palm Springs while leaving musical duties to his assistant conductor and the orchestra's first-chair players.[35] At the end of the first year of Wallenstein's term, several of the best orchestra members defected to the film studios.[36] By contrast, that year music critic Alfred Price Quinn wrote that Yates's "Evenings On the Roof concerts . . . have now become the most widely discussed private musical enterprise in the city." In 1945 Quinn, a Leipzig-trained pianist, stated baldly in the *B'nai B'rith Messenger* that "Wallenstein is not the leader the orchestra needs."[37] By the early 1950s the orchestra was in dire straits, provoking further pressure for a new conductor.

In 1948, as growing right-wing paranoia in California precipitated the first anticommunist investigations and persecutions in Hollywood, Yates published his accusation that Wallenstein was developing a conservative patronage that remained in "pleasant inertia." In private, Yates wrote to a friend that the *Los Angeles Times* had replaced crusader Isabel Morse Jones for what Yates called "refusing to go along with the right people." (Mildred Norton of the *Daily News,* who had studied with Schoenberg, took up Jones's role of independent advocate.) Yates further attacked the "Chamber of Commerce" attitude in Los Angeles, which, through the Philharmonic's programming, refused to recognize the important émigré composers who were continuing to settle in the city.[38]

These disappointing developments in Los Angeles' classical music world aided the success of Yates's chamber concerts. Many of the Philharmonic's finest players took the almost nonexistent pay offered by his "Evenings on the Roof" series in order to play repertoire that challenged them. While the Philharmonic ignored the city's growing community of European émigré composers and performers, Yates gave them special recognition, thus drawing a substantial émigré audience, hungry for the challenging fare they had known in their homelands. He published essays on what he called his "tough" programs, and as his writing came to national attention, so did the achievements of the Roof concerts. These concerts, spurring musical sophistication by their balance of adventures into both the present and the past of serious music, provided a focus for the scattered intelligentsia of Los Angeles. The vacuum caused by the loss of Klemperer's stimulating leadership of the Philharmonic opened the door for the Roof's enduring leadership in innovative chamber music, as it also provided shorter—but important— terms of entrepreneurship for the orchestral conductors Janssen, Waxman, and Byrns.

4

Performers, and Klemperer's Return

Music remains above you. The better you become at it, the music moves higher, so it becomes unreachable.

—Gregor Piatigorsky

It was not only the beauty and Mediterranean climate of Southern California but also a network of relationships that drew the fleeing European performers. At first, Klemperer was at the center of this network. Of the many European artists he invited to Los Angeles to perform, the soprano Lotte Lehmann, the violinist Joseph Szigeti, and the cellist Gregor Piatigorsky all made their homes in Southern California, where the force of their personalities resounded in varying ways among the musical community for several decades. The cellist Emanuel Feuermann, on the faculty at the Curtis Institute in Philadelphia, also taught master classes in Pacific Palisades the last two summers of his tragically short life. The pianist Artur Schnabel, although not a resident, did much to further the local cause of chamber music, at that time a difficult product to sell in Southern California.

Joseph Szigeti exhibited unwavering integrity, nonconformist musical attitudes, and a cultural curiosity he had drawn from his early experiences with the violinist Joseph Joachim and the pianist and composer Ferruccio Busoni, as well as the influence of Schnabel, his recital partner. Szigeti's programming choices were courageous for the time. His first Los Angeles recital, at Klemperer's invitation in 1933, offered a Bach sonata for solo violin, the Debussy sonata, a Brahms sonata, and works of Ernest Bloch,

Joseph Achron, and Manuel de Falla. Critic Jones wrote in the *Los Angeles Times* that Szigeti's performance represented a "new age in virtuosi, the day of an intellectual awakening in music." After his initial appearance with Klemperer and the Los Angeles Philharmonic in January 1936, Jones noted that Szigeti "is not the usual sensationalist who breaks into American music like a meteor and goes out as quickly. . . . He has brilliant technical equipment but his distinguishing virtue is serious, interpretive musicianship." In an interview at the time, Szigeti told Jones he never started practicing a composition until he had first memorized it. He also observed, "I think jazz has sharpened the receptivity of the listener. Great music will benefit from that."[1] His idea of artistry was "to reach out for an ever wider and more universal audience than our performance was originally destined for." Following up on this idea, in 1938 Szigeti persuaded his friend and colleague Béla Bartók to accept a commission from the clarinetist and swing band leader Benny Goodman, which resulted in a highly successful trio, *Contrasts,* for their three instruments.[2]

Szigeti and his wife emigrated to America in 1939, and the decision to live in California grew out of "a summer vacation that perpetuated itself" as he fought in 1940 to overcome a depression that persisted while he endured torturing uncertainty about his relatives and possessions in Europe.[3] By 1942 he and his family were living in a house on the Palos Verdes Peninsula southwest of Los Angeles. When not on his annual tours, performing for Canadian, Russian, and American soldiers, raising thousands of dollars in War Bond sales, or appearing for all the relief agencies during the war years, Szigeti began to involve himself in Los Angeles' musical affairs. In 1942 he played the Brahms Violin Concerto with fellow Hungarian George Szell conducting the Philharmonic in the Hollywood Bowl, where Jones noted that "the audience listened with an intentness that bespoke the keenest enjoyment."[4] His 1943 solo appearance in the Pasadena Civic Auditorium with Werner Janssen's orchestra included the *Stempenyu* Suite, a work dedicated to Szigeti by the Lithuanian-born violinist-composer Joseph Achron, who had recently died in Los Angeles.[5] The following year, as part of a widespread cultural effort to understand America's new allies the Russians, Janssen presented an all-Russian program, including Szigeti's performance of the Prokofiev Violin Concerto, at the Wilshire-Ebell Theater. In 1945 Szigeti repeated the work for a Russian War Relief concert, conducted in the Hollywood Bowl by Bruno Walter. In 1950 he generously offered Yates's "Evenings on the Roof" a memorable benefit concert consisting of

Joseph Szigeti, 1942. Otto Rothschild Collection, Music Center Archives, Los Angeles.

J. S. Bach's three sonatas for solo violin, which drew a large audience to the Wilshire Ebell Theater. Los Angeles violist Milton Thomas, who later played with Casals, Heifetz, and Dame Myra Hess and taught on the music faculty of the University of Southern California, remembered Szigeti's recital as his single most influential musical experience.[6]

The enterprising program that had introduced Szigeti to Yates's concerts was the first American performance (in June 1947) of Hindemith's unpublished realization of five of the "Rosary" violin sonatas by Heinrich Ignaz Franz von Biber, titled *The Passion of Our Lord,* presented by the harpsichordist Alice Ehlers with her fellow émigré, the violinist Adolph Koldofsky.

Austrian-born Ehlers had toured in Europe with Hindemith, playing these sacred violin sonatas by Biber, after her studies in Vienna with Leschetizky and Schoenberg and in Berlin with the pioneering harpsichordist Wanda Landowska and the musicologist Curt Sachs. She left Germany for England in 1933, when her friend and mentor Dr. Albert Schweitzer, with whom she had studied the works of Bach, warned her of the approaching danger to Jews in Germany. In 1938, during a temporary appointment to the Juilliard School of Music in New York, Ehlers visited her younger daughter in Los Angeles. The German-Swiss film director William Wyler heard her perform and cast her to play her own harpsichord in his 1939 film *Wuthering Heights*.[7] Bing Crosby asked her to play twice on his radio show *The Bing Crosby Hour*. By then the situation in Europe was so dangerous that Ehlers's Los Angeles agent, Dorothy Huttenback—a German-trained pianist—told her not to go back to Europe and put her in touch with Max Krone, dean of the University of Southern California's School of Music.

USC's School of Music had experienced a severe decline during the Depression. During its struggle with low enrollments and little money for faculty salaries in the 1930s, a generous gift of funds for a building, an auditorium, an ensemble, a trio, and free concerts—all established with his name on them—was provided by the eccentric Captain G. Allan Hancock, a wealthy oil man, developer, banker, aviator, sea captain, railroad engineer, marine biologist, cellist, and philanthropist. In 1942, a year after her appointment as a full professor at USC, Alice Ehlers was named to the School of Music's "artist faculty," whose salaries were paid by Captain Hancock.[8]

For twenty-five years at USC, Alice Ehlers took on the challenge of introducing her instrument and early music literature to students for whom this was a fresh experience. Beside teaching both piano and harpsichord and three classes in music history, each year she organized an eighteenth-century music festival, for which she coached singers and worked with conductors in performance practice. Choral conductor Roger Wagner, harpsichordist Malcolm Hamilton, and mezzo-soprano Marilyn Horne were among her many students. Ehlers dedicated the festivals—which occurred in the Christmas season and involved the sacred music of Bach—to her mentor, Schweitzer, and made a point of taking donations that then were sent to help his medical work in Africa. Ehlers performed continually, in solo recitals, oratorio and festival concerts, and in small ensembles. Her complete performance of Bach's Goldberg Variations at a Roof concert in 1945 brought a capacity crowd, which listened with "rapt attention" and rewarded her with a long and enthusiastic ovation. "Had this near miracle

Alice Ehlers, 1951. Otto Rothschild Collection, Music Center Archives, Los Angeles.

not been witnessed, skepticism as to its truth would have been my reaction," wrote critic Alfred Price Quinn.[9]

Although Artur Schnabel had settled in New York City in 1933, his relationship with Los Angeles, developed through friendships with Klemperer and others, proved strong and enduring. At his first Los Angeles performance in 1938 of both Mozart's Piano Concerto No. 21 and Beethoven's "Emperor" Concerto with Klemperer and the Philharmonic, there was an unprecedented demonstration of appreciation. Schnabel continued to make frequent visits to the city. In 1943, although he had dropped his New York concert management, he attracted an overflow audience to UCLA's Royce Hall for a program of piano sonatas attended by Klemperer, and he returned several times in the 1940s for further recitals.[10]

Through his colleague and fellow Leschetizky pupil Richard Buhlig, who lived in Los Angeles, Schnabel became interested in the uncompromising programming of Yates's "Evenings on the Roof." In 1946 he learned that the newly formed Music Guild, in proposing to present such celebrity performers as himself, was on the point of threatening the future of the artistically successful but financially insecure Roof concerts, which used only local musicians. Schnabel successfully urged that the Music Guild subsidize the Roof concerts, making his appearance contingent on this collaboration.[11] Further, when the London String Quartet, scheduled to perform for the Music Guild with Schnabel, canceled at the last minute, Schnabel chose as substitutes the young American Art Quartet, a Los Angeles ensemble formed for the Roof concerts with Yates's encouragement. The success of their performance with Schnabel established the young quartet and brought its members (violinists Eudice Shapiro and Marvin Limonick, violist Virginia Majewski, and cellist Victor Gottlieb) many further opportunities— both professional and informal—among Southern California's stellar European instrumentalists.[12]

The violinist Jascha Heifetz, a member of the earlier wave of White Russian émigrés, was living in Beverly Hills in 1937. As European colleagues began gathering in Southern California in the mid- and late 1930s, he suggested to the RCA Victor recording company that he would like to record piano trios with the pianist Artur Rubinstein and either Feuermann or Piatigorsky.[13] In 1938 Feuermann emigrated to the United States and immediately applied for citizenship. That same year, Rubinstein demonstrated against Mussolini's adoption of Hitler's anti-Semitic laws and was banned from further performance in Italy. Poland, Rubinstein's homeland, made threatening publicity out of this event and also banned his performances. Rubinstein and his wife, living in Paris, were then cut off from their families by the German invasion of Poland. The American ambassador to France arranged for them to be evacuated along with Americans leaving France by boat for the United States in October 1939.

Rubinstein's tours to the West Coast became more frequent after his recital in Philharmonic Auditorium in February 1938, when, critic Jones wrote, he "aroused a Los Angeles audience to demonstrate genuine enthusiasm and excitement in a way that has not been equaled in years." Rubinstein returned to the city in 1939 to play Tchaikovsky's First Piano Concerto with Klemperer and the Philharmonic, "a thing to remember among concert experiences. . . . octaves faster than the ear could follow, or the eyes either."[14] Like Heifetz, Rubinstein was attracted by the glamour of Hollywood. A summer vacation in the Los Angeles area convinced him to buy a

Emanuel Feuermann, January 1939. *Los Angeles Examiner* **Collection, University of Southern California.**

house and settle there in 1941. Feuermann spent that same summer in Pacific Palisades teaching master classes gathered by his students.

With the 1941 conjunction of Heifetz, Feuermann, and Rubinstein in Los Angeles, RCA Victor was at last able to bring the three major artists together for recordings. A newspaper publicity clipping from September 7, 1941, showed the three laughing together as they prepared to record piano trios of Brahms, Beethoven, and Schubert.[15] Serious tensions developed, however, between Rubinstein and Heifetz, whose temperaments and opinions on musical interpretation, particularly regarding tempos, constantly clashed. Feuermann, in a gentlemanly letter to Rubinstein indicating his

Artur Rubinstein with his son, Alina, 1945. Otto Rothschild Collection, Music Center Archives, Los Angeles.

cautious enthusiasm over the recording takes, clearly felt himself walking a tightrope. Rubinstein later referred to Feuermann as "an artist after my heart. A supreme master of his instrument, he was a source of inspiration through-out our recordings. In the Schubert and the Beethoven, I had constant argu-ments with Heifetz, never with Feuermann. . . . The Brahms Trio did not quite satisfy any of us."[16] The ensemble scheduled a public performance to coincide with the release of the recordings the following spring (1942), but at that very time Feuermann's ascent as a brilliant performer—along with his tremendous promise as a teacher—was tragically cut short by his sudden death following routine surgery. To honor Feuermann, Heifetz waited seven years before forming another piano trio with Rubinstein and Piatigorsky.

Rubinstein felt that Hollywood was "simply bursting with vitality" during the war years.[17] He performed regularly in the Hollywood Bowl, and in the 1950s he was the soloist for Alfred Wallenstein and the Philharmonic in all the Beethoven piano concertos. He taught a few students privately but admitted, "I am not a pedagogue." Instead, he relished socializing among Hollywood celebrities, and took on several film recording assignments. At his Beverly Hills home, Rubinstein hosted informal chamber music evenings to which he invited Thomas Mann and others of the émigré community. He also liked to bring émigrés together with Hollywood stars. In 1949 he took up the cause of the new Los Angeles Chamber Symphony Orchestra and gave an afternoon benefit concert in a tent on the lawn of his mansion, playing a Mozart piano concerto with the orchestra and its founder-conductor, German émigré Harold Byrns. This event gathered a crowd of about 200, most of them movie stars; Robert Craft, who was there with the Stravinskys, remarked, "I had never seen so many familiar faces in one place."[18]

In the absence of performances of new orchestral music by the Philharmonic during the Wallenstein years, conductor Byrns offered works by area émigré composers Schoenberg, Stravinsky, Toch, Hindemith, and Eric Zeisl, thereby contributing "with intimidating severity . . . a highly worthwhile addition to the local musical scene," according to critic Mildred Norton.[19] Born Hans Bernstein in Hanover, he had been thoroughly trained in Berlin as a composer, coach, and conductor and until 1933 had conducted in various North German opera houses. After emigrating from Italy to the United States in 1936, he guest conducted in New York and Boston. By 1948 he was working in Hollywood as an uncredited orchestrator for MGM's film scores. Byrns's successful Los Angeles Chamber Symphony Orchestra was initially a group of thirty players selected in 1949 from the film studios' finest musicians, with the Roof's American Art Quartet as principals. The enterprising Byrns became acquainted with Alma Mahler Werfel in Los Angeles, orchestrated early songs by Gustav Mahler, and in the year before her death was able to convince her to break her ban on performances of musicologist Deryck Cooke's completion of Mahler's Tenth Symphony. Byrns premiered Korngold's Symphony in F-Sharp with the Vienna Symphony in 1954 and thereafter performed often in Europe.

In 1929 Russian-born Gregor Piatigorsky had met with an extraordinary reception to his first Los Angeles concert appearance with the Philharmonic, the program of which included the Dvořák Cello Concerto and Richard Strauss's *Don Quixote*. The orchestra's founder, William Clark,

"brought my cello on-stage, insisting that I respond to the demands for encores. Movement after movement from various Bach suites followed, and
the last orchestral piece on the program was not played at all," Piatigorsky
remembered.[20] He subsequently performed in Los Angeles on tours in
1934 and 1935, and in 1936 with Klemperer and the Philharmonic. In 1939
Klemperer brought Piatigorsky back to play the Schumann Concerto.
About this occasion Jones wrote in the *Los Angeles Times*, "There are few
players who can make the instrument sing in this Schumann but when Piatigorsky plays it, strong men and fellow-musicians in the orchestra become
dewy eyed. [There is] a compassionate gentleness about his playing. . . .
Nothing is too hard for Piatigorsky. . . . He dominates the instrument but
he woos it, too. The audience was enchanted with his playing and with the
personality of this giant of the steppes."[21] Piatigorsky returned to Los Angeles several times in the 1940s to give recitals and to play in the Hollywood
Bowl, always to unusually large audiences.

In 1949 Piatigorsky left the Curtis Institute in Philadelphia, where he
had taught since 1942 as Feuermann's replacement, and moved with his
wife and two children to Brentwood. That year Heifetz, Rubinstein, and
Piatigorsky were brought together for four programs of piano trios at
Chicago's Ravinia Festival, and some of these were recorded. Rubinstein
did not like the nickname "The Million Dollar Trio," which *Life* magazine
attached to the ensemble. There were further musical squabbles between
Heifetz and Rubinstein. After making recordings in 1950, followed by short
television films of the celebrity trio, Heifetz and Rubinstein never performed
together again and avoided social contact, although they both continued
to live in Beverly Hills.[22] As Heifetz and Piatigorsky wound down their solo
careers, however, they undertook a series of Heifetz-Piatigorsky concerts, an
association into which they brought additional performers for the chamber
works they played on tours and in recordings through the early 1960s. Their
relationship was compatible and friendly, doubtless enhanced by the fact that
their characters were opposites, yet complimentary.[23]

By the 1960s teaching became Piatigorsky's central interest. USC convinced Heifetz and violist William Primrose to teach master classes in a
special division of the Music School, and, from 1962 until his death in
1976, Piatigorsky joined this endeavor.[24] Piatigorsky's own words show his
positive approach to his students:

> You don't have to be a genius to know your shortcomings, because
> there are so many of them. But you have to be a mighty intelligent per-

Gregor Piatigorsky (right) with Jascha Heifetz, 1963. Otto Rothschild Collection, Music Center Archives, Los Angeles.

son to know your strong points. That is your obligation: to know what is good. And if possible to enjoy. And everything that you don't like, to convert into something that is likable. That is the only way I know. Otherwise you will live in the negative all your life. You can't live in that, you can't prosper in it. . . . I never met a really, truly conceited musician. Because they know what they don't know—especially before the concert. . . . Music remains above you; you are just striving to reach it. And the better you become at it, the music moves higher, so it becomes unreachable.[25]

Piatigorsky's master classes, two per week, were more demanding than those that students experienced anywhere else. Each cellist was expected to be ready at any moment to play any work he had in his repertoire. Yet Michael Tilson Thomas, who served as a piano accompanist for these classes in his student years at USC, reports that Piatigorsky believed students should be able to do that with a maximum of three hours' concentrated practice a day, for it was equally important that they "live life!" This understanding maintained among the class a sense that "we were all members of a family." Cellist Nathaniel Rosen remembered Piatigorsky intuiting the essence of the student, enabling each one to express that essence in music and to look upon technique as the ability to express oneself. Cellist Laurence Lesser observed that Piatigorsky "was psychological as a teacher," primarily interested in building one's ability to stand on one's own.[26] Lesser grew up in Los Angeles, his musical education guided by émigrés. He remembers that the area was "like a mecca, because there were all of these astonishingly high-level instrumentalists . . . [who] became teachers. . . . The European influence formed my life."[27]

In 1937 Klemperer appointed the twenty-six-year-old violinist Bronislav Gimpel to the post of concertmaster for the Philharmonic. A year later his older brother Jakob, a concert pianist who had been touring the United States as accompanist to the violinist Bronislaw Huberman, also settled in Los Angeles. The Polish-born Gimpels had received their early training in Lemberg (Lvov) from their father, a theater conductor, violinist, and pianist who had played the clarinet under Mahler.[28] Early celebrity as a child prodigy, which had placed Paganini's instrument in Bronislav's hands and brought him invitations to play recitals with Vienna opera stars Leo Slezak, Maria Jeritza, and Selma Kurtz and to perform for the Pope, Mussolini, and King Umberto of Italy, resulted in a deterioration of his technique after he "began to think" at age seventeen. During study at the Berlin Hochschule, Carl Flesch gave Bronislav discipline and practicing techniques, advising him to join an orchestra for one year. At eighteen Bronislav became concertmaster for conductor Hermann Scherchen, and for twenty years he held similar posts.[29] Klemperer presented him as soloist with the Philharmonic several times and in 1940 encouraged him to found and conduct the Hollywood Youth Orchestra, which was curtailed when Bronislav was drafted into the American Army in 1942. After his war service, which included playing in the Army Air Force String Quartet, Bronislav returned to his solo career, at first in New York and then in Europe, where he was in such demand that he played up to 100 concerts per season.

Before emigrating in 1938, Jakob Gimpel made his orchestral debut playing the Rachmaninoff Second Piano Concerto with the Concertgebouw Orchestra under Pierre Monteux and later soloed with Huberman's Palestine Symphony. In 1939 and 1940, to introduce himself to Los Angeles, he gave recitals in the Biltmore Hotel's Music Room. His programs often included works of contemporary composers. In Los Angeles he be-

Bronislav and Jakob Gimpel, 1942. Otto Rothschild Collection, Music Center Archives, Los Angeles.

came a particular advocate for Ernst Toch, who composed for and dedicated piano works to him. Jakob appeared with the Los Angeles Philharmonic in the Hollywood Bowl in 1940 under Albert Coates, was briefly signed as a recording artist for Columbia Records, but then turned to work as a "featured pianist" in films. In 1942 the *Los Angeles Times* reported that he would play Chopin's First Piano Concerto in the Hollywood Bowl with conductor Edwin McArthur, calling him "a pianist of unusual attainments to be waiting out here in Southern California for an occasional film. He has the equipment, the style and the experience for a full concert career." While he regularly gave recitals in small halls in Los Angeles, it was not until Jakob Gimpel was sixty that he began to be presented in the prestigious concert series at UCLA's Royce Hall and—at seventy—in the celebrity series at Ambassador Auditorium. These late-career presentations came about through the insistence of his many devoted fans.

Musicians were awed by Jakob's ability, evident since childhood, to read at sight even the most difficult scores. In 1946 Jones called him "a pianist of international rank . . . whose temperament is poetic, Polish in its intensity, but used with discernment and balance. . . . Not content playing a familiar program brilliantly, he gives his listeners new and provocative works [as well]."[30] In 1948 critic Albert Goldberg discovered "some of the year's most polished piano playing" to be by Jakob Gimpel at the Wilshire-Ebell, describing him as "a pianist of extraordinary dexterity and remarkable tonal control . . . the creamy quality of his keyboard technique is such that it tends to obscure the very intelligent and discerning musicianship which lies back of most of his interpretations."[31] Throughout his career Jakob's performances of Chopin impressed critics as revelatory. Recordings from his film work drew New York management, but "the rewards were in keeping with his own modesty; few crumbs were thrown in his direction," his son Peter recalls.[32]

Jakob Gimpel's self-taught knowledge of literature, history, and the arts attracted many artists as friends. He would ask his piano pupils if they had read and understood Shakespeare; yet there was no academic situation into which he could fit in Los Angeles until 1972, when the accumulated awareness of his stature as an artist earned him a residency, which he held until 1984, at California State University, Northridge. Given his frustrations, and the fact that he was primarily a performer, Jakob was at first an impatient piano teacher. In his sixties, with greater recognition, Jakob mellowed and understood better his students' points of view.[33] Like his brother, Jakob returned to Europe to concertize to great acclaim and spent periods living there. Yet both brothers were living in Los Angeles at their deaths: Bronislav's at sixty-eight from an overdose of the tranquilizers he had long used to manage the stress of his concert life, and Jakob's ten years later at eighty-three.

It had been Klemperer who, in 1912, had engineered Lotte Lehmann's first success in a major role at the Hamburg Opera, where she began her career. He had urged her to substitute as Elsa in *Lohengrin,* at a time when no one else considered her an artist of promise. In that performance, she remembered, "For the first time I felt my inhibiting shyness fall away and I sank into the flame of inner experience. I had always wanted to sing like this. . . . [Klemperer was] dragging my terrified voice into the vortex of his fanatical will."[34] She told Klemperer's biographer, "He was always a terrible demon. . . . one was hypnotised . . . one can't explain it."[35] By 1916 she was at the Vienna Court Opera and on her way to a career as one of the greatest singers of her time, chosen by Richard Strauss for leading roles in the premieres of several of his operas. She and Klemperer remained lifelong friends; he named his daughter after her, and her performances with him and the Philharmonic in the Hollywood Bowl in 1939 and 1944 were deeply satisfying artistic collaborations.

Lehmann's husband died in a New York sanatorium in January 1939. Her emotion-laden Hollywood Bowl concert with Klemperer on August 24, 1939, preceded the conductor's brain surgery by only a few weeks. Knowing that he was ill, the orchestra paid him tribute on that occasion with a fanfare of welcome as he entered the stage. He conducted Beethoven's First Symphony, Wagner's *Lohengrin* Prelude, and—with Lehmann singing— "Dich, teure Halle" from *Tannhäuser* and Elsa's Dream from *Lohengrin,* which "fell like a benediction" upon critic Jones's ears. Lehmann, with a pianist, then sang a group of lieder by Richard Strauss, Schubert, and Mendelssohn, after which Klemperer conducted Stravinsky's *Petrushka.* Jones wrote, "Out of [her] grief of the past year Mme. Lehmann has brought significant beauty. The wonderful quality of maturity without age was heard in her ringing voice. . . . There was a rapture of the spirit in [Elsa's Dream] which is communicable only by music. . . . Her voice is rich in all the colors of an artist's palette."

Five years later, Klemperer chose Lehmann as soloist for his July 1944 return to the Hollywood Bowl. Jones described the excitement: "Otto Klemperer was welcomed back to the podium of Hollywood Bowl last night by thousands of the faithful. His program of classic and romantic German works was enhanced by the presence and beautiful singing of Lotte Lehmann. In spite of the physical handicaps of long illness, this great conductor was able to bring the Bowl orchestra to a high point of achievement. . . . [Lehmann's performances of Dido's Lament from *Dido and Aeneas,* and Wagner's orchestral lieder "Schmerzen" and "Träume"] were of outstanding beauty, the long line being preserved with sustained legato. Lehmann's voice floated over the orchestra and Klemperer kept the ensemble in balance and yet supported the solo." Her voice, reported Jones, was "small in size for the great amphitheater but its quality had such carrying power that the effect was far-reaching in emotional impact. . . . This collaboration of the two famous musicians last night created a satisfying musical evening which will not soon be forgotten."[36]

Lehmann's voice, according to Gwendolyn Williams Koldofsky, her West Coast accompanist from the mid-1940s, was unique in sound and seldom accurately captured in recordings; her gift for interpretation was "something quite magical."[37] Conductor Bruno Walter, Lehmann's close friend and musical colleague, described the elusive but solid-gold quality of her art when he wrote to her, "I ask myself whether this unique directness of your manner is not the true secret of your so successful career."[38] Lehmann's California years, which saw the waning of her vocal and physical powers, were fraught with psychological terrors—to Walter she described herself as a hysteric—yet with triumphs as well, won by her indomitable nature and deep emotional resources. The birthday announcing each new decade of her age brought on a personal crisis. As she approached fifty, her 1937 lieder recital (probably arranged by Klemperer) in Los Angeles' Philharmonic Hall provoked a dyspeptic review by Richard Saunders of the *Hollywood Citizen News,* who found it "unfortunate that Lotte Lehmann possesses such a limited concert repertory. The song recital program was devoted almost entirely to the concert war-horses ridden . . . by all singers. Even these familiar German lieder, in her own language, she had to read from a book."[39] In the early 1940s Lehmann gave up her New York home; her opera appearances grew rare and ceased in 1946. The last period of her recital singing, from 1947 to 1951, was one of growing self-doubt.

Lehmann's artistic insecurities probably contributed to her seduction by Hollywood, which she encountered first while on a world tour in 1937. At that time she visited MGM's studios, which she found magnificent. Starstruck, she was disappointed that her camera was taken away from her at the entrance, and that Greta Garbo did not show up for their prearranged meeting. However, Jeanette MacDonald, "the queen of MGM," met her and later became one of her pupils.[40] In 1947 Lehmann, now nearing her sixtieth birthday, was again obsessed about her age. Rather than accepting Walter's invitation to sing at the new Edinburgh Festival that summer, she signed a seven-year film contract with MGM and bought a house in the Hollywood Hills to facilitate her new career. "I am so at the edge of a breakdown," she wrote to Walter at the time. "I don't even expect you to believe me. . . . I know that at this moment I am losing Europe. . . . I am very, very unhappy about this whole matter." By December the movie was completed. "You will be shocked," she wrote, "but it was always, always my dream to be able to play a real actor's part, *without music.* I wanted to test myself whether I was a real 'actress.' . . . I must say I have enjoyed the whole thing."[41] In April 1948, however, after she saw the film (*Big City*), she confessed to Walter that she found herself awful. Her contract expired without another film being made.

In 1950, reflecting on her recent experience, Lehmann wrote an autobiographical novel titled *Of Heaven, Hell, and Hollywood,* which she somewhat defensively called "a satirical fantasy." In it a famous tenor star of the Metropolitan Opera dies and dreams of life proceeding without him. He refuses heaven for Hollywood, which is smothered in smog and looks "unreal as always . . . houses hanging over abysses, the walls blinking with glass and steel, violent red flowers seeming to burst from nowhere—blue swimming pools between stones, and blossom-covered walls." As he observes an aspiring actor being conveyed in a Cadillac from his makeup session to the movie set a few steps away, the tenor muses, "How can anyone bear Hollywood who has not a sense of humor?" The only solution is to go to heaven, where Bruno Walter, Gustav Mahler, and Thomas Mann talk seriously; Schubert is trying to contact Goethe; and Richard Strauss longs for his abusive wife, Pauline. The tenor wakes from his illness—not dead, but considering a Hollywood career. His aunt tells him, as Lehmann must have told herself: "You made your way, Vienna could not hold you, the world was your stage. You conquered it with your great art, only your art. You went your way with a certain ruthlessness following your inner urge—following it for good or bad—never questioning whether you hurt someone else, never considering established rules because you created your own world. . . . You were never commercial. You never sold your art by cheapening it. . . . Don't cheapen it now. . . . You are not just a singer. Your art embraces the whole world of art, not just music."[42]

Indeed, this was true of Lehmann's life in Santa Barbara, where she wrote her books and took up painting with an extraordinary passion; she filled her home by the ocean in Hope Ranch with several beloved dogs, mynah birds, and her ceramics; she created gardens, a swimming pool, fountains, fish ponds, terraces, and winding walks; she rode a white horse on the beach. As her vocal powers waned, Lehmann frequently confided in Walter, from whom she felt she learned more than from any other person. She recalled "the beautiful careless time of youth," when she had no trouble with her voice. After years of describing in letters her vocal problems to him, in 1951, her final year of performing, she wanted Walter to know that "It was an unforgettable and wonderful . . . life. It was worth having lived . . . to sense the love of the audience."[43]

On a 1940 concert tour, Lehmann had commented in an interview with Jones that Santa Barbara would be a perfect place for a summer music festival similar to the Salzburg Festival. In 1945 the Curtis Institute proposed a branch of its music school for Santa Barbara, with Lehmann as dean. Lehmann, who had begun teaching privately in Santa Barbara, responded,

"Santa Barbara *has* to become a kind of 'Western Salzburg'—I have to see this dream come true in my lifetime."[44] This project transformed Lehmann's last years. Its practical aspect was initiated by the ever-courageous Isabel Morse Jones, who in 1946 began the process of gathering musicians and music patrons to form the Music Academy of the West, which opened in the summer of 1947 on the campus of the Cates School in Santa Barbara. At that time Jones was replaced as a critic on the music staff of the *Los Angeles Times* by Albert Goldberg; before retiring to Italy, Jones served as the first director of the Music Academy.

From the Music Academy's earliest seasons, the region's European émigré musicians involved themselves in the endeavor. Conductor Richard Lert, who had learned his profession in studies with the renowned Arthur Nikisch, Felix Weingartner, and Richard Strauss, was hired as conductor, then became music director in 1949. Lehmann gave frequent benefit recitals for the new festival and school. Rubinstein, Szigeti, William Primrose, Pierre Monteux, and the Russian choreographer Adolf Bolm served on the board of advisors; violinist Roman Totenberg was on the faculty. Darius Milhaud was named honorary director in the second season; Madeleine Milhaud coached students in French diction; and Arnold Schoenberg came as composer-in-residence for six weeks. Piatigorsky was on the faculty from 1950 to 1953 and continued with occasional master classes through 1975. In 1954 Maurice Abravanel, long a protégé of Bruno Walter, succeeded Lert as conductor and music director.

In 1951 Lehmann joined the faculty and began directing productions of operas, a new endeavor for her. Her first, in 1951, was *Fidelio*. She telephoned her beloved Bruno for advice and wrote to him in gratitude for his immediate response, "You have explained everything, so that I have to do the right thing, [even] if I haven't a spark of talent." In 1954 she communicated to Walter her joy in directing opera: "At first I had thought that I would not be able to do [Debussy's] *Pelléas*. I thought that my internal unrest would not permit it. How I have under-estimated the power of losing oneself! *Pelléas* is my salvation. I forget everything while I am working. What an opera! What a drama! What BLISS to create people. Instead of 'singing machines' I create human beings. Does this sound very arrogant? . . . I don't know if it is crazy to say this: it is almost *more* beautiful than to sing oneself. . . . Forgive me for going on so long. Perhaps you find me getting childish with 66 years? It is *nice* then to be childish."[45] In her ten years of teaching at the academy, Lehmann found great satisfaction and new creative inspiration. Her presence lifted the fortunes of the new endeavor.

Probably owing to her presence, a luxurious estate named Miraflores was donated to the academy to house its administrative offices and most of its classes, recitals, and other events. Lehmann's master classes with auditors, the first of their kind, became the central events of the academy season. Among her pupils for these classes were Grace Bumbry, Marilyn Horne, Carol Neblett, Maralin Niska, and Benita Valente.[46]

From 1955 on, the annual opera production was staged in the Lobero Theatre in Santa Barbara. The 1955 production was Richard Strauss's *Ariadne auf Naxos*. In 1957, to celebrate Lehmann's 70th birthday, the opera chosen was *Der Rosenkavalier*, all three major soprano roles of which Lehmann had sung, conducted by Strauss himself, when the work was new to the Vienna State Opera. The success of these opera productions and of the vocal program at the academy helped Lehmann convince the Metropolitan Opera to admit West Coast singers to its annual auditions for the first time. The first winner was Grace Bumbry.

Lehmann's seventieth birthday was another "tragedy" for her, and she found the exhausting work of directing opera "a little too much for me." Walter responded, "I would like to talk you out of your desperation concerning your approaching seventieth birthday. . . . I do not believe that you will ever be truly grown up. And, consequently, this big event should really strengthen your self-esteem."[47] Lehmann's decision to retire in 1961 from her teaching at the academy brought a National Educational Television crew to make a documentary film of her master classes. The documentary is stilted, and Lehmann is so eager to perform that she grasps each chance to illustrate, saying, "Shall I do it for you? I'm so glad for this excuse!"— leaving the young singer she is teaching sadly upstaged. Yet kernels of Lehmann's wisdom and approach are revealed in her remarks: "You have to take the music out from the piano [accompaniment] into your being"; "With great emotion, with an *outbreak* of emotion!"; "This is not *simple* enough—to me, the high point of art is the expression of great emotion with great simplicity"; "Inner drive and determination is more important than talent or other gifts." Finally there comes her observation about the moment when the Marschallin knows she is losing her young lover: "Everything has its time. . . . One has to say good-bye with a smile."[48]

Bruno Walter first conducted at the Hollywood Bowl in 1927 and 1929 on American tours, and chose Los Angeles in 1939 for respite after the horrifying murder of his musically talented younger daughter, Gretel. He brought his conducting to a temporary halt and sought peace in Southern Califor-

Lotte Lehmann at the Music Academy of the West, Santa Barbara, n.d. Lotte Lehmann Collection, PA Mss 03, University of California Santa Barbara Libraries.

nia at the very time that the Los Angeles Philharmonic was in crisis because of Klemperer's surgery and sudden leave of absence. When guest conductors were hastily invited to lead the Philharmonic, Walter agreed to take the season's first five performances.[49] Although he was under contract to the Metropolitan Opera and the New York Philharmonic at the time, Walter, his wife, and daughter rented a house in Beverly Hills, and he commuted across the country. Walter wrote, "I am thankful for the warmth of the sun that beautifies life in this part of America."[50] As France fell in 1940, he accompanied Lehmann in a rare benefit recital in Los Angeles for the French

Bruno Walter, Beverly Hills, 1940. Otto Rothschild Collection, Music Center Archives, Los Angeles.

and American Red Cross. In her *Los Angeles Times* column, Jones proudly noted that Lehmann and Walter had collaborated for such a performance in only one other city in the world, Salzburg, and that the Los Angeles audience was witnessing the most complete and authentic representation of the "great central tradition of German culture" possible to obtain. Walter established a relationship with USC, where he lectured on the symphonic literature and was granted an honorary degree in 1941. He enjoyed conducting at the Bowl, and he continued his guest conducting with the Los Angeles Philharmonic. Jones admired his "fervor which creates great art. This conductor creates music of the spirit and labors to perfect his own. . . .

Let us try to keep him here with only those absences necessary for his opera and occasional appearances elsewhere. He draws the best from our players. He has the personal power to pull Southern California together, musically speaking."[51] However, when asked in 1943 to take on the post of permanent music director for the Los Angeles Philharmonic, Walter refused gracefully: "I know I am too old to be [the Philharmonic's] director, I will be its friend."[52]

In 1945 Walter purchased a house on North Bedford Drive in Beverly Hills, next to the home of Franz and Alma Mahler Werfel, and remained there until his death in 1962. In his last decade he concentrated his energies on leaving a legacy of recordings through Columbia Records. For his 1953 recording of *The Marriage of Figaro*, with Los Angeles' own George London as the Count, the "Columbia Symphony Orchestra" was made up of Los Angeles musicians. After Walter's heart attack in 1957, Columbia Records' president, Goddard Lieberson, arranged for Walter to make recordings not far from his home, and this work continued in Los Angeles through early 1961.

Klemperer's relationship with music in Los Angeles did not end with his brain surgery in 1939. While still far from well, with his bipolar disorder exacerbated by the surgery, in 1940 he made a premature attempt to perform Beethoven's huge *Missa solemnis* with Bronislav Gimpel's Hollywood Youth Orchestra and an amateur chorus. At the time, Vicki Baum, who knew Klemperer well, described his appearance—a black patch over one eye, his roaring voice, and his paralyzed walk—as "Hoffmanesque."[53]

In April 1941 Klemperer conducted the youth orchestra in Hindemith's *Nobilissima visione* suite and his own orchestration of a Bach organ sonata. Although the symptoms of his illness were still present, his extraordinary musical gifts and command of orchestral playing were gradually reasserting themselves. A musician remembered that Klemperer's rehearsal with Los Angeles' WPA orchestra (for a performance that was ultimately canceled) was "awe-inspiring, if not terrifying. . . . He led us through a Brahms First Symphony that in all my years . . . has been unequalled. . . . He drove, as in a huge chariot, to the highest planes of expression, stopping not at all for corrections or interpretative advice. It was the essence of great conducting."[54]

Through the efforts of Florence Irish, Klemperer was invited to conduct a single concert at the Hollywood Bowl in August 1943. A large audience, including Bruno Walter and George Szell, welcomed him. Alfred Price Quinn called Klemperer's return to conducting "a veritable triumph. . . . As he appeared, . . . [Klemperer] was accorded the warmest and most sustained applause of any conductor appearing in the Bowl this summer. His musical memory and mentality are still tremendous and as he proceeded through his program those assets became more and more pronounced."[55] The next summer Irish arranged two more return concerts at the Bowl for Klemperer, including the celebrated 1944 appearance with Lehmann. In February 1945 he was invited to appear as guest conductor in the regular season of the Philharmonic. Again he received a stirring welcome, for a program in which he introduced Schoenberg's Second Chamber Symphony. Quinn contrasted the orchestra's performance with that achieved by the current conductor, Wallenstein: "The orchestra seemed to have absorbed the firm but quiet authority radiated by [Klemperer] and hence was able to function with relaxed nerves. [There was] a feeling of easy assurance . . . a tonal quality that was euphonious rather than tense, and a smoothness in ensemble details. These are characteristics our Philharmonic Orchestra does not consistently display."[56] Klemperer's March 1945 appearance conducting a chamber orchestra in Bach's Brandenburg Concertos, to inaugurate the Los Angeles Music Guild, left critic Lawrence Morton in "a state of highest exaltation." These works were little known to Los Angeles audiences, and Morton himself was discovering them. He wrote in *Script* magazine, "Given a chance to be heard, and honestly performed, [this music] reaches out to all that is good in the human spirit. A comparable goodness is required of the performer, and Klemperer subscribes to that kind of musical morality."[57]

As Russian and American military forces met on the Elbe in Germany in the spring of 1945, bringing the war in Europe to its violent end, Klemperer joined Stravinsky—who had settled in Hollywood in 1940—to conduct an emotional benefit concert for the Russian-American Club, presented before 6,000 people in the Shrine Auditorium. In January 1946 Klemperer conducted the first West Coast performance of Alban Berg's Violin Concerto (1935) with Szigeti as soloist, but the players treated the work (later considered one of Berg's most beautiful and inspired) with insolence and had to be chastised by Klemperer. Audience and critics were also baffled by the piece.

The adoration Los Angeles had felt for Klemperer faded when he needed it most. He was now sixty, grown more cautious, depressed, and terribly thin. Schoenberg failed to persuade the president of UCLA to invite Klemperer to teach conducting classes at the university. Stravinsky fruitlessly recommended to Stokowski that he share conducting tasks with Klemperer for a new orchestra Stokowski proposed founding in New York City.[58] In June 1946 Klemperer returned to Europe for the first of many subsequent visits. In spite of inevitable tensions that arose over the Nazi past, the many invitations he received to conduct in cities throughout Europe lifted his spirits and brightened his future prospects. His September return to his Los Angeles home unfortunately coincided with one of his manic phases. In November he received insulin shock treatment at a sanatorium in Illinois where Ernst Toch had been treated for depression. At the beginning of January 1947, Klemperer conducted a benefit to aid the Los Angeles Philharmonic's new pension fund, followed by another Bach program later that month. On March 12 he gave a final concert with the Music Guild, ending the program with Haydn's "Farewell" Symphony in anticipation of his imminent return to Vienna. While visiting Los Angeles's jazz scene at a downtown bar the next evening, Klemperer was beaten up, robbed, and left in the street.[59] A photograph of the conductor, bandaged from this "mean streets" incident, appeared prominently in the newspapers; it was a sad farewell to Los Angeles.

Klemperer's return to Europe the following summer was the beginning of a long and ultimately successful rebuilding of his international career. Because in this period his work was initially concentrated in communist Eastern Europe, where he served as music director of the Hungarian State Opera in Budapest, Klemperer's American passport was put under restrictions that hampered his international travel. His last appearances in Los Angeles were at the Hollywood Bowl on September 1 and 3, 1953. Again huge audiences greeted him, but the critics were cool.[60] In 1954 Klemperer moved to Zurich, qualified for a German passport, and gave up his American citizenship.

Klemperer's son, the actor Werner Klemperer, remarked that Los Angeles was not his father's kind of place.[61] The conductor was a solitary man, uncomfortable attending social functions for fund-raising. On the other hand, critic Morton wrote that "[Klemperer's Los Angeles] achievement was a very great one, not only because of his actual conducting skill, but also by virtue of the qualities of intellect he gave to the whole musical scene."[62] While his American period was the most difficult in his professional life, it was through Klemperer's efforts that orchestral music in Los Angeles was brought to maturity. Countless music lovers heard, and remembered for the rest of their lives, his inspired performances of great works.

5

Innovative Teachers in the Performing Arts

Blessed land that can now sprout from cracks and crannies such perfecting intelligence!

—Peter Yates, describing the Los Angeles City College Opera Workshop

Inspired by the evident need for their expertise, the teaching of Southern California's émigré musicians—much of it extraordinary—filled many gaps in Los Angeles' classical music culture. One large gap was opera. Los Angeles had left the founding and decades of support for a symphony orchestra to a single wealthy citizen and found it easier to rely on touring companies from elsewhere than to build a local opera. In 1934 the San Francisco Opera began annual visits to Los Angeles under the administration of Gaetano Merola.[1] To the growing throng of European émigrés, these occasional tidbits of their favorite musical art were frustrating. The arriving composers were almost all opera composers. One of them, Ernst Krenek, found it lamentable that opera in America should be an exotic, expensive import, provided as entertainment primarily for the rich. Moreover, he found it comical that opera was never performed in English, and that society patrons did not expect opera to be innovative theater in the way Europeans knew it.[2] It was particularly strange to Europeans that American-born singers rarely appeared on any of the few American opera stages. After the war, highly talented American singers would be compelled to find their opportunities abroad—in their own "exile," as one of them described it.[3] Much of this vocal talent came from Southern California, inspired, trained, and mentored by the refugees from Nazism.

In 1936, just as Merola's miniseason of six operas was being put together for the Hollywood Bowl, there appeared in Los Angeles a tall, gangling, forty-year-old refugee who would change the state of affairs for young American singing talent. Berlin-born Hugo Strelitzer had considerable background as an opera coach and assistant conductor for the leading German opera conductors. "He knew opera inside and out," said Natalie Limonick, who worked with him in Los Angeles.[4] He had earned a doctorate in musicology at the Westphalian University of Münster in 1921, had become a leading choral director in Germany, and after working in several German opera houses had taught from 1926 to 1933 in the opera department of the Berlin Conservatory.[5] After his release from the SS's Berlin prison, Strelitzer, a musician of boundless energy, intensity, and devotion to his art, felt confined working in the Jüdische Kulturbund and resolved to go to America.

This idea seemed hopeless because Strelitzer had no relatives in the United States to help him. Frances Cheney, a young Californian who met him in Berlin, not only assisted him with the language and plans for his escape, but sailed with him to New York in February 1936. In spite of letters of recommendation from Klemperer and Artur Schnabel, once Strelitzer was in New York he could not obtain an immigration visa. Cheney, whose father was a developer of the Palos Verdes Peninsula south of Los Angeles, believed Strelitzer would have a promising future on the West Coast. With the approval of her family, she offered marriage as a solution. Strelitzer would only agree to an engagement, pleading his old-world compunctions against marriage at a time when he had no money or position. Through coaching work with a Metropolitan Opera singer in New York, he was introduced by correspondence to Merola, who promised to meet him in Los Angeles in mid-July. At the same time, through the Cheneys' contacts, he applied for and became a top choice for an opening on the music faculty of Los Angeles City College, a two-year junior college that had been established in 1928 on the former site of Teachers College, the predecessor to UCLA, and was well equipped. In order to obtain a more permanent visa, Strelitzer—like most of the musical émigrés—had to exit and reenter the United States. He chose to go to Cuba, but in Havana his visa was denied by the American consul, who advised him to marry immediately. The generous Cheney family was amenable and smoothed many bureaucratic difficulties for Strelitzer through their contacts in Washington. Strelitzer and Frances married hastily in Florida, hurried to Havana to obtain the visa, and rushed back to Florida to catch the only boat available to convey them

Hugo Strelitzer, ca. 1936. Photo Dick Farrell, Los Angeles. Courtesy of Barbara Zeisl Schoenberg.

through the Panama Canal to Los Angeles in time for his professional interviews.

Immediately upon his arrival in California, Strelitzer met Merola and won a contract as assistant conductor and choral director, under Richard Lert, for the San Francisco Opera's Fall 1936 season in the 25,000-seat Hollywood Bowl. His work brought him an invitation from Klemperer to prepare the chorus for *Parsifal,* the Philharmonic's final performance in the Bowl's summer season. In addition, Max Reinhardt awarded Strelitzer a lucrative contract to train a chorus of 100 and conduct a sixty-man orchestra in the September run of his famous production of Hugo von Hoffmansthal's pageant, *Everyman,* at the Bowl. In contrast to the difficulties of his life in Germany, Strelitzer now found his talents in demand; he relished his arduous schedule. He wrote to his family that this transformation of his fate seemed to him the result of a "powerful game of destiny," in which, from total despair and hopelessness, without money, work, or visa, he had miraculously gained in Los Angeles honor and recognition beyond anything he had attained in his homeland. He wrote ecstatically to his family, describing the fantastic success of Reinhardt's $100,000 production, the beauty of the scenery and costumes, and the unforgettable impression of the set's giant cathedral as it appeared in the Bowl under the starry blue-black night; it all seemed a ghost of the Salzburg Festival's past, now translated to the gigantic dimensions of Hollywood, which was to him "the symbol of strength, inhibition, and lack of concern."[6]

At the conclusion of his strenuous conducting engagements at the Hollywood Bowl, Strelitzer was faced with the choice of taking either the City College appointment or an offer from Lert to assist him as a conductor in the Federal Music Project. The government-supported WPA Orchestra, offering paid employment in the Depression to the many unemployed musicians across the country, presented ambitious concert programs in Los Angeles from 1935 until 1941.[7] Lert planned to present opera performances in Los Angeles using the WPA Orchestra and a professional chorus he asked Strelitzer to form. Strelitzer, however, cast his lot with the academic position, assuming that it would provide him with not only greater security but also more substantial future opportunities. In 1936 the gradual phasing out of the government project had been announced in the press; however, the WPA Orchestra proved to be important to his teaching as Strelitzer's plans developed.

In his probational first year at City College, Strelitzer taught harmony, counterpoint, voice and vocal interpretation, and conducted a chorus, all the while discussing with the college's president and the head of the music department his pioneering plans for opera training, which he considered important for both the musical education of the young and for the musical life of Los Angeles. He was given a short leave of absence to take assignments as assistant conductor under Fritz Reiner at the San Francisco Opera, and in this period he quickly learned much about opera in the United States. He established a private vocal studio in Los Angeles, where he taught singers attracted by the film industry. He bought himself an eight-cylinder Ford "with built-in radio," and drove "proudly as a King" with his "good angel," Frances, from their small Hollywood apartment to Beverly Hills, to

Santa Monica and the sea, or into the mountains. Hollywood seemed to him a paradise, and the surroundings reminded him of the Italian Riviera. Reporting all this to his relatives, he remarked again at his continued astonishment that he was respected, after having been imprisoned and treated as a nonperson in Germany. His desire was to work in his new situation "as one possessed."[8] It was perhaps this strenuous quality that ended the marriage to Frances in 1940, although Strelitzer remained on friendly terms with her and her parents.

In September 1937, beginning what he considered to be the most meaningful epoch in his life, Strelitzer opened at City College the first state- and city-supported opera workshop in America. He faced much skepticism. Serious music education in the United States was costly to an aspiring performer, as it was offered only in private conservatories; the musical training in public universities and colleges was generally not yet adequate preparation for a professional performing career. Now, at City College, a talented young singer without considerable financial means would be able to prepare seriously for a career in opera without having to move to the expensive East Coast or to Europe to find the necessary training. For City College's program, Strelitzer envisioned schooling "a new, modern type of singer for the demands of the modern stage, film and radio."[9] Along with required vocal training and music history, he planned courses in ear training, sight-singing, and the fundamentals of harmony. Language courses would be taught by native teachers; the drama department would offer courses in pantomime, speech, and fundamentals of acting; fencing and dance would be offered by the department of physical education. A studio with a technician and the latest equipment for recording and radio transmission would be available, along with training in microphone technique for singers. To bring his vision to reality, Strelitzer argued for the necessity of this training in numerous conferences and debates with academic authorities and in speeches at society dinners and luncheons. He found strong support in the film studios.[10] The Chandler family, owners of the *Los Angeles Times,* were eager for Los Angeles to compete with the East Coast (and San Francisco) in cultural development. They saw to it that the project was publicized and encouraged in their newspaper. Other newspapers followed suit. This wave of public support was decisive in winning official agreement from City College, the state Board of Education, and the Los Angeles school system to sponsor the opera workshop. The fact that many of the great musicians of Europe were now settling in Los Angeles strengthened Strelitzer's determination to contribute to the development of a new musical metropolis. He would counteract the current American model by producing opera in English; opera without snobbery; opera without stars. American opera would be performed, along with new operas by European émigrés. European classics not yet heard on the West Coast would be offered. Productions would aspire to the most professional standards and yet reflect American society. It was his ambition to see in his lifetime the founding of a firm government-supported opera ensemble in America, such as he had known in Germany.[11]

Through his continuing choral assignments from Klemperer, Lert, and the Hollywood Bowl, Strelitzer was working with professional singers. It was not difficult for him to cast a wide net of publicity to discover the most gifted young vocal talent available. He accepted forty-eight singers for the first workshop. In the first full production in June 1938, *The Marriage of Figaro*, Susanna was played by a Japanese soprano and Cherubino by a Korean. In May 1939 George Burnstein, a nineteen-year-old with an exceptional bass-baritone voice, was cast in a minor role for the Los Angeles premiere of *The Magic Flute*. He was too nervous to sustain the part, but with Strelitzer's encouragement George Burnstein eventually became George London, in subsequent decades one of the world's greatest singers, himself an ardent advocate for opera in English and for subsidized "ensemble theater."[12]

From the beginning, the ensemble aspect of Strelitzer's opera workshop productions was outstanding. The 1938 *Figaro* was presented with no stage, curtain, sets, or lighting and no orchestra—only two pianos for accompaniment—yet music critic José Rodriguez wrote that "The reduced apparatus in no way diminished the exquisite style, excellent singing, masterful and yet magical acting, offered by an ensemble to which any ambitious and expensive opera production would aspire. The intimacy, the zeal and the inner enthusiasm—not to forget the pure musicality and the solid ensemble—brought one nearer to Mozart than all the artistic paraphernalia most opera companies in America regard as important."[13] By 1939 Strelitzer had won—for his production of *The Magic Flute*—an auditorium with stage, lighting, costumes, scenery, and an orchestra, so that young singers could be confronted with all the challenges of opera performance. His ability to inspire talented artists drew stage and makeup professionals from Hollywood. Donald Alden of the City College English department wrote a new and lively English translation, using topical American humor. The college orchestra was not up to Strelitzer's standards, but with the intervention of composer Louis Gruenberg, whose opera based on Eugene O'Neill's *Emperor Jones* was a recent success at New York's Metropolitan

Opera, Strelitzer prevailed upon the Musicians' Union to finance a professional orchestra in three rehearsals and three performances. The audience that gathered for this premiere production in English—with no "stars," in a star-crazed city—was in itself unique for the time. A blend of poor and rich, Asians and Americans, Otto Klemperer and the musical elite, attended alongside casually dressed students and formally attired city leaders. Critic Isabel Morse Jones noted the "modern functional design" of the scenery, the "streamlined" action, the excellent ensemble. "Dr. Strelitzer is an inspired conductor, and indefatigable," she wrote.[14] To Strelitzer it all seemed a moral triumph. The skepticism and negativity he had so ardently fought now melted away, and, until the entry of the United States into the Second World War, the workshop grew and thrived.

Strelitzer's next ambition was to broaden the American audience for understandable opera, and to achieve this he offered in 1940 a "swing" version of Otto Nicolai's mid-nineteenth-century comedy, *The Merry Wives of Windsor.* In this production, jazz was used sparingly, only in the musical numbers that ended with a repeated refrain. The jiving variation would begin subtly at the repetition, then gain in intensity as the singers improvised vocally on the stage, dancing in their heavy Shakespearean costumes. The success of this unconventional experiment, following on the triumphs of the two Mozart productions, firmly established the opera workshop in the public's mind. In 1940 a bill of one-act operas—Hindemith's *Hin und Zurück,* and Mozart's *The Impresario*—was produced with small ensembles from the student orchestra.[15] For larger projects in subsequent years—Donizetti's *Don Pasquale,* Johann Strauss Jr.'s *Die Fledermaus* in 1942—Strelitzer brought the City College to an agreement with the WPA Orchestra. This arrangement guaranteed needed employment for the orchestra's musicians and provided the necessary professional standard for the workshop. With the state and city now supporting both workshop and orchestra, Strelitzer believed he had created the basis upon which a future subsidized opera company could be built in America.[16]

The City College Opera Workshop could now draw the most gifted musicians from the West and Southwest, and the artistic level rose accordingly. Singers who later became internationally known took much of their schooling from Strelitzer. The demands created in wartime, however, took their toll upon the workshop. Singers were drafted, and some were subsequently killed in the war. The WPA Orchestra was dissolved in 1941. The last production of the workshop until its postwar resumption was a June 1942 offering of Douglas Moore's *The Devil and Daniel Webster.* The choice of this opera was timely, for following the December 1941 attack on Pearl Harbor there was a strong demand for Americanism in the arts. At the time this opera was produced, Jones wrote, "American music is a thoroughly alive issue. A movement is on foot to ask for one American composer on every program, at least. The time is ripe for native recognition and the growth which is inevitable if the program makers show critical discrimination." After the workshop had closed for the duration of the war, Jones regretted that "Time lost in the education of youth can never be made up. In order to have music there must be musicians. Musicians are not made in a day or during an emergency. It takes years of study under expert guidance to develop an artist or a composer."[17]

The reopening of the workshop in 1945 necessitated complete rebuilding. The organization now reflected the changes in society created by the war. So many young people had been either drafted or pressed into war production jobs, particularly in the aircraft industry that had sprung up in and around Los Angeles, that the pool of available talent was severely limited. The workshop therefore became a part of an evening division created by the college to accommodate adult students' work schedules. Singers and production staff arrived for coaching and rehearsals at the end of a full day of work. Strelitzer's anecdotes from his European musical experiences woke the tired students to their tasks and revived their ambition to excel, but for two years the vocal talent available remained beneath the prewar level. There was now no WPA Orchestra to draw upon. Strelitzer's imaginative solution was to inaugurate an evening performance class in the operatic literature for orchestra players. This course drew leading studio players as well as amateurs. Managers of the Musicians' Union objected strenuously to the arrangement, but Strelitzer countered with his passionately held point of view that each American should not only have the right to attend college or university but also the right to perform the works studied. The union had to withdraw. For the 1948 production of Beethoven's *Fidelio*, a work that had never before been performed in Los Angeles, MGM's and Warner Brothers' players alternated in the difficult horn solos, while the union leaders listened benevolently in the auditorium.[18]

With this production the opera workshop resumed its prewar artistic level. Singers again flocked for the training they could receive from Strelitzer and the outstanding collaborators he attracted. The liveliness of their experience is suggested by the operas produced: little-known works by Weill, Ibert, Respighi, and Auber, Puccini's *La rondine,* and Tchaikovsky's

Eugene Onegin, as well as Verdi's *La traviata.* In May 1952 the workshop gave the world premiere of Eric Zeisl's *Leonce und Lena,* a work composed in 1937–38, before Zeisl's emigration from Austria. Zeisl had many friends in the Los Angeles émigré community, and his premiere was the occasion for a reception given by the Austrian consul; the audience included Alma Mahler-Werfel, Igor Stravinsky, Erich Wolfgang Korngold, Josef Szigeti, Richard Lert, and Vicki Baum. In the cast, the baritone Heinz Blankenburg, who was to become a leading singer at the Hamburg Opera, sang Second Policeman in the chorus.[19] Encouraged by the interest aroused by this premiere, in 1953 Strelitzer scheduled two new short operas by other émigrés: Lukas Foss's *The Jumping Frog of Calaveras County* and Darius Milhaud's *Le pauvre matelot.*[20]

Several singers of this period, all of whom received in the City College Opera Workshop the grounding required for their professional work, went on to make their careers in various German opera houses: Essen, East Berlin's Komische Oper, Mannheim, Hanover, Gelsenkirchen, West Berlin's Deutsche Oper, and Bonn. Soprano Ella Lee went from training in Germany to the San Francisco Opera, and three others (tenor Brian Sullivan and sopranos Maralin Niska and Jean Fenn) became members of the Metropolitan in New York.[21] Their training under Strelitzer began with an audition and proceeded with thorough role-coaching sessions, at first in private, then with the ensemble. Strelitzer rigorously conducted all these sessions himself. "In no instance did one have the feeling that one was a student of a [junior college], rather one was treated as a professional singer," wrote Marilyn Hall. Strelitzer also rehearsed the orchestra and chorus. His Prussian discipline and sense of duty to art sometimes clashed with the laid-back attitudes of young Californians, to whom he was a tough taskmaster. While he occasionally expressed himself in outbursts of temper, he was also generous in his support for those students willing to strive for the highest standards, and the result was above-average achievements in which "one sprang over one's own shadow."[22] The students were aware they were working with an extraordinary musician with great musical gifts. "From the first note . . . his passion for the music was evident. His conducting style was loose-jointed and unorthodox, but produced amazing results," commented another student, who also found Strelitzer "dogmatic and anything but gentle. . . . His physical appearance alone was forbidding, and no passing stranger could mistake him for someone other than a musician, for he was a stereotype. Well over six feet tall, thin and somewhat hunched, he moved through the halls with a pile of manuscripts clasped to his chest. His long gray hair was wildly swept back from his hawkish face dominated by a beak-like nose. Small blue eyes peered intently at those he met."[23]

Recognizing the light quality of soprano Marni Nixon's voice when she was a freshman at City College, Strelitzer first introduced her to German lieder: "His love of the music, and of art song, I have never forgotten. It set me up for the rest of my life," she recalled. "He played the piano terribly! We didn't care, we didn't know the difference at the beginning. . . . He conducted the first Mozart opera I ever did, *The Impresario*. His hands were so big, his fingers so long; he was so bony and he had tufts of hair sticking out on the sides of his bald head . . . his jowls were very loose. Instead of giving us the cue, it seemed as if he reached over the orchestra and tapped us on the shoulder [with] this huge hand, against the light of the desk below. He was a very colorful character."[24]

In the 1950s Natalie Limonick was beginning her career as a pianist for opera and vocal music at UCLA while teaching musicianship in the City College Evening Division. Upon hearing that Strelitzer's musical assistant, Adolf Heller, had been killed in an automobile accident, she offered to take on Heller's role of accompanying at Strelitzer's rehearsals. "Hugo was a wild man," she recalled. "He came in at the [class] break, ran over, grabbed me, and said, 'I hear you can be had! I mean musically!' I began to assist him. He was one of those people who, if he recognized a talent, wanted to push it." Strelitzer gradually developed Limonick's opera repertoire and experience, from accompanying single scenes to two-piano arrangements of full operas. The next step was his order to "Conduct! I'll play, you conduct." After some practice in this manner, he assigned Limonick to conduct the orchestra in Pergolesi's *La serva padrona*. When she shied away from getting up in front of an ensemble of men, Strelitzer told her she could conduct while sitting at the harpsichord. "He did throw you into things, and you just had to do it," she remembered.[25]

Strelitzer took a sabbatical leave in 1955 to return to Europe. As he traveled through Germany, Switzerland, and Austria, he saw that everywhere his students were making decisive contributions to opera performances. His study of the new movements in theater and the opera experiments of Wieland Wagner, Walter Felsenstein, and Günther Rennert renewed his creative energies. When he returned to Los Angeles in 1956, however, he was confronted with the death of Vladimir Rosing, his longtime stage director. Through Limonick he discovered Lotfi (Lotfollah) Mansouri working in the UCLA opera workshop that had been established by Jan Popper.

Mansouri, an Iranian-born premedical exchange student, loved theater and American movies and sang tenor roles, but had never seen an opera before coming to UCLA as a psychology major.[26] When his passion for opera became clear to his family in Iran, they cut off financial support for his medical studies, and he began to make his way by working in American opera. Mansouri realized that singing was not his field, and Strelitzer gave him every possible opportunity to learn stage direction. From 1956 to 1960, while an assistant professor of psychology at UCLA, Mansouri directed Strelitzer's productions of Mozart's *Così fan tutte* and *The Impresario*, Puccini's *Suor Angelica*, and, finally, Mussorgsky's *Boris Godunov*, the culminating production of Strelitzer's workshop. Limonick, who was accompanying this production with Leonard Stein, remarked that it was "one of the most beautiful productions I can remember."[27]

Yet by this time tensions were high, because City College had decided that the opera workshop productions were "too professional" for a junior college and that money spent on opera was needed to retrofit buildings to meet earthquake standards. By 1960 there was no longer adequate rehearsal space for the orchestra, and the auditorium in which *Boris* was performed was scheduled to be torn down. Strelitzer did not give up his workshop without a fight. George London and other prominent musicians testified to Strelitzer's twenty-five years of pioneering in this field, noting that his students were now known from Vienna to Melbourne, and emphasizing how clearly his work had served as the model for opera workshops in the two Los Angeles universities and subsequently in others across the country. Nevertheless, the workshop ended in 1961 with a modest concert performance of *Carmen* in a small hall with no orchestra, and Strelitzer retired from City College soon thereafter at age sixty-five.

The unprecedented success of a local community college building professional standards into a pioneering opera workshop motivated the city's two larger, wealthier universities—the University of California, Los Angeles (UCLA) and the University of Southern California (USC)—to follow suit. Carl Ebert, the prominent German actor and stage director, was invited to establish an opera department at USC in 1949. The same year, UCLA brought the Czech pianist and conductor Jan Popper from Stanford University to UCLA for a similar purpose. The expanded opera workshop movement in Los Angeles subsequently drew vocal talent from greater distances and produced increasing numbers of impressive performers who made careers worldwide. *Los Angeles Daily News* music critic Mildred Norton, who was taking on Jones's role as a crusader for cultural enterprise, wrote about the prodigious wealth of musical talent gathered by 1949 in Southern California. She urged the production of new operas by resident European opera composers Toch, Korngold, Castelnuovo-Tedesco, Krenek, Schoenberg, and Stravinsky, commissioned by a new local opera company, in which Los Angeles' excellent directors and conductors would "give our brilliant young singers a few innings on their own sand lot."[28] Unfortunately, this did not happen for almost four decades. The city lacked the cultural will to create an enduring Los Angeles Opera company until 1986, long after the émigré opera composers, stage directors, and conductors were gone.

By February 1950 the *Los Angeles Times* had replaced Jones with Albert Goldberg. In the growing tensions of the Cold War, Goldberg wrote an article titled "The American Musician and the European Invasion," in which he complained that American music was inundated with Europeans. When readers' responses accused him of fascism, jingoism, and decadent nationalism, Goldberg countered with a report of conversations with Strelitzer and Ebert. Strelitzer declared in his interview that, although he sincerely believed American talent to be second to none, in ten years of searching for a gifted student to take over his student productions as a conductor he had discovered not a single young American willing to undergo the long and strenuous routine. He had found that American students were too impatient: when they realized that the necessary preparation involved attending endless rehearsals, playing accompaniments and coaching all the singers in their roles, learning every note and every word of the score, performing such menial backstage duties as giving curtain and light cues, drilling the chorus, and all the other unglamorous functions that attend an opera production, not one of them had the stamina to endure the apprenticeship. "They all went back to practicing the Tchaikovsky Concerto," Strelitzer remarked to Goldberg. Although Carl Ebert had only recently arrived in Southern California, he told Goldberg he was hopeful that he would be able to train not only singers but producers, stage directors, and conductors as well.[29] In an interview a few months later with Norton, Ebert confessed that he had given up an offer from La Scala to come to Los Angeles, where he felt the possibilities of creating a major, modern opera company were unlimited.[30]

Carl Ebert had been an illustrious figure in theater during the Weimar Republic, first as a brilliant actor, then as a stage director and administrator. His refusal to collaborate with the Nazis in 1933 had led to his voluntary exile. By the time he came to USC to develop an opera department in the School of Music, he was renowned as a cofounder in 1934 of England's Glyndebourne Opera Festival in partnership with the conductor Fritz Busch, with whom he had also led the Berlin Municipal Opera and the German opera seasons at the Teatro Colón in Buenos Aires. From 1935 to 1945 Ebert had directed the newly founded Ankara State Conservatory for theater in Turkey. Part of his task there—in a culture which knew little of Western music—was to establish an opera school. It was the kind of challenge upon which Ebert thrived. The illegitimate child of a brief liaison between an aristocratic Polish count and an Irish American music student in Berlin, he had developed a resourcefulness and an ever-youthful sense of adventure that thrived on adversity. Throughout his life, he found any obstacles thrown into his path to be stimulating. His birth parents had deserted him in infancy, and he was brought up in the lower-middle-class household of his adoptive parents. (He kept this history under wraps, for it was advantageous that he was rumored to be the son of the revered first president of the Weimar Republic, Friedrich Ebert.) His training at the Deutsches Theater in Berlin under Max Reinhardt sharpened Ebert's intuitive approach to acting through intense study of psychological motivation. In the fast-paced 1920s Reinhardt, an Austrian, returned to Vienna to expand his theater empire. His departure enabled Ebert to emerge at the forefront of innovation and experiment in Berlin.

Ebert first turned to opera in 1927, when he accepted the post of Intendant (general director) at the Darmstadt State Theater. He had long harbored a love affair with music and found in music theater a large and satisfying field for reform. "I have always looked to the music for the profound realization of the right expression," he commented.[31] Ebert was never daunted by his lack of training in music. Limonick remembers playing opera scores for him in California, as he visualized his directorial approach through hearing the music. Marta Feuchtwanger commented that "Ebert was the greatest theater man of Germany and the Weimar government, but mostly for the opera. If he were not this rather democratic personality, he could have been an autocrat there."[32]

The uncertainty of Glyndebourne's funding after the war gave Ebert no immediate hope of a permanent assignment there, and so he decided to accept the invitation from USC. As he was not able to afford a car, he made the ninety-minute commute daily by bus from West Los Angeles to the university, where each week he gave production classes and two lectures. Many unregistered students were attracted to his lectures and enjoyed his informality. Privately he called Los Angeles "Los Ankara." He wrote to his son Peter, "I have come here 20 years too soon, because it is impossible to accelerate a development which is still in its infancy. There is a chance that it will bring forth a rich harvest in the end. . . . I still cannot tell whether our move will be for good nor whether it was sensible at all. . . . I think I would grab the chance if La Scala came back to me. . . . No one can tell at this moment whether Glyndebourne will ever rise again."[33] However, the promising vocal talent he attracted stimulated his interest.

After nine months of intense work, Ebert felt the USC opera students were ready for their first public performance, which was to be Richard Strauss's *Ariadne auf Naxos*. Norton testified to the production's great success in May 1949: "After seeing the brilliance, grace, lightness, and finish of [Ebert's] work as it was reflected in USC's young people, . . . it is doubtful that anything short of an earthquake, a tornado, and an extraditing army will induce us to surrender him to any other city from this day forward." She noted the particular impact of two talented young singers, soprano Lucine Amara and baritone Theodor Uppman.[34] Ebert's second production at USC, Benjamin Britten's *Albert Herring*, was shaped in its final rehearsals by Britten himself, who was visiting the Pacific Coast with tenor Peter Pears in November 1949 to premiere his new *Saint Nicolas* cantata. Another singer attracted to working with Ebert was the mezzo-soprano Nan Merriman, whose career already had encompassed broadcast and recorded performances with Arturo Toscanini and Bruno Walter.[35]

The Los Angeles Opera Guild, originally founded to support the annual visits of the San Francisco Opera, approached Ebert in 1950, proposing that he present annual seasons of professional opera in English at the Shrine Auditorium for 5,000 schoolchildren between the ages of nine and eleven. These productions were to be sponsored by the Los Angeles County Board of Supervisors and the Department of Education. After an abortive 1949 experiment with Mozart's *The Abduction from the Seraglio*, which the children did not understand, the organization reversed its name and became the Guild Opera, a performing organization run by the indefatigable Florence Irish. Beginning in the spring of 1951, Ebert mounted *Hansel and Gretel, The Bartered Bride, La Cenerentola*, and *The Magic Flute*, rotating them in a cycle. Schoolteachers were sent materials and recordings with which to prepare the children for the experience. USC students benefited from the professional standards demanded in these productions, each of which ran for twenty performances. Marilyn Horne was given her operatic debut in 1954, when Ebert—whose understanding of voices was profound—

cast her in her first mezzo role as Háta in Smetana's *The Bartered Bride.* Horne had until then considered herself a soprano, but under Ebert's guidance began to discover her true vocal range. She was twenty at the time and found it "fabulous" to work with Ebert, who subsequently cast her as the Sandman, then Hansel in *Hansel and Gretel,* and in the mezzo-coloratura title role of Cinderella in Rossini's *La Cenerentola* in 1956. She later commented that Ebert not only had a great deal to offer in the staging of opera but also in the interpretation of Rossini's musical style, which eventually became her most celebrated specialty. Immediately after these experiences, Horne began her European career at the Gelsenkirchen Opera in Germany.[36]

Marni Nixon, who had studied acting at the Pasadena Playhouse in her early teens, also felt that Carl Ebert was one of the great mentors of her life. Like Horne, she won a scholarship to USC and worked with Ebert for four or five years in the early 1950s. "He could mold me," she said. "He would help me set what I could and would do. In [Menotti's] *The Consul,* he cast me as the Italian foreign woman. I said, 'I can't do that.' He said, 'You can, and you will.' His style, the depth of his understanding of acting, using the music and threading it through your voice, was astounding. His involvement was like Strelitzer's. Ebert . . . understood each person's particular talent, what they could do, and how to approach them. He would do that in different ways. You could watch what he did with other people, sometimes telling them nothing, sometimes everything. He had great musical taste, but approached operatic roles with a real acting intent, using the voice to serve that. It changed my life."[37] Nixon remembered traveling up and down the West Coast in Guild Opera productions, performing at 10 a.m. for audiences of schoolchildren. Under Ebert's direction, she played Norina in *Don Pasquale* opposite Theodor Uppman; Gretel in *Hansel and Gretel;* Miss Wordsworth in *Albert Herring,* also with Uppman; and Blonde in *The Abduction from the Seraglio.*

As had been the case in Europe, in his Los Angeles posts Ebert was the general director as well as the stage director. He engaged as conductors Jan Popper from UCLA and Wolfgang Martin from the Metropolitan Opera. He also hired Strelitzer as choral director for the Guild Opera productions. In 1950 Glyndebourne resumed its festival and recalled Ebert and Busch for the summers. By 1954 Ebert realized that his hopes for a full-scale Los Angeles opera company were not developing. As he saw it, the situation was blocked by the fact that almost all support for artistic enterprise lay in the hands of committee women of the social upper crust. Being, in Marta Feuchtwanger's phrase, "a rather democratic personality," he felt awkward

Carl Ebert at California Club reception, 1952. Otto Rothschild Collection, Music Center Archives, Los Angeles.

soliciting funding from these women and withdrew.[38] He returned to a permanent post as general administrator of the Municipal Opera in West Berlin, while his son, Peter Ebert, came to direct the Guild Opera productions. At the end of his career Carl Ebert chose to retire to Los Angeles on his Berlin pension. In Pacific Palisades he bought the first house he had ever owned and became a devoted gardener, specializing in choice orchids that he sent to his friends.

Czech émigré Jan Popper was an able concert pianist as well as a conductor. After accompanying and coaching singers in San Francisco, he taught from 1939 to 1949 at Stanford University, where he established the second opera workshop in the West. He shared with Strelitzer the characteristic of always being completely obsessed with his subject matter. In 1949 he was invited to develop UCLA's opera workshop, where he served as musical director until 1975, bringing in stage directors while he prepared the students musically and conducted the productions. "In Europe," he reminisced, "you are just a cog in the wheel: you are in charge of the music; you have no say-so about anything else. But here I suddenly was a director of an opera workshop and had to make decisions about stage design, about costumes, about staging, and the total picture of opera, for the first time, opened up to me completely."[39] Popper's opera workshop was organized in UCLA's Extension Division, which enabled him to accept outsiders who were often young professionals seeking experience. Maralin Niska, Irving Beckman (later a coach and conductor at the Hamburg Opera), and his future wife, Judith Beckmann (who became a leading soprano in Austria and Germany), all worked with Popper. With the experience gained under Popper as well as from Strelitzer, Lotfi Mansouri was "discovered" at Santa Barbara's Music Academy of the West by the stage director Herbert Graf, who took him to Zurich and Geneva. Mansouri subsequently became general director of the Canadian Opera in Toronto and later of the San Francisco Opera; he guest directed productions worldwide.[40]

Like Strelitzer, Popper began the UCLA opera program under primitive conditions but was gradually able to attract excellent singers. With this talent at his command, Popper's ambitions grew and gradually outstripped UCLA's budget. "We had seven fat years and seven lean years," he later remarked. He took students on summer tours to resorts and ventured into unexplored repertoire. One early venture was the world premiere of Lukas Foss's *The Jumping Frog of Calaveras County* (1950), conducted by its composer on the site of the original jumping contest in Northern California. The set was erected on what proved to be some cows' path to their stable, and in mid-production the music had to stop while the cows sauntered through between the orchestra and the stage. For Benjamin Britten's 1949 visit to Southern California, Popper produced several Britten operas (*The Turn of the Screw, A Midsummer Night's Dream,* and Britten's adaptation of Johann Christoph Pepusch's and John Gay's *The Beggar's Opera*). He presented Luigi Dallapiccola's protest opera, *Il prigioniero,* Virgil Thomson's *The Mother of Us All,* and operas by Eugene Zador (with whom he had studied in Vienna), Ibert, Milhaud, and Janáček. He mounted revivals of operas by Cimarosa, Meyerbeer, and Alessandro Scarlatti, and the first staged version in America of Monteverdi's *Orfeo.* He soon developed the UCLA Opera Theater, which presented touring productions nationwide, using a chorus trained by Los Angeles' famed Roger Wagner. In the 1950s and '60s Popper produced prize-winning televised shows of opera scenes for National Educational Television. Another offshoot of Popper's work at UCLA was the Musical Theater Workshop, which fostered such talents as Carol Burnett and Jon Rubinstein, the actor son of the pianist. By the mid-1960s Popper was taking leaves of absence from UCLA to guest teach in Europe and Asia and to produce opera elsewhere in the United States. His productions at UCLA grew in size; in 1971 he even tackled Meyerbeer's five-act grand opera *Les Huguenots*. In 1975 he retired from UCLA, but not from his wide-ranging operatic activities elsewhere. His own critique of his time at UCLA was that "Production became more and more challenging and bigger and bigger, until we nearly busted our seams. . . . The students appreciated the discipline that they had received as they went out into European theaters."[41]

Conductor Richard Lert's contributions to opera in Los Angeles included a 1936 concert version of Beethoven's *Fidelio* in English at the Pasadena Music Festival. The chorus was "far too large, the orchestra rather under-sized, and Lert masterly," in this "splendid musical contribution," wrote critic Jones in the *Los Angeles Times*.[42] The orchestra, the Pasadena Symphony, was to grow in importance under Lert's thirty-six-year guidance, presenting full seasons of orchestral programs, providing educational and cultural activities, and supporting a youth orchestra.[43] In 1939 and 1940 Lert conducted concert performances of Handel operas for the Pasadena Festival, and in 1949 he conducted Guild Opera performances of Mozart's *The Marriage of Figaro* for Franz Waxman's Los Angeles Music Festival. Lert's influence was tangible and lasting, yet he was modest, as described by Jones: he "did not pose, put forth ambitious manifestos as to his high estate in Europe, criticize the American public or try to stage a revolt. He was content to look around, listen, and fit into the musical scene here."[44] Starting in 1945, he taught conducting at USC. He gave unstintingly of himself to the Music Academy of the West. He later taught at Rice University and for many years served as a master teacher for summer institutes of the American Symphony Orchestra League; conductors of orchestras all over the country list him as their prime teacher and mentor. His knowledge of the traditions of Mahler and Richard Strauss in particular inspired his students, to whom it was clear that he loved and valued the importance of teaching.

An older conductor, Fritz Zweig, whose illustrious performing career had ended when he emigrated, also concentrated on teaching in his new life. He had studied with Schoenberg in Vienna, had settled in Berlin in 1923 as a conductor at the Volksoper, and had been instrumental in bringing Klemperer to the Kroll Opera, where he continued as Klemperer's associate. Zweig was on the conducting staff of the Berlin Municipal Opera when he was removed from his post in 1933. He first fled to Prague, where he was a conductor for the New German Theater (now the Prague State Opera). When Czechoslovakia fell to the Nazis in 1938 Zweig went to Paris, and at the fall of France in 1940 he fled yet again to the United States. In 1947 he settled as a private teacher in Hollywood. His availability and significant gifts are gratefully remembered by students such as Limonick, who revered his integrity and knowledge and frequently went to him for coaching. She remembered his astonishing facility for reproducing the sound of the orchestra when sight-reading an opera score at the piano: "In *Salome* you would *hear* the cymbals! The orchestral sound was in that man's ears, and the passion."[45] As a teacher, Zweig's most fruitful contribution to Los Angeles music was not realized until six years after his death, when his student, the Los Angeles–born Lawrence Foster, returned from a blossoming international career to conduct Verdi's *Otello*, with Plácido Domingo in the title role, as the inaugural production of the new Los Angeles Opera in 1986. Foster had begun his far-ranging professional career in Los Angeles in 1959 and has regularly returned as a guest conductor for the city's world-class company.[46]

Pia Wertheimer Gilbert brought her high level of piano and improvisational skills when she emigrated as a teenager from Germany with her family in 1937. In New York she used these skills to become an accompanist for dancers Lotte Goslar, Doris Humphrey, Martha Graham, and Charles Weidman. Marriage eventually brought her to Los Angeles, where UCLA's Department of Physical Education hired her as an accompanist and encouraged her to develop an innovative approach for teaching music to dancers.[47] In 1961 the publication of a book she coauthored with Aileene Simpson Lockhart, *Music for the Modern Dance*, spread knowledge of "the Gilbert method" to newly established departments of dance in universities across the United States.[48] Gilbert believed strongly that dancers must be musical and must be musically educated. She taught them to be able to read a musical score and to analyze music. "[Dancers] hear differently from musicians. They [must] learn musicians' terms," she claims. She taught the concept of musical notation through the dancers' physical movement rather than through notation itself, then encouraged dancers to read and write rhythmic and melodic notation. She developed dancers' composi-

Pia Gilbert with UCLA students, early 1960s. UCLA Library, Pia Gilbert Papers. Courtesy of Pia Gilbert.

tional abilities by having them devise musical instruments upon which they played their own short works, often improvising vocally as well. Most of the great choreographers had been trained musicians; Gilbert insisted on that basic grounding—a discipline too often disregarded—for all dancers.[49]

A later arrival, the conductor Herbert Zipper, born and trained in Vienna, chose in his late years to give the experience of classical music to the youngest children he could reach, as a necessary step in the continuity of the art. After employment as a conductor in Germany, Zipper returned to Vienna in June 1933 but, as a Jew, found little employment. He occupied himself as a composer for left-wing underground cabarets, where he met the well-known Viennese poet Jura Soyfer. On May 31, 1938, Zipper was arrested and sent to brutal imprisonment in the concentration camp at Dachau near Munich, which became the model for subsequent concentration camps. There Zipper composed, to a text by Soyfer, his fellow prisoner, the "Dachau Song." This call to courageous humanity (*Menschheit*) was not written down but was passed from prisoner to prisoner, to be sung and remembered for decades. It is a rousing march, the refrain of which uses the motto of the camp, "Arbeit macht frei" (work makes us free):

Lost to us the world of laughter,
Lost our homes, our loves, our all;
Through the dawn our thousands muster,
To their work in silence fall.

Refrain
But the slogan of Dachau is burnt on our brains
And unyielding as steel we shall be;
Are we men, brother? Then we'll be men when they've done,
Work on, we'll go through with the task we've begun,
For work, brother, work makes us free.[50]

While in Dachau, Zipper formed, in an unused latrine, a secret orchestra for the prisoners. He and Soyfer were transferred in September to the concentration camp at Buchenwald, where Zipper, whose job in both camps was to haul pails of excrement from the latrines, was fortunate to survive; Soyfer and many others died of typhoid that winter. Zipper's parents, who had escaped from Vienna to Paris, managed to purchase his freedom in mid-February 1939. Zipper first found a position conducting the Manila Symphony but then suffered the Japanese bombardment and occupation of the Philippines. During these life-threatening experiences, his conviction grew that the arts are essential to human existence and that his life's mission was to spread the gift of classical music to those who might not otherwise experience it.

Zipper followed his emigrating family to the United States in 1946, bringing his zeal and indomitable energy to decades of work as a conductor and teacher in New York, Brooklyn, and Chicago, where he developed several community arts programs. A late arrival to the Southern Californian émigré community, in 1972 he was called by USC to Los Angeles, where he quickly realized how musically deprived the inner city's elementary schools were. His conviction that music must be given to the youngest children was carried out in various ways, beginning with USC's efforts to develop an arts-oriented approach to elementary education at the 32nd Street School near the university campus. With support from a Rockefeller Foundation grant, Zipper demonstrated that even teachers inexperienced in the arts could find a way "through which the arts can become an integral part of elementary education."[51] At the Crossroads School in Santa Monica he

Herbert Zipper conducting at the 32nd Street Magnet School, Los Angeles, 1988. Herbert Zipper Archive at Crossroads School for Arts & Sciences, Santa Monica, California.

helped design a music curriculum that subsequently produced the school's top academic achievers. He convinced USC to become involved, leading to the Crossroads/USC performing arts majors program in 1977.[52] He professionalized the USC Music School's preparatory school, which offered after-school instrumental lessons; the school then became the USC Community School of Performing Arts.

Richard D. Colburn, one of Los Angeles' rare benefactors of classical music, had come to know Zipper's work with children in Chicago, and he funded a concerts-in-the-schools program in Los Angeles. Thousands of children whose elementary schools offered no music programs had opportunities to hear Zipper conduct and explain classical music provided by excellent student musicians, many of them from USC. "[Zipper] acted as if he were going to let us in on the greatest secret of mankind. And in many ways he was: the world of classical music, the composers who gave it to us, and the instruments that continue to translate it," wrote one parental fan.[53] When it was clear that USC was going to discontinue its Community School of Performing Arts, Zipper talked Colburn into purchasing the school. In 1988 it was renamed the Richard D. Colburn School of Performing Arts, and it now has its own well-equipped building, with the impressive Herbert Zipper Auditorium, centrally located near the Los Angeles Music Center.

After retiring in 1980 from USC, Zipper continued his pioneering efforts in arts education, reaching preschool children and their parents. In these Los Angeles crusades, Zipper was pursuing the goal he had discovered for himself on his thirteen-hour forced boxcar ride from Vienna to Dachau. When bullied by a Nazi guard to sing, with all his strength Zipper had sung Beethoven's setting of Schiller's "Ode to Joy." He later said, "It was in defiance of the barbarism at Dachau that I truly became a human being."[54]

Energized by their passionate relationship to their art, Ebert, Lert, Popper, Strelitzer, Zweig, Gilbert, and Zipper each possessed the resilience characteristic of those who have known and triumphed over extreme adversity. Their personalities were stimulated by challenges. For the sake of music, and in their desire to give music to others, they displayed toughness and adaptability, sparing no effort to move those they taught into the realms of art.

6

Arnold Schoenberg

I only teach the whole of the art. . . . As a composer I must believe in inspiration rather than in mechanics.

—Arnold Schoenberg

Arnold Schoenberg had just turned sixty when he made the sudden decision in mid-September 1934 to leave the East Coast for California. He wrote to his friends that in Los Angeles he faced "a completely blank page, so far as my music is concerned."[1] With no other alternative after his prestigious Berlin position was terminated in October 1933, he had accepted a low salary to teach at the brand-new Malkin Conservatory in Boston, with adjunct teaching in Manhattan. The strenuous commuting in the harsh winter climate had severely damaged his health, and he had gone to the summer home of the Juilliard School of Music in Chautauqua, New York, to recover. All his efforts to obtain an adequate teaching salary at an established institution on the East Coast had come to nothing. Carl Engel, the president of G. Schirmer (his American music publisher), had recommended Schoenberg as a lecturer to forty-seven institutions, but the results were meager. Prospects for the financial security he wanted looked so bleak that Schoenberg had even contacted Hanns Eisler and the conductor Fritz Stiedry about making connections for him in the Soviet Union. On September 12, the day before his birthday, he wrote to Stiedry (still working in Leningrad), "We are going to California for the climate and because it is cheaper." After he was temporarily settled in a rented Hollywood house with his wife, Gertrud, and toddler, Nuria, he expressed in a letter to Anton Webern his initial enthusiasm for the beauty of his surroundings: "It is

Switzerland, the Riviera, the Vienna Woods, the desert, the Salzkammergut, Spain, Italy—everything in one place. And along with that scarcely a day, apparently even in winter, without sun."[2] He recovered his health and energy and could indulge his intense desire to play tennis. By 1935, Leonard Stein—who would be his teaching assistant from 1939 to 1942—recalled, Schoenberg was "fit and roly-poly," springy, full of vitality, and tanned a dark bronze.[3]

Resistance to modern music in Los Angeles, however, gave Schoenberg major problems. Upon his arrival in New York a year earlier, Joseph Malkin had arranged extensive publicity that led to several receptions and performances. In Los Angeles there was no such greeting. Schoenberg's primacy as a cultural leader in Europe had been enhanced by a devoted circle of disciples—both students and performers—who, following the tradition of master-apprentice training, in many ways helped but insulated him. From his first years in California, memories of past repudiations and his sense of his own importance as a composer made him hypersensitive to any slight, even if imagined. While he was acutely aware of his music's need for "propaganda," as he called it, he had little ease in the American art of public relations.[4] Starting over at his age in the haphazard cultural environment of Los Angeles—at first with no institutional backing—his assumptions and expectations were often frustrated, and his relationships were frequently difficult as he struggled to make a living for his young wife and their growing family.

Otto Klemperer's position with the Los Angeles Philharmonic undoubtedly counted as an advantage to Schoenberg. Yet the month after his arrival, he refused an invitation to a banquet honoring Klemperer because he felt that the organizers of the event owed him greater recognition than a "walk-on" part.[5] At first he took some pains to entertain the society matriarchs dominating Los Angeles' music, but in November 1935 his approach to the manager of the Philharmonic, Bessie Bartlett Fraenkl, was peremptory in tone. He invited her to attend a class of his at the University of Southern California (USC) because, he wrote, "I know what I am doing there is of the greatest importance for everybody who is interested in music. . . . There will certainly be in perhaps twenty years a chapter in the musical history of Los Angeles: 'What Schoenberg has achieved in Los Angeles'; and perhaps there will be another chapter, asking: 'What have the people and the society of Los Angeles taken of the advantage offered by Schoenberg?'"[6]

Schoenberg assumed that he would conduct his own works in Los Angeles; his European royalties had diminished to nothing, and he needed the fees. Klemperer offered him a guest program with the Philharmonic in March 1935, after himself achieving an extraordinarily enthusiastic response the previous December to Schoenberg's 1917 orchestration of *Verklärte Nacht*. In his own program Schoenberg repeated that work and conducted his Bach transcriptions in celebration of the 250th anniversary of Bach's birth, as well as Brahms's Third Symphony. His performance of the Brahms was severely criticized for its leisurely tempo, which "irritated and baffled the players," and although the audience applauded the composer warmly, one critic hoped that "we should have much more Schoenberg to hear—with Klemperer conducting."[7] The following December Schoenberg again met with disaster conducting the Philharmonic, this time in an all-Schoenberg program that included the full orchestral arrangement (made in April 1935) of his Chamber Symphony No. 1 (1906). Peter Yates remembered the musicians in rehearsal deliberately sabotaging the music—which they dubbed the *Jammersymphonie* (a pun on *Kammersymphonie*)—by playing wrong notes and "horsing around." Leonard Stein suspected the players were tipsy from Christmas holiday revels; he found Schoenberg's patient efforts to educate the orchestra heartbreaking.[8]

Schoenberg took on no further conducting with the Philharmonic. In his helpful and strongly worded plea for a 1936 Philharmonic fund-raising drive, he expressed what bothered him about American culture: "As the materialism of our time seems to endanger the whole sphere of spiritual culture, I believe it is the duty of every man to fight for the existence of one of the most vital symbols of man's higher life."[9] He conducted the Federal Symphony Project's WPA Orchestra, which must not have helped him financially, for the concerts were free. Studio musicians, eager for challenging musical experiences, invited him to conduct a reading orchestra they had organized in Hollywood. Critical response to his conducting remained poor, while critical acceptance of Klemperer's performances of his music with the Philharmonic emphasized "the Schoenberg luminosity and romanticism."[10]

It soon became clear to Schoenberg that his twelve-tone music would not fare well in musically unsophisticated Los Angeles. In November 1934 he confided to Carl Engel in New York, in his new and struggling English: "Have I now to appear as only the composer of the *Verklärte Nacht* ... or as the devil in person, the atonalist, the constructor, the musical mathematician etc.? I hate this kind to consider a composer only from the view-point of history instead to enjoy (or not) what he says. I would like to learn your opinion about this matters."[11] The Third String Quartet (1927), played in

March 1935 by the local Abas Quartet, received newspaper notice only. Leonard Stein, who was at that time beginning his lifelong devotion to new music, found it "the strangest music I'd ever heard."[12] In January 1938, Schoenberg's 1933 Concerto for String Quartet and Orchestra (after Handel), in Klemperer's performance with the Philharmonic and the Kolisch Quartet, struck critic Isabel Morse Jones as a "derangement" of Handel. She wrote, "It was interesting chiefly as evidence of the progress of Schoenberg's remarkable theories and it had moments of fleeting beauty. As a musico-intellectual demonstration of Schoenberg's powers it was a work to study and to marvel at rather than to revel in."[13]

Practically none of Schoenberg's music was available in libraries or music stores in Los Angeles. In 1937 Schirmer published a collection of writings by and about Schoenberg, edited by the Los Angeles impresario Merle Armitage. With this information, Jones attempted a more probing discussion of Schoenberg's musical ideas in the *Los Angeles Times*. Her October 1938 report on the premiere by members of the Fox Studio Orchestra of Schoenberg's recently completed *Kol nidre* expressed her new attitude: "We are indeed on the threshold of a profound change in musical art. . . . Schoenberg, like Einstein, is essentially a simple man of truth."[14] In his own writings excerpted for the Armitage book, Schoenberg articulated his philosophy of composing:

All I want to do is to express my thoughts and get the most possible content in the least possible space. . . . If a composer doesn't write from the heart, he simply can't produce good music. . . . I have never had a theory in my life. . . . I write what I feel in my heart—and what finally comes on paper is what first coursed through every fibre of my body. It is for this reason I cannot tell anyone what the style of my next composition will be. . . . What can be constructed with these twelve tones depends on one's inventive faculty. The basic tones will not invent for you. Expression is limited only by the composer's creativeness and his personality. . . . In the time of the [Chamber Symphony No. 1, 1906], I understood better what I had written and I had more personal pleasure with that, than with the music which followed. Then to compose was a great pleasure. In a later time it was a duty against myself, it was not a question of pleasure. I have a mission—a task . . . I am but the loudspeaker of an idea! . . . All music, in so far as it is the product of a truly creative mind, is *new*. . . . It is no use to rail at new music because it contains too many ideas. Music without ideas is un-thinkable, and people who are not willing to use their brains to understand music which cannot be fully grasped at the first hearing, are simply lazy-minded. Every true work of art to be understood has to be thought about; otherwise it has no inherent life. . . . The artist is content with aspiration, whereas the mediocre must have beauty. And yet the artist attains beauty without willing it, for he is only striving after truthfulness.

The same book included an interview by the Los Angeles critic José Rodriguez in which Schoenberg discussed his reliance on instinct. When queried about feeling versus intellect in his music, he replied, "It might astonish some critics that I am somewhat the creature of inspiration. I compose and paint instinctively. . . . I see the work as a whole first. Then I compose the details. In working out, I always lose something. This cannot be avoided. There is always some loss when we materialize. . . . I am somewhat sad that people talk so much of atonality, of twelve-tone systems, of technical methods when it comes to my music. . . . I wish that my music should be considered as an honest and intelligent person who comes to us saying something he feels deeply and which is of significance to all of us."[15]

Schoenberg tried for the remainder of his life to convince a wider public that this was his true intent as a composer. He wrote succinctly to the composer Roger Sessions, "That I write in this or that style or method is my private affair and is no concern to any listener — but I want my message to be understood and accepted."[16] His relative isolation in Los Angeles, however, combined with Klemperer's illness and subsequent resignation from his Philharmonic post, hindered informed and sympathetic performances of Schoenberg's orchestral works.[17] He lacked the performing skills that enabled such composers as Béla Bartók, Paul Hindemith, Ernst Krenek, Igor Stravinsky, and Ernst Toch—as concert performers—to promote their works in person to American audiences. With the exception of his own recording of *Pierrot lunaire* in Los Angeles for Columbia (in 1940), Schoenberg's works were not taken up by major American recording companies until after his death.[18]

Although Schoenberg received prestigious and well-paid commissions from Elizabeth Sprague Coolidge, the Koussevitzky Foundation, and Harvard University, all based in the East Coast, obtaining commissions on the West Coast was difficult and unrewarding in terms of fees and publicity, and he managed to get only four. The first came in 1938, when he contacted Los Angeles' most influential Jewish leader, Rabbi Jacob Sonderling. Schoenberg had received desperate pleas from friends and relatives trapped in Austria and Germany. While he wrote many testimonials for these supplicants, he was unable to meet the requirements that would guarantee their financial stability in the United States, and he thus hoped to interest wealthy members of Rabbi Sonderling's congregation at the Fairfax Temple in providing the necessary affidavits. To support this effort, his *Kol nidre* was commissioned by the rabbi, who collaborated with Schoenberg on the text, for performance at a Yom Kippur service that fall, a month before the disasters of Kristallnacht. Schoenberg's free treatment of cantus firmus chant prevented the work's first performance in a synagogue, and so the service, narrated by Sonderling, took place in the Coconut Grove nightclub at the Ambassador Hotel.[19] G. Schirmer rejected it for publication in 1941. The second commission, for the Piano Concerto (1942), was originally to have been a "piano piece" for which Schoenberg's pupil, the pianist Oscar Levant, put up $100. When the work grew into a concerto, Levant got cold feet over Schoenberg's fee and performance requirements and withdrew.[20] The fee ultimately was paid by a wealthy UCLA student of Schoenberg's, Henry Clay Shriver. Another pupil, Nathaniel Shilkret, who had been a member of Schoenberg's Malkin Conservatory–sponsored Manhattan class in 1933–34, provided a third commission in 1945. He had come to Hollywood in the mid-1930s, composed for several film studios, and was associated with Victor Records. He commissioned each of the composers Mario Castelnuovo-Tedesco, Darius Milhaud, Stravinsky, Alexandre Tansman, Toch, and Schoenberg to write a short single movement for a suite for narrator, chorus, and orchestra on sections of the book of Genesis. The work was recorded by Victor Red Seal Records after its November 1945 performance by the Janssen Symphony Orchestra. Shilkret's own movement, "Creation," followed Schoenberg's five-minute "Prelude" for textless chorus and full orchestra. The composers each received $300—except Stravinsky, who held out for $1,000.[21] Schoenberg's Phantasy for Violin (1949) was commissioned by the Canadian violinist Adolph Koldofsky. A friend of Rudolf Kolisch, he had moved to Los Angeles in 1946 and played the first West Coast performance of Schoenberg's String Trio in May 1948 at "Evenings on the Roof."

Peter Yates's concert series did the most of any American musical organization to promote Schoenberg's music in a sustained way during his California years. Yates, inspired in part by Schoenberg's Society for Private Musical Performances in Vienna (1919–21), aimed to gather performers and audiences willing to venture outside the standard repertoire. Particularly interested in undervalued genius, he celebrated Schoenberg's residence in Los Angeles from the first season of his concerts in 1939–40. Yates programmed most of Schoenberg's chamber works, some several times.[22] His articles on Schoenberg, whose difficult personality he relished and endeavored to understand, appeared beginning in 1940 in the California periodical *Arts and Architecture,* and from 1949 on in various national publications. Yates's belief in his audience's ability to understand Schoenberg's music gradually encouraged other performances in Los Angeles.

In Yates's first discussion with Schoenberg (in 1939), the composer declared that his newly published Violin Concerto could not be performed by anyone living, as Heifetz had said he could not play it.[23] José Rodriguez had reported to Schoenberg that "a virtuoso" had told him the concerto would be unplayable until violinists could grow a new fourth finger. Rodriguez described Schoenberg "laughing like a pleased child" at this remark and continuing, "Yes, yes. That will be fine. The concerto is extremely difficult, just as much for the head as for the hands. I am delighted to add another *unplayable* work to the repertoire. I want the concerto to be difficult and I want the little finger to become longer. I can wait."[24] Undaunted by this attitude, Yates convinced a Hollywood Bowl Young Artists Auditions winner to learn the concerto with his wife, pianist Frances Mullen. When they took two movements to Schoenberg (on February 10, 1940), he was pleased enough with their work that he arranged for them to perform one movement on NBC radio. He wrote kindly on the young violinist's score, "Now I heard this for the first time and I am satisfied, about you and the composition too."[25]

These extremely contradictory responses illustrate both Schoenberg's concern for students and his anger toward those who crossed or belittled him. Leonard Stein remembered that "Schoenberg never made a fuss about how well one performed his works. He realized performers were doing their best. He'd be glad if you came to him beforehand to practice. He wouldn't have much to say. He wasn't going to spend his time goading the performers." Yet Stein also remembered Schoenberg's bearing such a grudge against Heifetz that even in the impecunious last years of his life he refused the violinist's offer of financial help.[26] Such paradoxes in Schoenberg's attitudes were basic to the complexity and intensity of his mind. While studying with him, Dika Newlin recorded in her diaries many instances of the "unresolvable contradictions" in his character.[27] His daughter, Nuria, offers her analysis: "He was gentle and he was severe, and he was angry and he was sweet, and he was happy and he was sad, and I think he was all of the things that everyone else is, to a much more intensified degree. . . . When he was angry, he was much angrier than anyone else was. And when he was happy, he was much happier."[28]

Carl Engel found that there was no one more *herzlich* or cordial than Schoenberg. Yet even Engel, along with other New York publishers, critics, radio, and recording companies, received doses of Schoenberg's frequently paranoid outbursts of spleen.[29] In Los Angeles, Europeans in the growing émigré community often were treated frostily by Schoenberg, who believed that they, more than Americans who lacked a sophisticated musical background, should certainly pay respect to his stature.[30] Anyone whom Schoenberg suspected of acting presumptuously toward him felt his anger, which could be spiked with irony and wit.

In 1948, at the beginning of his bitter altercation with Thomas Mann over the author's "pirating" of twelve-tone theory in the novel *Doctor Faustus,* Schoenberg sent Mann an invented "1988" encyclopedia article by an imaginary musicologist named "Hugo Triebsamen," which recorded that the composer Thomas Mann was the real inventor of the twelve-tone system, but having become a writer he had allowed its appropriation by the thievish composer Schoenberg. (Mann had indeed pumped Schoenberg for material on music and the life of a composer when he began writing the novel in May 1943.)[31] Schoenberg was not only enraged about the book's possible impact on his musical stature but also particularly insulted that the composer in the novel was afflicted with syphilis. Marta Feuchtwanger remembered Schoenberg in the Brentwood Mart, shouting to her his denial of the disease. She was taken aback but glad that he was speaking in German.[32]

Mann's major source for his novel's information about Schoenberg's twelve-tone method was Theodor Adorno, a near neighbor of both Mann and Schoenberg in the 1940s. Although Adorno believed he was elevating Schoenberg's reputation in his polemic *The Philosophy of New Music,* Schoenberg avoided him. Mann, who used Adorno's essay in his novel, remembered that "much as [Adorno] revered Schoenberg he had no intercourse with him."[33] Schoenberg, who persisted in calling Adorno "Wiesengrund," Adorno's Jewish father's name, vented his feelings against Adorno in a 1950 memo titled "Wgr." This began, "I never could bear him" and criticized the bombast, pathos, and grandiosity of Adorno's book. An unbridgeable chasm between himself and Adorno lay in the fact that in this book Adorno discusses Schoenberg's dodecaphonic "system," whereas Schoenberg himself declared that "mine is no system but only a method. . . . One follows the row, but composes on the whole as before."[34] Schoenberg wrote to his European student Josef Rufer, "Naturally [Adorno] knows all about twelve-tone music, but he has no idea of the creative process. . . . The book will give many of my enemies a handle, especially because it is so scientifically done." In a 1950 codicil to his will, listing possible advisors to his wife on the disposition of his legacy, Schoenberg demanded that "Wiesengrund should be excluded altogether."[35]

On the other hand, Hanns Eisler, whose loyalty to his teacher had resumed in the 1930s, was a frequent guest of the Schoenbergs after his 1942 move to Los Angeles. Schoenberg had corresponded with Eisler about creating a music school in the Soviet Union just prior to his move to California, and he demonstrated his interest in Eisler's family by using money confiscated in Germany to order Eisler's father's book on philosophy sent to him soon after settling in Los Angeles. As a tribute for his teacher's seventieth birthday, Eisler dedicated his favorite chamber work, *Fourteen Ways to Describe Rain,* to Schoenberg, who was very pleased with it. A week after Eisler's reunion with Bertolt Brecht in Hollywood, Brecht commented in his journal on Eisler's relationship with Schoenberg: "schönberg is an old tyrant and eisler . . . trembles and worries about his tie being straight or arriving 10 minutes early."[36] On July 29, 1942, Eisler took Brecht—about whom Schoenberg knew little—to hear Schoenberg lecture at UCLA on modern composition. They were invited afterward to the Schoenberg home. Before the occasion Eisler warned Brecht, who was known for his uncompromising rudeness, that if Brecht lost control and made any malicious comments to Schoenberg then he, Eisler, would break off all relations with his longtime collaborator. Brecht was deeply impressed by the keenness of Schoenberg's intellect and so charmed by his dry, sharp wit that he sent Schoenberg a poem in gratitude for the visit, during which Schoenberg had told a story of how he learned from a donkey the easiest way to climb a hill.[37]

Eisler felt that Schoenberg's home life with his second, very young family, was "a twelve-tone hell" and a "mess of disorganization." But when young Ronald Schoenberg needed an emergency appendectomy at the age of five, Eisler offered to lend the necessary money. He only managed to get Schoenberg to accept this gesture by saying that repayment would not be necessary if Schoenberg would give Eisler some lessons instead, to which Schoenberg replied, with relentless logic, "If you still haven't learned it I can't teach you."[38] Schoenberg helped Eisler get a teaching position at USC and recommended him for several other academic appointments, but he grew nervous over Eisler's politics. In 1944, when the witch hunt for leftists was already under way in Hollywood, Schoenberg publicly stated that politics was a dangerous game best left to politicians, and that artists who dabbled in politics should be treated like immature children.[39] When it became clear in late 1947 that Eisler would be deported, Schoenberg wrote Joseph Rufer, "If I had any say in the matter I'd turn him over my knee like a silly boy and give him twenty-five of the best and make him promise never to open his mouth again but to stick to scribbling music. That he has a gift for, and the rest he should leave to others. If he wants to appear 'important,' let him compose important music." After Eisler's deportation in 1948, Schoenberg again wrote Rufer, "We who live in *music* have no place in politics and must regard them as something essentially alien to us."[40]

Eisler maintained his respect—even reverence—for Schoenberg, and soon after his deportation gave a lecture in Prague in which, while he criticized Schoenberg's "petit-bourgeois attitudes," he remarked, "One could almost say that the characteristic feature of Schoenberg's music is fear. . . . He is the lyric composer of the gas chambers of Auschwitz, of Dachau concentration camp, of the complete despair of the man in the street under the heel of fascism. That is his humanity. It is proof of Schoenberg's genius and instinct that he gave expression to all these emotions at a time when the world seemed safe for the ordinary man in the street. Whatever one may say against him, he never lied."[41] Upon learning of Schoenberg's death in 1951, Eisler expressed an ambivalence echoed by several of the closest of Schoenberg's students: "Schoenberg's death shook me most profoundly. I have learned from him everything I know. . . . It was difficult to stand up to such a master."[42]

It was Schoenberg's own awareness of his mastery as a teacher that convinced him he could support his family in Los Angeles when he first arrived in 1934. However, he had no contacts with the two major universities, UCLA and USC, and the music divisions of both institutions were in a weak financial and academic condition because of the Depression. His initial idea was to teach film composers, for film was the one industry that was flourishing financially. He may have had creative motives partly in mind, for in Europe Schoenberg had long been seriously attracted to film as *Gesamtkunstwerk* (the combination of arts in one work). In particular, the staging difficulties of his one-act opera *Die glückliche Hand* had led him in 1913 to suggest a filmed version to be designed by Oskar Kokoschka, Wassily Kandinsky, or Alfred Roller.[43] During the development of sound in film, Schoenberg composed his *Begleitungsmusik zu einer Lichtspielszene*

(Accompaniment Music to a Film Scene) in 1929–30 and, at Klemperer's suggestion, considered creating a film for it with the Bauhaus artist and designer László Moholy-Nagy. Now that economic survival was uppermost in his mind, however, it was his confidence and interest in teaching that he leaned upon, and these strengths determined his life in America.

He knew from his year with the Malkin Conservatory that, in comparison to his European pupils, American music students were ill prepared. He hoped film composers would be better equipped to make use of his teaching and better able to pay him a comfortable living. This turned out to be partly true. Soon after his arrival in October 1934, he advertised himself in local newspapers as a teacher. He gave public lectures in Hollywood and soon developed a heavy schedule of private teaching, which remained lucrative until a 1937 strike in the film studios. Many of his private students were film composers, some of whom must have been told, as was David Raksin, a self-taught musician who came to Hollywood in his twenties to arrange music for Chaplin's *Modern Times,* "First you must learn something about music."[44] Gerald Strang, Schoenberg's teaching assistant from 1935 to 1939, commented on Schoenberg's work with film composers: "He was very much respected among musicians. . . . Right from the beginning there was a steady stream of people from the motion picture industry who took private lessons from him. . . . He more or less charged what the traffic would bear with the motion picture people in order to make a living. And in part, this enabled him then to take as well talented young people who couldn't afford to pay his prices. So a lot of young Americans, whom he did not charge at all, or charged a pittance, benefitted indirectly." Strang knew of no occasion when Schoenberg helped a composer with a film score, but he commented that the film composers who sought lessons with Schoenberg were anxious to be recognized in the concert world and "were always working on a symphony, a string quartet, an overture, or a concerto."[45]

Oscar Levant studied with Schoenberg from April 1935 through 1937. A prodigy on the brink of popular success as an impudent musical know-it-all on the radio show "Information Please" and his subsequent career as the highest-paid concert pianist in America, Levant paid eloquent tribute to his teacher:

> To my mind, Schoenberg is the greatest teacher in the world. The very contact with such a person either brings out something that is in you or lets you see that there is nothing to be brought out. Either way, it is helpful to know where you stand. Schoenberg not only permits each of

his pupils to be completely himself, he insists on it. Father of the atonal system, he is passionate in his reverence for the classics and classic form. From him I learned that modernism is not merely a matter of hitting the keys with your elbow and seeing what happens; it is logical, and formed with an utterly logical if unconventional development. No one has to like modern music, but every serious musician owes it to himself to keep his ears open and listen to what is going on.

Schoenberg set Levant, who thought musically in terms of the piano, to studying the language of strings in the quartets of Mozart and Brahms. The piano trios of Schubert, on the other hand, were studied for thematic development. Schoenberg, Levant said, "taught me to write piano music for the piano, chamber music for chamber groups, orchestral music directly for the orchestra."[46]

Levant's close friend George Gershwin met Schoenberg in the summer of 1936. Their mutual love of tennis and painting cemented a friendship between the two musicians. Gershwin can hardly be categorized as a student of Schoenberg's, but he was working on a string quartet at the time and may have brought it to Schoenberg on May 28, 1937.[47] On July 12, the day after Gershwin's tragic sudden death from a brain tumor, Schoenberg expressed his respect for Gershwin's music in a radio eulogy, which began, "George Gershwin was one of the rare musicians for whom music was not a matter of greater or lesser ability. Music for him was the air he breathed, food that nourished him, drink that refreshed him. Music was that which he felt, and music was the feeling that he received. Originality of this sort is only granted to the great, and without doubt he was a great composer."[48]

Alfred Newman, who was at Twentieth Century-Fox from 1935 and was its music director from 1939 to 1959, studied with Schoenberg from 1936 through 1938 and thereafter maintained a social relationship with him (including frequent tennis dates) through 1940. Newman was a key Hollywood figure for Schoenberg; he talked Samuel Goldwyn into allowing the Kolisch Quartet to record the four Schoenberg string quartets on a United Artists sound stage in 1937 and provided the Twentieth Century-Fox orchestra to perform the premiere of *Kol nidre* in 1938.[49] In 1938 Newman even asked Schoenberg to present the Oscar for best film score along with a short speech at the Academy Awards ceremony. Schoenberg was unable to attend the ceremony but sent his speech, in which he expressed a hope that "there will soon come a time, when the severe conditions and laws of modernistic music will be no hindrance any more toward a reconciliation with the necessities of the moving picture industry."[50] Others from the film capital who studied briefly with Schoenberg were Hugo Fried-hofer, who attended Schoenberg's seminar at USC in 1935; Edward Powell and David Raksin, who met Schoenberg through Levant and had lessons between 1935 and 1937; Leonard Rosenman, who later composed the first twelve-tone film score (*Cobweb*, MGM, 1955); and Franz Waxman, who began lessons in August 1945, although Schoenberg then became ill and could not continue. Two members of Paramount's music department, song-writers Ralph Rainger and Leo Robin, studied more extensively with Schoen-berg between 1936 and 1939.

Schoenberg was tempted to investigate the kind of salary a film composer could command, and in Los Angeles his students were often the key to composing possibilities. Robin and Rainger may have arranged an intro-duction to Boris Morros, head of the music department at Paramount Studios, where Schoenberg had appointments in 1936, 1937, and 1938.[51] Another contact came through pianist Edward Steuermann's sister, Salka Viertel, who was then writing scripts for Greta Garbo at Metro-Goldwyn-Mayer. In January 1936 an appointment was made for Schoenberg to meet with MGM's Irving Thalberg, who was producing a filmed version of *The Good Earth*, Pearl S. Buck's best-selling novel about Chinese peasants. Salka Viertel wrote about the encounter:

> A lot of protocol went on before the meeting was arranged and a stu-dio car sent for the Schoenbergs. . . . At 3:30 there was still no sign of the Schoenbergs. . . . Schoenberg had found it perfectly reasonable that he should be shown around the studio before deciding to work there. We sat down in front of Thalberg's desk, Schoenberg refusing to part with his umbrella. . . . I still see him before me, leaning forward in his chair, both hands clasped over the handle of the umbrella, his burning, genius's eyes on Thalberg, who, standing behind his desk, was explaining why he wanted a great composer for the scoring of *The Good Earth*. When he came to: "Last Sunday when I heard the lovely music [*Verk-lärte Nacht*] you have written . . ." Schoenberg interrupted sharply: "I don't write 'lovely' music.". . . Schoenberg had read *The Good Earth* and he would not undertake the assignment unless he was given complete control over the sound, including the spoken words.[52]

Thalberg proposed a $30,000 salary, but Schoenberg's demand for such artistic control naturally caused a delay in the discussion, during which

Gertrud Schoenberg suggested the (then) unheard-of fee of $50,000, which ended the negotiation. Gertrud wrote to her brother Rudolf Kolisch that they were pretty sure composing for the film studio was not for Arnold, and Schoenberg wrote to Alma Mahler-Werfel, "It would have been the end of me." He regretted the loss of the money, since had he managed to win it, such a sum would have allowed him to complete his opera *Moses und Aron,* the oratorio *Die Jakobsleiter,* and some theoretical works he had begun.[53] He was interested enough, however, in the film project to make sketches for it in two notebooks. In July of the same year, the director William Dieterle approached Schoenberg about collaborating on a film biography of Beethoven. Schoenberg replied that he could not join the project because "it would not be in keeping with what people are entitled to demand of me, namely that I should create *out of my own being.*"[54]

Schoenberg's true feelings about the Hollywood film industry were published in an April 1940 article in *Arts and Architecture* titled "Art and the Moving Pictures." It effectively ended the possibility that he would have any further appointments with film studios. In it he recalled having expected from the advent of sound in film a renaissance of the arts, dealing with the highest problems of mankind. For this exciting new medium he had envisioned audiences who could recite by heart whole pages of Shakespeare, Schiller, Goethe, and Wagner. He did not expect the "vulgarity, sentimentality, and mere playing for the gallery" that followed. Moving pictures had now become a mere "industry, mercilessly suppressing every dangerous trait of art." Films were "cut down to that zero point which allows for a happy ending," intended only for "ordinary people." He concluded that ways must be found to satisfy the demands of the more highly educated, as well as the demands of art itself.[55] After the publication of this article, Schoenberg's interactions with the film industry dwindled. Yet Schoenberg urged Kolisch to find work playing in studio orchestras during difficult times in his brother-in-law's career, and Gertrud Schoenberg attempted to sell a movie script when they faced lean years themselves in the 1940s.[56] Both Schoenbergs maintained friendly social contact with the Dieterles, Salka Viertel, and the Korngolds, who had arrived in Hollywood the same month as the Schoenbergs. Gertrud Schoenberg had been a close friend of Erich Korngold when they were teenagers in Vienna, and their children became friends in Los Angeles. Even the icy relationship between Schoenberg and Julius Korngold, the former enemy of musical modernism, melted. The elder Korngold wrote that in California "Schoenberg behaved more like a bourgeois husband and tender father than a musical revolutionary. He could be very amiable. . . . He seemed to have grown tolerant, very tolerant, and tolerance is not one of the characteristics of a real revolutionary."[57]

In May 1936 the prospects of a faculty appointment at UCLA encouraged the Schoenbergs to buy their own home nearby in Brentwood, where they employed domestic help and began holding Sunday afternoon gatherings that were known for excellent coffee and Viennese pastries. Klemperer, who studied composition privately with Schoenberg in California beginning in April 1936, was a frequent guest. When in town, members of the Kolisch Quartet would be there, joining visiting pianists Eduard Steuermann, Artur Schnabel, and Richard Buhlig, who was performing Schoenberg's piano music in his recitals in California and New York at the time. Ernst Krenek, whose desire to live in California brought him for late-summer visits, paid yearly homage with a visit on Schoenberg's birthday. Adolph Weiss, a fine bassoonist and a twelve-tone composer who had been Schoenberg's first American student in Berlin, was a member of Schoenberg's circle after 1938. The composers Edgard Varèse, Joseph Achron, Louis Gruenberg, and Ernst Toch came for frequent social engagements, which mingled prominent German-speaking émigrés with actors such as Harpo Marx and Peter Lorre. Once Schoenberg began teaching at UCLA, members of the music department and the administration of the university were invited to the Sunday afternoons in Brentwood. Schoenberg also proudly hosted formal celebrations of his UCLA students' compositional achievements. Their music would be performed, and they would have the opportunity to mingle with a select group of Schoenberg's distinguished musician friends over Viennese refreshments.

Many comments from Schoenberg's American students echo Levant's praise for him as "the greatest teacher in the world," one who invested extraordinary care and energy in this work and whose methods were unique.[58] But because he recognized that the ability to compose was inborn, Schoenberg's attitude was paradoxical. He himself frequently made this comment about his own teaching: "I always called it one of my greatest merits to have discouraged the greatest majority of my pupils from composing. There remain, from the many hundreds of pupils, only 6–8 who compose. I find such who need encouragement must be discouraged, because only such should compose to whom creation is a 'must,' a necessity, a passion, such as would not stop composing if they were discouraged a thousand times." Rather than encouraging his pupils, he showed them that "I did not think

Arnold Schoenberg in Brentwood with his dog, Roddi, 1937. Used by permission of Belmont Music Publishers.

_ _ _ _ _ _ _ _ _ _ _ _ _
_ _ _ _ _ _ _ _ _ _ _ _ _
_ _ _ _ _ _ _ _ _ _ _ _ _

_ _ _ _ _ _ _ _ _ _ _ _ _ _ _ _ _ _ _ _

May we request the pleasure of your company at a reception on

Sunday, February 18, 1940
from 3 o'clock to 7 o'clock

At this reception (to which, among others, my classes have been invited) compositions of some advanced students will be played. Although the actual training of these students comprises only three semesters, they have arrived, thanks to their intelligence, talent and earnestness at an astounding degree of ability and maturity.

It is likely that this opportunity to be heard by this audience of distinguished and selected personalities will give them a great encouragement.

The concert will start soon after 3 o'clock.

We hope to see you among those on whom we count and look forward to that with our

most sincere regards

EAST →
SONSET · SEPULVEDA BLVD →

WEST →

12931

N. ROCKINGHAM AVE

BRISTOL AVE

116

me and others Arnold Schoenberg

There will scarcely be more than 60 minutes of music R. S. P.

PHONE: W·L·A· 35077

Arnold Schoenberg invitation, 1940. Used by permission of Belmont Music Publishers.

too much of their creative ability. . . . All my pupils differ from one another extremely. . . . They all had to find their way alone, for themselves."[59] He did not attempt to teach a style or to give his students "tricks." Gerald Strang described the acute analytical ability that lay behind the way in which Schoenberg was a "destructive rather than a constructive critic" for his students: "He had the knack . . . of putting his finger on the reason why something went wrong. . . . Schoenberg recognized that nine times out of ten the weakness was a result of something that happened earlier, and could go back and say [why]. This must have had some influence on the criticism and self-criticism of the people who worked with him."[60]

John Cage, at age twenty-two, was among a group of three private students who, joining together to save on their fees, studied at the Schoenberg home on Canyon Cove in Hollywood in the fall of 1934. In spite of the harsh criticism he received, Cage believed that "Schoenberg was a magnificent teacher," one who put his students in touch with musical principles:

> I studied counterpoint at his home and attended all his classes at USC and later at UCLA when he moved there. I also took his course in harmony, for which I had no gift. . . . He told me that without a feeling for harmony I would always encounter an obstacle, a wall through which I wouldn't be able to pass. My reply was that in that case I would devote my life to beating my head against that wall—and maybe that is what I've been doing ever since. In all the time I studied with Schoenberg, he never once led me to believe that my work was distinguished in any way. He never praised my compositions, and when I commented on other students' work in class he held my comments up to ridicule. And yet I worshipped him like a god.[61]

Peter Yates passed on to Cage Schoenberg's recollection of Cage as "an inventor of genius. Not a composer, no, not a composer, but an inventor. A great mind."[62] Bernice Abrahms Geiringer, a member with Cage and George Tremblay of the initial threesome, remembered that Cage's relationship with Schoenberg was "affable." Cage was highly verbal, precise in his counterpoint exercises, and analytical; he "had one of the clearest minds, and he came unencumbered. He just went his way." Like Tremblay (who was already well trained as a musician) and Cage, she continued to study with Schoenberg at USC, then at UCLA. She discovered that "Schoenberg did not teach composition. . . . You had to *really know* what preceded you. You just didn't start with yourself. You had to have the most disciplined background. . . . What he was really focusing on was a foundation." She was one among several who testified that—contrary to the impressions of those who did not know him—Schoenberg was a very emotional person and extraordinarily perceptive. She had been encouraged by her piano teacher to compose, yet her family situation was difficult. She remembered Schoenberg advising her, "Miss Abrahms, you're not made of glass."[63]

Pauline Alderman, a member of USC's music faculty who was one of Schoenberg's first private students in Hollywood, arranged his invitation to teach in USC's summer school in 1935. Because USC's President Rufus von KleinSmid ruled the university like an "absolute monarch" and strongly disapproved of modern music, the summer appointment led only to a part-time position, the Alchin chair in composition, in the academic year 1935–36 and another appointment the following summer.[64] In 1936 UCLA, which, thanks to its state support, was a much richer institution than USC, a private institution, "discovered" Schoenberg and with Klemperer's recommendation offered him a tenured appointment as professor of composition, at a beginning salary of $4,800.[65]

The USC summer teaching gave Schoenberg a great deal of trouble, for he found himself facing a class of thirty to forty public school and college teachers, middle-aged and older, who were in the class primarily to earn a few credits that would improve their salary schedules.[66] Strang, who came to study with Schoenberg on scholarship from the San Francisco Bay Area, where he had worked for Cowell's New Music Society, believed that Schoenberg was "completely at a loss" in that situation. "He had no idea what grades meant, or what kind of expectations he could ask of his students." His English was not adequate to a class situation, and Strang volunteered to sit beside him and supply necessary words. Schoenberg got Strang another scholarship—with funds from Samuel Goldwyn—for the fall semester. Leonard Stein enrolled on the advice of his piano teacher, Richard Buhlig, and volunteered to play musical examples from Beethoven piano sonatas for Schoenberg's classes. Both Stein and Strang continued with Schoenberg at UCLA in 1936, Strang serving as Schoenberg's first teaching assistant. Stein took on that role at UCLA from 1939 to 1942. Both men helped Schoenberg write his textbooks until his death in 1951 and in many ways supplied the aid Schoenberg's European students had provided. Beside correcting students' papers, Strang said, he helped resolve Schoenberg's personal problems, advised him on the purchase of his house, and acted as a chauffeur. This role of amanuensis enabled Strang to see Schoenberg's difficulties and adjustments in his new situation:

It was in many ways a very frustrating period for him and for everybody else. He had come to us with the reputation of being extraordinarily difficult to get along with, being very autocratic, very domineering and intolerant. But the effect of being so completely dislocated and having to find these ways through an educational system which was so completely foreign to all the European models that he had been accustomed to, apparently made him much less domineering than he had been. I never saw any of that. He was sensitive. [His] feelings were easily hurt. He was constantly misunderstanding people's motives. He was resentful, for instance, if someone on one of the faculties on which he taught gave a party and didn't invite him and Mrs. Schoenberg. . . . If he saw somebody on campus, [who] didn't come and shake hands with him, he thought that he had done something to offend them. Or—vice versa—perhaps they were intending to offend him. All this kind of personal sensitivity made it very difficult for him, but somebody had to act as a buffer and a bridge. That was my role for the first two-and-a-half to three years he was in Southern California.[67]

Strang and Stein both commented that neither USC nor UCLA allowed Schoenberg the influence he deserved. Although Schoenberg never reached the salary he hoped for at UCLA, his new position helped him withstand the reduction in his private teaching in 1937, when, because of a "little catastrophe in Hollywood," his film students stopped their lessons owing to cancellation of their film contracts.[68]

In the 1930s UCLA was converting from its past as a school of teacher education and becoming a full-scale university. Strang believed that UCLA had hired Schoenberg as an outstanding and controversial international figure who would enhance the reputation of the newly emerging academic institution. At first Schoenberg was given hope that he would be allowed to develop—and be director of—the music department's theory and composition program. With the same force and zeal he had earlier applied to the rescue of European Jewry, he drew up memos and plans. His July 1937 plan for graduate students in the UCLA music department outlined his principles of artistic commitment: a devotion "only comparable to that to religion or to the fatherland"; and a respect for laws of morality, which are stricter than those of everyday life. He deeply believed that artists "have to be models for ordinary everyday citizens and have to behave accordingly. It has to be one of the foremost task[s] of every school of art to develop the character of the students. . . . [Artists] belong to the leaders of mankind."[69]

From the start Schoenberg's classes were overlarge. In 1937, teaching twenty-five students in composition, twenty-five in analysis, and sixty in counterpoint, he petitioned Robert G. Sproul, the president of UCLA, for salaries for his teaching assistants; he also requested funds to build a library of scores for students in analysis and composition.[70] With prodigious energy, intellect, and self-assurance, Schoenberg envisioned whole new educational structures. He proposed a conservatory-like domain within the music department, which he called a "Music Club."[71] It would contain a number of divisions he called "schools": an orchestra school, a school for conducting, and a school for orchestration whose pupils would orchestrate works for the conductors and the chamber orchestra and would attend rehearsals of the Philharmonic and the Federal Orchestra. There would also be a choir school and a school for copyists. There would be a fixed time when students would listen to recorded works while following scores. These same works would be performed in concerts by prominent local artists of Schoenberg's choice, in which the choir and the orchestra would also perform.[72]

Schoenberg proposed elevating the university's musical training to a European level. His projected "Curriculum for Composers" (1941–42) was intended to "sharpen prerequisites" in order to separate the more talented students from those aiming only to fulfill average requirements: "It seems to me that a great number of talented students to be found in this community could be stimulated to take a more serious attitude towards art if they were forced to," he wrote. His suggested plan involved progression through six undergraduate courses in harmony, counterpoint, and analysis to a seventh, "Composition for Composers" (with the consent of the instructor). Graduate classes for composers would explore different aspects of composition.[73] Following the precepts of the great Viennese musicologist Guido Adler, Schoenberg wanted to require of graduate students a thorough knowledge of specific works. He recommended that students be informed of what they must study for their oral examinations and what they should expect to be asked.[74] The committee for such an examination should consist of not only three members of the music faculty but also one member from the art department and one from philosophy or physics. The theory or composition student should undertake a thesis on a problem of composition, including analysis and comparison of two or more works in regard to the problem and an independent investigation, idea, or theory, with illustrations.[75] Schoenberg often expressed his opinion that aspiring composers should study intensively for a minimum of five (sometimes he demanded six to eight) years.

Another radical vision Schoenberg suggested for UCLA in 1940 was a faculty forum of the arts and aesthetics. He hoped to engage teaching colleagues from the sciences and the humanities in regular discussions regarding what effects recent changes in technology, sociology, and economics might be having on the arts and aesthetics. He foresaw culture-altering changes overtaking a society that neglected full communication between the arts and sciences. Among the problems for which he sought the help of his colleagues was the possible "end of art," caused by the erosion of a class structure and the consequent inability of artists to resist the temptation to satisfy the demands of the masses.[76]

None of these plans were realized during Schoenberg's tenure at UCLA. Instead the hiring emphasis in the music department turned toward musicologists, and staff positions were not developed to achieve the graduate program in composition Schoenberg had in mind. "The situation at UCLA was always very frustrating to him," remembered Strang; Schoenberg did not "fit" at UCLA. But he "had an active, wiry mind which was constantly grabbing hold of and tussling with something. If it was something which he couldn't resolve . . . his tendency was to push it aside and concentrate on something else."[77]

Although Schoenberg was unable to convert the administrations of either university to his views, his influence on his students was considerable and long-lasting. He saw clearly that he needed to adapt his expectations to American levels of musical background. He found talent, inventive ability, and originality in American students, but it was his opinion that the general level of their music education was "superficial and external." In a 1938 article Schoenberg described his students' musical experience as akin to "Swiss cheese—almost more holes than cheese."[78] Because of this, he wrote, "I had to change many of my ideas which I developed within almost forty years of teaching."[79] His curriculum at UCLA covered harmony and basic analysis for beginners (taught by his assistant), composition for beginners, counterpoint for beginners, structural functions of harmony, analysis of larger forms, and orchestration. He asked beginning students in composition to write complete rondos, which he presented at his home with formality and pride in carefully planned celebrations. Using approved radio broadcasts of concert music, he assigned student listening reports.

For these he worked out, in careful detail, rigorous and comprehensive questionnaires.

Leonard Stein recalled that while Schoenberg's musical examples and exercises remained in many ways similar to those he had used for his European pupils, his teaching and theory texts written in America, while maintaining his basic principles, were adjusted toward the needs of "beginners." Schoenberg grew proud of his ability to teach noncomposers and even boasted to Stein that he could teach composing to tables and chairs.[80] Stein said, "I was appalled at the poor sort of material that students would turn in . . . and Schoenberg would always try to turn them around into something, patch them up. . . . He worked his head off." Schoenberg would give each student a separate exam and would usually change the grade Stein gave on an exam to a higher one. "He countenanced mediocrity. He knew what to expect from these students."[81]

Indeed, in perhaps the most surprising of his paradoxical attitudes, Schoenberg declared several times the worthiness of support for the artist who might not achieve great creative mastery. By 1939 he had developed his idea of "ear training through composing" to help beginners in the understanding of music: "Just as almost anyone can be trained to draw, paint, write an essay or deliver a lecture, it must also be possible to make people with even less than mediocre gifts use the means of musical composition in a sensitive manner. . . . Every good musician should submit to such training."[82] In the 1940 edition of *Music and Dance in California,* he published an article titled "Encourage the Mediocre" that was aimed at "the protectors, the patrons, [and] the customers of the arts." He pointed out that "it is the mediocre artist on whom a rapid expansion of cultural goods depends, more than on the genius who gives the impulse and produces momentum and acceleration." He noted that while people of moderate means were willing to buy landscapes or order portraits from second-ranking painters, too few cared to pay to hear concerts or acquire recordings of works by contemporary composers. "Is there no way to do justice to sincere artists?" he asked.[83]

It was his view that musical study must be based on the works of the masters. His teaching dealt with the profundity with which great composers of the past carried out their ideas, and inquired into the many ways they handled musical problems. Stein believed that Schoenberg's ideas were continuing to evolve. The manner in which he taught harmony considered the ambiguity and multiple meanings of chords. "Instead of modulating from key to key, he is considering [the structural functions of harmony] in terms of regions of one key: monotonality," Stein explained. "This [process of discovery] occupied him as much as his composition did: How and why. Principles of composition. A kind of middle ground between practice and theory, which is not easy to explain. . . . He wasn't interested in pure theory but in the explanation of why certain things happened in composition. He always started in a very intuitive way, through the writing itself."[84]

Schoenberg's students were stunned by his "improvisations" on a given problem, written at tremendous speed on the blackboard in the style of Beethoven, Haydn, Mozart, or Brahms. The composer Leon Kirchner remembers feeling so awed by such demonstrations that at first he thought it hopeless to become a composer. The students' exercises were to be done in these styles; Schoenberg never drew on his own music. "One had to master the past and the forms out of which the present came. . . . What was terrifying was his acute analysis of a student's weakness. He would correct, immediately, in whatever personal style the student was using. . . . It took me years to really understand deeply what Schoenberg taught. At the time I would think I understood, but there was such depth to it, it took a long time to realize its implications."[85] Although he studied with Schoenberg for only two years at UCLA (1937–38 and 1940–41), Kirchner believed that Schoenberg's influence was formative for him. Schoenberg's command of musical tradition and his music's connection to the past encouraged Kirchner to follow his own line of thinking regardless of musical fashions and trends; he ultimately chose not to be a serialist. "Although Schoenberg was extremely systematic, he defied and denied system," Kirchner observes. He remembered Schoenberg being annoyed at the phrase "the twelve-tone system." "He somehow, inherently or intuitively, realized that there was no system in which there could be a final formula. . . . The [twelve-tone technique] is only one parameter in his work: something which I respect very much. But beyond that are the other qualities [such as] his immense musicality. . . . Behind that twelve-tone row is a giant musical mind."[86]

Schoenberg believed that modernism, like composing, "cannot and ought not to be taught. But it might come in a natural way, by itself, to him who proceeds gradually by absorbing the cultural achievements of his predecessors." Although he was persuaded by his first students at USC to present an in-class analysis of his twelve-tone Third String Quartet, and UCLA asked him to deliver a public lecture on the "Method of Composing with Twelve Tones" in March 1941, he usually avoided the subject in class. From the time of his arrival in America he had been tormented by those inquisitive about his "trademarks": the twelve-tone composer, the atonalist.[87] Dika Newlin, who studied with Schoenberg during the same period as Kirchner, remembered Schoenberg's irritation when students approached him with their own twelve-tone efforts. He confessed that he could not teach or correct others' work in this method, for it "seemed to be a matter so personal to him . . . which he himself had been able to attain only after profound thought and deep inward struggle." It was a bone of contention that in 1940 Krenek published his *Studies in Counterpoint,* "a slender volume . . . in which certain twelve-tone principles are set forth in a rather schematic manner."[88] In a 1939 letter to Krenek about teaching, Schoenberg had remarked, "American young people's intelligence is certainly remarkable. I am endeavoring to direct this intelligence into the right channels. They are extremely good at getting hold of principles, but then want to apply them too much 'on principle.' And in art that's wrong."[89]

Lou Harrison was one Los Angeles pupil who did obtain Schoenberg's help in composing a twelve-tone work. He studied privately with Schoenberg in 1941–42, supporting himself by playing the piano at Lester Horton's dance studio. He had heard a performance by Frances Mullen of Schoenberg's Piano Suite and was determined to compose and dedicate to her his own twelve-tone Piano Suite. He reached a point of blockage in his work and steeled himself to ask Schoenberg's help. Peter Yates recorded Harrison's description of the lesson: "I played the Prelude. There was a rather long moment of silence, and then he asked thoughtfully, 'Is it twelve-tone?' I simply said, 'Yes.' He reached for the page, saying, 'It is good! It is good!' . . . By the time I had played to the point of blockage in Movement III, he plunged directly in, already aware of my structure, and, with splendid illuminating instructions, permanently disposed of not only that particular difficulty but also any of the kind that I might ever encounter." Yates reported that Harrison followed Schoenberg's instruction that the tone row is not a composing formula.[90] Harrison later told Vivian Perlis that Schoenberg was a great influence on him, "in some ways more of an influence [than his mentor Charles Ives] because Schoenberg represents the more fundamental control. . . . It was this sense of order that I needed from Schoenberg."[91]

In informal ways, those with relatively easy access to Schoenberg learned from him by taking opportunities to inquire about his composing. Stein once asked whether there was a definite extramusical program in the First Quartet. Newlin recorded Schoenberg's reply, which was "Oh yes, very definite—but private!" In her diary Newlin noted Schoenberg asking studio musicians, "How can you compose without writing your own life?"[92] Strang also noted that "Schoenberg was certainly devoted to the idea that music expresses the feelings and attitudes of the composer." Stein was working closely with Schoenberg at the time of the composer's near-fatal heart attack in the summer of 1946. When he returned to work on his String Trio a month after his illness, Schoenberg told Stein about reflections of his experiences of "death and restoration" in that work. Stein came to the conclusion that Schoenberg had "a very programmatic mind." Both Strang and Stein were closely involved with the writing of Schoenberg's *Fundamentals of Musical Composition,* in which he encourages the student to keep in mind a special character, a poem, a story, or even a moving picture to stimulate the expression of definite moods while composing even the smallest exercises.[93]

On the other side of the coin, Pauline Alderman remembered Schoenberg remarking that a composer needs to be able to write a canon as easily as he would write a letter; following Brahms's example, he wrote one every morning to keep in practice. At a social occasion the young Viennese composer Eric Zeisl asked why Schoenberg kept up the practice of writing complex double canons that no one would ever hear. Schoenberg replied, "That is for the satisfaction of the inner logic."[94]

The challenges of teaching occupied Schoenberg until the end of his life, as he set down his principles (with the help of Strang and Stein) in texts for students. The preface to his *Structural Functions of Harmony* recorded his "dissatisfaction with the knowledge of harmony of my students of composition at the University of California, Los Angeles."[95] The four books he worked on in California (the others were *Preliminary Exercises in Counterpoint, Fundamentals of Musical Composition,* and *Models for Beginners in Composition*) were all intended for the average American university student. They gave him many years of trouble but were clearly important enough to the legacy he intended to leave that he was willing to sacrifice much time from his own composition.

A part of his effort to educate was his concern about the climate for the arts in America: How, he wondered, would serious musicians be able to make a living? His opinions about music in America (expressed in radio and newspaper interviews on the West Coast and in several essays unpublished in his lifetime) went largely unnoticed by the musical establishment in New York. In 1934 he pointed out that high concert and opera ticket prices and the emphasis on box-office returns narrowed both the class of concertgoers and the compass of repertoire available to music students in the United States.[96] In his letters Schoenberg often expressed his feelings about the American "commercial racket." In 1945, after he had retired from UCLA, his comments sharpened: "No serious composer in this country is capable of living from his *art*. Only popular composers earn enough to support oneself and one's family, and then it is *not art*"; and "If it is art it is not for the masses. And if it is for the masses it is not art." The pervasiveness of advertising in American life and media provoked Schoenberg's remark in a 1946 letter to his old friend Oskar Kokoschka that he was living in a "world in which I nearly die of disgust."[97]

In a 1948 article for the newsletter of the League of Composers, he challenged the morality of the marketplace. Why was it the aim of composers, artists, and writers to produce something similar to the latest success on the stage, the movies, the radio, novels, and music? "Has originality lost its appreciation? Does it interfere too much with the commercial success? One can understand that fear for one's life may cause a man to bow to dictatorship . . . but must one tolerate the moral and mental baseness of people who bow to the mere temptation of profits? . . . Is it aesthetically and morally admissible to accommodate to the listener's mentality and preference? If so, is there not a limit how far such accommodation is allowed to go? Does such accommodation promote the artistic culture of a nation? Does it promote morality? Is it not more healthy to give a nation a chance to admire its heroes than to applaud the fleeting success of an ephemeron?"[98]

Such remarks were a part of his duty as a teacher, Schoenberg believed. This calling demanded the highest ethical standards. He had always tried to convince his students "that there is such a thing as artistic morality and why one must never cease to cultivate it and, conversely, to oppose as forcefully as possible anyone who commits an offense against it."[99]

The tremendous energy Schoenberg gave to teaching "the whole of the art" took a toll on his health to which he had difficulty admitting. In her student diary Newlin noted many occasions when he would continue teaching although he was in no condition to do so. Nuria Schoenberg Nono believed that her father's great interest for teaching was "what really saved him and kept him strong and alive during all of the time he was here in the States. . . . Retirement [in 1944, at the age of seventy] was one of the worst things that happened to him." Beyond losing the activity of teaching and university contacts, the pension he had accrued in only eight years on the UCLA faculty was a mere $38 per month, at a time when the children of his second family were thirteen, eight, and four. He continued to hold classes in his home, but the state of his health and the relative poverty in which the family found itself prevented him from attending events or concerts. During the period's undistinguished leadership of the Los Angeles Philharmonic, he remembered Mahler and lost interest in the orchestra.[100] The deaths of his close friends and students in Europe burdened him. Carl Engel's death in 1944 severed his one lifeline to the New York musical establishment and ended a relationship he had come to depend upon. The rejection of his application for a Guggenheim Fellowship in 1945, combined with his feeling that he had been systematically excluded (by those who ran the Philharmonic and the Hollywood Bowl) from Los Angeles' public musical life, contributed to his withdrawal into bitterness.[101] Schoenberg Nono remembers when the Sunday afternoon gatherings, rather than drawing him out, reinforced his intellectual loneliness: "After a while my father realized that these people were coming here to meet each other and not to talk with him. . . . Daddy would be sitting . . . maybe completely alone, not talking to anyone, and so he decided one time that we weren't going to do this anymore. . . . For a long time on Sunday afternoons at two o'clock . . . we would get in the car and drive around the block . . . while these people came and found no one at home and went away."[102]

After he recovered from his serious heart attack in the summer of 1946, Schoenberg's spirits rallied. He continued teaching privately and, in spite of a long catalogue of serious health problems, recaptured his gusto. In response to an award of $1,000 from the National Institute of Arts and Letters, he gave the credit for his accomplishments to his opponents, saying that while he never understood it, it was their enmity that helped him continue swimming against the tide without giving up.[103] Critic Virgil Thomson printed Schoenberg's speech in his column in the New York Herald Tribune, adding, "[The statement] shows indeed, through its passionate and disjointed phraseology, how deeply touched the great man is by the belated recognition of his professional colleagues, not one of whom he considers his musical equal. . . . Coming from the conqueror at the end of a long aesthetic civil war, it is a sort of Gettysburg Address."[104] The Los Angeles music critic Lawrence Morton called on Schoenberg in Brentwood in order to show him the Thomson article, which had not been forwarded from New York. Morton later wrote to Thomson, "Since his eyes are not too strong—he must save them for his writing and composing—he asked me, in his very gentle and polite manner, to read it to him. I must tell you that the old gentleman was touched, very deeply moved; so much so that I did not dare look at him while I read, for fear of losing my own voice, in the emotion of seeing the tears well up in his eyes. . . . I think you should know how much joy your column brought to a man who has known much less joy than his genius should have earned him."[105]

Los Angeles' celebration of the composer's seventy-fifth birthday in 1949 underscored a growth of understanding and appreciation for his chamber music. After programs of his work presented by Yates's (by then well-established) "Evenings on the Roof" and the newly formed local branch of the International Society for Contemporary Music, Morton wrote in a review that "[Los Angeles was] given the opportunity of reviewing within a few short weeks almost the whole scope of Schoenberg's art, except for his dramatic and choral music, from a song of Opus 1 to the violin *Phantasy* composed this year for Adolph Koldofsky. . . . The repertoire might have been selected to illustrate a formal critical analysis of the development of Schoenberg's art. . . . There were no cries of anguish and no anti-modernist demonstrations. On the contrary, there was real enthusiasm. . . . History will record us as the audience that applauded, however belatedly."[106] Albert Goldberg noted in the *Los Angeles Times,* "There is a large and willing public for [Schoenberg's] music in our town. . . . There were more people on hand and more enthusiasm over what they heard than the most sanguine prophet would have dared to predict."[107]

There was no local opera able to attempt Schoenberg's early and middle-period operas, however; this may have discouraged his completion of *Moses und Aron.* In this anniversary year, the newly formed Los Angeles Chamber Symphony Orchestra presented the composer's Chamber Symphony No. 1 under the German émigré conductor Harold Byrns. The same year, Alfred Wallenstein offered an Interlude and the "Lied der Waldtaube" from the *Gurrelieder,* the only Schoenberg work Wallenstein attempted during his long tenure (1943–56) with the Los Angeles Philharmonic. In a February 1945 guest appearance with the Philharmonic, Klemperer had performed Schoenberg's Chamber Symphony No. 2, but the neglect by Wallenstein added to Schoenberg's bitterness as he reached seventy-five. In gratitude to his many birthday well-wishers, both European and American, he sent a letter that began, "To become recognized only after one's death- - -!" He realized that he could not hope for "plain and loving understanding" of his work in his lifetime, as he had felt "commanded to express certain ideas, unpopular ones at that, it seems, but ideas which had to be presented."[108]

As Schoenberg found European interest in his compositions growing in the postwar period, he wrote, "There is nothing I long for more intensely . . . than that people should know my tunes and whistle them."[109] What happened was the opposite. Leonard Stein commented, "Schoenberg was not responsible for the twelve-tone concept taking over. People like [René] Leibowitz [whose *Schoenberg et son école* was published in 1947] would come in the late forties and explain his music to him!"[110] At the time Leibowitz was reinterpreting Schoenberg's serialism for young European composers who had been deprived of modernism for the duration of the war. In 1948 Leibowitz encouraged Adorno to complete the manuscript on Schoenberg's method that had provided so much material for Thomas Mann's *Dr. Faustus*.[111]

In 1949 Adorno published his *Philosophie der neuen Musik* in Germany. The same year, on a visit sponsored by the U.S. State Department, the German critic Hans Heinz Stuckenschmidt told Albert Goldberg of the *Los Angeles Times* that Schoenberg's twelve-tone system was being widely adopted by young composers in bombed-out Germany "because it gives them a sense of order."[112] Gertrud Schoenberg told Milton Babbitt, who was instrumental in interpreting Schoenberg's work in mathematical terms to Americans, that Schoenberg was repeatedly baffled by the accusations that he was a "mathematical composer. . . . My husband didn't know any mathematics, and didn't even know of what they were accusing him."[113] Schoenberg himself had said in 1949, when he was too ill to accept an invitation to teach at Darmstadt, Germany, the center for the new serialism, "I am still more a composer than a theorist. When I compose, I try to forget all theories and I continue composing only after having freed my mind of them. It seems to me urgent to warn my friends against orthodoxy."[114]

The irony of America's perception that Schoenberg was the influence behind postwar composers' conformity to serialism is that this was a development he did not ultimately intend. While his violin and piano concertos, the Fourth String Quartet, the "Genesis" Prelude, the String Trio, the Phantasy, and *A Survivor from Warsaw* are serial works, in his California period Schoenberg also composed a number of works in which he yielded to his "longing to return to the older style," which included tonality.

(Schoenberg listed the Suite in G for String Orchestra; the Second Chamber Symphony; the Theme and Variations for Band; and "several others" as his tonal works.[115] "Others" could include *Kol nidre;* Variations on a Recitative for Organ; and *Three Folksongs,* op. 49, for mixed chorus.) The intensity of his teaching, which took more hours of his life than it had in Europe, and the depth of his homage to and analysis of the works of earlier masters in response to the needs of his American students, might seem to have influenced this change. In replying to questions on the subject from Josef Rufer, whom he particularly trusted, however, Schoenberg wrote that for him composing had always meant "obeying an inner urge," even when that meant changing styles to accommodate his "upsurge of a desire for tonality."[116] This was but another dimension to his creative work, which was always developing in surprising ways. There is a notable easing of serial restrictions in Schoenberg's American twelve-tone works. He also used tonal vocabulary in serial works when he felt the meaning demanded it (in the *Ode to Napoleon,* his protest against dictatorial tyranny; and in the Piano Concerto, the program of which outlines the emotions of being uprooted from one's homeland). In his texted works composed in Los Angeles, Schoenberg continued exploring new expressive uses of *Sprechstimme* and narration to project his meaning, right up to his last work, the fragment titled "Modern Psalm No. 1," a setting of his own words for chorus with speaker and orchestra.[117]

In his last public lecture, presented November 29, 1949, at UCLA, Schoenberg discussed his "evolution," not his revolution. He paid tribute to those who educated him musically, from his early musician friends to his composer models Brahms, Bruckner, Liszt, Mahler, Richard Strauss, Wagner, and Hugo Wolf. Lacking a basis in traditional theory, he had learned to rely on "the miraculous contributions of the subconscious . . . the power behind the human mind, which produces miracles for which we do not deserve credit." This evolved into a belief that seems, if we look beneath all Schoenberg's paradoxes and complexity, deeply consistent throughout much of his life: "What I believe, in fact, is that if one has done his duty with the utmost sincerity and has worked out everything as near to perfection as he is capable of doing, then the Almighty presents him with a gift, with additional features of beauty such as he never could have produced by his talents alone."[118] Beauty in Schoenberg's music has come to the ears of the American public only as performers have gradually become at ease with its accompanying challenges. It does not come to the ear through systematic analysis, but through awareness of the intuitive expressivity—the implicit romanticism—in his musical ideas and language.

An important aspect of Schoenberg's character remained essentially European. He was an elitist who believed in fighting for "spiritual culture," humanity's "higher life," the spiritual and intellectual realm of *Geistigkeit*. The American idea of market forces—which necessarily lower the aspirations of the individual in order to satisfy the greatest number of consumers— remained alien to him, as was the Southern California culture of entertainment and hedonism. In 1950 Albert Goldberg asked Los Angeles' émigré composers how separation from their homeland had affected the character and quality of their work. By then, suspecting that he would not live to complete his spiritual testament in *Moses und Aron* and *Die Jakobsleiter*, Schoenberg had withdrawn to compose his last choral psalms, works reflecting the tender acceptance foreshadowed at the close of the work based on his earlier brush with death, the String Trio. Stravinsky, who had so often been transplanted, gave Goldberg a curt response: "I do not think that this subject is really worth a column of your pen." Schoenberg, thinking back over his efforts to continue composing while giving so much of himself to teaching, replied with some resignation—but added a final fighting gesture: "If immigration to America has changed me—I am not aware of it. Maybe I would have finished the third act of *Moses and Aaron* earlier. Maybe I would have written more when remaining in Europe, but I think: nothing comes out, what was not in. And two times two equals four in every climate. Maybe I had four times four times harder to work for a living. But I made no concessions to the market."[119]

7

Ernst Toch

Art, true art, is mysterious. . . . In its essentials it is religious, no matter how remote it may be to any preconceived religious program.

—Ernst Toch, "The Credo of a Composer"

After the United States entered the war in 1941, Southern California's tremendous response to President Roosevelt's call for an "Arsenal of Democracy," combined with the new emphasis on war propaganda in Hollywood films, produced a civilian warrior mentality that extended to young musicians in Los Angeles. Their pride in the great Europeans who had settled in their midst caused ideological battles for differing streams of contemporary musical thought. Partisans of either Schoenberg or Stravinsky joined opposing camps to debate with or shun each other in the foyers of the city's concert halls. An equally partisan but less vocal third party turned to and studied with the independents, whose figurehead was Ernst Toch.[1]

Toch himself would have been reluctant to acknowledge this role. For him the prime condition was sincerity to one's self. His early self-training through secret study of Mozart's scores caused him to question the cerebral attitudes in postwar composition. In 1955, as the merits of serial techniques versus the formal restraints of neoclassicism were argued around him, he remembered himself at the forefront of German musical modernism in the Weimar era and remarked that he was "the forgotten composer of the century."[2]

When one considers the quality of Toch's output in all genres of composition, it is astonishing that only recently have his works been rediscovered. Nikolai Lopatnikoff, one of his European students, offers as explanations Toch's modesty and stubborn integrity: "Toch was by nature an individualist, a loner who stayed aloof from artistic trends . . . and went quietly on his own way. This was his strength and this also partly accounts for the undeserved neglect of his music in the postwar period—a time when his creativity worked at a high pitch and when some of his most significant music was written."[3] Toch himself commented on his psychological makeup in 1957, when he was awarded, at the age of seventy, the Order of Merit from the German government in expiation for his emigration: "By my distinction of being different from my environment I was lost in my childhood and lonesome at home and in my town [Vienna]. I was, if not the black sheep, the awkward sheep, and I was never fully accepted. I roamed the world, partly by choice, partly by fate. Possibly, today, I substitute fatherland for father and, in a most primitive way, I am proud of a father's blessing. But most of all I am proud of being a descendant of the music which sprang up in Germany and Austria, . . . an heir to the greatest of all masters, and I humbly accept the acknowledgement that I belong to their spiritual family."[4]

Toch was born to compose, yet music, literature, and the arts played no part in his family's ghetto background in Vienna. His father, the first of the family to emerge from poverty, hoped his son would enter his leather business or become a doctor. It was believed in the family that the father's early death from a heart attack was caused by his discovery that Ernst, at sixteen, was obsessed with composing string quartets.[5] Although the pain of such a conflicted background stayed with him all his life, Ernst Toch also treasured the lonely musical discoveries of his childhood. Because his ear canals were abnormally large, he was exceptionally sensitive to sounds. Stone breakers building cobblestone streets, faucet drips, steam whistles, sticks he clacked along a wooden picket fence, and the different pitches of glasses of water— all enthralled him. (Some of these remembered sounds would return in his late symphonies.) When he first discovered a pawned piano in his grandmother's house at the age of four, his mother brusquely dismissed his excitement as foolishness. He heard no concerts, only organ grinders and military bands. He was gifted with perfect pitch, and at the age of seven or eight learned the meaning of notation by watching the lines on the music staff while a lodger in his parents' home practiced the violin. So ridiculed was his interest in music that Toch came to believe that his composing was shameful. When he was ten, however, the revelation of Brahms's fame at death showed him that it should be possible to follow his obsession to live as a composer. "I am [trained] by Mozart, by Bach. . . . How would anybody know? Nobody played an instrument with [me], nobody sang with [me], and I did all this in secrecy. These were my only masters. I never had any other," he told the musicologist Robert Trotter, one of his most trusted pupils in Los Angeles. By the age of eighteen he had composed six string quartets; the sixth, his op. 12 in A minor, had been passed by a schoolmate to Arnold Rosé, concertmaster of the Vienna Opera and leader of the Rosé Quartet, which performed it. The year his father died, Ernst saw a notice for the Mozart International Competition of the city of Frankfurt. With a portfolio of required new works he won the competition, which gave him free tuition at Frankfurt's Hoch Conservatory and a living allowance for four years.

Feeling that he had been granted a miracle, Toch left Vienna in 1909 for Germany and his upward spiraling, prolific career as a composer that brought him early fame in the exhilarating years of the Weimar Republic. In the midst of his World War I military service (in 1916) he married Lilly Zwack, the daughter of an aristocratic Jewish banking family in Vienna. She was a violinist who had also been schooled in French, painting, and piano; her commanding strength of character and cultured background provided nurturing support and practical capabilities he relied upon increasingly. As an antidote to the early discouragement by his parents, the encouragement of three strong musical women—his wife, Elizabeth Sprague Coolidge, and Marian MacDowell—helped him build his creative confidence.

The doctorate in music Toch had earned in 1921 facilitated his family's 1934 flight from Europe. He was first appointed to a position lecturing on modern music at the New School for Social Research in New York. There he met George Gershwin, who helped him obtain a Hollywood film contract. Toch was forty-eight when in 1935 he interrupted a summer holiday in Austria to respond to Paramount's call to compose the film score for a George DuMaurier tale, *Peter Ibbetson*. He was paid $750 a week, but he had to wait seven weeks before the film was ready for him to begin work. He lived alone at a Santa Monica beach hotel, socializing with émigré friends such as Vicki Baum and Richard Lert at their magnificent house on Amalfi Drive in Pacific Palisades. Lert had known and admired Toch in Mannheim and was aware of his extraordinary facility for orchestrating as he composed. Yet Paramount's music department told Toch that he could not orchestrate his own film scores.[6] Toch found the pressure of Paramount's music deadlines intolerable.[7] His *Peter Ibbetson* score won the unusual distinction, however, of being reviewed by Olin Downes in the *New York Times* and was nominated for an Academy Award. In the fall of 1935 Toch returned to his teaching in New York, where he wrote an article for *Modern Music* that shows his hope for composing "film-opera," as well as some early disgruntlement with studio attitudes:

> The sound-film, equipped with such potentialities and having so great a scope, is adapted as no other medium is to bring music to "the masses." . . . The decisive factor . . . of course, is the selection of the music, its quality, placing and apportionment. On the whole, little attention has been paid to these questions, and music has been treated merely as a necessary evil. . . . Few people, so far, realize that the music as well as the costumes must be made "according to measure" if it is to "fit." . . . There is no doubt that if the people in charge would devote as much attention to the quality of the music as to the other items in a film they would deserve great credit. Nor would they harm the box-office—in all probability, it would be helped. This state of affairs once achieved, the composer could begin an extremely promising collaboration with the films. . . . The road will lead . . . finally to the real film-opera . . . the genuine film-opera of today. Of its eventual success . . . there is no question.[8]

Toch sought film assignments the following year, but found this difficult while teaching in New York. Realizing that "music in Hollywood is a closed shop," he moved his family to Pacific Palisades in the fall of 1936.[9] From 1936 to 1939 his composing skill was used only for uncredited piecework or B movies.[10] Yet Toch was highly respected among Hollywood musicians, several of whom studied and formed lasting bonds with him. Among his early American students were composers Hugo Friedhofer, Alex North, André Previn, and Douglas Moore.[11]

Toch's labors in the film industry became a heavy burden for him. The necessity to compete with others to earn his living went against the grain of his reticent personality. His granitic integrity, his strong convictions that could not be overturned or even argued, and his lack of patience for small talk separated him from the culture of the film world. The greatest commitment in his life was to his own nonfilm composing. His character was deep and inward; he tended toward melancholy and suffered from depressions, yet possessed a pronounced vein of humor. In private, when comfortable with friends whom he trusted, he enjoyed entertaining guests with his imitations of clowns, his extraordinary ability to mimic, his witticisms, and long narrative jokes.[12] He had little ability or instinct for publicizing himself or his music, and he could turn sarcastic and hostile when he felt misunderstood.

Lilly Toch described her husband as "utterly unassuming, so simple and modest, nearly shy." She assigned herself the role of fighting his battles, for she felt that "his unpretentious, undemanding ways never changed. . . . The pattern of his childhood situation had much to do with this attitude. . . . He considered his gift as something given to him without merit on his part."[13] To counteract her husband's growing despair over his lot as a composer, in the early California years Lilly maintained a stimulating social life. She enjoyed inviting the Thomas Manns (whom she introduced to the Stravinskys) and the writers Emil Ludwig, Bruno Frank, and Salka Viertel with her film director husband, Berthold, along with local professors. Other friends included Alma Mahler Werfel and Ernst Krenek, who came to dinner with his German wife, the former actress Berta Hermann. Over the years Lilly's social occasions became increasingly painful to Toch because his hearing was overly sensitive to several groups conversing at once. In the Tochs' Pacific Palisades period, young John Cage appeared on their doorstep, full of admiration for Toch's experimental spoken choral work, *The Geographical Fugue* (1930). Cage's interest stimulated Toch to compose a companion piece, *Valse* (1961), mocking the party conversation that eventually became auditory bedlam for him.[14]

From 1938 until after the war, Toch was pressed by conscience to save sixty-four Austrian cousins who had been trapped by the Anschluss; some had been sent to concentration camps, but some were able to emigrate. Toch accepted every kind of film work he could find—most of it uncredited—in order to be able to help them financially. He contributed uncredited music for the finale of Alfred Newman's score for *The Hunchback of Notre Dame* (RKO, 1939); he orchestrated Korngold's score for *Devotion* (Warner Brothers, 1943); he orchestrated for David Raksin, who respected Toch and helped him find work at Twentieth Century-Fox. "He was a wonderful musician, a wonderful composer, and a darling man. He worked very hard," remembered Raksin.[15] At Fox, Toch contributed to three films, including *Heidi*, starring Shirley Temple. He also orchestrated and composed background music for Bing Crosby's radio appearances on the *Kraft Music Hall*.[16]

In 1939 Paramount gave Toch the opportunity to compose his own full score for a Bob Hope film, *The Cat and the Canary,* the murder plot of which Toch found unpleasant.[17] The dissonant, modernist idiom he had developed after his World War I experience was well suited to mystery and suspense, and Paramount exploited this quality in three more films. His contribution to *The Ghost Breakers* was reported by music critic Isabel Morse Jones to be "manifestly original" in its "ultra-modern idiom. . . . Its efficacy for betraying the minds of accomplished crooks and for creating fear and suspense in an audience, is amazing."[18] In the period after Pearl Harbor, Toch composed four full scores for Columbia, two of which were nominated for Academy Awards (*Ladies in Retirement,* 1941, and *Address Unknown,* 1944).[19] Credit for the nominations was taken by Columbia's music director, Morris Stoloff, and Columbia reused Toch's themes—uncredited—in *forty* other low-budget films. Paramount and Fox also reused Toch's music.

During this period Toch wrote to friends, "Everything has become grotesquely improbable: With every success that my film scores have, everything gets more difficult for me. The favorites of the music departments close their ranks . . . in order to keep me out."[20] He hired at least three agents in succession to help him find film work and even asked his wealthy American cousin, John Bass, to exploit an industry contact. Lilly Toch described Toch's struggles with film producers for a degree of musical autonomy in the pictures he was assigned: "In the beginning films gave him tremendous joy because he got in touch with situations wholly of music: he was always trying to find in films those places to be kept open to music and not spoken. . . . He fought to have [some dramatic situations] turned over to music and to take out music where it didn't belong. This fight really spoiled his joy, by and by, because he very rarely could get through with his ideas. . . . If he was given a free hand, as in a very few cases, some music came out which is quite remarkable."[21]

In the decade (1935–45) that he worked in Hollywood, Toch came to despise composing for films as a prostitution of his talent. Occasionally his letters to close friends would reflect his hopes for a new film assignment, but by 1944 he had renounced all his enthusiasm for "picture work." "One has to realize that the access in matters of music is blocked by such an amount of ignorance, stupidity, and bad taste that it is really hopeless," he wrote.[22] Around the same time he drafted a bitter personal memo:

I often wondered why the tremendous effects that music *could* have in sound-film, never as yet have been exploited. . . . Music in sound-film is . . . a queer step-child. . . . The composer is brought in . . . to *paste on* music in his comparatively best way; and this by hustling and rushing, for it's "only" music and the film is ready and has to be released. . . . Music becomes very often a spot of embarrassment not only for the producer and director, but also for the composer himself. . . . If they only would allow the composer to collaborate with them *in time,* that is from the start of the script! . . . [The listener is supposed to be] *unaware* from where it comes. This is the real task of film-music. . . . Success: do a good job in the safe way. . . . Great success: do a great job in conventional lines. Tremendous, sensational and enduring success is reserved, and always was, to him who dares the first step towards what is bound to come, and forces the rest of his competitors to follow him.[23]

By 1944, when he wrote this, Toch was desperate about being thought of in America as merely a film composer; his own creative frustrations were mounting.

In 1936 his chamber opera *The Princess and the Pea,* produced by a New York WPA group, had run for six weeks on Broadway with great success. In California, later the same year, Toch eagerly composed—but then shelved in disappointment—a vibrant String Trio, which was too modernist for the tastes of the film musicians who had requested it. That year he also felt the sting of loss when the American division of the International Society of Contemporary Music invited him to compete in its international competition, for which he had often been a jurist in Europe. Yet he also humbly recognized the invitation as a "feature of the American hospitality, for which I never cease feeling grateful."[24]

In 1937 his mother died suddenly in Europe. In her memory, while Hitler was occupying Austria in 1938, he composed the *Cantata of the Bitter Herbs,* op. 65, a work for vocal soloists, narrator, chorus, and chamber orchestra on the exodus of the Jews from Egypt. At the suggestion of Rabbi Jacob Sonderling, it was first performed at a Hanukkah celebration for children at the Fairfax Temple south of Wilshire Boulevard (near the present Los Angeles County Museum of Art). The work's premiere was produced with Hollywood assistance. The great German émigré stage director Leopold Jessner, reduced at the time to a mere script reader for MGM, arranged the text (the Haggadah, traditionally read at the family table at Passover) and staged it; Boris Morros, head of music at Paramount, provided his studio's best musicians and conducted.

Klemperer and the Los Angeles Philharmonic performed three of Toch's orchestral works: *Music for Orchestra and Baritone* to a text by Rilke, composed by Toch in 1931 in response to the rise of Nazism, and premieres of *Pinocchio: A Merry Overture* (1935; his second American work, which proved to be one of his most popular),[25] and a suite, *The Idle Stroller* (1938). The work for orchestra and baritone was performed at a 1936 concert to benefit the effort by Prince Hubertus Loewenstein to maintain "the continuance of cultural writing, art, and compositions by foreign exile artists and scientists now residing in the United States." It was described by critic Jones as "bitter, acid music, strong with suffering."[26] In contrast, *The Idle Stroller* "represents the thoughts that flit through one's mind strolling in the woods," Toch told Jones in April 1939. This work reflected Toch's uncertainty over Americans' reception of his modernist idiom; the *Daily News* music critic called the series of six mood sketches "skillful, clever, but not significant. . . . Ernst Toch, I am sure, has on his shelf emotionally and musically more important and profound works."[27]

After Klemperer's resignation, Toch's orchestral works were infrequently played by the Los Angeles Philharmonic, yet his works appeared on more programs than was the case for most other émigré composers in Los Angeles. Visiting conductors John Barbirolli, William Steinberg, Leopold Stokowski, Alexander Smallens, and André Kostelanetz all chose to perform Toch's works with the Philharmonic, while the orchestra's music director, Alfred Wallenstein, gave him only one performance.[28]

While embroiled in film work, Toch had little time and patience for negotiations with American music publishers, all of whom were based on the East Coast. With Gershwin's help he became a member of the American Society of Composers, Authors, and Publishers (ASCAP), which collected royalties for him. Lilly Toch, who handled most of her husband's practical affairs and could be an obsessively tough negotiator, hammered out a contract for him with Associated Music Publishers (AMP), Schott's American representative. In the 1940s ASCAP's rival, Broadcast Music Inc. (BMI), became the collection agency for Associated Music Publishers. This put Toch at a disadvantage with AMP because he belonged to the wrong collection organization, yet to change his membership to BMI would jeopardize his European rights with Schott, should they be reinstated. He therefore began scattering his works among smaller publishers. These businesses subsequently suffered the bankruptcies and buyouts of American capitalism, which gave little heed to the needs of the creative artist. In 1950 Toch published an article in Europe, in which he summed up this confused situation: "The [music] publishing business functions very unfavorably for the composer in America. The American publisher is first of all a businessman, and as such wants to sell his goods quickly and profitably. European publishers, on the other hand, have realized in the course of their long experience that current commercial considerations are inappropriate for music publishing and should not be applied to this particular kind of merchandise. Such an understanding of the cultural mission of the publisher is generally not to be found in America." Since the major music publishing firms showed interest mostly in school music, works for wind bands, and many kinds of didactic works, Toch continued, "the propagation of serious music is, if at all, mostly undertaken by minor publishers of small financial capacities."[29]

In early 1937 a sudden telegraphed commission from Elizabeth Sprague Coolidge brightened Toch's life. A pianist herself, Coolidge asked for a piano quintet to be premiered at her Berkshire Festival near Pittsfield, Massachusetts, in the summer of 1938, with Toch performing. Toch disliked intensely the combination of piano and strings, but he set to work in the "Villa Majestic," a studio he had constructed from two huge crates that had conveyed the Tochs' furniture from Europe. The studio's site was three miles north of Malibu in a camping area at Coral Beach, where Toch could compose undisturbed. A $30 upright piano, a cooking ring, and a sofa provided his luxuries. The rugged landscape and the relative simplicity of the coast in those days gave him a much-needed sense of freedom. His wife observed that for a time he was utterly happy.[30] Toch never told Coolidge his reservations about the instrumental combination, and because of his film commitments he was not able to take part as pianist in the world premiere of the Piano Quintet, op. 64. He did, however, play in the Los Angeles premiere in September 1939.

Coolidge continued to encourage him and through many years did a great deal to promote his work. In 1938 she premiered his neglected String Trio—which he dedicated to her—at the Library of Congress in Washington, followed by performances in 1939 at the New York World's Fair and the Golden Gate International Exposition in San Francisco. As their correspondence grew, Toch found in Coolidge someone to whom he could entrust his inner thoughts and upon whom he could always rely. He could express to her his anguish over the injustice and violence of events in Europe and, in sleepless despair, the contrasting comfort of thinking of her. "By you," he wrote her at the end of 1940, "I would like to be known to the last recess of my heart." She returned his affection with gratitude, for, in spite of her energetic activity as patroness, her deafness caused her to complain of loneliness and boredom as old age wore on. In the war years, when Coolidge traveled infrequently to California and was often ill, both Ernst and Lilly kept in close touch with her through their affectionate letters, birthday flowers, and holiday greetings. Letters on both sides reflected mutual despondency over the war. Coolidge felt that the entire musical world had been so affected by efforts for defense that her funds for concerts were temporarily depleted, and by 1942 there was little she could do for Ernst Toch's music.[31]

The war years particularly depressed Toch. Letters to the many relatives he was trying to help in Europe were often returned, stamped "Address Unknown," and contact was entirely cut off when the United States entered the war in 1941. In his efforts to earn as much as possible to help his extended family, Toch obtained an appointment in 1940 to the Alchin chair of composition at USC. This appointment reflected USC's desire to rival UCLA's appointment of Schoenberg.[32] The offers from President von KleinSmid were miserly, but Toch agreed to put aside financial considerations in order to build up an important center of composition tuition, teaching part-time for $1,500 per year; his lectures were to be arranged on two weekdays. Von KleinSmid also invited him to lecture on "Music Direction for Cinema" at $5 per lecture hour, $360 maximum per year. This small fee irritated Toch, who had understood from the chairman of the Department of Cinema that he would be paid twice that amount per lecture hour.[33] To increase his income, Toch continued to expand his assignments at USC: in 1942 he took on twelve weeks of summer teaching for $550; in 1942–43 he also taught a class in harmony for USC's Preparatory Department, year-round, for $120 per quarter; in 1943–44 he added private instruction in composition (at his home) for a minuscule $3.75 per half-hour lesson. His contracts consistently stipulated such underpayment, but his university appointments seemed to him to promise more stable financial security than did his sporadic and frustrating film work.

Two benefits resulted from Toch's academic appointments. The first was the purchase of property on the Franklin hill in Santa Monica and undertaking to build a house. By this time Lilly's mother, Ernst's sister, his cousin, and her daughter all were living with the Tochs. Lilly Toch decided against hiring their friend the German architect Richard Neutra to plan the

Ernst Toch (second from left) experimenting, October 1941. Associated Press Photo. *Los Angeles Examiner* Collection, University of Southern California.

house, because she believed he was tyrannical, dogmatic, and extremely orthodox in his ideas about living, and she was not fond of Neutra's Los Angeles houses, designed in the International Style.[34] Lilly's own design for the house gave prime space to Ernst's studio and buffered it acoustically from the family living quarters. The extraordinary view from his desk, looking toward the Santa Monica and San Gabriel mountain ranges over eucalyptus and palms bordering the Brentwood golf course, distracted Toch when he was working; he drew the curtains to block it out.[35]

The second benefit from his academic appointments would be realized only much later. Because he was having a painfully dry time creatively, and because he always learned much from teaching, Toch decided to distill his thinking about composition into a book, *The Shaping Forces of Music*, still highly respected today, over which he labored from 1942 until its publication in 1947. The book's dedication "to the country which gave me shelter when shelter was taken from me" includes the wistful sentence, "I may hope perhaps that this book will reach and help also some of those whom my music will not reach or affect." The drawn-out process of writing his thoughts about music firmed his creative convictions.

The depth of research and contemplation he gave to the book, the year-round pressures of his teaching, his despondency about conditions in Europe, his responsibilities for far-flung family members, his disillusionment about film music, and his creative despair wore upon Toch. He was listed as a "film composer" in Aaron Copland's 1941 book *Our New Music*. Toch wrote bitterly to Copland, asking him to correct this impression in the next edition.[36] Lilly wrote to Coolidge, "Ernst is becoming more of a hermit every day." A young man (Joseph Haft) approached Toch that same year with poems he had written following the death of his adored young wife, Martha. Only months later, the young man himself died. The poems gripped Toch in his own sadness, and he composed *Poems to Martha* for baritone and string quartet in 1942–43. Toch wrote Coolidge, "He was a simple man, only a merchant and nothing of a poet; but it was the very simplicity and sincerity of his words that moved me deeply. The poems were written partly during her life, partly after her death. . . . It comes from the heart—may it go to hearts."[37] This was Toch's only nonfilm composition and his only commission between 1938 and 1944.

By 1943 Toch was deeply depressed. To Coolidge he described his despair about his "creative pause" and, to feel close to her in spirit, sent—and dedicated—to her his Sixth String Quartet, which he had composed in 1905 when he was seventeen.[38] This quartet had been his first played in public, the work miraculously chosen for performance in Vienna by the Rosé Quartet. Sending it to Coolidge, he recalled the "immense amount of strife, of doing and undoing, possessing and losing, groping along since I wrote this . . . child of my childhood." In the Old World, he confessed, "I felt I reached people's heart and mind, there was a living process of sensible communication, justifying my work and endearing it to myself. I never questioned the 'raison d'être' of my doings. Here I feel terribly lonesome. If somebody would wake me in the middle of the night and shoot this question at me: for whom are you going on? I might say: for Elizabeth Coolidge. . . . You might easily say I speak as a bitter, disappointed, frustrated composer. Please don't say so. . . . My music is being more and more performed. That is beside the point. I do not mean the test by success, I mean the test by truth, sincerity, and devotion. Whatever my work may be worth . . . it is addressed to you as the essentially sympathetic soul at all times." Lilly wrote that Coolidge's friendship for Toch and his deep affection for her, "such as I have never known in him," had given him "anchorage, refuge, poise, strength."[39]

Toch and Schoenberg, his near neighbor in California, had first met as soldiers in the early years of World War I. Schoenberg respected Toch sufficiently to inform him in 1943 of his pending retirement from teaching at UCLA and to tell him he would recommend Toch as his successor—if he was asked. Toch, apparently worrying about the "if," and remembering that Klemperer had played an important role in Schoenberg's appointment, immediately wrote to Coolidge, asking her to help by writing important conductors to suggest that they put pressure on UCLA for Toch's appointment. This she did, but nothing developed for Toch at UCLA.[40]

In 1944 Coolidge, who lived part of the year in Cambridge, Massachusetts, was able to arrange that Toch lecture for the music department at Harvard, and she turned over her nearby apartment to the Tochs for their stay. These lectures gave additional impetus and shape (and the title) to the book Toch had begun writing two years earlier. He described to Coolidge his fascination with his work on *The Shaping Forces of Music,* the vast amount of material he had assembled for his survey, and his investigations into the relationship of modernism to previous theory and practice. As a composer schooled only by examples from the past, he felt himself to be the "product of a long line of [musical] ancestors, and that each creating artist, involuntarily, is placed as a link in this chain."[41] The question he now posed was whether there had been a break along the recent line of this chain, "either discrediting our contemporary work or everything which has been derived from the past."[42] In the face of American resistance to the dissonant modern style, in 1938 Toch had said about his European musical idiom, "Although I pass for a modernist and even atonalist, my music is in no way atonal, nor has it anything to do with the twelve-tone system. Rather, it is rooted in tonality, which is, however, treated in a hovering, gyrating manner, gravitating always towards definite tone centers." In 1941 he emphasized his belief in "the conciseness and concentration of musical expression, in well balanced form, in utter economy of artistic means, in the functional life of independent voices more than in the compilation of harmonies." He defined his fundamental architectural design as "a natural balance of tension and relaxation."[43]

It was Toch's intent in *The Shaping Forces in Music* to "bring out and emphasize the timeless and permanent features of music as against the time-bound and transient ones. In doing so [the book] attempts to reconcile the at-times-'classical' with the at-times-'modern.'"[44] To that end, in 1945 he developed his "Credo," in which he stated that he was ready for a "reaction against the reaction" that overthrew nineteenth-century hyper-emotionalism. "Art supposedly reflects the essential spiritual content of its period," he wrote. Life—and therefore art—should revolve around love, death, suffering, struggle, hope, despair, and the urge and search for God. These were the things that great art of all ages and cultures had encompassed. True art is mysterious, religious, naive, not "interesting," but immediate and stirring. The "Credo" continues:

> Technique of art may be learnable and teachable (though even it is learnable and teachable to a very limited degree). The other part of art, the one of religion and naivety, is unlearnable and unteachable. This is the part that makes art not modern or oldfashioned, but timeless. . . . It is the part that makes us *love* true art and stirs us to the depths of our soul. . . . [In much contemporary music] something seems to have been lost. . . . There is no lack of esteem for contemporary music, but the signs of love, of irresistible love, seem to be missing. There is a prevailing inclination to blame atonality for that phenomenon. This accusation must be rejected. The development into the musical idiom of today was natural, logical, and inevitable. It means no destruction of the old but an extension of it. . . . If music of our century has, so far, failed to compel general devotion, as in the past the reasons for it should not be sought in technicalities. They most probably lie in the spiritual sphere.[45]

The ideas in his "Credo" dominated Toch's composing after 1945, the year he quit the film industry.[46]

The end of the European war brought heartbreaking reports from the Tochs' friends and relatives. "How can one possibly stand what has been stood by millions and millions of suffering people?" Toch wrote Coolidge.[47] Devastated by the reports from Europe and overworked as well, in the summer of 1945 Toch took leave from USC to undergo psychiatric treatment in Illinois, after which he withdrew from his campus classes, opting to teach his USC composition students privately at his Santa Monica home. The completion of his book in 1946 enabled him to resume his composition, which made him feel "like a horse released to run." Schott reestablished his publishing contract, and that summer Toch composed a new string quartet (his twelfth, op. 70), the first in eighteen years. This accomplishment was a sublime delight to him. "I am slower now and more critical," he told Coolidge.[48]

During the period when Toch was on medical leave, Max Krone, dean of USC's School of Music, involved himself in preparations for the publication of Toch's book. Krone proceeded with revisions, made his own arrangements for publication, and stipulated that he would receive 50 percent of the royalties for his work. Lilly recalled that when she and Ernst learned this, "We sat on the terrace, on a very beautiful afternoon, and I remember very clearly that my husband's face turned to stone." Toch reported the problem to the university but was given no help because, Lilly explained, Krone "was a tremendous businessman for the university." He had bought land at Idyllwild privately and developed it into the Idyllwild School of Music and the Arts (ISOMATA), a summer school that promised financial success for USC. "So the man was taboo," stated Lilly. "He was a money bringer."[49] Krone was also all-powerful in academic appointments. In March 1947 Toch wrote to Krone, following several drafts contributed by his wife and Coolidge, politely appreciating Krone's efforts and suggestions for the book and stating that the publisher he (Toch) had contracted with wanted to use another editor. For this purpose, Toch had chosen Schoenberg's assistant Gerald Strang, then studying with Toch as a doctoral candidate at USC. Toch enclosed a check to compensate Krone for his interest and time. The next month Krone withdrew Toch's faculty appointment at USC.[50]

Private teaching at home was now Toch's only source of income, and he found himself easily exhausted by it. "I had so many students," he told Robert Trotter. "I was such a fanatic teacher. Half of my students were very poor and did not pay me anything, and I gave them lessons although I never had lessons myself, but through my knowledge I expanded and expanded, and I loved to teach music."[51] Lilly Toch recalled that sometimes "when Ernst came out of the room with students who were elated, I had a shock [at] how he looked." He would extend an hour's lesson to two or three hours; the two would emerge, Ernst "haggard and pale and really very visibly exhausted, having struggled with the soul of the student," and the student "beaming with the feeling he could do it, now he has it."[52] Toch's ability to empathize with the needs of his students and to quickly see and continue a student's way in a composition resulted in many impressive successes. Douglas Moore, already a teacher of composition himself and later a Pulitzer Prize winner, was composing film scores when he studied with

Toch in 1940. When the younger composer's opera *The Devil and Daniel Webster* was produced by Hugo Strelitzer at Los Angeles City College, Toch wrote to Moore, "There is not a dead spot in it." Moore responded that he would keep the letter among his most treasured possessions.[53] Emmy-winning film composer Alex North continued to study with Toch from New York, sending his compositions for comment. Mantle Hood, a young jazz/pop performer and UCLA student who was to become an influential American ethnomusicologist, began studying with Toch in 1945. They worked together for five years, and lessons sometimes lasted the whole day. Toch never imposed a system of composition, Hood pointed out. Studying with Toch was "very humbling . . . . He was always very honest, never offering great praise." In 1950 Toch's termination of Hood's studies included the advice, "The man you must study with is YOU." Hood felt that Toch's teaching was a major influence in his life.[54]

Mel Powell (later another Pulitzer Prize–winning composer, but at the time a pianist at MGM), studied with Toch from 1946 to 1948. Powell noted that, in the Hollywood studios, Toch was given "a special admiration that was his due, certainly from all his fellow composers, and indeed from the musicians who . . . would always look forward to the pleasure of playing his scores." Although Powell eventually subscribed to a more intellectualized aesthetic than Toch's and did not include his name in his list of teachers—which hurt and annoyed the older composer—he appreciated that Toch "was able to provide a great deal of what proved to be of value to me. . . . We would talk about structures, structures, structures, always large contexts. . . . We would take as models the best teachers anyone could find." Powell remembered Toch's "melancholia, a tautness, a highly tensed man virtually throughout those two years; clearly not a serene or contented soul." Yet he was also "a very warm and concerned teacher." Powell did not want to compose film scores and was ambitious to go east to study with Paul Hindemith. Toch, who had known Hindemith well since their student days at the Frankfurt Conservatory, helped Powell prepare, and warned him of certain characteristics, saying, "Well, you know, Hindemith is a genius." Powell thought Toch's attitude "elegant." Later he found that Hindemith—whom he described as "a murderer," "cold as ice," a teacher whose classes were "strewn with corpses"—expressed great esteem for Toch as a composer.[55]

In those years Toch was being particularly severe with his own composing. In February 1947 he accepted Coolidge's commission for a work for chamber orchestra, to be performed at Harvard and in Washington, where she had established a series of concerts at the Library of Congress. Toch's private teaching schedule, however, interfered with his composing. In August, after an excruciating struggle with himself, he wrote to Harold Spivacke, chief of the Music Division at the Library of Congress, that he must withdraw his work, as he felt it was inadequate. His decision caused him extreme pain, but he "could not act differently if my life depended on it." His attitude toward his composing had changed radically in the recent years of personal crisis: "While in former times a commission with a set date was always welcome and most stimulating and never found me failing, another attitude gradually became domineering, with an extremely despotic claim that whatever I write and pass to the outer world must first completely satisfy my own demands. . . . The more or less empty toying with sounds, the repetition of certain fashioned patterns or 'isms' assumed a quality unbearable for me to the point of repulsion. . . . I cannot fully approve of what I wrote in the present case. . . . My craftsmanship . . . could easily bridge the gap and few, if anybody, would know the difference. But I cannot abide by such a solution; least of all with a work supposed to remain connected with the name of the person for whom I have more veneration than for anybody else in this country." Coolidge was touched, thoroughly understood his attitude, and honored his rare idealism. He expressed his gratitude by proposing to compose for the Coolidge Foundation a vocal work based on Martin Luther's text, "God's Time Is the Best Time."[56]

The lack of a local opera company and the cold shoulder offered by the Los Angeles Philharmonic and the Hollywood Bowl were others factors stifling Toch's composing in Los Angeles. His chamber music, however, was played by various groups, such as the London Quartet (sponsored in free concerts by Coolidge), the Roth Quartet, the Brodetsky Ensemble, and the Los Angeles Chamber Orchestra under its conductor/founder Harold Byrns. Violinist Louis Kaufman and pianist Jakob Gimpel championed his work; Heifetz and Piatigorsky also performed it. In the postwar years, Peter Yates's "Evenings on the Roof" presented a steady stream of Toch's chamber music, including the composer's 1947 performance of his Piano Quintet, op. 64, with the American Art Quartet.[57] Violinist Eudice Shapiro, leader of the quartet, recorded Toch's violin sonatas and developed a friendship with the composer.[58]

When in 1954 "Evenings on the Roof" changed its name, management, and philosophy to become the "Monday Evening Concerts," directed by Lawrence Morton, the chamber series' policy toward Toch's music also reversed. Lilly reported, "In Monday Evening Concerts, if you wrote music which still threw anchor, so to speak, [to] tonality, unless you were Stravinsky you were banned." While granting that Toch had been a central figure in Los Angeles music, Morton admitted in a later interview that "[Toch] represented a period in music that Monday Evening Concerts was not particularly eager to promote any more."[59] In 1959 émigré composer/conductor Ingolf Dahl, who had wielded influence in the concerts' management since the early Roof years, contradicted this trend by conducting members of the Los Angeles Philharmonic in the world premiere of Toch's *Five Pieces for Winds and Percussion*. Dahl undoubtedly also brought his influence to bear on the concerts' decision to honor Toch's 75th birthday in a 1962 program that acknowledged the composer's debt to Mozart.[60] Hollywood joined in the tribute; the Screen Composers Association contributed funds for the performers and distributed tickets to its members. Toch wrote to Morton expressing his surprise, delight, and gratitude, but the assumption that his music was passé galled him. Musical "fashions," "technique in the vacuum," and the postwar emphasis on systems made him deeply angry. "Our time," he declared in 1964, "has produced music that is based on systems, that makes do with systems, and which therefore could very well have been devised by a congenitally deaf person."[61]

In 1948 the Tochs' only child, Franzi, married while still an undergraduate at UCLA. Toch wrote a tenderly sorrowful string quartet movement titled "Dedication" for the wedding.[62] Weariness, overexertion, and frustration were pressing upon him, and a few months later he suffered a near-fatal heart attack. His doctor ordered total bed rest. He stopped his private teaching and withdrew entirely into his composing. Once recovered sufficiently, he returned to Europe in hope of rediscovering the world he had lost. He longed for winter, snow, and the peace of an Austrian village. He was also entering a new creative period, characterized by an obsession to compose symphonies for full orchestra and to convey through them his "messages" to the world, strengthened by the convictions he had expressed in his "Credo."[63]

At the end of November 1949, the Tochs set off for the first of many anguished searches for a composing refuge in Europe. The composer wrote back his first impression to Trotter: "Crossing the Swiss border into the countries which have gone through the war seems crossing a deeper ocean than the one between Europe and America. The burden of [Europe's] past weighs horribly on everything and most horribly on the perspective of the future. It is hard to imagine a young generation shouldering it and one feels deeply sad for its sake."[64] The Tochs chose to settle in the American sector of Vienna, where, at age sixty-three, Ernst wrote his First Symphony. He would compose seven symphonies and an opera before his death in 1964 at seventy-six, and all of them would embody large themes he felt psychologically pressed to articulate. The "despotic claim" he had mentioned to Spivacke sometimes induced Toch to work on several compositions at once, always dominating and determining his relationships to others and the world around him—which he increasingly blocked out.

The first three symphonies (1950, 1951–52, 1955) make use of literary mottoes, which provide only a slight idea of what was on Toch's mind to express. He was convinced that formal analyses and stylistic discussions "lead nowhere and help nobody."[65] The motto for the First Symphony (dedicated to the schoolmate who had initiated Toch's career by taking his string quartet to Arnold Rosé) is "And though this world with devil filled / Should threaten to undo us, / We will not fear, for God has willed / His truth to triumph through us," a quote from Luther's hymn "A Mighty Fortress Is Our God." Toch wrote that the form of the symphony is not traditionally classical but derives from the course of a drama.[66] The drama may have been his inner struggle with depression, as expressed to Coolidge in 1947, for which Luther's texts seemed the solution. William Steinberg premiered the First Symphony with the Pittsburgh Symphony in January 1953. (In Nazi Germany, Steinberg had not only conducted Toch's opera *Der Fächer* [The Fan] in 1933, in spite of Nazi intervention, but also his Second Piano Concerto for the Jüdische Kulturbund.)

The Second Symphony was composed in Zurich in 1952. It is dedicated to Albert Schweitzer: "To the lonely seer in a time of darkness, / To the only victor in a world of victims."[67] Toch identified with Schweitzer's struggle against awesome odds to fulfill his medical and spiritual mission in Africa, where the doctor was at first thought to be an evil demon so feared by the natives that they wanted to kill him.[68] Toch, in his own struggle to complete his artistic mission, wrote that the symphony's motto, from the story of Jacob wrestling with the angel (in Genesis 32:26), "became the ever-so-imperious summons coming from the work itself back to its author, from its first nebulous conception on to the last stroke of the pen: 'I will not let Thee go unless Thou bless—complete—me.'"[69]

In 1952 the Tochs returned from Europe to an altering situation in California. Feeling persecuted in the climate of Cold War investigations, the Brechts and the Manns, with whom they had enjoyed stimulating evenings, had moved back to Europe. The Tochs' social circle was further diminished by the deaths of Schoenberg, Lion Feuchtwanger, Erich Korngold, and Franz Werfel. Alma Mahler Werfel, who was fond of Ernst, had left for New York. The Tochs now received little income other than his commissions. The Third and Fourth Symphonies were commissioned in 1954 and 1957; the Louisville Symphony and the Koussevitzky Foundation commissioned other orchestral works in 1953 and 1956; two German commissions came in 1957 and 1959.

Toch believed that these composing commitments demanded retreat from Los Angeles. He and Lilly left California in 1952–53 for Des Plaines, Illinois, where Ernst lived and composed in an empty farmhouse seventeen miles from the sanatorium where he had earlier received psychiatric treatment and where Lilly, who had studied psychology at the Jung Institute in Zurich, worked. "A somewhat queer setup," Toch wrote to Coolidge, but he was "obsessed with writing symphonies" and needed "concentration, solitude, and most of all, peace from students."[70] During this peripatetic period, he received invitations from and composed at the Huntington Hartford colony in Pacific Palisades in 1954, 1957, and 1959; Yaddo in Saratoga Springs, New York, in 1955; and the MacDowell Colony in New Hampshire five times between 1953 and 1957.

In Los Angeles, meanwhile, little attention was paid to Toch's new symphonies. After a performance of his Second Symphony by Wallenstein in 1952 (the year it was premiered by Charles Munch and the Boston Symphony), the Los Angeles Philharmonic scheduled no further Toch performances during its regular concert seasons. Two local commissions did come to Toch in 1953–54. One was from the University of Judaism, requesting a chamber work for soprano, tenor, and five instruments on a biblical text, *Vanity of Vanities, All Is Vanity*. The other was from the Coleman Chamber Music Association in Pasadena for its fiftieth anniversary. For this organization Toch composed his Thirteenth, and last, String Quartet, completed in 1953. In this work he used twelve-tone technique toward his own ends, thinking of it as "a musical parlor game." Eudice Shapiro remembered him declaring, "Anyone can write a twelve-tone piece, and if [he or she] is a good composer it will come out something like the composer." His "sounded exactly like Toch," Shapiro reported. In his introduction to the printed score, Toch wrote, "My ultimate belief is that twelve tone writing can be an enrichment—by liberal incorporation . . . of the past—as well as it can be an impoverishment—by dogmatic rejection of everything outside of it. . . . I wish to state that I do not belong to the 'school' of twelve tone composers and that I do not intend to join it. My stand is individual and personal and the reservations are made merely to indicate and demarcate my position. It gave me considerable pleasure to write this quartet, perhaps because of the challenge, perhaps because of the gratification to feel strong, even within restrictions."[71]

Toch's insistence on his individual stance in the face of the musical fashions of the day erupted into controversy in January 1954. It began with an interview for *Los Angeles Times* music critic Albert Goldberg, in which Toch expressed his withdrawal from developments in contemporary music. In line with the "Credo" he had established for himself in 1945, he now believed that the state of music had sunk very low: "I am amazed at the confusion today and the shifting of importance to things I cannot think of as important. . . . I try to convey something, to let music talk. Most contemporary music coughs and belches but it does not talk. I am convinced that 95% of the composers of today would not have dreamed of writing a note if they had lived a century ago. . . . If [composers] are to be content with mathematics, why should not everyone compose? . . . I stopped teaching from despair. . . . You cannot learn to be creative." Goldberg's article appeared under the gruff and misleading headline, "Toch Gives Up Teaching Musical Composition, Declares It Futile."[72] *The Musical Courier* picked up the controversy, printing the interview and responses to it from composition teachers across the country in three articles in March, April and May. Several prominent composer-teachers defended their teaching against Toch's statements.[73] One of them, Lukas Foss, by then teaching composition in Schoenberg's former position at UCLA, remarked sardonically, "Mr. Toch, may we congratulate you upon accepting [a coveted invitation] to teach composition at Tanglewood this coming summer?" In June *The Musical Courier* gave Toch a chance to respond. He stated that he did not consider it defeatism to take stock of the situation of one's time. In response to the brouhaha about teaching composition, Toch quoted Schoenberg: "You can learn only what you already know," and added, "You cannot make a composer out of somebody who would not be a composer without you." After an agonizing interlude at Tanglewood, the summer home of the Boston Symphony, Toch accepted few similar teaching engagements.[74]

At the Huntington Hartford Foundation retreat in Pacific Palisades, and then at the MacDowell Colony, Toch composed his Third Symphony (1954–55), which he spoke of as his musical autobiography.[75] The commission, from a Chicago committee celebrating the 300th anniversary of Jews' entry to America, coincided with his desire to base a symphony on the notion of the Wandering Jew and on his own wanderings in exile. He took as its motto a bitter sentence from Goethe's early novel, *The Sorrows of Young Werther,* which had moved him as he read it in the trenches of World War I: "Certainly I am but a wanderer, a pilgrim on the earth—are you anything more?"[76] Within the strong structure of the symphony there are frequent reminders of the part expressionism had played in uncovering psychological truth in the years before and after the First World War. The symphony's arpeggiated, wandering opening theme and countertheme, chromatic and tonally indefinite, are characteristic of his late period stance regarding tonality and atonality. The work is organized around cyclical elements of importance to its dramatic conception. Talking about the symphony in 1957, he mentioned that "crusts of decades had crumbled and laid bare old strata of memories," which helped him form the work. By 1962, however, Toch's reticence was greater, and he would not discuss its emotional component. He remarked, with some irony, "I fear I am revealing myself as being a Romantic, and I do not need to remind you how very detrimental this [is] to any reputation today."[77]

An important element of Toch's symphonies is a throwback to his boyhood interest in unusual sounds. These are used as components integral to the meaning of the works. In the Second (Schweitzer-dedicated) Symphony, glissandos in the timpani appear like ominous distant jungle roars in the first movement; the harp combined with piano four hands provides a liquid depth of light and shadow in the second movement, against which a quasi-pentatonic theme contributes a sense of the exotic. In the final movement, the ultimate struggle with the angel is represented in great percussive blocks of dissonant chords in harp and four-hand piano, gradually dominated and silenced by the increasing strength of the kettledrum.

In the Third Symphony, Toch went further, incorporating instruments such as the glass harmonica (invented by Benjamin Franklin and used by Mozart in solo works), glass balls, and the "hisser," a sound created by the release of a tank of compressed gas. (In the published score the vibraphone replaces the glass instruments, and the hisser is reproduced by a crescendo on a cymbal hit with hard sticks.) The hisser, which functions as an aural symbol of a concentration camp's extermination chamber, appears devastatingly at climactic moments in the first and last movements to alter and then snuff out life and character. It is followed in the first movement by a kind of limbo created by the glass instruments or vibraphone and the Hammond or pipe organ. This strange atmosphere is disconcertingly broken by the snare drum, temple blocks, and Turkish cymbals, introducing an increasingly distorted military march. The march briefly gives way to a flowing, romantic, contrapuntal treatment in the strings of the arpeggiated wandering theme, much altered and lyrical, which in turn is jolted back into the march as the structure of the movement returns in a curve to its beginning elements, everything altered.

William Steinberg premiered the Third Symphony with the Pittsburgh Symphony Orchestra in December 1955, taking it to New York in November 1956. At a press conference before the New York performance, Toch was asked about his unusual instruments and refused to answer, saying, "If you have nothing else to ask me but about the instrument [the hisser] then I have nothing to tell you." According to Lilly, the critics tore the symphony to pieces.[78] Nevertheless, that year it was awarded both the Pulitzer Prize and the Huntington Hartford Prize, and Toch was elected to membership in the National Institute of Arts and Letters. Here was belated recognition that he was no longer "the forgotten composer of the century."

Lawrence Weschler, the composer's grandson, believed that Toch's flights from Los Angeles, from teaching, from obligations to friends, family, and grandchildren, were almost desperate after the Third Symphony; there was a sense of his having wasted time, of having still too much to compose.[79] Certainly the increased pace of his composing as he approached and moved through his seventies was astounding. Ten more orchestral works (four of them symphonies), an opera, nine chamber works, six piano works, and five vocal works were to be written before his death. In order to achieve this productivity, Toch isolated himself further from responsibilities and poured himself into his compositions.

After Coolidge's death at eighty-nine in November 1953, Toch relied on her close friend Marian MacDowell, to whom Coolidge had introduced him in 1952, and who had invited him to the MacDowell Colony in the summer of 1953. Although MacDowell was ninety-six at the time, Toch felt an instant bond with her. "I will never forget her laughter," he told Robert

Trotter. "There was no senility in her. We could talk about anything and she would be the winner. I hardly know any person whom I adored so much as I adored her."[80] Although she had been forced to use crutches much of her life, she showed him around the MacDowell house at Peterborough, claiming that exercise was good for her. When he told her that he had lived and studied in Frankfurt, she roguishly answered him in genuine Frankfurt dialect; Frankfurt was where she had studied piano with Edward MacDowell, who had died insane at age forty-seven. Her courage and spirit in caring for her composer husband, then founding and funding the MacDowell festivals and artists' colony through her own concert tours, moved Toch, who wrote her in 1955, "Albert Schweitzer is, in my veneration, your only rival."[81] She died in 1956 at ninety-eight. Toch's Fourth Symphony, begun while he was completing the Third and finished in 1957, is his homage to her. The work is his most lyrical in character; even the timpani sing melodies in the third movement. He inserted his own emotional tribute to her, a text to be spoken by an unseen speaker between the movements.[82]

Toch's ambition to write operas resurfaced in 1959, when he wrote to the publisher Mills Music that his composing was tending "more and more to the stage," and that he was "frantically" looking for a libretto or librettist.[83] The search ended when he found a text by the well-known émigré Hungarian playwright Melchior Lengyel, who had been the screenwriter for *Catherine the Great* (1934), the first film Toch had scored, and was living in Hollywood.[84] Lengyel's story was Scheherazade's last tale to her captor, the sultan: the truthful account that her lover is at that moment storming the city in revolution. Her colorful tale results in her deliverance from the sultan, who, fascinated and driven mad by her story, is captured and taken away. However, Scheherazade is spent, and she dies in the arms of her conquering lover. Toch wrote to his publisher that the scenario "not only satisfies me in every respect but makes me extremely happy. It is a drama of great inner tension." Weschler comments that the text served Toch as "an autobiographical allegory on themes of tyranny and defiance, blockage and release."[85] Unfortunately, in 1960 Lengyel was leaving Hollywood to resettle in Italy. Lengyel's son provided an English translation of *The Last Tale,* and Toch's Austrian friend Herbert Zipper retranslated it into German as *Das letzte Märchen.*

While working on this opera, Toch described it as "the best piece I ever wrote."[86] Opera director Hugo Strelitzer remembered the composer describing the violence with which his music came to him in dreams in this period.[87] Toch traveled to New York to work in Columbia University's electronic music studio, hoping to find new sounds to convey Scheherazade's dreams of the thousand tales she had already told the sultan. He became discouraged, however, by the difficulty of achieving what he heard in his mind and returned to conventional composing. In spite of the symptoms of incipient colon cancer, which he ignored, Toch completed *The Last Tale* as a one-act opera in 1962, his seventy-fifth year.[88]

In April 1962, shortly before the opera was completed, the Tochs' son-in-law was killed in an automobile accident. Toch was faced with the choice of whether to care for his widowed daughter and her four young children or to reserve himself, in his own last days, for his work. His compulsion to compose drove him to write in a diary entry of "deepest depression, sick of life, with bad premonitions that I may end through suicide [or] delivered to an asylum as Schumann, Hugo Wolf, Nietzsche."[89] He decided to express his grief for his daughter in yet another opera, based on Lion Feuchtwanger's final historical novel, *Jephta and His Daughter*. The novel's story was taken from the biblical book of Judges. Jephta, a "ferocious, bloody, grandiose, and ill-fated bandit leader," battling for Israel's conquest of the land of Jordan, vows to his warrior God, Yahweh, to deliver as a burnt offering whoever first comes running toward him from his home if he is victorious.[90] The outcome of the battle is as he wishes, but when he returns home his lovely daughter runs out to greet him, and he realizes he must sacrifice her. He tells her of his vow. She accepts her fate, for she has always seen Yahweh in her father. Together they plan her death. Ultimately Jephta is forced to recognize that his sacrifice was futile; he had made his terrible vow in order to buy the support of a god who did not exist. Although he has saved Israel in its hour of greatest need and helped achieve its unification, he has paid such a price that he does not rejoice in his victory. He yearns for death. In an epilogue, Feuchtwanger ruminates on man creating God in his own image.

Weschler describes Toch at this time as "driven—and to some extent wracked as well . . . So driven that he couldn't wait for his librettist to translate the novel into a workable text."[91] Again Toch composed from his inner state; using themes that had gripped him in the novel, he produced the tragic Fifth Symphony in one movement, essentially an opera without words. Toch called it a "Rhapsodic Poem." Eloquent, expressive reverie is conveyed in chamber music textures or solos. These moments are violently broken in upon by short but harshly contrasting tutti segments; the high violins repeat mad glissandos, tension is built and climaxed by large dissonant chords and percussive emphases. The initial *dolcissimo* theme—in a flexible, swaying rhythm presumably representing the daughter—is followed by an expressive cry from the cellos. These themes return in various ways throughout the work, until at the end the daughter's theme is gradually snuffed out.[92]

In this final period the well of Toch's musical imagination seemed inexhaustible. His work intensified in the last months of his life as he completed three "pantomimes" for orchestra (*Capriccio, Puppetshow,* and *The Enamoured Harlequin*); the Sixth and Seventh Symphonies; a Sinfonietta for String Orchestra; a Sinfonietta for Wind Orchestra and Percussion; and a Quartet for Oboe, Clarinet, Bassoon and Viola. This acceleration left little room for anything else and none for attending to his health. Matthew Doran, Toch's student and a fellow composer at the Huntington Hartford Foundation in 1963, observed that by then Toch seemed to realize his end was drawing near. "He was in hard seclusion. . . . nothing else was important to him. He would swim in the pool about 10 minutes in the morning at six o'clock, and then go to a cabin and compose all day long."[93] Toch wrote to Nicolas Slonimsky, "I am so flooded with music at present that everything vanishes in my days." He reported that he had "made up for too much tragedy" by writing *Capriccio* and *Puppetshow*.[94] Three Impromptus, op. 90, individual solos for Jascha Heifetz, Gregor Piatigorsky, and William Primrose, who were teaching together at USC, preceded the orchestral works.

Toch may have had the artistry of these great performers in mind in the Sixth Symphony. A fascinating variety of sound and texture from the full orchestra is used, but tutti sections are rare. The prevailing chamber music lightness, especially in the textures of the first and second movements, is offset by the unifying cyclical treatment of expressive themes, which offer a passionate climax in the more robust final movement. The result often seems fragmented and certainly more demanding of virtuosity than do the earlier symphonies. Having composed the work with ease between September and November 1963, Toch wrote to his publisher in great excitement, "Hardly ever within the last 50 years have I experienced the realization of a score like the one I just finished . . . in such an unbroken flow, in such a short time. . . . I can hardly wait to have [conductor William] Steinberg see that score."[95] Steinberg's lack of response was a blow to him, but Toch's Seventh Symphony was already under way, begun in early December 1963 and completed at the end of March 1964.

Whether or not Toch knew that the Seventh Symphony, op. 95, would be his culminating symphony, that is its effect. There is a Mozartean grace and wit in the play of themes and in the structural clarity of the three movements. The first movement continues the ruminative, interrupted manner of the Sixth Symphony yet uses the full orchestra in its discourse. Brass and percussion break in with critical comment against the lyricism of the themes. The second movement offers a tight-knit but effortless elfin scherzo contrasting a blithe Viennese waltz with its own variation. The final Allegro risoluto provides the serious counterweight to the earlier movements. An opening dramatic recitative, fateful wedges driving up through the orchestral texture, a trumpet theme reminiscent of the theme of Jephta's daughter, and repeated hammering on the anvil (an instrument Toch had used less conspicuously in the Third and the Fifth Symphonies) are elements that punctuate the otherwise classically organized form.

The symphony was completed in Zurich on the Tochs' last European trip, during which Ernst and Lilly revisited Mannheim, where he had taught in the 1920s. There they learned that there were no more Jews living in the city. In June 1964 Ernst was glad to return to his Santa Monica home on the Franklin hill, where he completed his last three works in greater peace than he had known since his joyful period in the "Villa Majestic." He died of cancer in October.

Toch's compositional legacy is gradually reappearing, particularly in Europe, through recordings. In America most of his work still remains untapped. He was averse to promoting himself, and what happened musically in California mattered little to the all-powerful New York musical establishment of the time. At one point Toch wrote in frustration to Serge Koussevitzky, "You know how much Los Angeles is out of the world and how little even a great success . . . here matters."[96] The legacy of his thought remains to be explored as well. "What is good music?" he asked frequently in the last decade of his life, as he pondered developments in systematizing all the parameters of "serious" music. He read widely and thought deeply about the relation of art to human existence, and much of his oeuvre was autobiographical. In a 1954 lecture, following the nationwide controversy over his remarks on the teaching of composition, he quoted the words of the poet Rainer Maria Rilke in *The Notebooks of Malte Laurids Brigge:* "One ought to wait and gather sense and sweetness a whole life long, and a long life if possible, and then, quite at the end, one might perhaps be able to write ten lines that were good."

In another 1954 address, "Just What Is Good Music?" presented at the

University of Minnesota, Toch insisted that "Good art is religious. . . . Good music is the kind of music that will never substitute sensationalism for progress. It is the kind of music that will never cater to dated modernity but only to timeless humanity." He passionately wanted music to speak to its audience: "Good art is the kind of art which never focusses [on] the vessel [i.e., style] but [on] its contents. It is the contents, not the vessel that the real artist is struggling for, suffering for, bleeding for," he wrote. He emphasized that *"It is better to adjust to the ages than to the age."*[97] Strelitzer, who revered his close colleague, commented that Toch was "so sincere, so honest in his artistic belief," that "he could not swim with the stream."[98] Toch's thought and the extraordinary creative flood of his last years were his profound and always individual response to the artistic heritage, as well as to the events, that had shaped him.

European Composers in the "Picture Business"

Hollywood is as hard as a diamond, beside which New York seems soft and a veritable rosebud.

—George Antheil, 1937

From their European points of view, both Arnold Schoenberg and Ernst Toch originally voiced optimism for film's potential as a new synthesis of the arts for the masses. Their hopes were dashed by 1940. By that time many more refugee European composers had flocked to Hollywood, hoping to find work in the booming film industry, one of the few American industries unchecked by the Depression. Their expectations were high. Sound film was young, and ripe, they thought, for the expertise of experienced, skilled composers. Like Toch, Kurt Weill and Mario Castelnuovo-Tedesco wrote articles before they traveled to California that declared their hopes for the new art form they predicted would emerge from film combined with fine music. Weill wrote in 1937: "In America the new musical art work may after all develop from the medium of the movies. For nowhere more than here has film attained that technical perfection and popularity which can smooth the way for a new art form."[1] Castelnuovo-Tedesco's article, "Music and Movies," written in French before he arrived in Hollywood and published only recently, observed that opera was a European "art phenomenon" which could probably not be transplanted to America. "Is it worth the effort of a young and new people to subject themselves to a form of art whose conventions, faults, limitations, and compromises are already known? Would it not be better to pursue something different, something new?" he asked, concluding that "musical cinema could become the true national art form for America, exactly as the opera [has] for Italy."[2]

Hanns Eisler, after a lecture tour to the West Coast in 1935, published a critical report that was closer to the reality Europeans actually found when they arrived:

> We have nothing in Europe to compare with the perfect organization and technical equipment. . . . The music is written by a number of people . . . sitting in offices. They are not excessively well paid and are in fact office workers, for they have to keep to appointed office hours every day, even if they have nothing to do. The composers are selected according to their special genres. One is chosen as a specialist in military music. . . . Another is for Vienna waltzes and operetta music of the old school. Yet another is a specialist for jazz and dance music, still another for lyrics, and the last writes the preludes and the accompaniments—he comes from serious music. . . . The music to a film is composed [by] five or six composers. . . . What hell for the composers, who year after year have to write the same type of music and thus are faced with the prospect of becoming hopelessly dim-witted. In addition, the standard of most of these films is abominably low, not only in subject matter, but also in music. Although films could be an excellent means of entertainment and education in modern society, in the hands of private industry [films] are solely for profit and a means of lulling the masses.[3]

Like Eisler, the composers who had worked in film in Europe, Britain, or Russia were accustomed to a culture where the composer—Dmitri Shostakovich, Sergey Prokofiev, Arthur Honegger, or William Walton—was regarded as an artist in his own right; his status as a concert or opera composer was valued, and his contribution to a film all the more treasured. He may even have been consulted on matters of artistic importance in the conception stage before filming began, and presumably his opinions carried weight. Yet what the European refugees found in Hollywood, which they derisively came to call the "picture business," was more like the dictatorships they had fled. After his first visit to Hollywood in 1935, Igor Stravinsky described the studios, "each of which is a kind of principality, with its own borders, trenches, police, cannons, machine guns, as well as its ministers for the various technical and artistic operations." He was granted an appointment with the vice president of MGM, Louis B. Mayer. "I was led through a grey corridor to a grey room crowded with others, waiting like myself. I remained there a long time, during which everyone talked about Mr. Mayer, though no one had seen him and he might have been a myth. But at long last a door opened and a little man with a large beak appeared, followed by two lieutenants. He approached me, nodded, said, 'I am a man like others, with a lot to do,' and, with this, shook my hand and left. At least I can testify that Mr. Mayer is not a myth."[4]

Max Reinhardt's son Gottfried, arriving in 1933 hoping to work at Paramount Pictures, expected paradise as his train wound through acres of orange and lemon trees between San Bernardino and Los Angeles. What he found instead in Hollywood was a profound clash between "no culture" and the culture of the arriving émigré Europeans; he concluded that "America was no paradise."[5] In the class system established by the founding Jewish studio moguls, arriving Jewish composers ironically found themselves below the salt, their art still obscured in the shadows of the silent films. Hans J. Salter, a Viennese composer who had studied with Alban Berg and Franz Schreker, came to Hollywood from Berlin's Universum Film AG (Ufa) studio in 1937. He recalled that at Universal Pictures' studio "Music was at the very bottom of the heap. . . . 'Keep that God-damned music down,' was a popular battle cry."[6] The moguls and the composers needed each other, however: movies had become the cheap diversion for the millions suffering in the Depression, and as the industry grew, from 500 to 600 scores had to be composed each year. These scores would be recorded under ideal conditions, using the finest technical equipment available. By 1942 around 7,000 musicians were engaged in Hollywood, as each studio developed its own full-time orchestra from a large pool of the most skilled orchestral players in the country.[7]

Film offered composers the best promise of financial survival, but the realities of the creative environment proved too daunting for many. In Europe, Paul Hindemith had acquired film experience composing for a 1918 black-and-white American silent cartoon, *Krazy Kat and Ignatz Mouse at the Circus;* in 1927 he revised the score for the cartoon's rerelease as *Felix the Cat at the Circus.* In 1939, anxious about his and his Jewish wife's future in Germany, he explored employment possibilities with Walt Disney. The accounts of his visit, written in his letters to his wife, are devastating. He found Disney on the set for *Fantasia,* at age forty-five, "evidently rather uneducated and clueless. . . . Disney spouted a crazy salad of his opinions on his musical impressions, obsequiously and without contradiction toadied to by twelve animators and seconded by world-wonder Stokowski, who has all this calamity on his conscience." When Hindemith visited the Tochs, he learned—"laughing through tears"—that what appeared to him more or less comic was more than shameful: "The whole is a nightmare, a gold-digger delusion. . . . Whomever you see and talk with is looking to find one of the gold nuggets lying around." The insurmountable fact that commercial interests superseded the artistic in Hollywood was difficult for most of the Europeans to stomach.[8]

Alexandre Tansman, for example, chose Hollywood for exile rather than emigration. The Polish-born Jewish composer, who lived most of his life in France, was on a tour to the United States as a pianist and conductor in the late 1920s when he met and dedicated his Second Piano Concerto to Charlie Chaplin. The actor then helped the Tansmans escape from France after the German occupation. Tansman spent the years 1941–46 as an exile in Hollywood, where he sustained his composing of concert works through his earnings from film duties. There he became an intimate of Stravinsky, whose biography he wrote. While enduring the indignities of the film studios, Tansman, who was forty-two when he arrived, was grateful for the "European ghetto" in Hollywood; he and his pianist wife found life there to be extremely artificial otherwise. "The film studio atmosphere was not terribly artistic," he wrote. "It was not much fun for us. Generally, producers were rather uncultured people. The entire city of Los Angeles was awaiting the latest film from MGM. Fortunately for us, however, there were those small gatherings of Europeans who provided an artistic and cultured environment. There, we were able to be ourselves. . . . In those days Hollywood was a kind of contemporary Weimar. All the European elite were in Hollywood or somewhere on the California Coast. As a result, I was surrounded by a most inspiring cadre of colleagues."[9] The film composer David Raksin remembered that "[Tansman] was very good. He was on the staff of MGM. He did a lot of scores, some very big pictures."[10] But Tansman did not get credit for most of these films. In 1945 he finally won an Academy Award nomination for his score for *Paris Underground*. The next year he returned to Paris for good.

Unlike composing for European films, being "a Hollywood composer" meant being rejected or ignored by musical circles in the rest of the nation. The demands of film composing and the isolation of Hollywood created a wall difficult for any composer to breach. The successful film composer in America—until Aaron Copland broke the mold in 1939—was not a concert composer and was not known outside Hollywood.[11] Eugene Zador and Mario Castelnuovo-Tedesco worked anonymously in film and therefore found it easier to maintain their identities as concert or opera composers. Those who ventured into concert or opera composing generally found it difficult to keep their lucrative studio contracts. As Toch commented, composing for the studios was a "closed shop." It was also, as Toch's story has shown, an experience of exploitation. Music department directors with backgrounds in managing chains of movie palaces, or in vaudeville or song writing, had little use for European conservatory-trained expertise or university doctorates in music. With the notable exception of Erich Wolfgang Korngold, those European composers who were prodigies found little acknowledgment of their special gifts. It helped if composers had contacts with producers or music department directors with European experience. The failures of Schoenberg, Stravinsky, Hindemith, Weill, and Ernst Krenek to secure continuing film-scoring opportunities indicate that the conditions of studio work demanded a great degree of adaptability. One must ask, given the humiliations and frustrations they experienced: how did those composers who stayed to earn their livings manage to save their artistic identities and achieve their own goals? How, as Korngold put it, did each "compose for himself"? Like Toch, some eventually managed to turn their backs on the industry to compose for themselves or for commissions. While they were working in film, some tried to bring producers and the Academy of Motion Picture Arts and Sciences to a greater awareness of the contribution of music to film, as well as the necessity for recognition of the very process of composing. Beyond their daily struggles within the system, these composers must have realized that their music was reaching the widest potential audience. In the 1930s and 1940s, film scores were forming the musical tastes of the American public. As Hollywood became the film capital of the world, film composers' music was heard everywhere.

A chronological review of the film experiences of some of the refugee composers shows that over time—as happened in Toch's case—tensions grew among the established studio composers against the influx of talented European émigrés; by the 1940s most Europeans' careers were safest if they did not demand credit for their work. The age of each composer at his time of arrival is noted; it was easier for the younger, more adaptable composers to comply with the studios' dictates.

Frederick Hollander was thirty-seven when Erich Pommer invited him to work for Fox Film Corporation in Hollywood in 1933. Pommer's musical (*The Only Girl*) flopped, and Fox's music department gave Hollander a return ticket to Germany in December of the same year. He cashed in the ticket. Following the advice of German film director William Dieterle, he went to Mexico to obtain an emigration visa on the British quota (by virtue of his London birth), then applied for American citizenship, which he gained in 1939. Hollander returned to Hollywood but found no easy entry to the studios; his experience and talents in several fields made him difficult to categorize.

Hollander then tried to re-create the world of cabaret in which he had been so prolific as a writer, composer, director, and actor in Europe. He re-modeled a garage on Santa Monica Boulevard into a theater and put up a large sign: "Frederick Hollander's Tingel-Tangel Theatre." He taught young actors English versions of his most successful songs and satires and invited Hollywood celebrities to his opening in May 1934. They all came and signed his guest book with praise and good wishes. Charlie Chaplin wrote that he had never laughed so much before. Only five feet four inches himself, Chaplin called Hollander "the great little man."[12] The cabaret skits' ironies, however, escaped the Americans, who still knew little about the Nazi menace that preoccupied Hollander, and his venture ended abruptly in November, when the cabaret's business manager absconded with the box office take. Hollander managed to land a three-year contract to direct Westerns for RKO Pictures. Westerns were "not my style," commented Hollander after completing one.[13] No further offers came. In the eighteen months since his arrival, Hollander had thoroughly confused the typecasting habits of Hollywood: was he to be considered a director? composer? lyricist? writer? actor? entertainer?

Hollander went into a deep depression and moved to the Santa Monica mountains to live in poverty for eleven months. His wife was reduced to shoplifting food.[14] Yet the Dieterles' door remained open to them, Vicki Baum invited him to use her Bechstein piano, and close émigré friends newly arrived in Hollywood, including Franz Waxman and Vienna's Billy Wilder, helped where they could, while Hollander settled into writing a novel titled *Those Torn from Earth*. In it he described the uprootings of 1933 via the intertwined stories of a German conductor, a German expres-sionist painter, and a high-living character modeled on the once-famous Austrian silent-film director, Joe May (born Joseph Otto Mandel), whose total failure in Hollywood is the book's central focus. Much material is taken from Hollander's own escape from Berlin, his experiences in Paris with Peter Lorre, Wilder, Waxman, and other refugees, and their subse-quent encounters with Hollywood. The conductor's Klemperer-like mad-ness becomes a major episode in the book, which is written in an expressionistic style.[15] Thomas Mann, the acknowledged leader of the anti-Nazi community of exiles in the United States, wrote a kindly foreword for the book's eventual publication in 1941.

After Hollander paid an agent to find him film-scoring work, he was given an option on a three-year contract by Paramount, where he was at first tossed "crumbs" as assignments. Hollander—who as a young talent in Berlin had collaborated not only with Reinhardt and Marlene Dietrich but with prominent expressionist poets, playwrights, and top cabaret artists—was famed for his gift for compositional improvisation at the piano. Yet this was sneered at by Nathaniel Finston, head of Paramount's music department, who called his music "piss in ice-water."[16] In desperation about his future, Hollander took Dietrich's advice to visit a soothsayer on the Santa Monica pier. The soothsayer—who possessed only one tooth in her upper jaw—said of his fortune, "It's not good. But it's not bad. Not bad at all." In a world so distant from the one in which his family name had carried considerable musical weight, Hollander realized that, in spite of all, he was still working at the piano. "It's not good—but not too bad" was his subsequent answer to himself during the remaining two decades of his Hollywood career.[17]

Finston was fired by Ernst Lubitsch, Paramount's chief of production at the time, and replaced in October 1935 by a chubby, sociable Russian cellist named Boris Morros. Morros was appreciative of émigrés' musical background and highly ambitious to improve music at the studio. Unknown to all, in 1934 he had become an undercover intelligence agent for the Soviet Union, gathering information and supporting other secret operatives in exchange for his Russian family's welfare. He gradually became "the longest-serving and possibly most flamboyant American ever involved with Soviet intelligence."[18]

From the time of Morros's arrival, Hollander described his period at Paramount, where he worked on thirty-nine films, as a "honeymoon."[19] His songs—written for newcomer Dorothy Lamour, Jack Benny, Betty Grable, and Gladys Swarthout—were sung by Bing Crosby on the immensely popular radio program *Your Hit Parade*.[20] Marlene Dietrich starred in two of Hollander's three Lubitsch-directed comedies. These successes enabled Hollander to buy a house with a swimming pool in the Hollywood Hills and to bring his family from Europe. He enjoyed Central Avenue jazz clubs and gospel churches as well as the rich gathering of émigré colleagues, which grew to include writers Alfred Döblin, Heinrich Mann, and Franz Werfel and actors Fritz Kortner, Peter Lorre, Fritzi Massary, and Walter Mehring. He settled into a regular bridge game with Billy Wilder and ensured Wilder's future by introducing him ("starving, undiscovered as a film writer") to Lubitsch.[21]

Paramount loaned Hollander to Universal for *A Hundred Men and a Girl* (1937), in which Leopold Stokowski appeared as himself, conducting Deanna Durbin, who sang both Mozart's "Alleluia" from *Exsultate, jubilate* and Hollander's hit song, "Music in My Dreams." ("Only in America," quipped Hollander.) In 1939 he moved to Warner Brothers, where he composed for "elegant comedies and cozy family tragedies full of comic bassoons." In the 1940s he composed three more musicals for Dietrich, who agreed to play a Nazi sympathizer in Wilder's *A Foreign Affair* (1948) only if Hollander would write her songs. (Hollander appears in this film at the keyboard, accompanying Dietrich as a nightclub singer.) He also worked on *Berlin Express* (1948) and *Sabrina* (1954). In all he composed for 175 Hollywood films. Some of them were B-pictures thrown his way like dog bones, he wryly commented, but many featured big stars.[22]

Hollander never orchestrated his own scores, but he played them so brilliantly on the piano that the studio orchestrators were able to hear the instruments he had in mind.[23] His songs were twice nominated for Academy Awards; his scores, always lively, witty, and sophisticated, won two Oscar nominations.[24] His favorite of these, according to his biographer, Völker Kühn, was the 1953 score for *The 5,000 Fingers of Dr. T,* a Stanley Kramer film on a story by "Dr. Seuss," which flopped on its initial release but has since become a cult favorite. Hollander was given the freedom to compose throughout the film, using classical methods such as fugal and variation techniques in colorful counterpoint to a little boy's fantasy of his terrifying piano teacher.

Only Wilder gave Hollander opportunities to compose to his own lyrics. His songs—even his popular hits—were often cut.[25] John Waxman comments that "Hollander's big mistake was that he went to the wrong place. If he had gone to New York to write for Broadway he would have been huge: a writer, director; he could have been in the league of Cole Porter."[26] Hollander himself appreciated his successes in Hollywood but never felt "at home." Grateful though he was for America's succor when he needed it, when he returned permanently to Europe in 1955 he wrote to his former colleague, cabaret composer Mischa Spoliansky, "Hollywood lies where it belongs: far behind me."[27]

Franz Waxman, the youngest—and therefore the most adaptable—of the group discussed in this chapter, developed an impressive career in Hollywood films following his arrival at the age of twenty-eight. After their Berlin collaborations and flight from Germany, Waxman and Hollander had lived and worked together in Paris. In the spring of 1934 Pommer brought Waxman from France to adapt for Fox a Jerome Kern–Oscar Hammerstein stage musical, *Music in the Air,* starring Gloria Swanson. Waxman, who had not seriously thought of himself as a composer until this time, became an acknowledged master of film composing through steady perseverance, completing 144 Hollywood film scores over a period of thirty-two years. Bespectacled and serious-looking, he was known for his integrity and thoughtful, erudite approach. He "gave himself, one hundred percent, to films he was interested in," says his son John.[28] His scores were often considered better than the films they accompanied. They were nominated twelve times and won a record-breaking two consecutive Academy Awards for *Sunset Boulevard* in 1950 and *A Place in the Sun* in 1951. In one of Hollywood's typically humiliating episodes, however, the director George Stevens ordered a third of Waxman's material for *A Place in the Sun* reworked after the score was completed.

Although Waxman's first assignment with Pommer flopped, James Whale, who had liked Waxman's previous work for Pommer on the French film *Liliom,* invited him to compose the score for *Bride of Frankenstein,* produced by Universal in 1935. Whale's first *Frankenstein* (1930) had used music only for the opening and end credits. Waxman's *Bride* was a fully realized symphonic score, using Wagnerian leitmotif techniques and considerable dissonance to reinforce the film's expressionist extremes and ironies. Such musical subtleties kept film composing fresh for Waxman; his tonally ambiguous theme for the monster conveys the film's dualistic view of him as both evil and good. For years Universal recycled themes from Waxman's *Bride* music for other films.

This early success led to an imprisonment of sorts, as Waxman was made Universal's music director, supervising, contributing to, and conducting some fifty film scores in two years. "He was a chameleon; he could write different styles. In the beginning he worked on everything that was given to him," remembers his son.[29] Waxman's move to MGM—from 1936 to 1943—enabled him to concentrate on composing, freed from administrative duties. In that period he was twice "loaned out" to producer David O. Selznick, most notably for *Rebecca* (1940), based on Daphne DuMaurier's novel. (This was Alfred Hitchcock's first film in Hollywood; Waxman later composed for three more Hitchcock films.[30]) The strong characterizations in his romantic themes for *Rebecca* and the subtlety of psychological comment in the score show Waxman's growing mastery. By the time he left MGM in 1943, he had gathered five Academy Award nominations.[31]

Waxman wanted more dramatic opportunities, and he moved to Warner Brothers, where Korngold and the veteran Max Steiner (a Vienna-born composer who had emigrated to America in 1914) captured the most interesting assignments. Waxman scored war pictures, and in 1945 he won another Academy Award nomination for *Objective, Burma!*[32] In 1947 he decided to freelance. He had known Billy Wilder in Berlin from the early 1930s at Ufa in Berlin, and in 1932 had composed a film musical to an uncredited Wilder screenplay.[33] Because of their studio commitments, Waxman and Wilder were not able to work together in Hollywood until 1949, when Wilder directed Gloria Swanson in *Sunset Boulevard* for Paramount. Waxman contributed one of the most sophisticated and fascinating of all film scores to this send-up of Hollywood unreality. Leitmotiv technique provides a unity that is constantly varied with wry touches of musical humor, in a sensitive score perfectly suited to the screenplay. Wilder was himself musically inclined, and Waxman felt free to make subtle use of musical references to deepen characterizations and situations in the film. From a swatch of J. S. Bach to a reference to Richard Strauss's opera *Salome,* from an expressionist tango to a slowed-down takeoff on newsreel music, the score is rich in musical irony. Because madness pervades the film, Waxman borrowed from Alban Berg's 1925 opera *Wozzeck* the essentially cinematic idea of wildly contrasting musical juxtapositions for the New Year's Eve party scenes.

In the mid-1940s Waxman gave interviews for *Film Music Notes* in which he described the lot of a movie composer and expressed the hope that "someday the movie tycoons will . . . accept their responsibilities toward the cultural and artistic progress of our country and, as eighteenth century royalty and nobility did, endow some of today's composers."[34] By 1959 he was more outspoken and specific. His assignment to *The Nun's Story* (a Robert Anderson screenplay for Warner) led him to complain to the producers about the notoriously late starting dates and short deadlines—sometimes less than four weeks—for completing a film score: "Babies are not born overnight . . . and so it is with music or anything completely creative. . . . Everyone else connected with this picture has now been thoroughly drenched in it . . . and has had time to give it adequate thought. How, then, can a composer, if he is to do a decent job of creating, see a film [for the first time] one day and start writing it the next morning at nine o'clock?"[35] To prepare himself for this film, Waxman traveled to Rome to research church music. He invested the rather bland story with his probing dramatic instinct, garnering another Academy Award nomination. A constantly working man, all of whose waking hours were devoted to music, Waxman even composed while driving to and from the studios. He told *Newsweek* magazine in 1955 that, for him, motion translated into music, and "since no one walks in Los Angeles, and I live on top of a mountain [off Mulholland Drive], I do a lot of moving"—which translated into a lot of composing.[36]

Waxman also achieved extraordinary success outside his film work. His ambition to develop as a conductor led him to found the Los Angeles Music Festival, which enabled him to breach the film industry's barriers against opera and concert music and to become internationally respected as a musician.[37] In the two decades (1947–67) of the festival, which he supported with the proceeds from his scores for television, Waxman contributed immeasurably to the growth of musical awareness in Los Angeles. He brought to UCLA's Royce Hall works from his European cultural heritage that Los Angeles had not yet encountered and invited living composers to perform their works. In the early years of the festival he honored William Walton and Arthur Honegger with performances of several of their concert works. He may have wanted to highlight the fact that their work in British and French films did their status as concert composers no harm, in contrast to the situation facing Hollywood film composers.

Waxman's list of Los Angeles Festival premieres is impressive. He introduced important orchestral works by Mahler and Shostakovich to the West Coast.[38] In 1956 the festival's West Coast premiere of Debussy's *Le martyre de Saint Sébastien* (1911), narrated by Louis Jourdain, was broadcast to Europe. Each festival introduced at least one premiere performance of an orchestral work by a contemporary composer—most of them, but not all, European. By far the largest number of premieres was given to Stravinsky, whose appearances as conductor were highlights of the festival. (Stravinsky's festival contributions are discussed in chapter 10.) In some of the festival programs featuring Stravinsky, his assistant and protégé, Robert Craft, conducted performances of works by Alban Berg, Anton Webern, and Arnold Schoenberg.[39] In 1955 the German composers Gottfried von Einem, Rolf Liebermann, and Werner Egk came to the festival to conduct their own works, and other works by Ralph Vaughan Williams, Carl Orff, and André Caplet received their West Coast and American premieres. The oratorio *Isaiah the Prophet* by Alexandre Tansman, who had returned to

Paris from his wartime exile in Hollywood, was given its American premiere the same year. These increasing numbers of performances of European works set the stage for the international editions of the festival in 1961–1963. There was an all-Russian program during the 1961 festival, featuring two works by Tikhon Khrennikov, a leading Soviet composer; Waxman was partial to Russian music and clearly enjoyed his reciprocal opportunities to conduct in the Soviet Union. Works by Americans John Vincent and Roy Harris (both then on the UCLA music faculty), Walter Piston, and Elinor Remick Warren were performed at the international festivals, along with concert works by Waxman's film colleagues Toch and Miklós Rózsa. Berlin-born Lukas Foss, who came from the East Coast to join the UCLA composition faculty in 1953, was featured as both composer and performer.

The festival eventually included chamber concerts, opera, ballet, music theater events, and children's concerts. Rudolf Serkin was featured in a cycle of the complete Beethoven piano concertos. Local excitement was provided when prominent émigré musicians who had moved to Southern California appeared as featured soloists: violinist Joseph Szigeti and soprano Lotte Lehmann performed in the first festival in the Beverly Hills High School;[40] Bruno Walter contributed personal notes about his European Mahler premieres; Richard Lert conducted the Guild Opera in a production of Mozart's *The Marriage of Figaro;* Carl Ebert and Hugo Strelitzer presented a production of Smetana's *The Bartered Bride* with the Guild Opera under Czech conductor Jan Popper; in 1959 André Previn—"by arrangement with MGM"—played Richard Strauss's *Burleske* for piano and orchestra and in 1961 returned for the first international festival, bringing jazz players Shelly Manne (drums) and Red Mitchell (bass) to improvise on themes from Leonard Bernstein's *West Side Story.*[41]

Over the course of the festival, Waxman presented only four of his own concert works: the *Carmen Fantasie;*[42] the American premiere in 1956 of his Sinfonietta for string orchestra and timpani; the West Coast premiere of his oratorio *Joshua,* written in memory of his wife, Alice; and, in the final festival concert (1966), the American premiere of his last work, a dramatic song cycle of children prisoner's poems, *The Song of Terezin.* These latter two acknowledgments of his Jewish heritage came at the end of Waxman's film career, when he no longer needed to be a musical chameleon. In his last work, the poignant lines written by doomed children in the concentration camp Theresienstadt (Terezin) are subjected to grotesque distortions of musical expressionism. The youthful victims' terror and pain, their longings for release, joy, and love are almost submerged in orchestral shrieks of horror. The following year Waxman died of cancer at age sixty in Los Angeles, still at the height of his powers. Although his major concert works had been published, and Jascha Heifetz recorded his *Carmen Fantasie,* Waxman's opera *Dr. Jekyll and Mr. Hyde* and a cello concerto remained incomplete.[43]

Among all the composers working in Hollywood during the 1930s and '40s, Erich Wolfgang Korngold must be considered the most fortunate and exceptional case. He was an internationally acclaimed composer—particularly celebrated for his opera *Die tote Stadt*—when he first arrived in Hollywood in 1934 at the age of thirty-seven. He had no experience in film music; in fact, he had turned down film score offers from Ufa in recent years while he composed and taught at the Vienna Staatsakademie. His exceptional mental capacities and rare dramatic and musical talents, however, soon made him the most admired among the Hollywood film composers, who were not always inclined to admire each other. In the words of film composer David Raksin, who could be sour in his opinions, Korngold was "the real McCoy, a marvel."[44]

In the fall of 1934, Korngold's assignment to adapt Felix Mendelssohn's music for Max Reinhardt's film of *A Midsummer Night's Dream* for Warner Brothers was intended to have been a short eight weeks' work. But Reinhardt's extraordinary demands developed the project into the most lavish and expensive movie made to that date in Hollywood, and Korngold's visit lasted six months. The two Austrian artists collaborated in a way unknown to the Hollywood studio chiefs. During the filming of certain scenes, Korngold conducted an orchestra onstage, concealed by artificial shrubbery. After determining what music would accompany spoken dialogue, he would also "conduct" the actor being filmed to make him speak his lines in the required rhythm, later recording the orchestral part.

As a conductor Korngold was unorthodox. (Since he had seen Gustav Mahler conduct his massive Eighth Symphony in 1910, young Korngold's ambition had been to follow in the footsteps of "Direktor Mahler.") Gottfried Reinhardt paints a vivid picture of Korngold conducting for Max Reinhardt: "Korngold did not conduct with his stick. . . . Once in the grip of his sausage fingers, it was lost to sight. . . . Korngold rowed. Heroically. And the stream of rhythm on which he launched his orchestra flowed freely, melodies rippled with laughter and surged with passion, while harmonies were pure and deep as an alpine lake; not one rubato, crescendo or

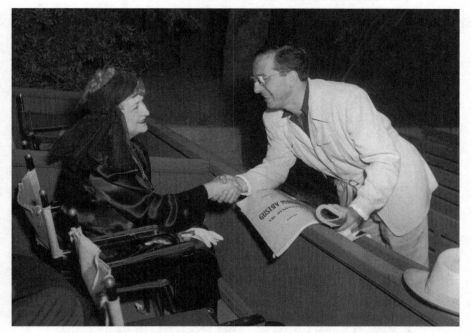

Alma Mahler Werfel and Franz Waxman, Hollywood Bowl, July 1948. Otto Rothschild Collection, Music Center Archives, Los Angeles.

diminuendo was calculated. . . . In obedience to some inner law of his, they were simply right and unassailable."[45] Teddy Krise, a member of the Warner orchestra in Korngold's time, remembered that the composer made music director Leo Forbstein hire extra musicians to transform what had been a pickup dance band: "[Korngold] really shook the place up and brought so much class to the department that in a few years the orchestra was the best there was, in my opinion," said Krise. Eleanor Aller, principal cellist of the Warner Orchestra in 1939 (also wife of the violinist/conductor Felix Slatkin and mother of conductor Leonard Slatkin), described recording sessions as "pure joy; unforgettable hours of music making. Korngold was not a conventional conductor by any means, and sometimes it was hard to follow his beat. In fact, he didn't conduct the orchestra, he *hypnotized* them." Along with his extraordinary musical gifts, so keen were Korngold's dramatic ideas and contributions that Max Reinhardt declared, "If he were not the great musician that he is, he would become a great dramaturg."[46]

Following the completion of *A Midsummer Night's Dream,* on the boat back to Europe in March 1935 Korngold and his wife, Luzi, found themselves wooed by fellow passenger Jack Warner, who was trying to talk Korn-

Erich Wolfgang Korngold, ca. 1930. Photo courtesy of Schott Music Gmbh & Co.

gold into a contract.[47] The increasingly ugly anti-Semitism in Austria convinced the Korngolds, who had two sons, to seriously consider possible refuge in California, and in the fall of 1935 Erich accepted a return engagement to compose a film musical called *Give Us This Night* (with lyrics by Oscar Hammerstein), for Ernst Lubitsch at Paramount. Mezzo-soprano Gladys Swarthout and tenor Jan Kiepura—who, with Lotte Lehmann, had premiered Korngold's opera *Das Wunder der Heliane* in Vienna in 1927— starred, and Korngold must have felt himself in familiar musical territory.

His wife and children accompanied him to California for this project. Before his work on it was finished, Warner asked him to compose the score for a completed swashbuckler, *Captain Blood,* starring Errol Flynn, and Korngold agreed.

At the beginning of each of his film projects, Korngold was plagued by bouts of anxiety; his children often heard him muttering, "I can't do it!" But these doubts were overcome by his enthusiasm for a good story. His talent for improvisation, along with his aptitude for drama, provided a natural basis for film composing. Sitting at a piano in a projection room, he would watch the completed film, and his fears would dissolve as he began to improvise musical ideas. Endowed with facile mathematical skills, Korngold quickly learned how to calculate the timing of background music with an astonishing exactitude, without resorting to such technical aids as the click tracks other composers used. While completing *Give Us This Night,* Korngold composed—in three weeks—a score for Warner Brothers that was nominated for an Academy Award and propelled *Captain Blood* to great popular success. The vitality in the score's quicksilver dramatic comment, the excitement and humor of the thematic invention, along with the polish with which it was achieved, showed the Warner executives that they had found a treasurable composer.

Korngold's film scores were conceived in the manner of Richard Strauss's tone poems. He used leitmotifs and developed them contrapuntally as character and plot demanded. Coherent key schemes were worked out according to the dramatic action, which would be swept along by his highly expressive, memorable melodies. Hugo Friedhofer, who orchestrated for both Korngold and Max Steiner and became an Academy Award–winning composer himself, remembered the Austrian composer's invaluable sense of theater, timing, and stagecraft (developed since his childhood), and the privileges he was accorded during his film work: "Korngold would go to the producer and say, 'Look, can you give me a little more footage at the end of' whatever scene it was. 'I feel that as the end of an act. I feel that there's a first act curtain there.' And he would always get his way. In some instances that I recall, he would suggest transpositions of scenes. He was acting like a producer . . . and they listened to him, much to their own advantage."[48]

For the next several summers, homesick for their native country's climate and scenery, the family left what Luzi Korngold called the "frictionless luxury" of Hollywood for the familiarity of their primitive and somewhat decaying country castle near Gmunden in the Salzkammergut area.[49] Jack Warner, always anxious to keep Korngold, offered him more generous contracts than were offered to other film composers, and his music director, Leo Forbstein, was happy to allow him unique liberties; Korngold would score only two films a year (while Steiner was composing on average eight to ten a year). Between 1934 and 1954 he worked on twenty-three films, for only sixteen of which—all for Warner Brothers— he composed the full score. No other film composer achieved the privileges granted to Korngold: His music remained his property; he had the right to refuse projects he felt were unsuitable; he was often involved in prefilming decisions; he could decide where music should be used in the films; he could work at home when he wished; he would have his own screen title; and his name appeared in advertising wherever the director's name appeared. He was also—at $12,500 per assignment—the highest-paid composer at the time in Hollywood.[50]

When their younger son, George, became ill with tuberculosis in 1936, the Korngolds moved him from Austria to California that fall, while Erich composed for Warner Brothers' epic *Anthony Adverse*, the most extensive score yet developed for a film.[51] Through the coherence of his musical ideas and structures, Korngold's score holds the disparate elements of this story together and sweeps the drama along. It won an Academy Award, and fan clubs—many of whose members watched his films repeatedly to appreciate their musical subtleties—began growing up around Korngold's movie music. Many fans requested piano scores; most went repeatedly to his films (one saw *Kings Row* sixty-eight times); all of them hoped his music would be issued in recordings "without dialogue, gun shots or airplane crashes."[52]

Although Korngold and Luzi eventually became U.S. citizens in 1943, it was not until almost the last moment before the Anschluss that they made the decision to emigrate from Austria to Hollywood. In January 1938 a telegram from Warner Brothers summoned Korngold to return from Vienna immediately to score another Errol Flynn picture, *The Adventures of Robin Hood*. Filmed in the new Technicolor, it was most expensive movie the studio had made to date, and Jack Warner wanted the vigor and professionalism Korngold could provide. The urgency of the appeal demanded Korngold's decisive action; he was advised by colleagues in Vienna that this was an omen he should obey. With only one day to prepare for the trip, the Korngolds returned to Hollywood. A screening of the film, however, daunted Korngold so severely that he sent a letter on February 11 to the producers refusing it: "*Robin Hood* is no picture for me. I have no relation to it and therefore cannot produce any music for it. I am a musician of the heart, of passions and psychology; I am not a musical illustrator for a ninety-percent-action picture. Being a conscientious person, I cannot take the responsibility for a job which, as I already know, would leave me artistically completely dissatisfied and which, therefore, I would have to drop even after several weeks of work on it. . . . Please do not try to make me change my mind; my resolve is unshakable."[53] Forbstein calmed Korngold, telling him he could work week to week on the film without a contract, with the proviso that he could quit at the end of any week. Korngold completed the score only because on February 12 he received a telephone message that Austria's demise was imminent; when summoned by Hitler to Berchtesgaden, Chancellor Schuschnigg had resigned. With the German annexation of Austria, the Korngolds' homes and property were confiscated, and their immediate challenge was to bring their older son and their parents unharmed to California.

The Korngolds thus became instant émigrés. Erich, whose life as a composing wunderkind had been carefully insulated from such worries by his overbearing father, the Viennese music critic Julius Korngold, took on the sole support of his family's three households.[54] Yet, in contrast to the dire drama of his own situation, the music for *Robin Hood* was vibrant and confident and is still considered one of the best in the history of film music. The score, which fills 73 percent of the film's running time, was completed in seven weeks. It won Korngold his second Academy Award.

When the European war broke out in 1939, Korngold sank into a deep depression. In 1941, responding to news of the increasingly desperate situation of Jews in Europe, he composed two religious works for Los Angeles' Fairfax Temple. (Like Max Reinhardt, who considered his own Jewishness a purely personal matter and could not bring himself to take his ancestry as seriously as Hitler did, Korngold had not thought of himself as particularly Jewish.)[55] *A Passover Psalm,* op. 30, to Hebrew texts, and *Prayer,* op. 32, to a text by the Korngolds' close friend Franz Werfel, were commissioned by Rabbi Jacob Sonderling and performed in Los Angeles the year they were written. Other than these religious works, Korngold wrote no music "for himself" for the duration of the war. "Even if I wanted to, I could not compose on my own level," he told his wife. His own level had been that of the Vienna Opera in the emperor's era, when he was composing for such stars as Maria Jeritza, Lotte Lehmann, and Richard Tauber. Sadness about his homeland was expressed in Korngold's interview for the *New York Times* in 1942: "I'm grateful that I haven't seen the swastika in Vienna, I have no bad memory. I can still dream of Vienna as it was. I am not a refugee and I am happy I had here a new country before I lost my own."[56]

In 1940 Korngold expressed what satisfaction he could find in film composing: "When, in the projection room or through the operator's little window, I am watching the picture unroll, when I am sitting at the piano improvising or inventing themes and tunes, when I am facing the orchestra conducting my music, I have the feeling that I am giving my own and my best: symphonically dramatic music which fits the picture, its action, and its psychology, and which nevertheless will be able to hold its own in the concert hall." Luzi Korngold wrote in her biography, however, that her husband probably would not have composed for films if financial circumstances had not demanded it.[57]

In 1941 Korngold's latent anger against the film industry's attitude toward music surfaced in his response to an invitation to become a member of the Academy of Motion Picture Arts and Sciences: "I, for my part, feel that we composers would fully deserve the *disdain* accorded us and our music in the film industry and in the press, were we to join an academy which contributes toward that very disdain of film music by calling itself an Organization of Actors, Directors, Producers, Technicians, and Writers, *even though it already has as members several composers and conductors of name.* As soon as the Academy calls itself an Organization of Actors, Directors, Producers, Technicians, Writers, *and Composers,* I will be the first to join it gladly."[58] Friedhofer saw at first hand that "[Korngold's] contribution was enormous and he influenced everyone working at that time. He was the first to write film music in long lines, great flowing chunks that contained the ebb and flow of mood and action, and the feeling of the picture."[59] Film scores by Max Steiner, Alfred Newman, Franz Waxman, Jerry Goldsmith, and John Williams all owe much to Korngold's influence.

Korngold's concert works, however, came hesitantly. Julius Korngold's domination of his son was noticeable in California. Eleanor Aller recalled that Erich always had his father present at film recording sessions: "After each take, Korngold would look round to his father to get a nod of approval."[60] Yet, against the advice of his father, Erich did not make the sustained efforts necessary to find an American agent, management, or even a publisher. Dr. Korngold, a once powerful critic deprived of his forum against musical modernism (in the Viennese newspaper, *Die Neue Freie Presse*), began advising Erich which of his film themes to use in the concert works he felt Erich should be writing. The Violin Concerto of 1945 is a product of the father's musical choices. Erich worked on it sporadically from 1937 to 1939, revised it in 1945 in the months before and after his father's death, and dedicated it to Alma Mahler Werfel.

In 1944, as Korngold saw streams of car headlights flowing through the Cahuenga Pass to the night shift at the Lockheed aircraft plant in North Hollywood, his depression began to lift. "There comes Hitler's downfall," he said to his wife.[61] For Christmas that year he gave her full sketches of his Third String Quartet, the first work he "wrote for himself" since he had finished his last opera, *Die Kathrin,* in 1937. The quartet was completed in 1945, the year his father died, and is dedicated to Bruno Walter, who had known him and performed his works since his childhood. A dramatization of his inner conflicts, it portrays the freeing of Korngold's spirit. While its movements follow classical forms, Korngold makes the most of the character and drama inherent in the form of each movement: the first a sonata form, the second a scherzo with trio; the third a song form with a contrastingly passionate center section; and the fourth a rondo, whose repeated themes present an energetic triumph over the themes of psychological depression that open the first movement. These initial themes contribute a disorienting but dramatically eloquent tonal ambiguity to the work. The first theme descends chromatically in distorted intervals that grow larger and more remote from tonality as they are developed and varied. The second theme at first ascends stepwise; its intervals also grow larger, until in the development section they become sevenths and octaves struggling for survival amid a complex texture of agitated rhythmic movement, trills, and rapid chromatic descending scales; at this point the composer writes *Avanti!* (Go for it!) in the score.[62] Only at the end of this first movement is one assured of the home key, D major. The Scherzo makes use of a staccato motoric rhythm accompanied by an elfin counterrhythm; this scintillating combination conveys the sparkle of moving car lights and hope in the night. A contrastingly serene melody (taken from Korngold's favorite and most recently completed film score for *Between Two Worlds,* 1944) provides the trio. The theme that dominates the third movement is a modal love theme built on rising melodic fourths. (Throughout his career, he used rising fourths to express an essentially cheerful spirit.) The final movement of the quartet (marked *con fuoco*) makes use of two rondo themes: a fiery, driving rhythmic motive and a contrastingly exuberant tune with changing meters.[63] Other themes from the earlier movements of the quartet are recalled and transformed by the driving rhythm of the finale. At its climax, a repeated motto built on rising fourths emerges triumphant. In the last measures, the two briefly reprised atonal themes of despair and hope from the first movement are cast away by a strongly tonal final cadence.

In 1946, after he decided not to renew his Warner contract, Korngold composed a virtuosic miniature Cello Concerto, in which he used further devices of modernism—extreme dissonance, avoidance of tonality, irregular rhythmic pulse, syncopation, and frequent changes of meter—for the film *Deception*. In 1947 Heifetz premiered Korngold's Violin Concerto to triumph in St. Louis, but the New York critics received it coldly: Irving Kolodin called it "more corn than gold" in the *New York Sun,* and Olin Downes dismissed it in the *New York Times* as "a Hollywood Concerto." Even the Vienna critics proved condescending.[64] That year, after recovering from a heart attack, Korngold began a symphony to celebrate the defeat of the Nazis, dedicating it to the memory of Franklin Delano Roosevelt; the moving funeral march of its Adagio third movement is the work's emotional centerpiece. While the work is titled Symphony in F-sharp, its tonal relationships are obscured by dissonance and excursions to remote keys. As in the Third String Quartet, melodic distortion, changing meters, disruptive and irregular rhythms, tonal ambiguity, and contradiction of traditional harmonic function are exploited and brilliantly orchestrated to express character, circumstance, and conflict. Resolution to the home key is long postponed but all the more satisfying. Korngold's quest to recapture his cheerful spirit—again in themes using rising fourths—is stated serenely by solo flute as the second theme of the first movement, more heroically by the horns in the second movement, and then gaily announced by solo piccolo in the final movement. Completed in Hollywood in September 1952 after two demoralizing trips to war-weary Europe, the symphony is a powerful, tightly organized work, filled with compelling vitality. It is a message of affirmation from Korngold's spirit, released from the grip of a controlling parent, the sorrows of emigration, war, and the loss of his dreams of renewed success. This last major work of Korngold's all-too-short lifetime of sixty years is a neglected masterpiece from a composer who said of himself, "I am a musician of the heart, of passions and psychology."[65]

In 1936, while the United States was still gripped by the Depression, an enterprising New York–based journal began to inquire into the aesthetics and procedures of Hollywood film music, publishing a series of articles by the peripatetic American composer George Antheil. He came that year to Hollywood after sixteen years of performing and composing in Paris and Berlin. Boris Morros took him on at Paramount. He was the same age as Kurt Weill and Ernst Krenek, and he hosted them, as well as Paul Hindemith, as they investigated work possibilities at Hollywood's film studios. Because he was well known in New York, Antheil was assigned a column, titled "From the Hollywood Front" (note the war language), in the League of Composers' journal, *Modern Music*. His first column at the end of 1936 noted the significance of Leopold Stokowski's move from his position as music director of the Philadelphia Orchestra to work in Hollywood films and claimed that "picture music—a new art form—is coming into its own. . . . Many Mickey Mouse films are operas in the purest sense of the word." However, Antheil cautioned: "Composers must be forewarned: no one should attempt to come out unless he can write piano scores at the rate of 15–30 pages a day. . . . Good scores . . . talk to Hollywood in its own language—the language of money."

By contrast, the next issue of *Modern Music* included an article by Antheil on "Breaking into the Movies," which describes what was to happen that year (1937) to both Weill and Krenek, and in 1939 to Hindemith: "Hollywood is a brutal city. It esteems its hired help solely in the symbols of how dearly it needs and how much it must pay for their services. . . . 'Once cheap, always cheap' is the rule. A composer who comes out here 'to show Hollywood' what he can do, will ultimately find Hollywood not interested. There are a number of such stranded men here right now. . . . Hollywood is as hard as a diamond, beside which New York seems soft and a veritable rosebud." With aptitude, Antheil reported, a composer (as a freelance) could earn $3,000–8,000 a picture. The job would be "short & sweet"; only three to four weeks at the end of the production process.

By the end of 1937 Antheil was warning that Hollywood music was a closed corporation; music favored by the studios was "unmitigated tripe," upon which music critics should turn a searchlight. In the spring of 1938 he noted a good Weill film score, making no concessions to Hollywood, for Fritz Lang's *You and Me*, made by Paramount. "There is only one trouble," he commented; "there are not enough intelligent and forward-looking music directors in Hollywood."[66]

Kurt Weill made at least ten trips from New York to find work in Hollywood between January 1937 and the end of November 1948. He quickly lost his illusions about film composing as a "new musical art" with his first project: his score for *You and Me* was ruthlessly cut and doctored at Paramount, and ultimate credit went to Frederick Hollander. Weill's considerable efforts in the film studios caused him intolerable artistic frustration, in spite of the fact that he went to Hollywood while two theater productions for which he had written the music—the biblical drama *The Eternal Road* and the antiwar musical *Johnny Johnson*—were running successfully on Broadway. He was helped in 1937 by introductions from members of New York's Group Theatre collective, who were also establishing themselves in Hollywood, and from Antheil, who had known him in Berlin in the early 1920s.

Weill's lack of experience with the film medium undermined his security in Hollywood, and he confessed to working slowly. In letters to his wife, Lotte Lenya, he expressed his constant anger and frustrations. In early 1937 he found the people in the business "jealous, ugly. . . . There's only one way to get on here: you have to take everything with a great sense of humor and make fun of it (to yourself, because you mustn't show it!) and just enjoy the beautiful scenery and make money."[67] The climate gave him constant headaches. Except for occasions with Max Reinhardt and an evening with Katia and Thomas Mann, he could not abide the German-speaking émigré social community or the company of other film composers, and he was "haughty" to Korngold. The socializing necessary to deal making heightened his inner tensions. Waiting for others to make decisions made him "insanely nervous." He found himself "fighting tooth and claw" for work in the "very monotonous and irritating atmosphere." Hollywood seemed like hell to him; he felt he was selling his soul. He took seriously Antheil's advice not to sell his talents cheaply, and his price was often too high to interest producers, most of whom had never heard of him. (Ironically, along the way he occasionally received healthy amounts of money, even when his ideas and music were scrapped.) In April 1937 he wrote that "A whore never loves the man who pays her. She wants to get rid of him as soon as she has rendered her services. That is my relation to Hollywood (I'm the whore)."[68] In the spring of 1938 he raged to Lenya about the immorality, viciousness, stupidity, and lack of culture he was encountering in his Hollywood experience. His constant—and unfortunately misplaced—aim was to "establish who I am." At Paramount he resented Morros for pushing him to work faster and to find a collaborator. He was sure his music was "original and unique. . . . I now realize just how much I could achieve in motion pictures if only they would let me."[69]

In the filming of his successful Broadway musicals *Lady in the Dark* (1944), *Knickerbocker Holiday* (1944), and *One Touch of Venus* (1948), his music was cut, fragmented, pushed to the background, and in many cases replaced by the work of others; credit and an Academy Award nomination for the score for *Knickerbocker Holiday* was given to its adapter, the German émigré composer Werner Heymann.[70] Weill's last Hollywood effort, in the fall of 1948, was a fruitless search for a film contract for his musical *Love Life*, which had just opened on Broadway, as well as a failed attempt to sell a new project (conceived with Alan Jay Lerner) that was judged too sophisticated by the studios. Weill's tensions, disappointments, and frustrations about his Hollywood ventures could well have contributed to the heart attack he suffered the following summer. In the spring of 1950 he died of another attack, at the age of fifty.

In contrast with Weill's struggles for recognition and creative authority, being anonymous was a relatively safe way to survive as a composer in the film industry. Italian composer Mario Castelnuovo-Tedesco (at age forty-five) and Hungarian Eugene Zador (at forty-six) both arrived at the MGM studio in 1940, when Louis B. Mayer had already become one of the richest men in the United States by providing "class for the masses," demanding perfectionism and spending lavishly for his studio's product. MGM's music department was organized for factory-like production, with twenty full-time composers, twenty-five arrangers, and forty copyists working first under Nathaniel Finston and later under Herbert Stothart, described among musicians as "God at MGM."[71] The composers already established at MGM allowed little opportunity to newcomers, and while both Castelnuovo-Tedesco and Zador had been well established in their European careers, they were also highly cultivated gentlemen, reluctant to fight their colleagues.

Castelnuovo-Tedesco was a contemplative man, modest and unassuming. His knowledge of literature was broad and deep. He thought of himself as having an "instinctive timidity," and his feelings and music were characterized by "tender melancholy."[72] In emigration, ejected from a culture in which he had moved easily among the most renowned artists of his time, Castelnuovo-Tedesco felt "an almost physical torment, a tearing asunder, a mutilation. It seemed to be a dress rehearsal for death; and indeed, since that time something in me has been absolutely dead: not hope, but illusion. What has kept me alive has been love for those dear to me and for music. However much affection I have come to feel over the years for my adopted country, I have no longer been able to become attached to people and things; I have lived as if suspended in mid-air, in a cloud, waiting."[73]

Jascha Heifetz and the American violinist Albert Spalding, both of whom had Hollywood connections, helped arrange an MGM contract for Castelnuovo-Tedesco. In 1933 he had been so interested in the possibility of film scoring that he had composed 2 Film Studies for the piano (inspired by Mickey Mouse and Charlie Chaplin) while still in Italy. In 1940, before reaching California, he wrote a piano suite entitled Stars, the four movements of which depicted Greta Garbo, Deanna Durbin, Marlene Dietrich, and Shirley Temple. At MGM, however, in the first job he had ever held, Castelnuovo-Tedesco was startled to be given employee number 11694 and to learn that his contributions to background scoring should have neither form nor personality. The major requisite for composing seemed not to have talent, but to have a good metronome. He found that he was no more than a cog in a well-oiled machine. His surname posed a problem for his colleagues, who at first called him Mr. Tedesco and then "Teddy," which he felt was slightly ridiculous.

Because he had great facility and a fluent technique, Castelnuovo-Tedesco composed—directly in ink—whatever was demanded of him with extraordinary speed and ease, orchestrating his own work without hesitation, an unusual divergence from the rule eventually allowed him by Finston because it saved the studio money. After he realized that music was the Cinderella of film production, Castelnuovo-Tedesco's illusions of a spontaneous and authentic form of musical film art vanished. Music was considered a necessary evil; more or less a "filler." Automobile and airplane noises were more important. In order to complete a score in the fiendishly short time allotted, up to thirteen composers would labor on it simultaneously. Finston once asked him to compose for an intimate scene a three-and-a-half-minute violin sonata in the style of "Oh, you know, Brahms, Franck, and maybe a little Debussy." The technique expected was inevitably the Wagnerian leitmotif technique, most motives reduced to puerile mosaics. Having come to Hollywood to offer his best, Castelnuovo-Tedesco felt that only his worst was requested. During the three years he worked at MGM, contributing to some 200 scenes a year, his name never appeared on the screen.[74] Credits were instead given to the old-timers who had contributed the least.

Castelnuovo-Tedesco's MGM contract contained a standard—but astonishing—clause, stipulating the studio's right to ownership of any of his compositions, including even those not written for films. Over eighty of his concert pieces thus came into the studio's possession.[75] Not surprisingly, when this contract expired in 1944, Castelnuovo-Tedesco chose to become a freelancer, working for Columbia (where he had several intelligent composition students and felt particularly welcome), Warner Brothers, Twentieth Century-Fox, and Universal Artists. He collaborated on films with Toch, to whom he was particularly close; with Miklós Rózsa, who had gained great success since his arrival in Hollywood in 1940; with Bronislaw Kaper; and with Daniele Amfitheatrof, a Russian émigré whom he had known in Italy. The two film scores Castelnuovo-Tedesco composed that came the closest to pleasing him were *And Then There Were None* (1945, an Agatha Christie film directed by René Clair) for Twentieth Century-Fox, and *The Loves of Carmen* (1948) for Columbia. Otherwise, not much that he composed for film satisfied him. It was his final judgment that the film experience amounted to little of significance in his artistic life. In the United States, however, he was inevitably labeled "a Hollywood composer." He stopped writing for films in 1958. He wrote in his autobiography that he did not hold any personal rancor toward the film industry; during the terrible war years he had been grateful to be assured a relatively tranquil life that permitted him to maintain his family and complete his children's education.[76]

During Castelnuovo-Tedesco's years of toil in the film studios, he never stopped composing concert works and operas. In 1946 his Overture to *The Taming of the Shrew* (composed in Europe before he emigrated) was called "an ingratiating piece by a master orchestrator" by the *Los Angeles Times* music critic.[77] Most of his thick catalogue of chamber music, piano pieces, a great deal of vocal music, and many works for guitar—much of it intended for Andrés Segovia—was written in his California years, when he had little contact with the eastern establishment. These concert works were infrequently performed in Los Angeles. Segovia, at his first appearance with the Los Angeles Philharmonic in 1950, performed the concerto Castelnuovo-Tedesco had composed for him in 1939. The composer performed his own chamber music for "Evenings on the Roof" and its successor series, the "Monday Evening Concerts." His opera *The Merchant of Venice* (1956) won the Campari composition prize at La Scala in 1958 and was first performed at Florence's Maggio Musicale in 1961; a Los Angeles production was mounted at the Shrine Auditorium in 1964. Following this success, he composed three more operas: *All's Well That Ends Well* (op. 182, 1955–58), *Saul* (op. 191, 1958–60), and *The Importance of Being Earnest* (op. 198, 1962; premiered in 1972 by the Rome Radio Orchestra). In 1959 he was named a distinguished visiting professor at Michigan State University, where he taught a course in opera composition.[78]

In his concert music, the composer retained a conservatively impressionistic tonal idiom throughout the onslaught of avant-garde fashions, about which he wrote, "I have never believed in modernism, or in neoclassicism, or any other -isms. I believe that music is a form of language capable of progress and renewal . . . yet music should not discard what was contributed by preceding generations. . . . What I have sought to do, during my artistic evolution, has been to express myself with means always simpler and more direct, in a language always clearer and more precise."[79] He was sought out by many students, among them such film composers as André Previn, Henry Mancini, Jerry Goldsmith, and John Williams.[80]

Even more than Castelnuovo-Tedesco's, Hungarian-born Eugene Zador's name remained obscured in the shadows of the Hollywood film industry. In Europe he had known Kodály and Bartók well, and he had studied composition with Max Reger and musicology with Arnold Schering. By 1939, when he fled Europe, five of his operas and a ballet had been performed, as well as several orchestral works. His mastery of classical technique and his accommodation of modern elements were commended by one of the most influential musical analysts of the time, Donald Francis Tovey.[81] His reputation as a master of orchestration, based on his admiration for and study of Richard Strauss's works, was established.

Upon his 1939 arrival in New York, Zador was given an auspicious early performance. His opera *Christopher Columbus* was performed before a live audience of 2,600 and broadcast nationally by the Radio City Music Hall Orchestra, conducted by a fellow Hungarian, Erno Rapée (well known as a conductor for silent films), with Metropolitan Opera stars Robert Weede, Jan Peerce, and Martha Lipton heading a fine cast. It won excellent reviews for its "thrill of adventure," "dash and color," "superb imagery," and "sharp-eared sense of tonal drama." Although Zador had been awarded three doctorates—the most recent from the New York College of Music— he believed that he could earn three times as much money in Hollywood as he could by teaching, and his Austro-Hungarian connections were useful to him. The Hungarian soprano Ilona Hajmássy had become Ilona Massey, a movie star at MGM, and she owed Zador a favor for his role in getting her accepted earlier at the Vienna State Opera.[82] She helped arrange a three-year contract for him at MGM, and he arrived in Hollywood in September 1940 to become a member of the music staff. He soon found himself ghostwriting uncredited cues for other composers (Waxman among them). Anonymity became Zador's way of life in film music.

The Hungarians in Hollywood were known for helping each other— or stabbing each other's backs. Starting in 1940, when Miklós Rózsa arrived from London with Alexander Korda's film company, Zador helped the younger Hungarian composer in many ways. Possibly through Zador's influence, the New York College of Music conferred upon Rózsa an honorary doctorate. Zador had known Eugene Ormandy in Budapest when they were in their twenties, and he introduced Rózsa's music to him in 1941

(Ormandy had become music director of the Philadelphia Orchestra in 1938). While composing his *Hungarian Fantasy* for Heifetz, Zador recommended two of Rózsa's early violin pieces and offered to orchestrate them. Ormandy programmed works by both composers, and in early 1943 he urged Rózsa to help Zador's situation at MGM. He was relieved to hear a year later that Rózsa had done so.[83] For twenty-three years Zador contributed to Rózsa's success by arranging and orchestrating his film scores without credit. Eventually the two had a falling out, and *The V.I.P.s* (1963) was their last film together. Zador left MGM at the same time but continued composing for and orchestrating films anonymously, amassing a total list of over 120. At the rare times when he was granted credit, he used a pseudonym to shield his Jewish family in Europe.[84]

Perhaps because of his chosen anonymity, Zador seems to have encountered less difficulty than others with the stigma of being a "Hollywood composer." His concert and operatic works received many performances. In the 1960s and early 1970s, he added to his list of operas until they numbered eleven. All five of his American operas were performed in the United States.[85] *Christopher Columbus* received performances in Vienna and Tokyo. His orchestral works were performed in the United States by Stokowski, Pierre Monteux, John Barbirolli, George Szell, and others. Zubin Mehta conducted Zador's *Festival Overture* (1964) at the December 1964 opening of the Los Angeles Music Center. The *Children's Symphony* (1940; revised 1960) received over 100 performances. A major orchestral work written in 1943, the *Biblical Triptych*, was inspired by Thomas Mann's *Joseph* novels. Dedicated to Mann, the work was premiered by the Chicago Symphony in December 1943. Mann wrote warmly to Zador, conveying his admiration and satisfaction.[86]

In his last years Zador produced chamber quintets for woodwinds (1972) and brass (1973), and concertos for "underprivileged instruments" such as the cimbalom, trombone, double bass, and accordion.[87] His works continued to reflect his roots in Hungarian folk music; expressive accessibility was important to him. Like Castelnuovo-Tedesco, he was thought of as a "traditionalist" or a neo-Romantic and was disturbed by the growing emphasis in the 1950s and 1960s on cerebral systems in music. Zador went his own way musically, refusing to capitulate to trends. In his own words: "Every work is worth however much emotional power it has, and that is why I write only when I am inspired. If one can relate to a piece only intellectually, then it isn't worthwhile; for good music must also reach that very old-fashioned and often cursed resource, the heart."[88]

Early in his American residency, Zador was amazed to hear harshly outspoken criticism of President Franklin Roosevelt. This signaled a freedom in democratic society that was entirely new and inspiring to him. He was deeply grateful to the United States for welcoming him and providing him with means to make a living. He expressed this gratitude musically when in the 1970s he added an epilogue for a cappella chorus to his 1939 opera, *Christopher Columbus,* using his own words: "God bless this world, protect this wondrous land, this land of the hope of man."

Of all the émigré composers, Hanns Eisler had accumulated the most prior experience in composing film scores when he arrived in Hollywood in 1942 at age forty-four. He had composed for films since 1926, when he was commissioned to write a chamber orchestra accompaniment for an abstract film performed at the 1927 Baden-Baden Music Festival. His European films, like his incidental music for plays by Bertolt Brecht, Erwin Piscator, Lion Feuchtwanger, and Karl Kraus, were politically motivated.

From February to May 1935 Eisler toured the United States to address rallies on the subject of Hitler's efforts to destroy the working-class music movement in Germany. In New York, Charles Seeger, at that time writing music criticism for the *Daily Worker* as Carl Sands, introduced Eisler to the Composers' Collective, whose members had promoted the "Peat Bog Soldiers" song, written in 1933 by concentration camp prisoners in northern Germany. Eisler used this song to climax each of the fifty mass meetings he addressed in most of the large U.S. cities, delivering his first-hand account of Hitler's lowering of German musical standards "so that Hitler could rid himself of a dangerous enemy."[89] Two of Eisler's propaganda films were shown in New York by the Workers Film and Photo League, where he met Joseph Losey, then director of educational films for the Rockefeller Foundation. This introduction would eventually send Eisler to Hollywood.

Starting in September 1935, Eisler returned from Europe yearly to lecture at the New School for Social Research in Manhattan. In these years he became an active member of New York's leftist Group Theatre collective and composed the score for a film documentary by Joris Ivens on the Chinese war of resistance against the Japanese invasion. In January 1938 he settled in New York, with the backing of left-wing columnist Dorothy Thompson, playwright Clifford Odets, and Eleanor Roosevelt. In difficulty with U.S. authorities in 1939 over obtaining a nonquota visa, Eisler worked on a film cartoon for the oil industry, written and directed by Losey for the 1939 New York World's Fair.[90]

In 1940 the director of the New School, Alvin Johnson, obtained for Eisler a $20,000 grant from the Rockefeller Foundation to research ways in which experimental music could be used in film. Eisler was named the composer/director of the project, which was to be free from any commercial demands by the film industry. Eisler's colleagues Ivens, Losey, and Theodor W. Adorno (whom Eisler had known in Germany since 1925) also received Rockefeller support. Film footage excerpts totaling approximately eighty-five minutes were chosen for the experiment from existing films.[91] Conductors Jascha Horenstein, Fritz Stiedry, and Rudolf Kolisch recorded Eisler's music for these excerpts. The project, which ran between February 1940 and November 1943, was to culminate in a book on film music commissioned by Oxford University Press.

Since 1937 Eisler had gradually abandoned his earlier stance against Schoenberg's influence. He had composed several cantatas to texts by Brecht on current events, using the twelve-tone method but in a more simplified, tonal style than Schoenberg's and retaining suitably Brechtian emotional distance.[92] In 1938, in New York and away from Brecht's influence, Eisler composed a twelve-tone string quartet in which emphatic (non-Brechtian) expression marks guide the quartet's process. The dialogue with and against the twelve-tone method is fascinating and entertaining throughout the work, which was Eisler's only string quartet.

In 1940, with the creative freedom afforded him by the two-year Rockefeller grant, Eisler used a new variant of the twelve-tone method in his experimental settings of film scenes. His purpose was to prove that various techniques of modern composition—electronic instruments or natural sounds, the twelve-tone method and its vocabulary, or stylization of traditional musical language—could be used to enhance dramatic meaning in films. He asked whether "it would be worthwhile to ascertain whether the motion-picture audience's aversion to modern music is not merely a legend, and whether it would not approve of modern music that adequately fulfilled its dramatic function. Such proof might help to break down the prejudice against modern music in the film industry."[93] Underlying the project was a general critique of film scoring as practiced in Hollywood, including the leitmotif technique, "mood music," the conventional demand for melody and euphony, "haphazard musical padding," and the general attitude that music should vanish as soon as it has accomplished its purpose.[94]

Eisler had no intention that his own film music should vanish. Since his earliest work in the medium, he had refashioned from his film scores six suites and five orchestral pieces as concert works. Further chamber and orchestral works emerged from the Rockefeller experiments. One of the best known of these pieces is *Vierzehn Arten, den Regen zu beschreiben* (*Fourteen Ways to Describe Rain*), op. 70, composed for Ivens's film *Rain* and then arranged as a suite in homage to Schoenberg and dedicated to him.

An important part of the Rockefeller project was the introduction of some of the film excerpts with their modern musical settings to both the American film industry and the public. In April 1942 Eisler went to Holly-wood with his recording engineer, Harry Robin, where they were able to continue technical work in the film studios; in October Eisler demonstrated his ideas to producers at the RKO and Warner Brothers studios. He made another presentation to the public at the Academy of Motion Picture Arts and Sciences in January 1943, in which two sections from *White Flood* (*Eis*) were shown. These segments, which later became part of the Chamber Symphony, op. 69, were composed in the twelve-tone method for fifteen instruments, including two electric keyboards. They were intended to be colorful, spontaneous, and easily understandable. In 1944 a second public demonstration of the film with its music was reported in *Film Music Notes:* "That the 12-tone technique is the last word for dealing with a dead Arctic world was conclusively demonstrated, and the opponents of the 12-tone system were not slow to point the obvious moral. But one suspects Eisler has more up his sleeve. . . . At all events, the picture was given an ovation by a highly mixed and general audience."[95]

Two of Eisler's important collaborators, Adorno and Brecht, settled in Brentwood and Santa Monica in 1941. In November 1942 Eisler began col-laborating with Adorno on the book for Oxford, *Composing for the Films.* Adorno's émigré years in America had confirmed his bias against mass cul-ture, and this attitude is strongly reflected in the book. It was completed in German in 1944, then translated in 1946 into English. In 1947, when it was published, Adorno withdrew his name as coauthor, hoping to avoid association with Eisler, who by then was under investigation by the U.S. government.

Soon after his own arrival in California in 1942, Eisler began setting Brecht's poems of exile. The forty-seven songs—many of them quite short—written between May 1942 and December 1943 became known as the *Holly-wood Songbook.* To the majority of poems by Brecht, Eisler added other poets' texts of alienation—including his own. In this collection, the first concert songs he had composed for voice and piano since 1927, Eisler's concentrated, objective, and antisentimental style accumulates a compelling expressive power reminiscent of the great song cycles by Schubert.

Eisler composed the songs quickly, as he was at the same time becoming involved in composing for Hollywood films. This was a situation he grew to hate because it was difficult to use his new theories in commercial films. Marta and Lion Feuchtwanger frequently invited Eisler and Brecht to their home in Pacific Palisades. She later remembered that Eisler's frustrations with Hollywood's film industry drove him to drink.[96] He composed scores for eight Hollywood films, working when he could with compatible colleagues. His first was *Hangmen Also Die* (1943), in which he worked with Brecht and Fritz Lang. This anti-Nazi film was conceived immediately after the assassination of Reinhard Heydrich, the Nazi "protector" of Czechoslovakia. The story, written by Brecht, involves a Czech conspiracy to accuse a Nazi of the crime, and Eisler's score was nominated for an Academy Award. Illustrative of his fresh attitude toward film composing is a striking scene in which Eisler counterpoints cheerful "entertainment music" against the psychological plight of the heroine, as she gathers her nerve to accuse the targeted Nazi in a restaurant. The contradiction between the tension of the moment and the gaiety of the music startles the viewer and heightens the drama in an unconventional way; this was a Brechtian technique Eisler called "antithetic relation."

Eisler received another Academy Award nomination for a Cary Grant film, *None But the Lonely Heart* (1944), written and directed by Clifford Odets. Odets wrote another film that Eisler scored, *Deadline at Dawn* (1946), directed by their Group Theatre colleague, Harold Clurman.[97] RKO contracted with Eisler for three films that he later declared he composed for money alone: *Spanish Main* (1944), *Jealousy* (1945), and *A Scandal in Paris* (1945). He was not paid as well as other Hollywood composers, but he made enough money that he was able to financially assist Schoenberg, Brecht, and Paul Dessau, a fellow émigré whom he employed as an assisting composer. (In July 1945, Dessau reported to Brecht that Eisler's nerves were shot, for he feared that Hollywood would ruin his ears.)[98] Eisler's other studio films were *So Well Remembered* (1947), directed by Edward Dmytryk, and *The Woman On the Beach* (1947), Jean Renoir's last film in Hollywood. Renoir said about Eisler, "He was a great [composer], without doubt, like Bartók or Schoenberg. One always felt his significance, even in company. His humor was explosive: he jerked one toward truths, often sarcastically, always with enormous intensity."[99]

In March 1946 Eisler was appointed to fill Toch's composition and counterpoint positions at the University of Southern California. He enjoyed teaching and was respected by his students. He was no longer in financial difficulty. He hosted popular Sunday gatherings at his rented house on the Pacific Coast Highway in Malibu and described to Odets the pleasure of having the Chaplins to dinner with Thomas Mann: "They got on very well. The rigid Dr. Mann was delighted with Chaplin, laughed like a schoolboy and lost a little of his German dignity. Chaplin admitted to not having read a single line of Mann's, but was very pleased with him as an audience and put on a Big Show." Eisler helped Chaplin with the composition of the score for Chaplin's *Monsieur Verdoux* (1946). When Eisler's siblings' deadly political feud over their opposed Trotskyist and Stalinist Communist ideologies surfaced in the Hearst press, and 1947 subpoenas for hearings in Washington terminated Eisler's collaboration on Chaplin's silent film *The Circus,* Chaplin rallied wide support for Eisler among artists in Europe. "In your family, things happen as in Shakespeare," was his wry comment to Eisler.[100]

Many of the émigrés from Hitler's Europe had socialist or left-leaning tendencies. Since 1938 the House Un-American Activities Committee (HUAC) in Congress had been planning an enquiry into leftists in Hollywood. In 1940 they began to study signs of what was called "premature anti-fascism" or "subversive" activity in the Hollywood film industry. The same year, the California legislature followed suit with its own Joint Fact-Finding Subcommittee on Un-American Activities, interrogating writers and artists and ordering undercover agents to follow suspects to meetings, which were then recorded in detail. The midterm elections of 1946, which swept the Republican Party back into Congressional power, resuscitated the languishing Un-American Activities investigation in Congress.[101] The Cold War began in earnest with Winston Churchill's 1946 "Iron Curtain" speech in Fulton, Missouri, and President Harry Truman's 1947 pledge to "support free peoples who are resisting attempted subjugation by armed minorities or by outside pressures" (known thereafter as the Truman Doctrine).

Eisler's sister, the Trotskyist Ruth Fischer, and his brother, the Stalinist Gerhart Eisler, had been politically opposed since 1922. Both had lived in the United States since 1941. In New York, Fischer, impoverished and isolated from most Communists' approval since Trotsky's 1940 assassination and her escape from Europe, began publishing a periodical on "Stalinist conspirators." She gradually became suspicious to the point of paranoia, claiming in April 1944 that she was being followed and that her two brothers were behind a plot to murder her. She outlined a book to prove her claim that Gerhart was the Soviet Comintern's top American agent. Fur-

(WX4)WASHINGTON, SEPT. 24--HOLLYWOOD COMPOSER DENIES HE'S A COMMUNIST--
HANNS EISLER, 54-YEAR-OLD HOLLYWOOD COMPOSER, DENIES BEFORE HOUSE UN-
AMERICAN ACTIVITIES COMMITTEE TODAY THAT HE IS A COMMUNIST. HE SAID HE
APPLIED ONCE FOR MEMBERSHIP BUT DROPPED OUT AND WAS NEVER ACTIVE. HE
WAS FIRST WITNESS AS COMMITTEE OPENED PROBE OF WHETHER ALIEN COMMUNISTS
HAVE BEEN PERMITTED TO STAY IN THIS COUNTRY ILLEGALLY.
(AP WIREPHOTO(SEE STORY)BEF4I233STF-NKW)1947

Hanns Eisler testifying in Hollywood, 1947. *Los Angeles Examiner* **Collection, University of Southern California.**

ther, she claimed that Hanns was well connected with the Russian consulate in Los Angeles and living there in a "Stalinist environment" (probably a reference to his artistic collaborators). As the country's political climate darkened, Gerhart was called to testify before HUAC in late October 1946. In November Fischer published a series of six articles in the Hearst press, in which she characterized both her brothers as secret agents for Soviet Russia. As a result of this exposure, a former managing editor of the *Daily Worker,* Louis Budenz, accused Gerhart Eisler of being the chief communications officer and de facto head of the U.S. Communist Party.[102] Gerhart was charged with being a foreign agent leading American Communist activities. He was barred from leaving the United States and arrested. Hanns learned of his brother's arrest through a telephone call from his New York agent, who demanded that Eisler should immediately prepare a declaration against his brother. Eisler refused. His persecution began.[103]

In April 1947 HUAC member Richard Nixon announced that a subcommittee would be sent to Hollywood "to conduct an investigation into Hanns Eisler, [whose case] is perhaps the most important ever to have come before the Committee."[104] After testimony in Los Angeles that May, Eisler was summoned to Washington for a three-day interrogation before the full committee in September 1947. At his hearing before HUAC, Eisler was not allowed to read his prepared statement to the committee. Martha Gellhorn, in the *New Republic,* called the hearings "a flawless travesty of justice."[105] Eleanor Roosevelt was reviled in the press for having tried to help Hanns and Lou Eisler obtain a nonquota visa in 1940. Although a member of the State Department reported finding no definite and convincing evidence that Hanns Eisler was a member of the Communist Party, HUAC recommended to the Justice Department that he be prosecuted for perjury and passport fraud and deported.[106] The Justice Department, bypassing any court of law, decided on a "voluntary deportation," which meant that Eisler, who could not afford a legal defense, would have to pay his own way back to Europe. Shortly after Eisler's hearings, Thomas Mann wrote to a close friend, "For personal reasons the case of Hanns Eisler touches me closely. I know the man very well; he is highly cultivated, brilliant, very amusing in conversation, and I have often had splendid talks with him, particularly about Wagner. As a musician he is, in the opinion of all his colleagues, first class. Since the Inquisition has turned him over to the 'secular arm' for deportation, there is the danger that he will land in a German camp. I hear that Stravinsky (a White Russian!) means to start a demonstration in his favor. But I have a wife and children and am not inquiring further into the matter."[107] However, Mann did bring considerable pressure to bear on President Edvard Beneš of Czechoslovakia to obtain a Czech passport for Eisler.

There were farewell concerts of Eisler's music in both Los Angeles and New York, accompanied by an outpouring of support from leaders in the world of music. Stravinsky, Copland, Roger Sessions, Toch, and Roy Harris sponsored the concert in Los Angeles at the Coronet Theater on December 14, 1947; Copland, Leonard Bernstein, Harris, Walter Piston, Randall Thompson, David Diamond, and Sessions sponsored the concert in New York at Town Hall on February 28, 1948. At LaGuardia airport, before his flight on March 26, 1948, from New York to Prague, Eisler said, "I feel heart-broken over being driven out of this beautiful country in this ridiculous way. . . . I take with me the image of the real American people whom I love."[108] In his suppressed statement to HUAC, Eisler asserted that he had never been politically active in the United States and declared that "music is the only subject on which I am qualified enough to speak." He listed his American activities since 1935, including the eight studio films, the book, and the many concert works he had written in Hollywood. He concluded: "That, Sirs, is my activity in the US, and I must presume that the committee considers it as un-American. . . . I am charged because I am the brother of Gerhart Eisler, whom I love and admire, and whom I defend and will further defend. Does the committee hold the view that brother love is un-American? . . . It is terrible to think what will come of American art if this committee can judge which art is American and which un-American. Hitler and Mussolini attempted just that. They had no success, and the committee to fight un-American activity will also not succeed."[109]

9

Issues of Identity

Ernst Krenek, Eric Zeisl, and Ingolf Dahl

Longing, nostalgia, loneliness, and strife. I would know of no better nourishment for the artist's soul.

—Eric Zeisl

Problems of creative identity, interlocked with questions of personal and professional identity, plagued émigré composers to a greater extent than performers. In America, Arnold Schoenberg turned back to tonality from time to time in hopes of gaining wider appreciation for his music. After Schoenberg's death and the premiere of *The Rake's Progress* in 1951, Igor Stravinsky turned from neoclassicism to serial techniques in his desire to stay current with postwar developments in new music. Even Ernst Toch, who chose seclusion after his 1948 heart attack, was willing to compose in the twelve-tone method and attempted electronic music. But Toch's twelve-tone work still sounded like Toch, and electronic tinkering strained his patience; Stravinsky's twelve-tone music remained recognizably Stravinskyan in its attitudes toward rhythm and style; and Schoenberg's scores remained dense and complex even when tonal. In their art music Mario Castelnuovo-Tedesco and Eugene Zador rejected trends and remained true to their established European creative personae, while Erich Wolfgang Korngold, after his father's death, extended his use of modernist vocabulary for expressive purposes in his last concert works. Any of these composers may well have felt—like Toch—relatively "forgotten" in the concert and opera worlds, with the dramatic exception of Stravinsky, who remained front and center in the public's eye and ear (with the help of others) while living in America.

Difficulties with creative choices and identity were more severe for the younger émigré composers born in the twentieth century than for their elders. In their youth they were acclimatized to the hectic pace of change in European musical styles and attitudes characteristic of the period between the two world wars. After the United States' entry into World War II, as they were faced with a new and widespread American nationalism, the question arose whether émigré artists were European or American. In a 1942 article questioning the inclusion of Schoenberg and Ernst Krenek in an "all-American" program at Royce Hall, critic Alfred Price Quinn wrote in the *B'nai B'rith Messenger,* "My own opinion is that those of foreign birth may be classified as American composers provided they are brought here as children, grow up here, and are educated in the American environment. How one can be considered an American composer who has already become internationally famous as an Austrian, Italian, or Frenchman and has reached mature age before immigrating to America, just doesn't make sense to this writer. Stravinsky, Koussevitzky, and Prokofiev, for example, lived for years in France but I never heard of France claiming them as French artists."[1]

This question festered in the shifting creative decisions and life choices of Ernst Krenek, born in 1900; Eric Zeisl, born in 1905, who suffered lasting depression over the loss of his Austrian roots, which were the source of his creative voice; and Ingolf Dahl, born in 1912, who worked hard to become accepted as an American composer but ultimately questioned this effort. Peter Yates's adventurous "Evenings on the Roof" concerts helped the situation in 1947 by instituting annual programs of works by young Los Angeles composers including émigrés, with no questions about their right to be called Americans. Yates continued this practice until his retirement from the series in 1954, when Lawrence Morton turned his attention as director of the succeeding "Monday Evening Concerts" to the postwar generation of avant-garde European composers. This change of focus exacerbated questions of creative identity for Krenek, Zeisl, and Dahl, as these concerts had been the primary outlet for their music in Los Angeles. Ironically, after the mid-1950s it was their postwar European peers' strong blast of well-propagandized compositional iconoclasm, formed in the traditionless rubble of their war-torn homelands, which created storms in Dahl's, Zeisl's, and Krenek's creative identities.

Ernst Krenek's life in California continued the complex course he had earlier pursued in Vienna, Paris, and Berlin. His record of employment in the United States was fragmented and left him impoverished. After a brief introduction to teaching at the Malkin Conservatory in Boston, he taught for three years at Vassar College in Poughkeepsie, New York. In June 1947 he deserted the financially limited Hamline University in Minneapolis, where since 1942 he had developed the music department, first as its head and then as dean of the School of Fine Arts. He left Minnesota for Southern California at the 1946 midwinter break to "see roses and violets blossoming at Christmas time," he wrote his old friend, Dimitri Mitropoulos, conductor of the Minnesota Orchestra.[2] Krenek's prospects for employment in California were dim. Nothing came of his expectation to be appointed successor to Schoenberg's position at UCLA. Theodor Adorno and George Antheil (who had tried unsuccessfully in 1937 to find him work in films) were not available to assist him and, without the help of their strong personalities, Krenek's diffident demeanor was at a disadvantage. He picked up ill-paid teaching positions where he could.

One of these was at the Southern California School of Music and Art, created to accommodate war veterans returning to complete their educations on the GI Bill of Rights. The school was housed in the Hancock mansion at the corner of Wilshire Boulevard and Vermont Avenue. The music faculty was mainly composed of émigrés: Richard Lert taught conducting; Eric Zeisl taught solfeggio and theory; Thomas Mann's brother-in-law, Klaus Pringsheim, also taught theory. Krenek taught composition, orchestration, and theory—enriching these with his penchant for musicological exploration. He believed strongly that "the study of music history, if properly conducted, should open the student's mind to the amazing varieties of musical expression and make him eventually more tolerant and appreciative of the creative efforts of our own time."[3] He would discuss the fifteenth-century composers Johannes Ockeghem and Jacob Obrecht, sight-reading at the piano their complex scores, explaining the notation, and singing in parts with a few eagerly interested students, while ex-GI jazz musicians played pinochle in the background, ignoring Krenek's teaching. They were biding their time at the private conservatory in order to collect their government allowance, disappearing periodically to play nightclub jobs.[4]

In 1948 Krenek added a part-time position in the evening division at Los Angeles City College, where he found himself teaching large music history classes at $5 per student. Franz Schubert's chamber music and sonatas were new to the class, and because of Krenek's knowledgeable and glowing praise of these works, the students' interest in Schubert grew over many years.[5] By 1949 the GI Bill program was winding down, and the Southern California School of Music and Art was about to fold. Krenek took on a third job teaching in the extension division at Los Angeles State College. At the same time he rejected helping offers from Vienna and the University of Wisconsin at Madison. He wrote to his friend Rudolf Kolisch (who had made the Wisconsin contact for him) that he was working very hard, teaching nine different courses with hundreds of students. "The pay is lousy, so that I can hardly make ends meet. . . . 75% of what I am doing here does not please me either, and it is uncertain too, but at least I live where I have always wanted to live."[6] Krenek then accepted a three-year appointment at the Chicago Musical College, from which he resigned after only a few months. Because he refused to take newly mandated qualifying courses for California teaching accreditation, he soon lost his appointments at both Los Angeles City College and Los Angeles State College. In the mid-1950s and mid-1960s, Krenek held occasional guest professorships at Princeton, Brandeis, the Peabody Institute in Baltimore, and the Universities of Maryland and Hawaii, yet in 1975 he told an interviewer that he felt teaching was not his main business.[7] While his third wife, the composer Gladys Nordenstrom, a graduate student of his from Hamline, worked as a public school teacher, Krenek resorted to writing pop songs under the pseudonym "Teddy Rivera."

The Roof and Monday Evening concerts were the only steady local forum for Krenek's music. Around two dozen of Krenek's chamber works were performed there between 1947 and 1971: two of these were world premieres, three were American premieres, and thirteen were West Coast premieres. Krenek occasionally appeared as pianist or conductor in his own works. He found the programs stimulating and attended them regularly; Frances Mullen's Roof performances in six recitals of the complete solo piano works of Mozart drew his constant attendance at a time when he was composing his Fourth Piano Sonata, op. 114. The operas that Krenek continued to compose to his own librettos, however, found no American outlet, with one exception: a one-act opera titled *Dark Waters,* composed in Los Angeles on an American subject and staged in 1951 by Carl Ebert at the University of Southern California (USC).

Krenek's response to Albert Goldberg's 1950 series of *Los Angeles Times* articles on the émigré composers' attitudes to their American lives was a pithy criticism: "One might say that musical life in America is conducted in a manner which apportions to the more refined, complex, and exacting artistic achievements . . . a smaller degree of significance and respect than they more frequently enjoy in the over-all picture of European public opinion."[8]

In 1952 Krenek completed an autobiographical article, his "Self-

Analysis." His stated intent was "to show why I think that my work will be more important to a future generation than it seems to be to the contemporary world at large." He concluded that "genius could be defined as the sovereign power that cuts across the patterns and creates a new historical situation. . . . I leave the ultimate judgement [about his own genius] to history."[9] In the 1950s he began returning annually to Europe, promoting interest in his music. Gradually commissions, performances, publication with royalties, and awards came from the reconstituted and largely avant-garde musical establishments of Austria and Germany. These helped boost his stature in modern music circles in his adopted country. In California these achievements were reflected in performances of Krenek's new works at the "Monday Evening Concerts," which were programming such trend-setters as Karlheinz Stockhausen, Pierre Boulez, Luciano Berio, and Luigi Nono in Europe, Roger Sessions and Milton Babbitt at Princeton, and the grantees of Paul Fromm's commissioning foundation in Chicago.[10]

During this period Krenek developed a relationship with Stravinsky. In 1957 the older composer was composing his first entirely twelve-tone work, *Threni,* on the biblical text *Lamentatio Jeremiae prophetae,* which Krenek had set in 1942. At this time—while Robert Craft was performing and recording the complete works of Anton Webern—both Stravinsky and Krenek were interested in Webern's serialism. Krenek's new ambition was "to attain the perfection that I saw in the music of Anton Webern; one of the extremely rare cases in history of the complete coincidence of creative imagination and strictly formulated technique."[11] In 1957 Krenek reported to Kolisch on his first piece in "organized time," *Sestina,* op. 161 (a Fromm Foundation commission), the text of which he had written in a serial verse form used in the twelfth century and later by Dante, Petrarch, and others. He also described the shock he felt when he was no longer admitted to the European electronic studios, "because the young gentlemen who have taken over those facilities have decided I am an old fogy who should not be allowed to waste their precious equipment." Embittered, he was "starting again from a 'tabula rasa.'" This rejection was a lasting torment: "I am treated by those contemporaries with whom I feel the strongest solidarity as if I never existed, and to [be] always compelled to [dig] my own channels somewhere else . . . has caused me a great deal of anguish."[12]

The Los Angeles music critics were rough on Krenek as his works were unveiled at the "Monday Evening Concerts." In 1957 an anonymous *Los Angeles Times* critic reported that Krenek's Capriccio for cello and chamber orchestra (written for the Darmstadt summer courses in advanced techniques of composition) sounded like a "rehearsal for a Halloween celebration . . . so macabre and so grotesque were the sounds." In 1961 Albert Goldberg found *The Santa Fe Timetable* (a 1945 choral work) "a tedious and joyless ride on a local that made all stops . . . and was a great advertisement for the superior advantages of air travel." In 1966 critic Burton L. Karson thought *Fibonacci Mobile* "another of those works in which a clinker wouldn't be noticed" and commented that Krenek conducted the chamber ensemble "for all the world as if he were in charge of a Beethoven symphony." In 1967 Walter Arlen found Krenek's *Quintina* (1965–66, for soprano, six instruments, and electronic tape) "more cerebral than effective," yet two years later he discovered a repeat performance of the work, conducted by Michael Tilson Thomas, to be "an impressive essay in mood-giving avant-garde techniques." Martin Bernheimer, reviewing the concert series' celebration of Krenek's seventieth birthday for the *Los Angeles Times,* noted that the audience had "stayed away . . . in droves."[13]

In 1966 the Kreneks moved from Tujunga Canyon in Los Angeles to a home in the desert near Palm Springs. At that time the University of California, expanding to San Diego, called upon Krenek to help constitute a music department there, built around creators rather than scholars. Krenek obliged, bringing his former Hamline students Will Ogden and Robert Erickson to form the faculty and to further recruit Tom Nee, John Silber, and Pauline Oliveros. Such a number of composers was unusual for a new faculty. John Stewart, who was brought in as provost from Dartmouth College to "get all the arts departments started," remarked that the tendency at the time was "to upset hypotheses and expectations." At first there were many performances of Krenek's works, but gradually Krenek's total serialism antagonized San Diego audiences, according to Stewart.[14] Other than being named an honorary fellow, Krenek played no further role at the university.

At age seventy-three, Krenek's anger led him to compose a work that echoed his earlier Schubert mode, the song cycle *Spätlese,* op. 218, set to his autobiographical text of an old man's ruminations on rejection by the young. In the cycle's sixth and final song, an abrupt scenic transition from the vineyard to a desert expresses regret: "Here where under the palm tree the sand whirls away / I, a [transient], sit and write late what should be permanent, / [incautiously] relying on the southern sand / for what northern fog did not grant."[15] Why, given the lack of opportunity and his relatively narrow success in Southern California, did Krenek stay in the area?

At seventy-five he looked back and answered: "I like it here better than elsewhere. . . . True to my style, I settled in the desert where there is no stream whatsoever, not to mention a mainstream. I shall never become an American composer." He explained the zigzags of his creative development as his own personal "knack for maneuvering myself out of the mainstream of contemporary developments." He told *New Yorker* critic Andrew Porter in 1979, "Observers were not quite able to follow my gyrations. But that is my nature. I can't change that. I was always concerned . . . with the idea of freedom of the individual, the liberation from inhibitions and such things."[16]

In 1978 (at age seventy-eight), feeling rejected by much of the musical world, Krenek composed a self-reflective vocal work, *The Dissembler,* to his own text, which takes its title from a Yiddish term for actor, *Versteller.* This twenty-minute work is composed for baritone and chamber ensemble and returns from his recent Schubertian mode to an exaggerated expressionist style. In it Krenek relives phases of his creative life: a scientist pondering and confused by the question, "What is Truth?"; a Catholic praying "to be saved from drifting into the absurd"; and finally himself as an actor making use of differing guises and exiting the stage. Krenek commented that the title "means that someone is not so much acting a part but rather hiding his identity and pretending to be someone else. My dissembler goes through this act in his search for truth":

> *I am an actor—*
> *pretending to be what I am not, acting out what I imagine*
> *I would do were I another self . . .*
> *I do it to exhibit myself, to arouse amazement, to become*
> *famous for how voraciously I devour the essence of those I observe,*
> *how glibly I slip into their empty hulls.*[17]

In this late period of his life, Krenek reportedly confessed to a close friend that he was living a lie in not admitting that he was Jewish. Gladys Krenek twice emphatically denied this account as untrue. Krenek's memoirs, written over a period of ten years to give "a detailed account" of his life and "to be published after a suitable lapse in time," are stored in the Library of Congress. Whether or not they will help sort out the puzzles of his creative as well as personal identity will have to await further inquiry.[18]

In 1982 the Austrian government extended to Krenek the honorary use of an apartment in Schoenberg's former home in Mödling, a Vienna suburb. While relishing the welcome back to his European birthplace, nowhere did Krenek find himself completely "at home," although he had become an

American citizen in 1945. "In Europe I am a composer-in-absence," he said. "I am not an American composer. . . . I just happen to live here."[19] When he was congratulated by friends upon having two homes in locations as desirable as Mödling and Palm Springs, his eyes teared up, and he said sadly, "I don't know where I belong."[20] A similar confusion of identity describes his facile musical output, numbering over 240 works, which covered an extraordinary number of changes in style—perhaps more than in any other twentieth-century composer. He admitted in his "Self-Analysis" that this fact had baffled observers and "surrounded my work with an unusual obscurity—almost anonymity."[21]

In total contrast to Krenek's frustrated attempts to join the postwar avant-garde, Viennese-born Eric Zeisl's composing in America was characterized by homesickness and longing for the past. For Albert Goldberg's 1950 series of articles on "The Transplanted Composer," Zeisl commented:

> I was a finished product of the old world. I could not change this even if I wanted to; it would only mean that I was trying to create from the surface rather than the core of my memories. . . . The artist as an individual is always unhappy and maladjusted to his society. . . . It is this very maladjustment and despair which prompts him to dig so deeply into the hidden resources of his soul, to find there new faith and strength for his weaknesses. The more harassed he is, the stronger the medicines with which he will come up for his own benefit and the benefit of mankind. . . . Longing, nostalgia, loneliness, and strife. I would know of no better nourishment for the artist's soul. . . . America looks only for the image of her own features in art. America can find in my work not her own image mirrored, but she can find there strong medicines against the ills of fate, which I have learnt to brew and which she may need one day. They are hers.[22]

Zeisl had no inclination either to become American or to relate to the disruptive movements of postwar European music.

Like Krenek, Zeisl was a Viennese of Czech background. He was extremely attached to Vienna and to his childhood. His music was bound to the romantic past, nurtured by the works of Mahler and Richard Strauss; as he matured it also reflected his Slavic and Jewish roots. His family's lack of support for his youthful composing led to many fruitless years of psychoanalysis, yet Zeisl could not bring himself to leave Vienna to further his musical career. His early publications of songs (starting at the age of sixteen) gained him notice. In 1934 he won the Austrian State Prize for composition. His ascending curve of prestigious performances by the Vienna Symphony, the Volksoper, the Galimir Quartet, and such singers as Alexander Kipnis and Elisabeth Schumann, however, was thwarted as the Nazis' stranglehold on Vienna's cultural institutions tightened. As a Jew, he was unable to gain further publications. Yet in early 1938 his hopes rebounded. A performance of his comic opera based on Büchner's *Leonce und Lena* was scheduled by Radio Prague, negotiations were under way for a Viennese premiere of the work at the Schönbrunn Palace theater, and he was appointed to teach theory at the Vienna Conservatory. After Austria became "Ostmark" under Nazi rule in 1938, all these promising arrangements were canceled. The day after Kristallnacht (November 9, 1938), Zeisl and his wife Gertrud, a lawyer, escaped to Paris.

"Yours is a tonal nature," said Alma Mahler-Werfel, who met Zeisl in the community of refugees in Paris, admired his music, and befriended him.[23] There, among the émigré community pondering its future, the Hebraic element in Zeisl's composing style became more pronounced. In 1939 Zeisl composed incidental music for a Joseph Roth novel, *Job: The Story of a Simple Man,* performed in memory of its author, who had recently died in Paris. In this dark account, the privations, tragedies, and despair of a Jewish family in prerevolutionary Russia are miraculously relieved when the family takes refuge in America. Roth's story continued to obsess Zeisl for the remainder of his life.[24] After arriving in New York, he continued to develop the story as an opera. He worked with the émigré writer Hanns Kafka, who broke off their collaboration to go to Hollywood as a screenwriter. Zeisl followed Kafka to California in 1941 at the age of thirty-six, hoping to finish the opera and basing the welfare of his family—by then including a baby daughter born in 1940—on a noncommittal invitation from MGM.

The full film contract Zeisl hoped for never materialized; he signed on instead to write a minimum of two minutes of music in assigned "moods" weekly for MGM, at $25 per minute. He also composed and orchestrated forty to fifty FitzPatrick Traveltalks, which paid $100 for each ten-minute documentary. Zeisl was naive in business matters. His lack of experience with English and his inability to break through the competitive resistance from established composers on the MGM staff put him at a disadvantage. From 1944 to 1955 his family's situation remained financially desperate.[25] As a composer, however, he enjoyed his film assignments, creating uncredited "moods" for more than twenty films between 1942 and 1958, including

Lassie Come Home, The Postman Always Rings Twice, Journey for Margaret, Reunion in France, Bataan, Above Suspicion, and two Abbott and Costello comedies. Although he delivered faithfully, MGM neglected to pay the $1,100 owed him for his first eighteen months. Gertrud Zeisl fought the matter out; the payment was made, but Eric's contract ended. In spite of an occasional further film assignment and a few private students, the Zeisls' struggle for existence continued. "In the summer, when private lessons stopped, it was really a matter of life and death. I mean, we didn't have money for the next day's meal," Gertrud remembered. To make ends meet, Zeisl transcribed and orchestrated operetta composer Rudolf Friml's music and took whatever teaching jobs he could find.[26]

Zeisl's connections with other members of the émigré community increased after 1943, when he was asked to compose incidental music for a play by the renowned German playwright Emil Ludwig, *The Return of Ulysses,* which was produced by the Pasadena Playhouse. Ludwig, supported by his non-German royalties and living comfortably in Pacific Palisades, was won over to Zeisl's incidental music by its conductor, Hugo Strelitzer, who befriended Zeisl and premiered his early opera *Leonce and Lena* at Los Angeles City College. At a New Year's Eve party given by Ludwig, Zeisl also met Ernst Toch. The two melancholy Viennese humorists immediately struck up a friendship and sat down at the piano together to improvise comical versions of Viennese waltzes. Like Toch, Zeisl was often unhappy, brooding in bitterness upon his situation. For one thing, California's sun and heat were injurious to his health, and he constantly wished for fog and rain.[27] As was true of Toch, the other side to Zeisl's melancholy was an irrepressible sense of humor. His zest for life, personal warmth, and the expressivity of his music won him close friends. The conductor Fritz Zweig, the Zeisls' neighbor in West Hollywood, recommended Zeisl's song cycle *Kinderlieder* (1933) for a 1948 "Evenings on the Roof" performance, which was so successful it was repeated the same evening. Through Zweig, Zeisl met Otto Klemperer, who enjoyed the young composer immensely. Hanns Eisler, who also admired Zeisl's music, gave him letters of introduction both to film studios and to study with Schoenberg. Zeisl never used the letter to Schoenberg; he felt he would not be able to afford the lessons and, in any case, he did not want to change his own music.[28]

Refusal to change was one of Zeisl's strongest instincts. When Gregor Piatigorsky commissioned a concerto from him, Zeisl refused to suit it to the cellist, who naturally desired a virtuosic part in which to shine. Rather than accommodating Piatigorsky, Zeisl conceived his work as a Concerto grosso (1955–56) in which the solo instrument was part of the ensemble, "an equal among equals." Piatigorsky told Zeisl he was selfish: "You are thinking only of what pleases you and not what you should do to please me," he complained; he never performed the work. Jakob Gimpel was another friend whose solo piano work from Zeisl, the *Sonata barocca* (1948–49), did not please its commissioner. Gimpel reportedly believed the work was too contrapuntal for his performance style.[29] Zeisl harmed himself by lacking diplomacy when approaching important figures in the publishing and performing field. Erwin Stein of Universal Edition publishers and conductors Eugene Ormandy and Bruno Walter were among those angered by his obduracy.[30]

Zeisl's Southern California friendships, however, were warm, enhanced by the pleasant parties given with full Viennese hospitality in the Zeisls' small house. The beds would be removed to accommodate their party guests, who could number from forty to fifty. The Korngolds became their close friends, and the two families vacationed together. Kurt Herbert Adler, who had performed Eric's work in Vienna, would bring the singers and conductors of the San Francisco Opera to visit the Zeisls when the company came to town. Zeisl met conductor William Steinberg, among others, through Adler. Darius Milhaud, who had befriended Zeisl in Paris, visited from Mills College, where he was on the faculty.[31] Social encounters with Schoenberg inspired both the Zeisls.[32] After Schoenberg's death in 1951, the Zeisls became close to Gertrud Schoenberg; their daughter, Barbara, married the Schoenbergs' son Ronald in 1965. Jakob Gimpel introduced the Zeisls to Alexandre Tansman, who in turn connected them with the Stravinskys, whose son Soulima and his wife lived for a time near the Zeisls. Zeisl venerated Stravinsky, and young Barbara studied French with the Stravinsky family's Swiss governess, Mina Svitalski. Of his many composer friends and acquaintances, it was Tansman who most helped Zeisl's return to his own composing, which was often autobiographical. The Tansmans had two small girls close in age to Barbara. After watching the three of them somersaulting in 1944, Zeisl, encouraged by Tansman, composed *Pieces for Barbara*, a piano work that recalled his own childhood and restored the confidence that he had lost in the hostile environment of the film studios.

At the war's end, Zeisl received news of his European family's tragedies. After his wife's death in 1940, Zeisl's father had married her sister. In July 1942 the two of them were deported from Vienna to Theresienstadt, and a few months later they were taken to extermination destinations where all Jews immediately perished.[33] The scope of Zeisl's feelings as he learned of

Eric Zeisl, Alexandre Tansman, and Mario Castelnuovo-Tedesco, ca. 1943. Courtesy of Barbara Zeisl Schoenberg.

the horrors of their deaths is reflected in his setting of the Ninety-second Psalm for soprano solo, chorus, and orchestra. Titled *Requiem Ebraico* and dedicated to Zeisl's "dear father and other victims of the Jewish tragedy in Europe," it is an impressive, memorable work, progressing through mourning to hope.[34] It was commissioned by Rabbi Jacob Sonderling, who also commissioned works by Schoenberg, Toch, and Korngold. In 1945 it was premiered in the First Methodist Church of Hollywood with the assistance of the Santa Monica Symphony. A later broadcast performance of the Requiem gained praise from Toch and others, encouraging Zeisl to compose another choral work, the textless *Songs for the Daughter of Jephtha,* first conducted by Harold Byrns on a program in which Stravinsky's Mass for mixed chorus and wind instruments was given its West Coast premiere.[35]

Zeisl enjoyed teaching courses in theory and composition for the City College's Evening Division, where he had full classes and a wide variety of students, including "window washers from Watts and mechanics from the aircraft industry, musicians from the Philharmonic and young composers . . . the best and the most unschooled." When frustrated with a student's work, Zeisl was heard to say, "If I were you I would jump out of the window, but close it first."[36] Among his students were Leon Levitch, a

Yugoslavian pianist who had studied composition in Italian concentration camps during the war; film composer Jerry Goldsmith; ragtime composer Robin Frost; and Julie Mandel, a composer of musicals for children. Most of Zeisl's serious students went on to study with older composers such as Krenek, Castelnuovo-Tedesco, and Toch. Levitch remembered how this hurt Zeisl, who was possessive about his students.[37]

In 1949 an inheritance from his brother Walter's sudden death enabled Zeisl to take enough time from teaching to compose four sonatas, all of which were premiered in the early 1950s. These were his Violin Sonata, dedicated to Tansman; a Viola Sonata; the *Sonata barocca* for solo piano (dedicated to Zeisl's brother and intended for Jakob Gimpel); and the Cello Sonata (intended for Piatigorsky). In 1953 Zeisl's Second String Quartet was performed by two excellent local quartets, and his *Little Symphony* was published. William Steinberg conducted the "Cossack Dance" from Zeisl's unfinished opera *Job* with the Buffalo Philharmonic in 1949, and Stokowski programmed the same work in the Hollywood Bowl.

Zeisl felt his music was otherwise neglected in Los Angeles by Morton at the "Monday Evening Concerts" and by Werner Janssen, whose orchestra performed much contemporary music. Heated correspondence from Zeisl to both these leaders demanded recognition that was not forthcoming. In the ideologically rigid musical atmosphere of the mid-1950s, which demanded the replacement of tonality by cerebral systems for composing, Zeisl asked Morton if his rejection was because of Zeisl's strong belief in tonality. After receiving a haughty reply, Zeisl responded, "You classify me as a 'lesser' composer. How can you be so sure of it, having heard so little of my work[?] . . . Perhaps by accident you will one day hear some of my music and change your mind about me." Zeisl kept after Morton, who was a near neighbor of his, asking him to visit to hear his chamber music and signing himself "your friend, Eric." Morton's second negative reaction drew an angry reply from Zeisl: "I am very glad that you find my music *not* interesting! The word 'interesting' alone means the death sentence of every good and great music. Music has to come from the heart and soul of a composer [if it] aims to be something much more vital and important than 'interesting.' How come you are so sure of yourself? You are wrong—very wrong! . . . There is always a supreme judge—the *public!* Your public is a special one. It is a selected, discriminating and very educated crowd. Why don't you let *them* decide the issue!"[38]

Zeisl's fiftieth birthday, in 1955, brought some of his work to publication by Doblinger in Vienna, and a gala concert was organized in his honor by his friends in Los Angeles. In the summers of 1958 and 1959 he won grants to continue work on *Job* at the Huntington Hartford artists' colony in Pacific Palisades, an enterprise modeled on New Hampshire's MacDowell Colony. Zeisl's desire to complete *Job* was so strong that he paid Hanns Kafka to finish the libretto.[39] At the time when he lived at the Huntington Hartford compound (where Toch, Roy Harris, and Ingolf Dahl were also composing in small cottages), Zeisl was suffering deep melancholy over his recent diagnosis of heart disease. Work on the opera was difficult; Zeisl completed the orchestration of the second act and began planning the third. Each fall he returned to teaching without a true vacation. At City College there were cuts in his program and problems with tenure that caused him deep aggravation; these may well have involved the same demands for accreditation that irritated Krenek. Zeisl's health suffered increasingly in the heat, and he felt unable to talk over his problems with Leslie Clausen, the head of the music department. After teaching a theory class on the evening of February 18, 1959, he suddenly dropped dead at the college, a complaining letter to Clausen in his pocket.[40] He was only fifty-four.

His family felt that unusually bad luck had dogged Zeisl through most of his life. He had been a prolific song composer in Vienna and was just beginning to achieve mature success at the time of the Nazi takeover. In the culture of his new homeland, he was unable to continue in that vein, and he forged his American works on a basis of passionate tonal lyricism at a time when doing so was considered out of step and retrograde. He minded the criticism and the rejection, but he did not mind being out of step. His was the durable Viennese musical attitude that what he wrote from his heart would find its way to others' hearts.

Ingolf Dahl was twelve years younger than Krenek and seven years younger than Zeisl. His professional training as a musician in Germany had begun just as Nazi rule made his future vulnerable. Although he was known for his integrity as he developed an extraordinarily multifaceted career, Dahl's denial of his Jewish heritage caused him constant inner tension. He claimed in biographical information that he was "a native of Switzerland," or "born in Sweden, raised in Switzerland," or "born in Hamburg of Swedish parents," and that he had come to the United States in 1935 or in 1938 before the major wave of refugees, rather than in early 1939 as one of them. Furthermore, at this time when homosexuality was closeted in the United States, he tried for a period to deny his own nature by marrying Etta Gordon Linick, who had befriended him in Zurich, once she had divorced.[41] He remained married for the rest of his life to this strong, spirited woman, who shielded him in every way, keeping his hidden life and secrets from his closest friends and even from her child, Ingolf's stepson. Otherwise, Dahl was "a musicians' musician," as his most prominent student, Michael Tilson Thomas, described him. He was a brilliant pianist, a conductor of wide-ranging abilities, a respected composer, and a scholar. As a teacher he took on a broad variety of subject matter and teaching tasks with great skill and devotion. His knowledge, abilities, and generosity, combined with his high standards of achievement, were inspiring and lastingly meaningful to his students, many of whom were strongly influenced by him.[42] Along with his many artistic talents, which had shown themselves at an early age, his abilities as a charismatic leader enabled him to contribute generously to the growing Los Angeles musical community.

Dahl's professional beginnings in California demanded all of his considerable powers of adaptability. In 1939 it was natural for him to turn to Europeans in his quest for work. He had written from Switzerland to Klemperer, but his first personal approach to the conductor in California gained him no help, for Klemperer was then ill. While Klemperer was recovering from brain surgery, however, he asked Dahl to organize and to prepare a Los Angeles choir in Beethoven's *Missa solemnis* and a work Klemperer had recently composed. Klemperer remained interested in Dahl's career during the 1940s, attended concerts in which Dahl's works were performed, engaged him to play the harpsichord in a memorable 1945 concert of the Bach Brandenburg Concertos, and praised Dahl to his parents in Stockholm in 1946.

Yet California reality was financially harsh for Dahl at first. The Musicians' Union's residence requirement in Los Angeles postponed for a year the possibility of a living wage performing in studio orchestras. Dahl found himself commuting to San Francisco to play light classics with a teatime orchestra and coaching singers for voice teacher Lazar Samoiloff in Los Angeles. This Russian entrepreneur was also president of the Crescendo Club, an association of local musicians that offered Dahl opportunities to demonstrate his skills as a composer and performer and to make such new friends as the violinist Sol Babitz, the pianist John Crown, and the composer George Tremblay. Tremblay probably acquainted Dahl with Schoenberg's circle of students; in April 1939 Dahl attended one of Schoenberg's classes at UCLA and spoke with the master, whose works he admired.

That same year, an all–Charles Ives "Evenings on the Roof" program impressed Dahl, who was to become an avid supporter of American composers. He adopted Yates's uncompromising attitudes toward programming and committed himself to the Roof concerts, making himself indispensable as a pianist, conductor, composer, scholar, and the first president of the musicians' board. With considerable force, Dahl wrote early articles proselytizing for Yates's cause. In a 1943 article for *Modern Music* titled "Tough Concerts in Los Angeles," Dahl described the nonsponsored, purely cooperative, and inexpensive series, in which excellent performers shared the profits at the season's end. "It is still a bewildering fact," he wrote, "that the city with perhaps the greatest number of important composers per square mile has a public musical 'life' in inverse proportion to its resident and transient talent." "Evenings on the Roof" was "a notable exception," playing for "a discriminating and steadily increasing audience."[43] These opportunities were to be central to Dahl's career for the rest of his life, but they always paid minimally.[44] At Yates's urging Dahl translated into English, with the composer's approval, Schoenberg's *Pierrot lunaire,* conducting it in a 1944 Roof concert that was broadcast.

Dahl's health was plagued by asthma, as it had been since youth. He exercised vigorously to combat this condition. He also kept himself strenuously preoccupied with the demands of his many musical talents. In May and June 1939 Dahl had his first conducting opportunity in America, a two-week theater run of a play for which Ernst Toch had composed incidental music. Dahl grew fond of Toch and later performed Toch's neglected new works to the older composer's total satisfaction and gratitude. Dahl's conducting opportunities increased gradually, including the presentation of opera scenes with the WPA Orchestra, readings with the studio musicians' excellent Hollywood Rehearsal Orchestra, and guest appearances with the Los Angeles Oratorio Society, which had become, under Richard Lert's direction, the official chorus for the Philharmonic. Dahl also performed as a pianist as often as possible: at annual Bach festivals and festivals of modern music sponsored by the First Congregational Church; in an ambitious solo recital (of works by Alexander Scriabin, Schoenberg, Krenek, Arthur Honegger, Hindemith, and himself) at City College; and in a recital with violinist Bronislav Gimpel at the Biltmore Hotel. He played in the orchestra for the Ballet Russe de Monte Carlo at the Hollywood Bowl in the summer of 1942.

Starting in 1941, Dahl began salaried commercial work, at first touring as pianist with Edgar Bergen and his puppets Charlie McCarthy and Mortimer Snerd, an opportunity that forced him to cancel scheduled performances of all of the Beethoven piano trios for a Roof festival. This tour was followed by various engagements between 1942 and 1956 as accompanist and musical arranger for the British comedienne Gracie Fields. To enhance his playing of popular music, he took lessons in swing, but he described swing as "the arch enemy of everything we are, and I believe there is no compromise available."[45] In 1945 Tommy Dorsey signed Dahl as an arranger for his RCA radio program. By then he was hired regularly for film studio work, playing in recording orchestras, arranging, orchestrating, and doing some uncredited film composing. In 1946, his last year of radio work, Dahl was comedian Victor Borge's arranger and conductor on NBC. With all this work in show business, Dahl gradually emerged from poverty, but he believed that his greatest bonus was his friendship with clarinetist Benny Goodman, who appeared regularly on Borge's show. Goodman was in the process of developing his classical technique and style of playing; he and Dahl played chamber music together, and he paid Dahl $20 each for private lessons in the classical repertoire. Their work together led to Dahl preparing several arrangements—including a cadenza in Mozart's Clarinet Concerto—for the "King of Swing."

Dahl's real world, however, was the world of the émigrés, and his longing for Europe was such that for years the only newspaper he read was the *Neue Züricher Zeitung*. He also maintained—as he had in Europe—notes and self-analysis in his diaries, which document his participation in the émigré social network. On one significant day, September 21, 1940, for example, he met Bruno Walter at Klemperer's house and enjoyed hearing them both reminisce about their mentor, Gustav Mahler. That afternoon Dahl also paid a visit to the newly built home of Thomas Mann, who had recently settled in Pacific Palisades. Dahl had known the Mann family in Zurich; the youngest son, Michael Mann, a violist with whom he frequently played chamber music, had been an official witness at his Los Angeles wedding to Etta. Later the same day, Dahl accompanied the violinist Sol Babitz to meet Stravinsky, who had settled in Hollywood only four months earlier. Together Babitz and Dahl played for Stravinsky his Violin Concerto, which Babitz was helping the composer edit. A month later Dahl heard Stravinsky conduct the Hollywood Rehearsal Orchestra in Tchaikovsky's Second Symphony. "He conducts like a dancing demon," Dahl commented in his diary.[46]

Dahl devoted much of his work in America to Stravinsky, who in turn valued Dahl as a respected and trusted colleague. At a Roof concert in January 1942, Dahl played Stravinsky's *Piano-Rag-Music,* which would become a staple of his Roof repertoire. From the following month through

December 1944, Dahl and Babitz together gave six Roof performances of Stravinsky's works for violin and piano. In April 1942 the duo played a private performance for Stravinsky of Ives's Third Violin Sonata, which they were jointly editing for publication at Yates's suggestion and with Ives's financial support. Impressed with Dahl's abilities, Stravinsky hired him (for the sum of $100) in 1942 to make a two-piano arrangement of his recently composed *Danses concertantes,* which had been commissioned by the Werner Janssen Orchestra as a concert work, but which Stravinsky was planning to adapt as a ballet score for George Balanchine. That year Dahl wrote to his family and friends in Europe, "I consider myself exceptionally lucky to get into such close contact with Stravinsky and to have been able to please him by my work. . . . I learned a great deal by doing this and I was more than fascinated to watch the work of one of our greatest masters at such close range."[47] Now clearly one in a long line of Stravinsky's assistants, Dahl began the translation of Stravinsky's Harvard lectures, which were published in 1947 as *Poetics of Music.*[48]

Among Dahl's Stravinsky-related friends was Lawrence Morton, whose work as a music critic in *Script* magazine Dahl admired. Morton was interested in the emerging new music scene in Los Angeles and was particularly enthralled by the presence of Stravinsky. In 1943 he may have helped Dahl publish, in *Script,* his first article on Stravinsky. In it—probably at Stravinsky's request—Dahl challenged Stravinsky's troublesome statement that "music is powerless to express anything at all."[49] Stravinsky encouraged Dahl to write several more articles, as well as the 1944 piano arrangement of *Scènes de ballet* and notes for the 1946 New York premiere of the Symphony in Three Movements (1942–45). While composing the symphony, Stravinsky called on Dahl to hear his latest work, even when it meant interrupting the younger man's Thanksgiving dinner.[50] By 1948 Dahl was performing with Soulima Stravinsky the Concerto for Two Solo Pianos, which the composer had written for his pianist son, and was writing further articles, performance notes, and even reviews of Stravinsky's new work.

Knowing Dahl's expert pianism, in 1944 Stravinsky took Dahl to play chamber music with Joseph Szigeti at his home in Palos Verdes Estates. Dahl returned the next year to read scores of Berg and Busoni with Szigeti; Klemperer was present and reminisced about Mahler and conductor Arthur Nikisch. Szigeti found in Dahl the most accomplished sight-reader he had ever encountered, and he developed a deep admiration for his other talents as well. In 1947 he and Dahl set to work on a collaborative reconstruction of a Bach Violin Concerto in D Minor, which was published in 1959. When he heard Dahl's Divertimento for viola and piano in 1948, Szigeti commented, "I wish you had written it for violin." For his part, Dahl considered Szigeti's recital of the solo violin sonatas of Bach (to benefit the Roof concerts) "one of the summits of experience."[51]

Under the constant and powerful influence of Stravinsky, Dahl had difficulty composing in the early 1940s. He was in close contact with a composer utterly opposed to the emotional and linguistic basis of his own European atonal, expressionistic compositional orientation. One example of this style was Dahl's woodwind quintet, Allegro and Arioso, requested in 1941 by Schoenberg's composition student Adolph Weiss, at that time a bassoonist in the Los Angeles Philharmonic. Although it was solidly constructed and well written for the instruments, when this score placed fourth in a contest for members of the Crescendo Club, Dahl felt "Very depressed . . . alone, lonely, forsaken, frustrated, terribly isolated."[52]

Beyond the conflicts operating in his creative work, Dahl's personal life was in difficulty. His despair, his searches for male companions, and his growing distance from Etta led to a crisis in early September 1942. His successful citizenship examination in January 1943 and his swearing-in the following September, however, made him "unspeakably happy."[53] His self-image as an American was further strengthened in February 1943, when he met Aaron Copland while preparing to play Copland's Piano Sonata in its Los Angeles premiere at a Roof concert in March. Critic Isabel Morse Jones reported in the Los Angeles Times that "Copland arrived with a coterie and seemed pleased with the performance. The audience was eager and vociferous in applause."[54] Copland also heard in private Dahl's Suite for piano, which Dahl was preparing for his debut as a composer in a Roof concert. Parts of the work had been composed years earlier and more recently were supplemented by a final movement titled "Mt. Hollywood." Copland was critical, finding the earlier movements dated and Middle European. Dahl discarded the criticized movements, and his next composition, Music for Brass Instruments (1944) was a complete departure in style, influenced by Copland's Rodeo, which Dahl had arranged into a piano version and played at the Crescendo Club in January 1944. Jaunty American folk dance rhythms and jazz elements emerge in the tonal, cheerful movements of the work, a quintet. It was a success; Morton commented in a review that the composer had "found what he has long been seeking—the matter and manner of his own music."[55] From this time, Ingolf Dahl established himself as an American composer.

Copland accepted Dahl as a friend and colleague, and when in 1944 a tour with Gracie Fields took Dahl to New York City, he was thrilled to be introduced by Copland to the circle of American composers that included Henry Cowell, David Diamond, Harold Shapero, Alexei Haieff, Arthur Berger, and Lou Harrison. He wrote to Morton from New York, "The longer I stay here the more I realize that *everything* happens in the East and that we in the West are just backward hick people."[56] The same tour went on to Boston, where Dahl found a lover who became important enough to him that Etta realized that she must accept the "real Ingolf" and agree to share him. Dahl managed infrequent visits to Boston, and one of his messages to his lover described his own feelings: "Suffer! and sigh for joy that your heart is alive, that you are able to be intoxicated by the pain of its beat, by the size of its agony. You know what it means 'the heart is alive.' It happens so seldom in life. . . . Suffer and sing, even if tears choke your voice." He thought of composing a work to be titled "Elegy," but he did not write it until the last months of his life.[57]

In fact the passions Dahl confessed to his diary were not usually evident in his compositions, which were more often intellectual challenges to himself. In 1944–45 he signed up for Sunday morning master classes in Los Angeles with Stravinsky's close friend and self-exiled colleague Nadia Boulanger. Under her influence he wrote "one of the toughest assignments I ever inflicted on myself," the virtuosic *Variations on a Swedish Folktune* for solo flute, dedicated to his brother Holger.[58]

Dahl found his professional niche when he was appointed in 1945 to the faculty of USC's School of Music to coach opera repertoire, teach film and radio music, and conduct the university orchestra. He was later to teach courses in the music of the Classical and Romantic eras and the first academic course in the music of Stravinsky. He quickly won respect among his colleagues, one of whom remembered his "simplicity, his complete integrity, his incredible musical expertise, and with it all, his beautiful humanity. A man for all seasons, to be trusted and revered."[59] He supervised individual students in conducting, orchestration, and composition, inviting the hardier of them on mountain-climbing expeditions as he "bagged" his 100 peaks and more for a Sierra Club competition. With the student orchestra he performed many works new to the West Coast, particularly by American composers, and he developed a collaborative relationship for the orchestra with "Evenings on the Roof" and the "Monday Evening Concerts." Between 1954 and 1970 this collaboration was enriched by his many performances of Stravinsky's works.[60]

Dahl's increased financial and professional stability spurred further

Ingolf Dahl, 1946. University Archives, University of Southern California.

composing in the late 1940s, resulting in a series of chamber works composed for leading Los Angeles musicians, several of whom were Roof performers. The *Concerto a tre* (1946) for violin, cello, and clarinet, was premiered in 1948 by Benny Goodman with violinist Eudice Shapiro and cellist Victor Gottlieb. Copland aided its publication. Dahl played in the premieres at Roof concerts of his Duo for cello and piano (1946, revised 1948 and 1968) and his Divertimento for viola and piano (1948), as well as the Hymn and Toccata (1947) for solo piano.[61]

A 1949 commission from the well-known saxophone virtuoso Sigurd Rascher for a concerto broadened Dahl's canvas and recognition. The resulting Concerto for Alto Saxophone and Wind Orchestra (1949, revised in 1953) has enjoyed long-lived success. Its premiere by Rascher with the concert band of the University of Illinois at Urbana encouraged Dahl to continue composing for college and university groups. Invitations began pouring in from all over the country to lecture, to demonstrate, to adjudicate, and to appear on panels on behalf of American composers or for the cause of music education. Dahl could not say no to any musical opportunity, for "he longed to extend his recognition beyond the confines of the West Coast," writes his stepson Anthony Linick. Dahl's hectic local activities as a pianist, conductor, and multifaceted teacher brought him recognition in the *Los Angeles Times* as "the resident-musician-extraordinary," but, Linick surmises, "his inability to focus his musical gifts may have cost him the celebrity he thought he deserved."[62] In the summers of 1952, 1953, 1955, and 1956, Dahl was invited to head a study group for amateurs, educators, and general music students at Tanglewood, an opportunity that brought him into contact with important East Coast musicians.

His first sabbatical year from USC (1953–54) was spent—as were his subsequent sabbaticals—in European mountains. When relieved of his academic duties, Dahl paradoxically often felt his creativity paralyzed. His new acquaintance with postwar European composing increased his own insecurities. When Stravinsky began writing twelve-tone music in the 1950s, Dahl felt a sense of betrayal. Nevertheless, he took the same direction—beginning with his *Sonata seria* for piano (1953)—adhering to tonal implications in the construction of his tone rows. By 1960 he was looking back in nostalgia to "a time (*Concerto a Tre,* or Brass Piece) when I was much more naive and surer and happier than I am now." When he became angered by the loss in his latest music of the kind of creative control and responsibility that was crucial to him, he admitted missing "those days of the forties [when] there was almost such a thing as a 'common practice' in the U.S."[63]

In spite of his frustrations, Dahl garnered an impressive array of prestigious awards in the 1950s and 1960s, including commissions from the Los Angeles Philharmonic and the Koussevitzky and Fromm foundations.[64] He completed all his commissions; however, his self-criticism and depressions about his composing were brutal. "If there is anything I *don't* have it is facility. I envy the solid 12-tone writers or neo-classicists their assurance," he wrote a trusted friend in 1960. To escape these creative issues, much of his sabbatical time was given to hiking and skiing, but he also worked long and meticulously to tighten and reshape his compositions. "My music is just between too naive and too difficult," he confessed to his diary in 1962, but the twelve-tone Trio for violin, cello and piano he composed that year (for a joint commission by the Koussevitzky Foundation and the Library of Congress) won compliments. Albert Goldberg, often sour to new music, wrote in the *Los Angeles Times,* "[Dahl] is too ingenious a composer . . . to resort to slavish adherence to serial principles. Rather, he has used the idiom freely and for his own purposes." He remarked on the work's flashes of wit, adroitness, and "technical skill in coping with involved problems."[65]

The continuing complexities of Dahl's personal life contributed to his insecurities and exhaustion. His inner unease also reflected the turmoil in music in that period. As the foundations of his art were assaulted by the new ideas coming from Europe, Dahl took to angrily booing at the "Monday Evening Concerts" programs of his friend Morton, who he felt was chasing worthless musical fashions by favoring the new generation of European iconoclasts. He criticized the early performances of Lukas Foss's *Time Cycle* (1960), which included improvised interludes between movements of written music. Whether or not influenced by Dahl's comments, Foss's later performances of the *Time Cycle* dropped the improvisatory interludes. In his swift development as a conductor in the 1960s, Michael Tilson Thomas enjoyed rising to the challenges presented by avant-garde scores. Dahl's message to his student, after hearing him conduct a work of "graphic" music (notated by visual signs that were inexact as to pitch and rhythm), was a package containing music paper notated with squiggles and blotches, a rubber eraser, a comb, and other objects—mailed to Tilson Thomas with no comment.[66]

In this period, when Dahl's desired professional goals often eluded him, he was overwhelmed by a sense of failure. He chose as his motto *Durchhalten!* (stick with it), and drove himself in a grueling schedule, but on July 30, 1966, he paused to take a significant look back, questioning himself: "All my life I tried to be something I wasn't—[to speak the Swiss-German dialect]—[to] be a Swede—a married man—[to] be a composer—[to] be a twelve-tone composer—is it too late to try to start being who I *am.* . . . Is it too late for 'honesty?'"[67] The story of Dahl's double life, with its almost operatic conflicts and passions, has recently been written about in *The Lives of Ingolf Dahl* by Linick, who learned the facts only after his stepfather's death.

Dahl's final resolution of his own musical identity seems to have come in the last months of his life, with the composition of his *Elegy Concerto* for violin and chamber orchestra.[68] This work was begun as early as 1944. Sorting the sketches in August 1965 at Alt Aussee in the Salzkammergut, Austria, Dahl must have remembered Copland's distaste for his early "Middle European" style, as he noted that the piece was "too Bergian, too chromatic." Yet he made steady progress on the work and on December 29, 1969, found "some soulful music there."[69]

In the summer of 1970—this time on sabbatical in the mountains of Switzerland—both the Dahls were seriously ill. Ingolf was racked by asthma, battling his partially paralyzed diaphragm with an inhalation machine. Etta underwent emergency surgery for abdominal cancer. Her death on June 10, the day after Ingolf's fifty-eighth birthday, struck him as the loss of both his anchor and his chain. A week later he returned to the *Elegy Concerto* and wrote in his diary, "Go away sun, go away nature, go away beauty, don't tease me, torture me." He began again on the score, revising and orchestrating it from its beginning. "I *must* finish!" he wrote on July 20. Before his lonely death on August 7, he composed and orchestrated in short score enough of the concerto that it could be completed by his former student, Donal Michalsky, who found Dahl's defensive—and Ivesian—comments noted in the margins: "Don't wail so much!" "courage—sing it *straight*," and "when 'they' say, as they will, 'how can somebody be so naive,' let 'em!"[70] When Morton—known for his antipathy to emotionalism—saw the score, he described it in a letter to Yates as "impassioned (less cool than [our] Ingolf was wont to be in his late years)."[71] The depth of feeling that Dahl had admitted only to his diaries compelled his return to the chromaticism of his early composing in this dramatically eloquent, often tortured, yet at times almost playful work.

Much of Dahl's music is available through publications and recordings. His struggle with identity shared with Krenek's and Zeisl's the profound strains imposed upon these creative artists not only by emigration but also by adaptation to an alien culture that, although it offered freedom, held its own prejudices. Teaching was Dahl's ladder to national recognition. He had more success in America, and left a more lasting legacy, than did either Krenek or Zeisl. Krenek, having retreated from teaching to desert isolation and bitterness, had little enduring influence upon the musical community in California, although he produced more than 240 works. Zeisl, deeply angry about the plight of his compositions, died at a time when the expressive values that he stood for seemed on their way to obliteration. All three experienced the impact of postwar trends in music as a profoundly disorienting force upon their creative identities.

10

Stravinsky in Hollywood

I never return—I only continue.

—Igor Stravinsky

Igor Stravinsky was certainly the most widely publicized of Los Angeles' musical émigrés. Because he had lived in exile since the Russian Revolution, he was among the most expert at adaptation, and, like many performers, he was able to make preparations for his emigration. As early as 1922, George Antheil got the impression from their frequent conversations in Berlin that Stravinsky was considering whether to "visit America to learn, first hand, just what Americans are like and how far they might be expected to understand his music." Antheil also noted with dismay Stravinsky's way of "invariably turning idealistic musical conversations into mercenary channels."[1] "The man was an electric shock," wrote critic Paul Rosenfeld in 1925, describing Stravinsky on his first American concert tour. Arriving late at a New York rehearsal, the composer seemed "a metallic insect all swathed in hat, spectacles, muffler, overcoat, spats, and walking stick; and accompanied by three or four secretarial, managerial personages." On this three-month tour Stravinsky was impressed by America's energy, and he reported on his return to Paris that he expected America to "bring us the new things in music."[2] In the 1930s, when the Nazis categorized him as a Jewish Bolshevik, blocked his German royalties, banned performances of his works, and displayed his music as "degenerate," Stravinsky toured twice to America, performing with the Jewish violinist Samuel Dushkin and each time making contacts with film studios in Hollywood.

Otto Klemperer, always a strong proponent of Stravinsky's music, performed *Petrushka* in his own initial 1933 appearance with the Los Angeles Philharmonic and for the 1935 season invited Stravinsky to conduct the orchestra in a pair of concerts of his own works, including his Violin Concerto with Dushkin as soloist. Stravinsky's trip to California that year was sponsored by the Los Angeles impresario Merle Armitage, who saw to it that Stravinsky was greeted at the train station by a delegation of musicians from the orchestra and a group of local music lovers. Among the large colony of White Russian émigrés who had settled in Hollywood, Alexis Kall, once Stravinsky's fellow law student in St. Petersburg, extended hospitality—as well as Stravinsky's required secretarial help—in his modest Beverly Hills home.[3] Reviewing the February 1935 Philharmonic performances, Isabel Morse Jones described the composer as sandy-haired, nervous, jerky, and small. "He wears thick goggles and dances on the conductor's stand. His capacity for showmanship is not equaled by any living composer."[4]

On that two-week first visit, as well as presenting an all-Stravinsky recital with Dushkin (arranged by Klemperer), the composer tackled the film industry. Stravinsky met and discussed a film project with Charlie Chaplin—which was never realized. Through Antheil's introduction, he also visited Boris Morros, who negotiated with him about another unrealized film possibility. At MGM Stravinsky was spurned by Louis B. Mayer, but he presented to MGM's chief composer, Herbert Stothart, a miniature score of *Petrushka* and a European photograph of himself, nattily dressed, arrogantly posed with hand on hip, glancing haughtily over his shoulder. Through an interpreter, he and Stothart conducted an interview, during which Stravinsky said that California had made a great impression on him, "an impression of nature and of the artistic life style."[5]

In 1936 Stravinsky was stung financially by the loss of the lawsuit he had brought in France against Warner Brothers for misusing his music for *The Firebird*. He prepared more thoroughly for his 1937 visit to Hollywood—again during a concert tour with Dushkin—partly through a correspondence with Morros at Paramount initiated by his personal manager, Dagmar Godowsky, who had been a silent-screen partner to Rudolph Valentino. A contract between Stravinsky and Paramount was drawn up on March 11. This contract, "effective in Paris and governed by the laws of France" but undated and unsigned, shows a savvy approach and high demands. It stipulated that Stravinsky would compose music for one motion picture on which no other composers would work. It gave him free, full, and unrestricted copyright for his motion picture score and stated that he would select the film scenario from those submitted to him. It allowed further unheard-of freedoms: ten months to write the piano score and one full year to orchestrate it, for the sum of $25,000.[6] Antheil's "On the Hollywood Front" column for *Modern Music* reported in June that Stravinsky had been engaged by Paramount, but in November commented that he "cannot find the right scenario."[7]

Stravinsky was forced by tuberculosis to cancel his tour to the United States in the winter of 1938. That September Mussolini and Hitler met in Munich and then forged their agreement for mutual military support in May 1939. In this uncertain period, faced with extreme financial needs due to illnesses in his immediate family, Stravinsky persevered in film studio negotiations.[8] In 1938 he was intrigued by the idea of composing for Disney's animated cartoons. He left Europe for a lectureship at Harvard on September 27, 1939, three weeks after France had declared war on Germany. In his December 1939 visit to Hollywood, he heard the score of *The Rite of Spring* cut, the order of its movements shuffled, and the music badly performed for Disney's forthcoming full-length animated film, *Fantasia*. He had lost control of the work in his contract with Disney, owing to the fact that the United States had not signed the Berne Convention on copyright. Yet Stravinsky kept his Hollywood options open; George Balanchine, accompanying him to Disney's prerelease screening, noted that Stravinsky did not object at the time to the changes made to his score or the use to which it was put.[9] In October 1940, after the success of Germany's spectacular campaign to conquer France, Stravinsky rewrote for Disney part of his 1916 burlesque *Renard*.[10]

Vera Sudeikin, who had been his mistress since 1921, left France for the United States in January 1940, and, during Stravinsky's residence as the Norton Lecturer at Harvard, they were married in Massachusetts. In May they traveled by train to Los Angeles and signed a contract for a small house in Beverly Hills on June 1, the day Vera recorded in her diary the bombardment of Paris and her tears over the newsreels. On a concert trip to Mexico in July and August, they filed U.S. citizenship papers; when they returned on August 9, Vera noted that Los Angeles felt like home. Jones commented in the *Times* that "[Stravinsky] has come to Southern California in chaos and turmoil of mind and found quiet."[11] Stravinsky, whose contract with his German publisher, Schott Music, had expired, became further immersed in studio negotiations. In spite of his earlier suit against Warner Brothers, he discussed appearing as himself in their film about George Gershwin.

Financial need apparently compelled Stravinsky to compose music for several film projects before contract details were settled and signed. In 1942 Miklós Rózsa observed him composing film music "in his immaculate hand, on paper where he had drawn his own staves with a little gadget of his own devising," before a contract had been drawn up for *The Commandos Strike at Dawn,* an MGM film on the invasion of Norway. Because it was his first attempt to write a film score, Stravinsky requested advice from his friend Alexandre Tansman, then on the staff of MGM and earning a comfortable living. Stravinsky demanded a larger orchestra than MGM would allow, was turned down by the studio, and told San Francisco critic Alfred Frankenstein in an interview, "Film music? That's monkey business, and for monkey business my price is too high."[12] Stravinsky later published the music he had composed as an orchestral concert suite, *Four Norwegian Moods.*

"Monkey business" continued in spite of its frustrations to Stravinsky. Intrigued in 1942–43 by a proposal that he compose the score for Lillian Hellman's wartime script about the defense of a small Russian village (it was eventually produced as *The North Star,* with an Academy Award–nominated score by Aaron Copland), Stravinsky created music that—after contract negotiations failed—eventually became *Scherzo à la russe* for Paul Whiteman's popular big band. Aldous Huxley, by 1943 a neighbor and close friend of the Stravinskys, was working at Twentieth Century-Fox with director John Houseman on a script for Charlotte Brontë's *Jane Eyre.* Huxley may have proposed Stravinsky as composer for this film to Orson Welles, who was to portray Rochester. Before contract negotiations with Fox were broken off, Stravinsky had already composed music that he then transformed into the central Eclogue in the *Ode,* commissioned that year in memory of Serge Koussevitzky's wife, Natalie.[13] Franz Werfel's suggestion that Stravinsky compose for the film of his best-selling novel, *The Song of Bernadette,* drawn from Werfel's experience of escape through the Pyrenees from occupied France, again enticed Stravinsky into premature film composing in 1943. His music for the "Apparition of the Virgin" became the middle movement of his war-inspired Symphony in Three Movements (1945).[14]

Considering this complex history of futility and frustration, in 1946 Stravinsky dismissed his film experiences angrily when he told Ingolf Dahl, who was teaching a new course on film music at the University of Southern California (USC), "Film people have a primitive and childish concept of music."[15] Nevertheless, in 1956 Stravinsky was willing to receive $10,000 for adapting *Petrushka* for a twelve-minute animated television cartoon, work that he admitted in a letter to Nadia Boulanger was "reprehensible, but understandable, too, considering the taxes that are so pitilessly gouged from us." (In 1963 he won the $50,000 Wihuri Sibelius Prize and became a wealthy man obsessed by income taxes.)

During his early years in Hollywood, possibilities in ballet were naturally more to Stravinsky's liking than were his searches for sources of income in film. During Stravinsky's exploratory 1937 visit, Klemperer discovered that he could not get permission to perform Stravinsky's works without the composer inserting himself, and receiving a fee, as conductor. Klemperer therefore offered him the Los Angeles Philharmonic for a full production of his 1911 ballet *Petrushka,* which the composer conducted in the enormous Shrine Auditorium on March 12 and 13. With Alexis Kall's assistance, the Theodore Kosloff Ballet collaborated in the production. Kosloff, trained in the Moscow Imperial Theater School, had been a member of Sergey Diaghilev's Ballets Russes. In Hollywood he had turned to an acting career in the silent-film era. With the advent of sound in film he had returned to dance, established a ballet school, and continued in films as a choreographer. Arnold Schoenberg's assistant, Gerald Strang, wrote in *Modern Music* that he found the Kosloff Ballet's performance of *Petrushka* "amateurish and formless. Done in the Hollywood manner with 250 lavishly costumed dancers cluttering up the huge stage, the pointedness and irony of the score were lost in tasteless vulgarity. The affair unfortunately added nothing to Stravinsky's stature as composer or conductor."[16]

When Stravinsky settled in Hollywood in 1940, he worked with the distinguished Russian-born ballet soloist and choreographer Adolph Bolm, whom he had known since Bolm had danced in Diaghilev's production of *The Firebird.* After a tour with Diaghilev's Ballets Russes, Bolm had remained in the United States choreographing for the Metropolitan Opera in New York and the Chicago Civic Opera. In 1928 he had choreographed and danced Apollo for the world premiere of Stravinsky's *Apollon musagète* (a commission from Elizabeth Sprague Coolidge) at the Library of Congress. The same year Bolm had settled in Hollywood to appear in and choreograph for films. In 1933 he helped found and establish the San Francisco Opera Ballet and its affiliated school. Bolm returned to Hollywood in 1937, and in August 1940 his presence and connections on the West Coast enabled Stravinsky to conduct at the Hollywood Bowl his *Firebird* Suite (recently reorchestrated, so that he would be able to secure its copyright) in a production choreographed by Bolm and designed by the Russian émigré

Nicolai Remisoff, a former member of Diaghilev's *Mir Iskusstva* circle in turn-of-the-century Russia.[17] Jones proselytized in the *Los Angeles Times* for the establishment of a local company that would present all of Stravinsky's ballets under Bolm's leadership. In a preview for the Bowl event, she wrote hopefully, "Adolph Bolm [and Stravinsky] have seen the great days of Russian art disintegrate before their eyes and have re-formed it in essence and in high tension in Paris and now in America."[18] Her vision of a local ballet using the internationally known talents at hand did not materialize.

Another welcome presence in Hollywood in the late 1930s and early '40s was that of Balanchine. He had produced a Stravinsky festival at the Metropolitan Opera House during the composer's 1937 visit and subsequently brought his American Ballet dancers to Hollywood in 1938 to work in films. He had married his ballet star, Vera Zorina, and while she developed her movie career he spent much time in Hollywood collaborating on new works with Stravinsky. In his book *Stravinsky and Balanchine*, Charles Joseph describes their wartime artistic companionship: "It was a casual time, a time for leisurely dinners, neighborhood walks, and hours of conversations about music. Balanchine saw the composer almost daily."[19] Balanchine's suggestion that Stravinsky compose *Tango* (1940, originally for piano); his 1941 choreography of the Violin Concerto; their 1942 collaboration on the *Circus Polka* for Ringling Brothers and Barnum and Bailey (choreographed for fifty circus elephants and fifty beautiful girls, with Zorina riding the lead elephant in the premiere performance at Madison Square Garden); and the *Danses concertantes* (1941–42, a ballet in 1944)—all were the outcome of this growing artistic relationship. The collaboration continued in infrequent but more intense meetings in 1946–48 and then again in the 1950s, as they worked on *Orpheus* (1948) and *Agon* (1957), both commissions from Lincoln Kirstein.

Stravinsky believed that the Southern Californian climate was good for his impaired health. Robert Craft has frequently described the dramatic changes his second marriage and Californian life wrought upon Stravinsky. The European Stravinsky had presented himself as a figure of unquestionable authority and had dressed in the latest cosmopolitan fashion. In California he turned upon occasion to denim, sandals with socks, conviviality, and impish wit. Hollywood society was delighted with him. The anti-Semitism he had expressed in the 1930s vanished; the musicians and actors he encountered and worked with in California were predominantly Jewish, warmly friendly, and unquestionably talented. In the 1940s the Stravinskys' social calendar was so filled by film star invitations that Vera (and Craft) felt the need to fight them off.[20] Their network of acquaintances among the émigrés and exiles was rich: the Werfels introduced them to the Manns, the Tochs, the Reinhardts, and the Rubinsteins; the Tochs introduced them to Szigeti, who frequently invited Stravinsky to his home in Palos Verdes for chamber music, at times joined by Benny Goodman. Szigeti and Stravinsky performed and recorded Stravinsky's *Duo concertant*—an experience Szigeti found "delightful if strenuous."[21] The Tansmans introduced the Stravinskys to the Zeisls and the Castelnuovo-Tedescos, with both of whose families they maintained cordial relationships. Artur Rubinstein, to whom Stravinsky had dedicated his *Three Movements from "Petrushka,"* the ballet's original pianistic core, commented that Stravinsky had one of the most interesting of personalities and was "endowed with a considerable charm and wit. I am proud to say that our vastly divergent points of view about musical matters never marred our warm friendship." Sergey Rachmaninoff bought a house in Beverly Hills at the time of his retirement in 1942, and, after his wife became friendly with Vera at the local farmers' market, invited the Stravinskys to dinner with the Rubinsteins. Rubinstein remarked that this meeting of such divergent composers seemed inconceivable, but that after three vodkas and dinner, the two masters became so happily engrossed in imagining the immense fortunes they might have earned in Russian royalties denied them by the Soviet Union that they parted in hearty friendship.[22] Stravinsky also continued his long-standing friendship with Klemperer through the conductor's difficult times. In the 1940s he and Vera visited the Klemperers first in Bel Air, later in their modest West Los Angeles dwelling, invited them for teas and dinners, and attended the conductor's concerts as he gradually recovered his powers.

A favorite gathering place for the émigrés was the farmers' market on Fairfax Avenue and Third Street, which reminded them of European markets. There the Aldous Huxleys and the Stravinskys became inseparable friends in the mid-1940s. Stravinsky looked upon Huxley as a guiding spirit; Huxley's profound understanding of and interest in music was rewarded by this lively contact. (Huxley had been a music critic in 1921–22 in London; music remained an important part of his life and his writing.) The two couples introduced Wystan Hugh (W. H.) Auden to the market when he came to work with Stravinsky—at Huxley's suggestion—on *The Rake's Progress* in February 1947. Through Auden, the English novelist Christopher Isherwood, then working as a writer at MGM, joined the circle in 1949 and remained a close friend of the Stravinskys until they left Los

Angeles twenty years later. Isherwood was not interested in music, but he found Igor "really one of the most uninhibitedly sweet people I know." The social times with Isherwood seemed to revolve around alcohol, about which Vera complained more and more frequently, while Isherwood observed in his diary that both the Stravinskys drank too much.[23] "Scotch was one of the dearest and most faithful friends of [Stravinsky's] life," observed Lawrence Morton, who became a close intimate of the Stravinsky family.[24]

America's entry into the war put a brake on Stravinsky's widespread conducting travels. He did not intend to teach, and his one elderly private pupil died suddenly after two years of lessons, which were scheduled whenever the Stravinskys' expenses seemed overwhelming. Stravinsky joined ASCAP but wondered whether it was worth the trouble when his first check for only $60 arrived. Klemperer's resignation from the Philharmonic left an artistic vacuum from which other European composers also suffered. The Philharmonic and Hollywood Bowl audiences remained hostile to new music. In September 1940 the Hollywood Rehearsal Orchestra invited Stravinsky—on the first of several such occasions—to conduct them in his Violin Concerto, with Sol Babitz, who had left the Philharmonic in 1937 to play for Twentieth Century-Fox, as soloist.[25] Babitz had been born in Brooklyn; his parents were Russian Jews. He was largely self-taught as a violinist, yet he had studied in Berlin with Carl Flesch in the early 1930s. During that time he had been present at the 1931 Berlin Radio Orchestra premiere of Stravinsky's Violin Concerto, conducted by the composer, with Dushkin, who had arranged its commission, as soloist. Soon after the Hollywood reading, Stravinsky, furious at mistakes in the published score, set to work with Babitz on corrections, fingerings, and bowings, unwilling to wait for Dushkin's help.[26] Babitz introduced Dahl to Stravinsky the same month, and the two served many collaborative functions for Stravinsky. Babitz published two Stravinsky interviews in 1942 and 1948, but the violinist was a crusty character who wrote in the interviews what *he* wanted to say; critic Alfred Frankenstein, quoting Babitz in a 1942 article on the new *Danses concertantes,* remarked that "Stravinsky said nothing remotely similar during the hour that I spent with him over the score."[27] Dahl subsequently took on the chores of expressing Stravinsky in writing until the 1948 arrival of Robert Craft.

The Los Angeles critics' responses were tepid to the February 1941 Philharmonic performances of Stravinsky's recently completed Symphony in C and other new works. The program was received "attentively but without demonstration," wrote Jones. *Jeu de cartes* (composed for Balanchine and the American Ballet in 1936) seemed to her "a brittle work of the new order, without sufficient melodic interest or heart interest. . . . Probably this is to-morrow's music. *Capriccio,* although more than ten years old, is of today. It is exhilarating, joyous, brilliant, provocative and young." The orchestra rose at Stravinsky's entrance and in performance gave him "everything he asked for. The fact remains that he did not ask for enough dynamically and, in the symphony at least, there were lagging tempi. . . . One mustn't listen to this new music with expectancy. There is no build-up. Stravinsky scorns effects."[28]

Because composition of the Symphony in C had spanned the deaths in Europe of his daughter, first wife, and mother, his own illness, his Harvard lectures, and his move to Los Angeles, there were several versions of the work. In November 1941 Stravinsky needed help with corrections in the score while he turned his attention to composing *Danses concertantes* (1941–42) for Werner Janssen's orchestra—and, ultimately, for Balanchine. Nadia Boulanger, since 1912 Stravinsky's Parisian friend and an advocate of his music, was happy to make herself available. In 1937–38 and 1938–39 she had been a visiting lecturer at the Longy School of Music in Cambridge, Massachusetts, and after escaping occupied France in November 1940 she accepted a three-year contract at Longy to teach theory and composition and to conduct a choral group. She spent little of the term of her contract in Cambridge, however. During the occupation of Paris, Boulanger had taken shelter in the French country home of Arthur Sachs, the Goldman Sachs investment banker, art collector, and philanthropist, who had known Stravinsky since 1924. In America, Boulanger spent much of the war period with the Sachses in Santa Barbara. Vera Stravinsky's diaries record frequent occasions from September 1942 through June 1945 when Boulanger worked with Igor or visited them in Los Angeles.[29] The Stravinskys enjoyed their many visits with Boulanger and the Sachses so much that in 1943 they contemplated moving to Santa Barbara. During this period, Arthur Sachs commissioned for the New York Philharmonic Stravinsky's Symphony in Three Movements, sometimes called the "War" or "Victory" Symphony.

Beside correcting Stravinsky's scores, Boulanger helped him write articles, lectures, and letters. She agreed to teach a select group of petitioning Hollywood musicians, who included Dahl and Babitz. She later remembered how happy he was when he was asked to write the *Circus Polka:* "When I went to California to see him, he'd just finished writing it. . . . He was euphoric at having succeeded in writing *Circus Polka*. . . . It had so entertained him." Along with this example of his whim, Boulanger also noted the rigor in his manuscripts: "This is a man in full control."[30] In December 1943 Boulanger, with Bolm as interpreter, gave an interview to critic Jones in the Stravinskys' hillside Hollywood home. "I came out [to California] for a month and am staying a year, I have some thinking to do," said Boulanger. "The difficulty in America is that you have the talent, but the training for composition begins too late. The gifted children of 8 and 9 should be in conservatories. . . . It is too late to begin as an adult." In answer to a question from Jones, Boulanger placed Stravinsky "nearer the masters of the 13th century than those of the 19th or 20th." In her article Jones again complained to her readers, "Here are two of the most interesting figures in music today, living in Southern California by their own choice. Why don't we make use of them?" The question remained unanswered, and in January 1946 Stravinsky expressed his dismay at the void he felt when Boulanger returned to Europe.[31]

Dahl was called upon for intimate involvement with the composition of the Symphony in Three Movements. Stravinsky had begun work on it in 1942; in 1943 he had worked primarily on revisions of *The Rite of Spring*. After the premiere of the symphony on December 28, 1945, Dahl wrote a long article for *Modern Music* titled "Stravinsky in 1946." He found "baffling surprises" in the fact that the symphony seemed to recall the spirit of *Les noces* and the *Rite*. "Stravinsky is very anxious for the listener to hear that he did not travel backwards into his own past, even though many passages of the new work seem to recall it," Dahl wrote. Interviewing the composer, he captured Stravinsky's abrupt, terse language: "I never return—I only continue. . . . People always expect the wrong thing of me. They think they have pinned me down and then all of a sudden—*au revoir*. . . . The form of my earlier works, *Sacre* [*Rite*] for instance, is not very developed. What a difference between that and the first movement of this symphony. The dialectic development of form has been growing in me for years, and it is just the realization of such a form in this work that makes me feel I am very far away from my earlier days. . . . [This new work] is the biggest form I ever approached." In response to Dahl's questions about his creative progression, Stravinsky insisted that each of his works followed its own biological point of departure, "just as asparagus doesn't grow like radishes." He gave Dahl no technical hints, however, about the work in question: "It is not up to me to explain and judge my music. That is not my role. I have to write it—that is all." Dahl concluded that Stravinsky trusted to the guidance and logic of his instinct, as the composer continued, "When a dog is on a track which excites him it will make the saliva run in his mouth—likewise my mental saliva will be running when I feel myself on an interesting and exciting track, which thus proves to be the right track." Dahl finished the interview by asking Stravinsky whether the language of the work represented a new departure for the composer, who replied that he could not answer that question; "I do not have any ultimate view point of composition and when I write my next symphony it will then be an expression of my will at that moment. And what that will is going to be I do not know now. I wish people would let me have the privilege of being at least a little bit unconscious. It is so nice sometimes to go blind, just with the *feeling* for the right thing!"[32] How like Schoenberg Stravinsky seems in this statement.

Yet Stravinsky was speaking at a time when his disciples and Schoenberg's were enemies in Los Angeles musical circles. The younger generation, immersed in war films and propaganda, found it only natural to escalate the longstanding feud between the composers on behalf of their musical beliefs. Schoenberg student Leon Kirchner described this in an interview: "Well I remember that there were rival gangs that roamed the beaches and canyons of Santa Monica. . . . These gangs centered about deities like Stravinsky or Schoenberg. . . . Both were commissioned (with others) to write a work based on *Genesis*. At the first rehearsal these two towering figures in the twentieth—or any century's—music appeared. They veered off like two opposing forces. They were cathode and anode, and with them were their surrounding bodies or antibodies following them into their separate zones or territories. Neither group looked at the other."[33]

The American-born members of the two "camps" (as they referred to themselves) reported later that the older European disciples, who remembered the original exchange of insults between the two composers in 1925–26, were the leaders in the rivalry. Since then, Schoenberg and Stravinsky had ignored each other and each other's music. Their animosities may have reawakened in 1939, after Ernst Krenek published his book *Music Here and Now*, in which he wrote, "In the beginning of my career, in the early 1920s, I simply used atonal material because it seemed to be the most radical I could find. . . . Psychological change was the decisive cause of my change of style. [In 1925–29] I came in closer contact with French music and with Stravinsky . . . [and] had the feeling better and gayer times would come. . . .

[After composing *Jonny spielt auf* I] conducted polemics against Schoenberg and twelve-tone technique."[34]

Leonard Stein, discussing the history of the feud in an article titled "Schoenberg and 'Kleine Modernsky,'" reported that the appearance in California of Nadia Boulanger strengthened the numbers of Stravinsky's followers. Gerald Strang believed that the cosmopolitan character of both Stravinskys attracted "a far wider variety of personalities and backgrounds and people," whereas, because of his asthmatic bronchial problems, Schoenberg rarely went out in the evening, and after his retirement from UCLA was "not in a position to have much influence on public taste nor to have much exposure."

Ingolf Dahl bridged the chasm by translating into English and performing Schoenberg's *Pierrot lunaire* for "Evenings on the Roof." As a member of the Stravinsky camp, the composer-pianist Mel Powell, Dahl's Hollywood colleague and later dean of the California Institute of the Arts, kept Schoenberg adherents Adolph Weiss and violinist Adolph Koldofsky "at arm's length." Powell remembered the toll these differences in aesthetic positions took on professional and personal relationships: There was little mingling between the camps, and Ernst Toch, who represented a middle position, "detested and loathed the whole thing . . . the cultism."[35] Adherents to Toch's position outside the Schoenberg/Stravinsky fray were conservatives such as Mario Castelnuovo-Tedesco and his student Leon Levitch, who felt ridiculed, along with the Austrians Eric Zeisl and Ernest Gold, for continuing to write tonal music.

The celebrations of Schoenberg's seventy-fifth birthday in 1949 briefly broke his isolation. That October Stravinsky attended the season's opening concert at the Wilshire Ebell Theater of Harold Byrns's Los Angeles Chamber Symphony Orchestra and saw Schoenberg receive the audience's standing tribute after the performance of his Chamber Symphony No. 1, op. 9. By this time Craft was in residence, urging his interests in serial music upon Stravinsky, who, Craft tells us, "wanted to be influenced."[36] About Stravinsky's "conversion" to using the twelve-tone method after Schoenberg's death, Stein observed that "Stravinsky was always the embodiment of 'modernism' in both its most fashionable and most characteristic aspects. . . . [He] did, indeed, make serialism fashionable," and "when the Princeton crowd—or Babbitt & Co.—learned directly from Stravinsky about twelve-tone writing, and when in 1957 Stravinsky approved of Boulez, *suddenly* academia discovered serial music."[37]

That same year Dahl conducted the USC student orchestra in Stravinsky's "Dumbarton Oaks" Concerto. When Dahl remarked to the composer how the previously difficult rhythms of the piece had worked their way into the blood of young musicians, Stravinsky responded thoughtfully, by then distressed by the neglect of Schoenberg: "That was written in 1937–38, 20 years ago, like the light of a star hitting the earth after 20 light-years. But the starlight *does* arrive. Can you imagine the *loneliness* of the man who invents something new and does not live to see the time when the light arrives?"[38]

In 1947 Stravinsky signed a publishing contract with Boosey & Hawkes that guaranteed him an annual retainer of $25,000. The publisher acquired twenty-five of his Russian-published works, which Stravinsky set to revising so that he could register new copyrights. He was able to embark upon his opera *The Rake's Progress* with no commission. With war restrictions on travel lifted, he began touring again to conduct his own works with frequent tremendous success, and he demanded increasingly fat fees.

In their first years in California, the Stravinskys had reveled in the "sun, the climate, the beautiful countryside, the charming homes. Everything is marvelous here, and life is less expensive than elsewhere." Their contributions to the war effort included raising noisy chickens and growing a vegetable garden. In 1941 and 1942, the peace of walks in Santa Barbara and in "the wonderland of crystal clear air and heavenly quiet" at the Mount Wilson Observatory above Pasadena were recorded in Vera's diary.[39] But after the war much changed locally for the Stravinskys. Boulanger and the Tansmans, who considered themselves exiles, returned to France. Franz Werfel died in 1945. Hanns Eisler's deportation in 1948 drew Stravinsky's sympathetic sponsorship of a farewell concert in Los Angeles, although his lawyer advised him not to attend the event because of the increasingly charged Cold War political environment.[40] Smog became an increasing torment, particularly on south-facing hillsides like the Stravinskys', where their second home (bought in 1941) above Sunset Boulevard in Hollywood looked out over the often invisible Los Angeles basin. In August 1949 Craft, in his first full year working as Stravinsky's assistant, wrote to his sister about the city, "I hate the sprawl, the vacant lots, the lack of a center to this godless horror." That November and December Stravinsky wrote to his friend Arthur Sachs that, because so many interesting people had left, for him Hollywood was now dead; furthermore, he observed, "All musical enterprises here are in an ultraprecarious situation at the moment. Only large and long-established organizations, with their committees, patrons, and subscriptions, can survive. And, unfortunately, these societies offer only the most popular repertory. Therefore we are obliged to count on the heroic sacrifice of some apostles along the lines of Robert Craft."[41] Craft, age twenty-six, disbanded the New York concert organization that had cost him severe financial losses and received poor critical reviews and moved to Los Angeles to commit himself to assisting Stravinsky.

Why, with these complaints, did Stravinsky—and Craft—remain in Los Angeles for another twenty years? The answer lies in their needs as artists and in the extraordinary but uneven growth of musical sophistication in Los Angeles, to which both Stravinsky and Craft made important contributions and from which both benefited. Although the situation for new orchestral music had deteriorated in the 1940s and there was still no enduring local professional opera or ballet company, Dahl saw to it that Stravinsky's works appeared prominently in the "Evenings on the Roof" repertoire from 1943 on. Through Dahl's and Babitz's involvement, Stravinsky discovered these chamber concerts in 1944, when he attended a program of English Renaissance keyboard works combined with works by Mozart (a violin sonata played by Babitz), Haydn, and Brahms. The experience reminded him of his early joy in hearing concerts that combined new and old music in St. Petersburg. In 1953, after a program that combined works by Giovanni Gabrieli, Mendelssohn, and Monteverdi, conducted by Craft, he expressed his pleasure by composing and dedicating "to Peter Yates, who kindled his roof in the Evenings for listeners so cool in the day," his *Three Songs from William Shakespeare*. Stravinsky wrote to his publisher, "I dedicated these songs to Evenings on the Roof, a Los Angeles organization which I greatly admire. It is made of the best musicians to be found anywhere, who are willing to accept nominal and ridiculous fees for the sake of music itself. The founding and acting brain of the whole thing is Peter Yates who is really worthy of every praise. I wanted to give them some proof of my sympathetic understanding."[42] Many of the works Stravinsky subsequently produced in Los Angeles were composed, revised, or arranged with these chamber concerts and their performers in mind. Stravinsky essentially found a workshop for himself through this arrangement, while Craft, at first with Yates's encouragement, was able to find in the Roof concerts an outlet for his conducting ambitions.

The Roof concerts had already programmed more of Schoenberg's music than any other single American organization. After Schoenberg's death, Yates mounted an unprecedented four-concert retrospective series of the composer's oeuvre in 1952. Craft eagerly accepted conducting assignments for these concerts: he led performances of Schoenberg's Serenade, op. 24, Suite for Septet, op. 29, *Ode to Napoleon*, Wind Quintet, and *Pierrot lunaire*. This new exposure to Schoenberg's works produced a crisis for Stravinsky. Craft tells the story of Stravinsky's breakdown on a trip to the Mojave Desert a week after being present at all the rehearsals as well as the performance of Schoenberg's Septet Suite. Stravinsky wept, "saying he was afraid that he could no longer compose. . . . He referred obliquely to the powerful impression that the Schoenberg piece had made on him. . . . This event was the turning point in his later musical evolution," and his conversion to twelve-tone composing.[43] It is noteworthy that although Stravinsky usually attended Craft's rehearsals and performances, he did not attend Craft's world premiere of Schoenberg's 1925 inflammatory anti-Stravinsky cantata *Der neue Klassizismus,* translated into English as *The New Classicism*.[44]

After Yates's retirement from the Roof concerts in 1954, his successor, Lawrence Morton, needed a lure to keep both the musicians and the audience coming when the series lost its earlier name and became "Monday Evening Concerts." The lure proved to be Stravinsky, and the agent to arrange Stravinsky's "major association" with the concerts was Craft.[45] Stravinsky's works appeared in the series every season from 1954 until he and Craft left for New York in 1969. Craft dominated as conductor in that period, leading five programs out of twelve in Morton's first season (1954–55) and four each season from 1956 until 1959, when Morton went to Europe on a Guggenheim Fellowship to research a book on Stravinsky. In Morton's absence, Craft demanded to conduct larger works, which were not only expensive for "Monday Evening Concerts" but augured problems with the musicians' union, which allowed the special rehearsal rates only for chamber music. Moreover, Craft was "double stringing"—using concert rehearsals to prepare for recording sessions, which was forbidden by the union. Stein and Dahl, managing the concerts for Morton, found that it was necessary to cut Craft's concerts to one or two a season to maintain the special relationship with the musicians' union.[46]

Stravinsky, using these concerts as a laboratory, could remain in charge as new works, translations, or new instrumentations of his early works were readied for premieres. "I can watch the job while it is in progress," he wrote his publisher. This situation contributed to Stravinsky's creative decisions; his earlier oeuvre contained few works for a variety of smaller chamber ensembles, and so now he arranged songs and piano pieces for instrumental and vocal combinations that would fit Morton's programming plans and budget. (Stravinsky never charged the series a fee for performing his works; in fact he made regular helpful financial donations as the years wore on.) Stravinsky's anxiety that "the only true performances [of my works] can stem from myself" was assuaged by his use of Craft as conductor, and Craft's conducting desires were satisfied in ways he had not found possible in New York.[47]

By preparing the world premiere of Stravinsky's *In memoriam Dylan Thomas* for Morton's 1954–55 sold-out opening concert, in which Stravinsky's close friend Huxley contributed a brief and moving eulogy for the poet, Craft gained Morton's confidence to the point that the younger man was often in control of programming. There would be eleven more Stravinsky world premieres—half of them new versions of earlier works—at the "Monday Evening Concerts" before Morton's retirement. Stravinsky's avid interest in the works of Heinrich Schütz, Claudio Monteverdi, the Gabrielis, Guillaume de Machaut, Johannes Ockeghem, Orlande de Lassus, Thomas Tallis, and Carlo Gesualdo and in J. S. Bach's cantatas spurred their revivals in these concerts. Morton and Craft devoted a great deal of energy and time to unearthing and transcribing masterpieces of early music for modern performers and instruments. For this work they took advice and assistance from Babitz, who was well ahead of his time in his theories on the subject; Babitz established his Early Music Laboratory in the 1950s with Stravinsky's backing.

In 1954 Stravinsky endorsed Craft's extended project of performing and recording the works of Anton Webern. He sent for the music from Europe, attended all the rehearsals, and generously donated to Craft segments of his own recording time with Columbia Records. Yates noted Stravinsky's attitude during this project: "To understand the power of Stravinsky you need to watch him sitting in the presence of music he honors, as recently he sat through a two-hour rehearsal of our Webern pieces, his nose in the score, while Krenek merely watched and the others, sophisticated, wandered around in and out of consciousness. Then he came to the [Roof] concert and did the same over again."[48]

Stravinsky found other resources of talent and organization in Southern California to advance his music. He chose USC's Carl Ebert to stage direct the 1951 world premiere in Venice of *The Rake's Progress,* which he himself conducted. Thereafter, Ebert repeated this production in three successive seasons at Glyndebourne. When USC's opera workshop wanted to produce the opera, Stravinsky refused, but he gave the university the manuscript score of the work. Organizations accommodating larger instrumental or theatrical forces contributed to Stravinsky's—and Craft's—musical well-being in California. In the summer of 1949 *Histoire du soldat* (*The Soldier's Tale*), with Nora Kaye (of the Ballet Theatre) as the Princess, was presented at the first Ojai Festival in the mountains northeast of Santa Barbara. At the subsequent invitations of Morton, who was director of the festival in 1955 and 1956, Stravinsky conducted his Violin Concerto (with Eudice Shapiro as soloist), and *Les noces;* and Craft conducted Monteverdi's Vespers and Brahms's Second Symphony, among many other works. Marilyn Horne had become a favorite soloist of both Craft and Stravinsky by 1954; she enjoyed her first festival successes in these Ojai performances and traveled to Venice with the Stravinskys to be a soloist in the September 1956 premiere of the *Canticum sacrum.* Before this premiere Stravinsky tried out at Ojai the companion piece for the work, his arrangement of J. S. Bach's Chorale Variations on *Vom Himmel hoch,* with the Pomona College Glee Club conducted by Craft.

Each June, Franz Waxman presented so many Stravinsky works at his Los Angeles Music Festival that Morton felt threatened, and he wrote to Dahl, "I hate seeing Waxman getting our Igor."[49] Waxman captured the world premiere of *Agon* for his festival, performing it in an all-Stravinsky program on the composer's seventy-fifth birthday, June 18, 1957. Stravinsky had suffered his first major stroke the previous October in Berlin. He refused medical advice to stop conducting but now took on easier tasks such as conducting his *Vom Himmel hoch* arrangement and the *Symphony of Psalms,* while leaving "the difficult young *Agon*" and the *Canticum sacrum* to Craft. Morton, reviewing the premiere for *The Musical Quarterly,* wrote, "[*Agon*] will doubtless be a more popular work than the *Canticum,* but that is only because most people (not excluding conductors) would rather dance than pray."[50] Huxley delivered a short talk on Stravinsky's importance at the concert. In his diary Christopher Isherwood recorded his impressions of the event:

> [Stravinsky] conducts with the most graceful, campy gestures, like a ballerina. Bob is stiff, sudden, birdlike. He jabs at the musicians with his fingers, and you feel an almost vengeful, birdlike harshness; a pecking and a dry, ruthless, demandingness. Of course, I didn't enjoy the music. I didn't expect to. It seemed chiefly to consist of nervous stab-

bing sounds, the creakings and squeaks of a door swinging in the wind, little fizzes of energy from the violins; short desert twisters of revolving noise, which soon passed. Yet I believed it when Aldous—looking more beautifully slim and distinguished than I've ever seen him—called Igor 'the great genius,' 'saint of music,' and the maker of 'the Stravinsky revolution.'[51]

After his 1956 stroke Stravinsky's increasing frailty was obvious to the musicians who worked with him, yet his energy could still inspire. In early 1957 Dahl talked with him after a concert and felt "re-charged by the most powerful 'life-source' imaginable. He has that vitalizing effect—it seems to come out of his pores, and I feel tremendously lucky that I know him so well."[52] Nadia Boulanger had noted that Stravinsky's confidences "were given in very few words."[53] Dahl's notes continue to reflect Stravinsky's verbal style: when congratulated (by Morton) on completing *Threni* in May 1958, Stravinsky replied, "I'm afraid it is a big bore—but it will be good to bore my enemies!" That spring Waxman's festival staged a full production of *Mavra* at UCLA's Royce Hall, after which Dahl noted his eagerness—"like a school boy who wants to be sure of getting a good mark"—as Stravinsky claimed that "the orchestration of *Mavra* is really so much like Webern." In 1959, walking slowly to his car after dinner at a restaurant, Stravinsky mused to Dahl upon his earlier love for rules that correct emotion: "Today—now—I am not so sure, not so sure at all if that is true or if I feel this way any more." Dahl suggested, "In order to enjoy a game one must know the rules," to which Stravinsky agreed, "One must be sure that there *are* any rules—otherwise, no game." In 1963 Dahl observed, "He speaks slowly, deliberately, is fading . . . but an old lion is still a lion." On that occasion, mulling over the increasing complexity of European trends, Stravinsky commented that "Stockhausen has gone far beyond serial writing—but I stay with it because serial twelve-tone-ism is what I know and am familiar with." Stravinsky had emphasized harmonic orientation in his twelve-tone approach, yet in conversation with Dahl he complained, "*How* can one teach *harmony* [in] this day and age?—it's impossible. There is no harmony. How *can* you teach harmony?? It seems so long ago that you could teach harmony. The linear design, yes! a line that stops and begins again—or a line that continues (*continues!!*) against others."[54]

In the 1960s Stravinsky spent at least half the year away from Los Angeles; he traveled to the Far East, Africa, the Arctic Circle, South America, and Is-

Igor Stravinsky, giving a piece of his birthday cake to Franz Waxman, June 2, 1957. Otto Rothschild Collection, Music Center Archives, Los Angeles.

rael, as well as making frequent trips to Europe and spending summer months in Santa Fe. His insatiable desire to travel and to perform was a concern for those around him. Before a particularly dreaded South American trip in the summer of 1960, Isherwood recorded Vera's poignant comment: "He is so accustomed to being a great celebrity that he has to keep making public appearances."[55] By 1964 Stravinsky was having difficulty walking unassisted. Before the world premiere at "Monday Evening Concerts" of the just-completed *Elegy for J.F.K.*, the clarinetist Mitchell Lurie, accompanying the composer the few yards from rehearsal to the concert hall, asked him how he still traveled all over the world, conducting orchestras almost beyond his endurance. Stravinsky's eyes flashed wickedly as he replied, "It is my revenge!"[56]

In this period of the composer's physical decline, many musicians witnessed Craft's rebelliousness toward Stravinsky. In 1960 Etta Dahl wrote to Morton, who was in Paris, "The old master doesn't really conduct anymore. [In rehearsals for *Les noces*] the musicians [including Ingolf Dahl as one of the four pianists] set the pace with Igor following. . . . Bob was very insulting to the old man. . . . Granted that Igor has accepted Bob as son and guide, why does he also stand for being insulted or doesn't he mind, and if not, is he masochistic in his old age? At any rate, it is sickening to watch."[57] Musicians who had played for Stravinsky "B.C.," as they called the time before Craft, were nostalgic for their earlier relationships with the composer. Don Christlieb, the bassoonist who had helped organize and maintain the Hollywood Rehearsal Orchestra, and whose Los Angeles Woodwinds performed and recorded for both Craft and Stravinsky over two decades from 1949 to 1969, wrote that Craft was "cool and methodical to the extent [that] we felt we were competing with him for accuracy more than for interpretation, and nothing we could do would satisfy him." Christlieb remembered incidents when Craft insulted players, no matter how experienced they were. "There was a mischievous tendency amongst us as performers to . . . perform better for Stravinsky than for Bob. . . . It was the only way we could express our resentment. . . . Even the Los Angeles Philharmonic members said they were made insecure by [Craft's] manner." In later years, "We as performers knew that Stravinsky would have occasional lapses of memory, especially in fractional bars, even in concert. . . . We [would] make adjustments and avoid breakdowns. . . . We all worshipped him as an idol, and his excellent stick technique allowed us some freedom that made for inspired performances. . . . Just to work with Stravinsky was an event we all savored."[58]

Audiences also felt this sense of privilege, as the diminutive Stravinsky, in Mutt-and-Jeff companionship with his tall friend Huxley, found his way to the front rows at concerts so that he could read, from the light on the stage, the music in score as it was being performed. Yates described his absorption in recording sessions: "Stravinsky sat at a table, the scores in front of him, his magnifying glass ready to be lifted for a quick analytic glance, his head bent to follow every gesture of the music he was hearing. In this self-concentrated self-oblivion he seemed a comic figure, adjusting two pairs of glasses up and down the narrow curve of bare forehead, glancing up through cherub-innocent eyes, face intent to hear what would be said to him, cheeks already quivering with the smile through which he would respond."[59]

As a young performer in Los Angeles, Michael Tilson Thomas enjoyed direct contact with Stravinsky. In part because of this experience, like others who benefited from their contact with the European musical émigrés, Tilson Thomas has in turn influenced and inspired countless young musicians. He provides a fitting summation of the master and his place in the forward-looking musical world he helped to create in Southern California: "Stravinsky was so alive, interested in the process of music making, and so intrigued with both the old and the new music. Every piece was a new adventure for him, and I think that spirit of being an explorer—even someone who was a master, as he was, having that spirit, saying 'I want to explore music, I want to know more about music'—I think that affected us all."[60] Yates observed about the eternal youth they all saw in Stravinsky: "At more than 70 he retains a young man's capacity to hear music the first time, to take it all in as a new experience with all the excitement of discovery."[61]

Epilogue

Like Stravinsky, most of the émigrés discussed in this book managed to find personal self-renewal through individual journeys of discovery in their Californian lives. They came from cultures in which the traditions of classical music were so deeply rooted in their nations' identities that their expulsion could be used to strike fear into the hearts and minds of the general populace, yet they settled by necessity in an area that Peter Yates in 1931 found to be a "veritable Sahara of artistic incomprehension."[1] Their individual struggles with changes in identity demanded by their uprooting, and their needs to realize their individual dreams, too often took tragic tolls on their personal health and mental welfare.

Yet they persevered. They came in increasing numbers, joining fellow German, Austrian, Polish, Czech, Hungarian, and Russian writers, actors, choreographers, directors, and producers in a great concentration of talent on the shores of the Pacific. They found inspiration in each other, breaching walls between them that might well have been insurmountable in Europe. If not the fame they had known or felt they should receive, most—with the shameful exception of Hanns Eisler—found for themselves the freedom to be, and to do, what they were born to be and do. Most of them overcame the cultural and personal deprivations of their uprooting by reaching beyond themselves to students and to the public. They made a huge difference, gradually building a shimmering new musical culture for the Southern California area, as well as the legacy, through their students' careers, that still lives and influences American music nationwide.

How did they manage, in such a raw, new land, to find the vast amounts of energy that Leon Kirchner (in chapter 2) remembered them providing?

Black and white illustration by Lotte Lehmann for her unpublished novel, *Of Heaven, Hell, and Hollywood* (undated). Department of Special Collections, Davidson Library, University of California, Santa Barbara.

They must have believed in silver linings—as Lotte Lehmann illustrated in her painting of clouds and sun over the Pacific. Perhaps they shared with Schoenberg a vision of artists as moral leaders and agreed with his battle against the materialism that endangers spiritual culture. Perhaps they heard his call to fight for music as "one of the most vital symbols of [mankind's] higher life." May this book serve as a monument to the character, as well as to the talent, of these musical émigrés and exiles from Hitler's Europe.

NOTES

ARCHIVES

California State University, Long Beach. Oral History of the Arts Archive.

Coolidge, Elizabeth Sprague, Collection. Music Division, Library of Congress.

Dahl, Ingolf, Archive. Doheny Memorial Library, University of Southern California.

Eisler, Hanns, Collection. Feuchtwanger Memorial Library, Department of Special Collections, Doheny Memorial Library, University of Southern California.

Fischer, Ruth, Papers (MS Ger 204). Houghton Library, Harvard University.

Kolisch, Rudolf, Papers (MS Mus 195). Houghton Library, Harvard University.

Krenek, Ernst, Papers. Ernst Krenek Institute, Krems, Austria. (Papers formerly in the Ernst Krenek Archive, Mandeville Special Collections Library, University of Southern California, San Diego.)

Koussevitzky, Serge, Archives. Music Division, Library of Congress.

Kuhnle, Wesley, Repository. Special Collections, California State University, Long Beach.

Lehmann, Lotte, Collection. Department of Special Collections, Davidson Library, University of California, Santa Barbara.

Los Angeles Philharmonic Archives.

MacDowell, Marian Nevins, Collection. Music Division, Library of Congress.

Margaret Herrick Library of the Academy of Motion Picture Arts and Sciences, Los Angeles.

Morton, Lawrence, Collection. Charles E. Young Research Library, Department of Special Collections, University of California, Los Angeles.

Music Scrapbooks, Art and Music Department, Los Angeles Central Library.

Oral History, American Music, Yale University.

Rózsa, Miklós, Papers. Special Collections Research Center, Syracuse University Library.

Schoenberg, Arnold, Collection. Music Division, Library of Congress.

———, Papers. Arnold Schönberg Center, Vienna (formerly the Arnold Schoenberg Institute, Los Angeles).

Slonimsky, Nicolas, Collection. Music Division, Library of Congress.

Toch, Ernst, Archive. Music Department Special Collections, University of California, Los Angeles.

UCLA Library Center for Oral History Research, University of California, Los Angeles.

Waxman, Franz, Papers. Special Collections Research Center, Syracuse University Library.

Yates, Peter, Papers. Mandeville Special Collections Library, University of California, San Diego.

CHAPTER 1 Europe

Epigraph: Berlin in Lights: The Diaries of Count Harry Kessler (1918–1937), trans. and ed. Charles Kessler (New York: Grove Press, 1999), 454.

1 August Kubizek, *The Young Hitler I Knew,* trans. E. V. Anderson (Boston: Houghton Mifflin, 1955), 290. Cola di Rienzi, a plebeian demagogue, grasped enormous power in fourteenth-century Rome, with the intent to lead the Roman people to power over their rulers.

2 Kubizek, *Young Hitler,* 192, 200, 172–73, 234, 245, 208–13. Hitler was infuriated to learn from Kubizek that there was little orchestral German literature prior to Johann Sebastian Bach.

3 Houston Stewart Chamberlain, letter to Hitler, October 7, 1923. Text in German and English available at http://www.hschamberlain.net; also in Chamberlain, *Arische Weltanschauung* (Munich: F. Bruckmann, 1938), 8. Chamberlain, British-born, chose to live in Europe in his teens. He met Cosima Wagner in Dresden in 1888. He lived in Vienna from 1889 until 1909, when he settled in Bayreuth. In 1916 Chamberlain became a German citizen, and in 1917 he joined the Vaterlandspartei, the forerunner to the Nazi Party.

4 Ernst (F. Sedgwick) Hanfstaengl, in his *Unheard Witness* (Philadelphia: Lippincott, 1957), 102, reports on Hitler's tirade in the Bürgerbräu Keller during the Munich Putsch, November 8–9, 1923: "Now is the time to do away with the sinners' Tower of Babel in Berlin."

5 For a full discussion of the development and decline of musical expressionism in this period, see John C. and Dorothy L. Crawford, *Expressionism in Twentieth-Century Music* (Bloomington: Indiana University Press, 1993).

6 Ernst Krenek, *Music Here and Now,* trans. Barthold Fles (New York: Norton, 1939), 52.

7 Alfred Heuss in Berlin's *Zeitschrift für Musik* 92 (1925): 583. Translated in Alexander L. Ringer, *Arnold Schoenberg: The Composer as Jew* (Oxford: Clarendon Press, 1990), 224–26.

8 Text from the 1925 choral cycle, *Four Pieces for Mixed Chorus,* op. 27, in H. H. Stuckenschmidt, *Schoenberg: His Life, World and Work,* trans. Humphrey Searle (New York: Schirmer Books, 1978), 310. In 1924 Schoenberg's "Position on Zionism" was published by *Pro Zion* in Vienna. *Der biblische Weg* was published in a translation, with an exhaustive and perceptive analysis by Moshe Lazar, in *Journal of the Arnold Schoenberg Institute* 17, nos. 1 & 2 (June & November 1994).

9 "The most German of the arts" was a phrase Goebbels would use at the opening of the *Entartete Musik* (Degenerate Music) exhibition in Düsseldorf in May 1938, on the 125th birthday of Richard Wagner.

10 From a clipping Schoenberg kept of the German translation by Ernst Kühnly from the original 1925 interview conducted in English in New York, titled "Igor Stravinsky über seine Musik: Ein Gespräch mit dem russischen Meister." The article was signed N. Roerig. Quoted in Leonard Stein, "Schoenberg and 'Kleine Modernsky,'" in Jann Pasler,

ed., *Confronting Stravinsky: Man, Musician, and Modernist* (Berkeley: University of California Press, 1986), 310–19. Stravinsky's reference to "music of the future" is a comment on Schoenberg's 1921 announcement of the development of his twelve-tone method.

11 Lawrence Weschler, "Talks on Toch," unpublished lecture on Wechsler's grandfather, Ernst Toch, given in 1973 at Cowell College, University of California at Santa Cruz. I am indebted to Lawrence Weschler for sharing with me this unpublished manuscript and other family materials on Toch.

12 Paul Bekker, *Musikblätter des Anbruch,* May 1924, quoted in Peter Heyworth, *Otto Klemperer: His Life and Times,* vol. 1 (Cambridge: Cambridge University Press, 1983), 191.

13 John Willett, *The Weimar Years: A Culture Cut Short* (London: Thames & Hudson, 1984), 96.

14 Schoenberg grumbled further about Klemperer's conducting music "so impoverished in content and material that an emphatic performance is not only unnecessary but damaging, as it would reveal its inner emptiness." Schoenberg diary, March 7, 1928, quoted in Heyworth, *Klemperer,* vol. 1, 290.

15 Heyworth, *Klemperer,* vol. 1, 251, 275, 374.

16 Stefan Zweig, *The World of Yesterday* (New York: Viking Press, 1943), 313.

17 Ernst Krenek, interview with Vivian Perlis, Palm Springs, CA, March 22, 1975, Oral History, American Music, Yale University. Also in Krenek, *Music Here and Now,* 85–87.

18 Artur Schnabel, *My Life and Music* (New York: St. Martin's Press, 1964), 78.

19 Ernst Krenek, "Jonny erinnert sich," *Österreichische Musikzeitschrift* 35, nos. 4–5 (April–May 1980): 189. The same year Hollander wrote this ballad, he used ragtime dance to a text ("Rag 1920") by Klabund (Alfred Henschke) as his metaphor for the cultural degeneracy of post–World War I Europe. Alan Lareau, "Jonny's Jazz: From *Kabarett* to Krenek," in Michael J. Budds, ed., *Jazz and the Germans* (Hillsdale, NY: Pendragon Press, 2002), 24, 40–41.

20 Ronald Taylor, *Kurt Weill: Composer in a Divided World* (Boston: Northeastern University Press, 1991), 147.

21 Albrecht Betz, *Hanns Eisler: Political Musician,* trans. Bill Hopkins (Cambridge: Cambridge University Press, 1982), 39–42. In his 1926 composition, *Tagebuch des Hanns Eisler,* op. 9, for female voices, tenor, violin, and piano, Eisler worked out his conflicts with his teacher; the work was performed at the 1927 Baden-Baden Festival.

22 Hanns Eisler, "The Builders of a New Music Culture" (1931), in Manfred Grabs, ed., *Hanns Eisler: A Rebel in Music,* trans. Marjorie Meyer (Berlin: Seven Seas, 1978), 27, 29, 37–55.

23 Hollander was musical director for Max Reinhardt's Berlin cabaret, *Schall und Rausch* (Sound and Smoke), when it reopened after World War I. His uncle Gustav, a violinist and frequently a conductor for Reinhardt, was founder and director of the Stern Conservatory in Berlin; his father, Viktor, was deputy director of the conservatory, as well as a composer for Reinhardt and for Berlin's Metropol-Revue; his uncle Felix was Reinhardt's dramaturg at the Deutsches Theater.

24 Ufa was founded during World War I to provide government propaganda.

25 Bruno Walter, letter to Gustav Böss, September 20, 1928, in Bruno Walter, *Briefe 1894–1962* (Frankfurt: S. Fischer, 1969), 220.

26 *Berliner Morgenpost,* June 19, 1929, quoted in Heyworth, *Klemperer,* vol. 1, 286.

27 Otto Friedrich, *Before the Deluge: A Portrait of Berlin in the 1920s* (London: Michael Joseph, 1974), 323.

28 Volker Kühn, *Spötterdämmerung: Vom langen Sterben des grossen kleinen Friedrich Hollaender* (Berlin: Parthas, 1997), 68–72.

29 Hollander used this concept in a parody of the Habanera from Bizet's opera *Carmen* to satirize Hitler's anti-Semitism. The absurd refrain mocks the famous technique Hitler used in his speeches, when with rhythmic force he whipped up closely packed crowds with a catalogue of existing evils and imaginary abuses, climaxed by his shout: "And whose fault is it?" to which the audience would rhythmically respond: "It's all / the fault / of the Jews!" See Carl Zuckmayer, *A Part of Myself,* trans. Richard and Clara Winston (New York: Harcourt Brace Jovanovich, 1970), 271.

30 Friedrich Hollaender, *Von Kopf bis Fuss: Mein Leben mit Text und Musik* (Munich: Kindler, 1965), 313.

31 Josef Goebbels, "Zehn grundsätze deutschen Musikschaffens" [Ten Principals of German Music Creativity], in *Amtliche Mitteilungen der Reichsmusikkammer,* 5 Jahr, no. 11, Berlin, Juni 1, 1938, cited in Albrecht Dümling, "The Target of Racial Purity," in Richard A. Etlin, ed., *Art, Culture, and Media in the Third Reich* (Chicago: University of Chicago Press, 2002), 55, fig. 3.

32 Zweig, *World of Yesterday,* 427–28.

33 Heyworth, *Klemperer,* vol. 1, 414.

34 Otto Klemperer, *Minor Recollections,* trans. J. Maxwell Brownjohn (London: Dennis Dobson, 1964), 89, and Heyworth, *Klemperer,* vol. 2, 14, 21. Arthur Judson, head of Columbia Artists Management in New York, tried to find posts for Klemperer with the New York Philharmonic, the Boston Symphony, the Philadelphia Orchestra, and the Chicago Symphony. Klemperer, in an interview, did not identify the intrepid woman. The author speculates that she may have been Isabel Morse Jones, music critic for the *Los Angeles Times,* who had relatives in Italy and eventually retired there.

35 Peter Ebert, *In This Theatre of Man's Life: The Biography of Carl Ebert* (Sussex, England: Book Guild, 1999), 69.

36 Strelitzer worked under the conductor Josef Rosenstock in the Jüdische Kulturbund. I am grateful to Alice Schoenfeld for graciously providing me access to her collection of Strelitzer's papers.

37 Report from Piatigorsky's daughter, Jephta Piatigorsky Drachman.

38 Taylor, *Kurt Weill,* 184, and Michael Kater, *The Twisted Muse* (Oxford: Oxford University Press, 1997), 88.

39 "Too bad! It would have been one Jew less," they shouted as they sped off. Lilly Toch, "The Orchestration of a Composer's Life," oral history transcript, UCLA Library Center for Oral History Research (1978), 213. Lilly Toch was interviewed in 1971–72 by Bernard Galm.

40 The widely admired concert pianists Walter Gieseking and Elly Ney, who had played Toch's First Piano Concerto to great acclaim, became Nazis and both dropped this work from their repertoire. Gieseking, who had enjoyed great success with Toch's playful *Three Burlesques* for piano, used a pirated edition of Toch's popular work "The Juggler," published under an Aryan pseudonym, for encores. Weschler, "Talks on Toch."

41 Robert Craft, ed., *Stravinsky: Selected Correspondence,* vol. 3 (New York: Knopf, 1985), 219.

42 Igor Stravinsky, letter to Willy Strecker, April 14, 1933, and Strecker, letters to Stravinsky, April 18, July 30, and November 30, 1934, in Craft, *Stravinsky: Selected Correspondence,* vol. 3, 218, 235, 237. Joan Evans's corrected translation, from "no one" to "one can regard," is used in quoting Strecker's April 14 letter; see Joan Evans, "Stravinsky's Music in Hitler's Germany," *Journal of the American Musicological Society* 56, no. 3 (Fall 2003): 537n49. Robert Craft is the source of the comment that Louis Strecker was a Nazi; see Craft, *Stravinsky: Selected Correspondence,* vol. 2 (1984), 218. Strauss's remark from an interview used in Strecker's article was published in the *Frankischer Kurier,* November 28, 1934, and is quoted in Vera Stravinsky and Robert Craft, *Stravinsky in Pictures and Documents* (New York: Simon and Schuster, 1978), 662n9.

43 V. Stravinsky and Craft, *Pictures and Documents,* 552. Craft states on the same page: "Stravinsky's attraction to the strong-armed government of Mussolini, beginning in the mid-1920s, is understandable. It follows, too, that a man with an obsessive, almost pathological need for order would feel comfortable with oligarchies and autocracies." In 1930 Stravinsky gave an interview to the music critic of Rome's *La Tribuna* in which he said, "I don't believe that anyone venerates Mussolini more than I. To me, he is the *one man who counts* nowadays in the whole world. . . . I have an overpowering urge to render homage to your Duce. He is the savior of Italy and—let us hope—of Europe." Harvey Sachs, *Music in Fascist Italy* (New York: Norton, 1987), 168.

44 Stravinsky, interview, July 29, 1937, in Craft, *Stravinsky: Selected Correspondence,* vol. 3, 219–20.

45 Joseph Goebbels, "Speech for the Düsseldorf Music Festival," trans. Robert P. Morgan, in Oliver Strunk, ed., *Source Readings in Music History,* rev. ed. (New York: Norton, 1998), 1396.

46 Stravinsky, correspondence with Strecker, May 27–August 6, 1938, in Craft, *Stravinsky: Selected Correspondence,* vol. 3, 265–70.

47 Evans, "Stravinsky's Music," 583–84.

48 Nicolas Nabokov, in *Old Friends and New Music* (London: Hamish Hamilton, 1951) wrote that Stravinsky's French publisher reported that "All [Stravinsky] wanted was to get out as quickly as possible, out of Paris, out of Europe, into America where life was still orderly." Quoted in Eric Walter White, *Stravinsky: The Composer and His Works* (Berkeley: University of California Press, 1966), 115.

49 CBS radio broadcast, March 13, 1938.

50 Eisler's film scores for this period included *Niemandsland* (1930), a pacifist film, script by Leonhard Frank; *Kühle Wampe* or *Wem gehört die Welt* (1931), about the workers' milieu in Berlin, script by Bertolt Brecht; *Komosol* or *Heldenlied* (Moscow, 1932), about workers in the Soviet Union, directed by Joris Ivens; *Dans les rues* (Paris, 1933), screenplay by Victor Trivas; *Le Grand Jeu* (Paris, 1934), about French foreign legionnaires, directed by Jacques Feyder; and *Abdul Hamid* or *The Damned* (London, 1934), a satire on Adolf Hitler.

51 Luzi Korngold, *Erich Wolfgang Korngold: Ein Lebensbild* (Vienna: Elisabeth Lafite, 1967), 64.

52 I am indebted to Leslie Zador for the use of materials by and about his father, the composer Eugene Zador.

53 Bruno Walter, *Theme and Variations,* trans. James A. Galston (New York: Knopf, 1947), 323–24, 328.

54 Erik Ryding and Rebecca Pechefsky, *Bruno Walter: A World Elsewhere* (New Haven, CT: Yale University Press, 2001), 187, 269.

55 Alan Jefferson states that Otto Krause was a Catholic converted from Judaism and suggests that part of Göring's pressure on Lehmann was concerned with Krause's being Jewish; see Jefferson, *Lotte Lehmann: 1888–1976* (London: Julia MacRae Books, 1988), 84, 149. This point is contradicted in the authorized biography by Beaumont Glass, *Lotte Lehmann: A Life in Opera and Song* (Santa Barbara, CA: Capra Press, 1988), which maintains that only Krause's wealthy wife was Jewish and that her four children were classified as "half-Jewish."

56 I am grateful to the late Lorenzo Tedesco, son of Mario Castelnuovo-Tedesco, for his interview of February 11, 1997, in Brentwood, Los Angeles, and for giving me access to materials regarding his father's life and work, including chapters from Castelnuovo-Tedesco's autobiography.

57 Jan Popper, "Opera Potpourri," oral history transcript, UCLA Library Center for Oral History Research (1979). Popper was interviewed in 1978–79 by Leslie K. Greer.

58 Britta Marcus Björnsson, letter to the author, March 5, 1998. I am grateful to Björnsson for her frank discussion of the Marcus family's issues of identity.

59 Marcus was struggling to prove himself bisexual. The Nazis sent thousands of homosexuals to concentration camps, where they were systematically and quickly exterminated. See Saul Friedlander, *Nazi Germany and the Jews,* vol. 1, *The Years of Persecution, 1933–1939* (New York: HarperCollins, 1997), 206. Kubizek reported that homosexuality "had long been one of [Hitler's] problems and, as an abnormal practice, he wished to see it fought against relentlessly." Kubizek, *The Young Hitler,* 237.

60 He did not legally assume the name, however, until the United States entered World War II. Anthony Linick, *The Lives of Ingolf Dahl* (Bloomington, IN: AuthorHouse, 2008), 673. I am deeply indebted to Linick, Ingolf Dahl's stepson, for sharing with me the 1996 draft of his manuscript.

CHAPTER 2 **Paradise?**

1 Vicki Baum, *It Was All Quite Different* (New York: Funk & Wagnalls, 1964), 336. She was called to Hollywood in 1931 to assist in the filming of her novel *Grand Hotel.*

2 Peter Heyworth, "The Golden Years: 1934–1969," in Orrin Howard, ed., *Festival of Music Made in Los Angeles* (Los Angeles: Los Angeles Philharmonic Association, 1981), 6; Otto Klemperer, letter to Elisabeth Schumann, December 16, 1933, quoted in Heyworth, *Otto Klemperer: His Life and Times,* vol. 1 (Cambridge: Cambridge University Press, 1983), 28; and Heyworth, ed., *Conversations with Klemperer,* rev. ed. (London: Faber & Faber, 1985), 98.

3 Mark Brunswick, "Refugee Musicians in America," *Saturday Review of Literature,* January 26, 1946, 51. When he wrote this, Brunswick was chairman of the National Committee for Refugee Musicians and president of the American Section of the International Society for Contemporary Music.

4 Carey McWilliams, *Southern California: An Island on the Land* (Santa Barbara, CA: Peregrine Smith, 1973); John Russell Taylor, *Strangers in Paradise: The Hollywood Émigrés, 1933–1950* (New York: Holt, Rinehart and Winston, 1983), 11.

5 Dione Neutra, interview with Brendan G. Carroll, Los Angeles, August 26, 1981, in Carroll, *The Last Prodigy: A Biography of Erich Wolfgang Korngold* (Portland, OR:

Amadeus Press, 1997), 289. Dione Neutra, born in Munich, came in 1925 to Los Angeles with Richard Neutra.

6 Annita Delano, letter to Sonia Delaunay, March 11, 1929, quoted in the introduction to Paul J. Karlstrom, ed., *On the Edge of America: California Modernist Art, 1900–1950* (Berkeley: University of California Press, 1996), 8.

7 Peter Yates, letter to Peyton Houston, September 18, 1933, Peter Yates Papers, Mandeville Special Collections Library, University of California, San Diego.

8 Clippings of newspaper announcement by Carl Bronson, n.d., and reviews by Gilbert Brown, *Los Angeles Record,* and Carl Bronson, October 23, 1925, Wesley Kuhnle Repository, Special Collections, California State University, Long Beach.

9 "Musical Americanism," in Catherine Parsons Smith and Cynthia S. Richardson, *Mary Carr Moore, American Composer* (Ann Arbor: University of Michigan Press, 1987), 177–79. Cowell organized his New Music Society workshops in San Francisco in February 1933; see Lita E. Miller, "Henry Cowell and John Cage: Intersections and Influences, 1933–1941," *Journal of the American Musicological Society* 59, no. 1 (Spring 2006): 51. Information on Goossens's programming from Carol Reese, "The Hollywood Bowl 1919–1989: The Land, the People, and the Music," *Performing Arts,* September 1989, 25.

10 Isabel Morse Jones, *Los Angeles Times,* March 12, 1933. A less omnipotent entrepreneur than Behymer, but more discerning, was Merle Armitage.

11 Peter Yates, meeting "the monumental Klemperer" in 1933, was aware that, because of Behymer and the film industry, the situation Klemperer was facing in Los Angeles was "art for money's sake." See Dorothy Lamb Crawford, *Evenings On and Off the Roof: Pioneering Concerts in Los Angeles, 1939–1971* (Berkeley: University of California Press, 1995), 18–19, 69, 141.

12 José Rodriguez, "The Western Academic Problem," in José Rodriguez, *Music and Dance in California* (Hollywood, CA: Bureau of Musical Research, 1940), 29–37.

13 Jones, *Los Angeles Times,* August 6, 1933.

14 Jones, *Los Angeles Times,* January 15, March 12, and May 21, 1933.

15 Richard Drake Saunders, *Hollywood Citizens News,* March 14, 1934.

16 See Crawford, *Evenings On and Off the Roof,* 7.

17 Meremblum's young players appeared in a 1939 Hollywood movie (*And They Shall Have Music,* Samuel Goldwyn). Isabel Morse Jones reported that Meremblum's Junior Symphony played well and acted so naturally that Heifetz was talked into performing with them for the film. Jones, *Los Angeles Times,* July 9, 1939.

18 Gottfried Reinhardt, *The Genius: A Memoir of Max Reinhardt by His Son* (New York: Knopf, 1979), 298–301.

19 Gottfried Reinhardt, "It Was No Paradise," lecture at the Hollywood Bowl Museum, April 22, 1991, transcribed in Carol Merrill-Mirsky, ed., *Exiles in Paradise,* Hollywood Bowl Museum, exh. cat. (Los Angeles: Los Angeles Philharmonic Association, 1991), 74–75.

20 Arnold Schoenberg, "Two Speeches on the Jewish Situation," in Leonard Stein, ed., Leo Black, trans., *Style and Idea: Selected Writings of Arnold Schoenberg* (Berkeley: University of California Press, 1984), 501–2.

21 Paul Pisk, interview with Vincent Plush, May 10, 1983, West Hollywood, Oral History, American Music, Yale University. Pisk had been a student of Schoenberg's in Europe for twenty years.

22 Ernst Toch, letter to David B. Brimm, Jewish Community Center, Santa Monica, CA, March 4, 1945, in Horst Weber and Manuela Schwartz, eds., *Quellen zur Geschichte emigrierter Musiker 1933–1950: Kalifornien* (Munich: K. G. Saur, 2003), 276–78.

23 Robert Craft, ed., *Dearest Bubushkin: The Correspondence of Vera and Igor Stravinsky, 1921–1954, with Excerpts from Vera Stravinsky's Diaries, 1922–1971,* trans. Lucia Davidova (New York: Thames & Hudson, 1985), diary entry April 12, 1945.

24 Thomas Mann, letter to Erich von Kahler, May 1, 1945, in *Letters of Thomas Mann, 1889–1955,* selected and trans. Richard and Clara Winston (Berkeley: University of California Press, 1990), 351.

25 Thomas Mann, letter to Bruno Walter, May 6, 1943, in *Letters of Thomas Mann,* 295. Homesickness "for what was, what we left, what was before and what we thought would never come again" made the writers pessimistic, according to Marta Feuchtwanger in her "An Émigré Life: Munich, Berlin, Sanary, Pacific Palisades," oral history transcript, UCLA Library Center for Oral History Research (1976), 1319. Feuchtwanger was interviewed in 1975 by Lawrence M. Weschler.

26 Jerome Moross, "On the Hollywood Front," *Modern Music* 18, no. 4 (May–June 1941): 261.

27 Aaron Copland, letter to Victor Kraft, June 1937, in Aaron Copland and Vivian Perlis, *Copland: 1900 through 1942* (New York: St. Martin's/Marek, 1984), 271.

28 Peter Yates, "Los Angeles Composers," in *Arts and Architecture,* May 1949, and Yates ms., "Charles Ives—An American Composer," written in 1968 (published in *Parnassas,* 1975), Yates Papers, University of California, San Diego.

29 Richard Lert, interview with Melinda Lowrey, January 13, 1976, Oral History of the Arts Archive, California State University, Long Beach.

30 Arnold Schoenberg, letter to the violinist Adolf Rebner, February 26, 1940, quoted in Reinhold Brinkmann, "Reading a Letter," in Reinhold Brinkmann and Christoph Wolff, eds., *Driven into Paradise: The Musical Migration from Nazi Germany to the United States* (Berkeley: University of California Press, 1999), 3.

31 Pisk, interview with Plush.

32 Feuchtwanger, "An Émigré Life," 1355, 1576–77, 1740–41.

33 Leon Kirchner, interview with Janet Baker-Carr, *Harvard Magazine,* November 1974, 48.

CHAPTER 3 Otto Klemperer and the Los Angeles Philharmonic

1 Isabel Morse Jones, *Los Angeles Times,* October 17, 1933.

2 Jones, *Los Angeles Times,* June 4 and 15, 1933. Klemperer's appointment was announced on June 17 in the *Times.*

3 Jones, *Los Angeles Times,* January 12, 1933.

4 Bertha McCord Knisely, *Saturday Night,* January 12, 1933.

5 Herta Glaz, interview with the author in Los Angeles, January 28, 1997. Glaz was a soloist in Klemperer's Los Angeles performances of Mahler's *Das Lied von der Erde* and Bach's *Saint John Passion.*

6 Jones, *Los Angeles Times,* October 20, 1933; Knisely, *Saturday Night,* October 28, 1933; José Rodriguez, *Script* magazine, October 28, 1933; Bruno David Ussher, *Beverly Hills Town Topics,* October 25, 1933.

7 Peter Heyworth, "Klemperer and the L.A. Philharmonic," in Orrin Howard, ed., *A Fes-*

tival of Music Made in Los Angeles (Los Angeles: Los Angeles Philharmonic Association, 1981), 6. Sven Reher had studied with Carl Flesch at the Hochschule für Musik Berlin.

8 Gottfried Reinhardt, "It Was No Paradise," in Carol Merrill-Mirsky, ed., *Exiles in Paradise*, Hollywood Bowl Museum exh. cat. (Los Angeles: Los Angeles Philharmonic Association, 1991), 75.

9 Otto Klemperer, letter to Johanna Klemperer, October 17, 1933, quoted in Peter Heyworth, *Otto Klemperer: His Life and Times*, vol. 2 (Cambridge: Cambridge University Press, 1983), 22.

10 Klemperer, letter to Dorothea Alexander-Katz, November 9, 1933, quoted in Heyworth, *Klemperer*, vol. 2, 28.

11 Rodriguez, *Script* magazine, November 25, 1933; Knisely, *Saturday Night*, December 30, 1933.

12 Peter Hayworth, *Conversations with Klemperer*, rev. ed. (London: Faber & Faber, 1985), 89.

13 Heyworth, "Klemperer and the L.A. Philharmonic," 62.

14 Jones, *Los Angeles Times*, February 23 and April 20, 1934.

15 Jones, *Los Angeles Times*, August 26, 1934.

16 Jones, *Los Angeles Times*, November 11 and December 12 and 14, 1934.

17 Heyworth, *Klemperer*, vol. 2, 55–61.

18 Ibid., 49.

19 Heyworth, *Conversations with Klemperer*, 94.

20 Klemperer, letter to Micha Konstam, May 22, 1935, quoted in Heyworth, *Klemperer*, vol. 2, 47.

21 Casals never played Schoenberg's work in public.

22 Jones, *Los Angeles Times*, April 2, 1936. Feuermann's pianist on this tour was Edward Wolfgang Rebner, who married an American and returned to Hollywood to work as pianist, arranger, and conductor in the film industry.

23 Arnold Schoenberg, *Los Angeles Herald Examiner*, April 15, 1936.

24 Heyworth, *Klemperer*, vol. 2, 72.

25 Jones, *Los Angeles Times*, August 30 and November 29, 1936. The music librarian in Los Angeles' Central Library at the time was Gladys Caldwell. She not only assembled the impressive music collection Jones mentioned but also kept large scrapbooks of press clippings on music in Los Angeles, now in the Central Library's Art and Music Department. Although some of these were damaged in recent fires, they were an invaluable source for this book.

26 I am indebted to Naomi Krasner, daughter of Louis Krasner, for her father's account of this event.

27 Kalman Bloch, interview with the author, January 23, 1997, Los Angeles. Bloch, born and educated in New York City, studied with Simeon Bellison, principal clarinetist of the New York Philharmonic, who recommended Bloch to Klemperer. Bloch remained with the Los Angeles Philharmonic until his retirement, enjoying his last years as co-principal with his daughter Michele Zukofsky, who then continued as principal clarinet.

28 Klemperer, interview with John Freeman, November 27, 1960, for BBC television program *Face to Face*, transmitted January 28, 1961.

29 Glaz, interview with author.

30 Jones, *Los Angeles Times,* February 9 and March 24, 1939.

31 Dieter Rexroth, ed., *Paul Hindemith Briefe* (Frankfurt: Fischer, 1982), 222–23.

32 The date of Klemperer's letter to Peter Yates is unknown; Yates copied it into a letter to his friend Peyton Houston, dated April 21, 1939. Yates's subsequent letter to Houston, n.d., was sent after July 23, 1939. Both sources in Peter Yates Papers, Mandeville Special Collections Library, University of California, San Diego. The Ives score that was loaned to Klemperer was not returned to Yates; its whereabouts is not known.

33 Jones, *Los Angeles Times,* August 25, September 2, and November 30, 1939.

34 Jones, *Los Angeles Times,* November 30, 1939.

35 Jones, *Los Angeles Times,* January 2 and December 31, 1944.

36 Lawrence Morton mentioned this fact in *Modern Music* 22, no. 12 (November–December 1944): 51.

37 Alfred Price Quinn, *B'nai B'rith Messenger,* January 26, 1943, and February 16, 1945. In his thirteen-year term, Wallenstein ventured few twentieth-century works with the Philharmonic. He conducted Stravinsky's suite from *The Firebird* (1905) and *The Rite of Spring* (1913) but otherwise brought the composer as guest to conduct programs of his own works. He conducted three works by Ernst Toch: *Music for Orchestra and Baritone* (1931), the overture to Toch's 1930 opera *Der Fächer* (The Fan), and the Second Symphony in 1952, after its premiere by the Boston Symphony Orchestra. He conducted two works by Mario Castelnuovo-Tedesco and one each by Alexandre Tansman, Ernst Krenek, and Arnold Schoenberg (the "Lied der Waldtaube" [Song of the Wood Dove] from the *Gurrelieder,* 1901). Wallenstein was replaced in 1956 by the well-known Dutch conductor Eduard Van Beinum, who died three years later of a heart attack at age fifty-nine.

38 See Yates's articles in *Musical Digest,* May and August–September 1948; *Music of the West* 4, no. 2 (October 1948); and *Arts and Architecture,* May 1949. See also Yates, letter to Peyton Houston, May 25, 1948, Yates Papers, University of California, San Diego. See also Dorothy Lamb Crawford, *Evenings On and Off the Roof: Pioneering Concerts in Los Angeles, 1939–1971* (Berkeley: University of California Press, 1995), 83–86.

CHAPTER 4 Performers, and Klemperer's Return

1 Isabel Morse Jones, *Los Angeles Times,* March 14, 1933, and January 12, 1936.

2 Joseph Szigeti, *With Strings Attached: Reminiscences and Reflections* (New York: Knopf, 1947), 332. Bartók, Szigeti, and Goodman recorded this work in New York in May 1940.

3 Ibid., 315, 324, 325–26.

4 Jones, *Los Angeles Times,* September 2, 1942. Szell lived for a time in Hollywood between his emigration in 1939 and his appointment in 1946 to the Cleveland Orchestra.

5 Joseph Achron had a distinguished career in Russia as a concert violinist until he emigrated to America in 1925. He moved to Hollywood in 1934, performed in studio orchestras, and continued his composing and concert careers. He premiered his Second and Third Violin Concertos with the Los Angeles Philharmonic in 1936 and 1939.

6 Milton Thomas, radio interview with the author, KUSC, January 16, 1987.

7 Ehlers played a Pleyel instrument with pedals; whether it was the Pleyel she had found, discarded by Mahler, in the Vienna Opera is uncertain.

8 These salaries were not advertised; Pauline Alderman remembered Max Krone, dean of the School of Music, moving in mysterious ways in these matters. She also remem-

bered her colleague Ehlers as "a truly great musical personality." Hancock, the grandson of a Hungarian count, became wealthy from seventy-one oil wells, drilled in 1907, which produced millions of barrels of oil annually on his family's 4,438-acre Rancho La Brea, which later became Los Angeles' well-known Wilshire District. In 1930 Hancock founded his own Pacific Conservatory of Music in the Hancock mansion at Wilshire Boulevard and Vermont Avenue. He built USC's Hancock Building and Auditorium, formed the Hancock Ensemble, subsidized and occasionally played in the professional Hancock Trio, and donated free concerts in Bovard Auditorium. Pauline Alderman, *We Build a School of Music* (Los Angeles: Alderman Book Committee, 1989), 92, 119, 177–78, 185, 192.

9 Alfred Price Quinn, *B'nai B'rith Messenger,* November 25, 1945. Among her many appearances, Ehlers performed with Soulima Stravinsky in Bach's Concerto for Two Harpsichords at Franz Waxman's Los Angeles Music Festival.

10 Jones, *Los Angeles Times,* April 15, 1938, and January 16, 1943.

11 Peter Yates, "Evenings on the Roof, 1939–1954," oral history transcript, UCLA Library Center for Oral History Research (1972), 134. Yates was interviewed in 1967 by Adelaide Tusler.

12 Eudice Shapiro, Virginia Majewski, and Victor Gottlieb were all graduates of the Curtis Institute of Music in Philadelphia. In the 1940s Shapiro and Majewski were the first female principals in studio orchestras; Gottlieb was a former member of the Coolidge Quartet, and Majewski of the Kneisel Quartet. During the war Shapiro was concertmaster of the Janssen Symphony Orchestra as well as the RKO and Paramount studio orchestras. Stravinsky chose her to perform his violin/piano arrangements and his Violin Concerto at the Ojai Festival; as concertmaster of Waxman's Los Angeles Festival Symphony Orchestra she recorded his *Agon* and *Canticum sacrum* for Columbia Records. She had a long and distinguished teaching career at USC. Majewski performed and recorded in the Heifetz-Piatigorsky concerts in the 1960s. Eudice Shapiro, interviews with the author, June 28, 1988, and January 31, 1997, Studio City, CA.

13 Harvey Sachs, *Rubinstein: A Life* (New York: Grove Press, 1995), 275. Lithuanian-born Heifetz had toured the United States in 1917 as a prodigy and became a citizen in 1925.

14 Jones, *Los Angeles Times,* February 7, 1938, and January 21, 1939.

15 Photo from *PM's Weekly,* September 7, 1941, in Annette Morreau, *Emanuel Feuermann 1902–1942,* catalogue of the RNCM Manchester International Cello Festival, May 1996. I am grateful to Annette Morreau for providing me with this catalogue.

16 Sachs, *Rubinstein,* 277, and Artur Rubinstein, *My Many Years* (New York: Knopf, 1980), 494.

17 Rubinstein, *My Many Years,* 500.

18 Robert Craft, *An Improbable Life* (Nashville: Vanderbilt University Press, 2002), 144.

19 Mildred Horton, *Los Angeles Daily News,* March 28, 1949.

20 Gregor Piatigorsky, *Cellist* (1965; repr., New York: DaCapo, 1976), 191. Piatigorsky was three times a refugee, first from the Russian Revolution to Poland and Germany in the 1920s, then from Nazi Germany to France, and finally to the United States. He became an American citizen in 1942. According to his daughter, Jephta Drachman, it was her mother, Jacqueline de Rothschild Piatigorsky, who in 1939 abruptly booked the family on a boat from France when she realized that the Nazis would take over. Jephta Drachman, telephone interview with the author, October 3, 1999. Jacqueline de Rothschild

was the middle child of three children of Baron Eduard de Rothschild, head of the French banking family. Her brother Guy became the Baron Rothschild upon their father's death. Piatigorsky, born in Ukraine, had grown up in poverty.

21 As well as the concert, Jones had attended a rehearsal, in which Piatigorsky played facing the orchestra. Players in the back row had stood to watch his cadenza and cheer. Jones, *Los Angeles Times,* February 9 and 12, 1939.

22 Sachs, *Rubinstein,* 278.

23 A recording producer remembered an interchange in Russian between the two that sent both of them into laughter during a recording break. He asked what the joke was. Piatigorsky had settled into a cigarette with his usual (and justly famous) interest in talking. Heifetz had interrupted him, in Russian, to ask if he could possibly be quiet for one minute. After thought, Piatigorsky replied, "It's difficult." From *The Piatigorsky Legacy,* a four-part radio documentary produced in 1985 by Gail Eichenthal for KUSC-FM, USC's radio station. I am indebted to Jephta Piatigorsky Drachman and Laurence Lesser for guiding me to this documentary.

24 William Primrose was afflicted with growing deafness at this time and soon dropped out.

25 *Piatigorsky Legacy.*

26 Ibid.

27 Laurence Lesser, interview with the author, July 7, 2004, Cambridge, MA. Lesser first studied cello with Gregory Aller, a member of the White Russian community in Los Angeles since the 1920s, father of Lesser's subsequent teacher Eleanor Aller, and grandfather of Leonard Slatkin. Lesser studied theory with the German pianist Gerhard Albersheim, counterpoint with Mario Castelnuovo-Tedesco, and performance with Gabor Reijto (a Hungarian émigré from Nazi Europe) and Richard Lert at the Music Academy of the West. He participated in the Piatigorsky master classes in 1962 and in 1966 was a prizewinner in the Moscow Tchaikovsky Competition. That same year Lesser performed in Carnegie Hall with the Heifetz-Piatigorsky Concerts. From 1983 to 1996 and again in 2006–7, he served as president of the New England Conservatory in Boston.

28 The Gimpel brothers' grandfather had founded, and the family had managed, the famous Lemberg Yiddish Theater.

29 In 1932, while still in prewar Europe, Bronislav Gimpel formed a duo with Warsaw pianist Wladyslaw Szpilman—focus of the 2003 film *The Pianist.* In 1963 the two founded the Warsaw Piano Quintet. Simon Collins, "Bronislaw Gimpel," *The Strad* 87, no. 1040 (December 1976): 645. I am indebted to Peter Gimpel, son of Jakob Gimpel, for material on the Gimpel brothers, and for an extensive interview in Los Angeles on February 16, 1997.

30 Jones, *Los Angeles Times,* August 27, 1942, and April 11, 1946.

31 Albert Goldberg, *Los Angeles Times,* May 15, 1948.

32 Michael Bonnesen, "Sublimity," review in *Politiken,* Copenhagen, August 15, 1985; and Peter Gimpel, "Jakob Gimpel: An Authoritative Sketch," notes for Cambria CD-1070, *Jakob Gimpel's All-Chopin Recital,* recorded May 11, 1978, at Ambassador Auditorium.

33 Among Jakob Gimpel's students were Jeffrey Kahane, Daniel Pollack, film composer Jerry Goldsmith, and Clara Silvers, a Schoenberg student who married Eduard Steuermann.

34 Lotte Lehmann, *Wings of Song,* trans. Margaret Ludwig (London: K. Paul, French,

Trubner, 1938), 117–18. American edition titled *Midway in My Song* (Indianapolis: Bobbs Merrill, 1938).

35 Lotte Lehmann, interview with Peter Heyworth, 1972, quoted in Heyworth, *Otto Klemperer: His Life and Times,* vol. 1 (Cambridge: Cambridge University Press, 1983), 75.

36 Jones, *Los Angeles Times,* August 25, 1939, and July 27, 1944.

37 Gwendolyn Koldofsky, interview with the author, June 18, 1988, on radio broadcast "Backstage at Royce," produced for KUSC-FM, Los Angeles, celebrating the centennial of Lehmann's birth.

38 Bruno Walter, letter to Lotte Lehmann, March 17, 1951, Lotte Lehmann Collection, (Performing Arts Mss 2), University Libraries, University of California, Santa Barbara.

39 Richard Saunders, *Hollywood Citizen News,* March 31, 1937.

40 Beaumont Glass, *Lotte Lehmann: A Life in Opera and Song* (Santa Barbara, CA: Capra Press, 1988), 185.

41 Lotte Lehmann, letters to Bruno Walter, August 14 and December 23, 1947, Lotte Lehmann Collection.

42 Lotte Lehmann, "Of Heaven, Hell, and Hollywood: A Satirical Fantasy," unpublished manuscript, Lotte Lehmann Collection.

43 Lehmann, letters to Walter, November 30, 1949, and February 28, 1951, Lotte Lehmann Collection.

44 Lehmann, letters to Efrem Zimbalist, July 15 and August 5, 1945, Lotte Lehmann Collection.

45 Lehmann, note to Walter, n.d. (spring 1951), and letter to Walter, August 13, 1954, Lotte Lehmann Collection.

46 Among the coaches for the master classes and annual opera production were Jan Popper, Gwendolyn Koldofsky, Fritz Zweig, Irving Beckman, Natalie Limonick, and Beaumont Glass.

47 Lehmann, letter to Walter, July 30, 1957; Walter, reply to Lehmann, August 5, 1957, Lotte Lehmann Collection.

48 *Lotte Lehmann: Master Classes,* vol. 1, Video Artists International, available at http://www.vaimusic.com.

49 George Szell, Albert Coates, John Barbirolli, and Artur Rodzinski were the other guest conductors.

50 Walter, letter to Helmut Fahsel, December 26, 1939, in Bruno Walter, *Briefe 1894–1962* (Frankfurt: S. Fischer, 1969), 252.

51 Jones, *Los Angeles Times,* July 21, August 4, and November 24, 1940.

52 Jones, *Los Angeles Times,* June 6, 1943.

53 Vicki Baum, letter to Grete Fischer, December 1940, quoted in Heyworth, *Klemperer,* vol. 2, 108.

54 Double bassist Richard T. Andrews, letter to Peter Heyworth, January 5, 1978, quoted in Heyworth, *Klemperer,* vol. 2, 127.

55 Alfred Price Quinn, *B'nai B'rith Messenger,* August 20, 1943.

56 Alfred Price Quinn, *B'nai B'rith Messenger,* February 16, 1945.

57 Lawrence Morton, *Script* magazine, November 3, 1945.

58 Heyworth, *Klemperer,* vol. 2, 138.

59 The local newspaper report was accompanied by a photograph of Klemperer in a police station with a bandaged head. Heyworth, *Klemperer,* vol. 2, 157.

60 Ibid., 242.

61 Werner Klemperer, interview in a 1985 BBC film celebrating Otto Klemperer's 100th birthday.

62 Lawrence Morton, "A Brief Resume of Musical Activity in Southern California (1939–1945)," Morton Collection, Charles E. Young Research Library Department of Special Collections, University of California, Los Angeles.

CHAPTER 5 Innovative Teachers in the Performing Arts

1 Merola was musical director and manager of the San Francisco Opera from 1923 until his death in 1953.

2 Ernst Krenek, *Musik im goldenen Westen* (Vienna: Hollinek, 1949), 36.

3 Marilyn Hall, "Los Angeles City College Opera Workshop: Ein Modell," an unpublished sixty-four-page history written in German at the University of Freiburg (1971) to satisfy state requirements for teaching certification (hereafter cited as the Hall ms.), 60. A soprano, Hall sang leading roles in the City College Opera Workshop from 1952 to 1954 and, like many of Strelitzer's students, began her professional career as an opera singer in Germany. In her European career she changed her name to Maria Zahlten-Hall. I am grateful for her permission to refer to this unique manuscript.

4 Natalie Limonick, interview with the author, Los Angeles, February 5, 1997. Limonick was engaged at the Bayreuth Festival in 1961 with several other Strelitzer students. She worked as an accompanist and coach under Jan Popper at UCLA for seventeen years and from 1974 to 1986 served as director of the opera workshop at USC.

5 Hugo Strelitzer, interview with Lawrence Weschler, September 7, 1973, Los Angeles, in the Toch Archive, Special Collections, Music Library, UCLA.

6 Strelitzer, letter to "Meine Lieben," September 17, 1936. Much of the story of Strelitzer's escape from Berlin and early life in Los Angeles is taken from his correspondence with his family, courtesy of Alice Schoenfeld and the executor of Strelitzer's estate, Melvin Small.

7 Bertha McCord Knisely reported in *Saturday Night,* February 17, 1934, the musicians' union's announcement of the creation of the WPA Orchestra, funded by the U.S. government "to employ professional musicians who would otherwise be assigned to pick and shovel jobs" and to give free public concerts.

8 Strelitzer, letter to "Meine Lieben," September 17, 1936.

9 Strelitzer, letter to his family, June 27, 1937.

10 Boris Morros, head of the music department at Paramount, and Nat Finston, in the same position at MGM, wrote testimonials enthusiastically endorsing Strelitzer's plan. Hall ms., 12–13.

11 Ibid., 30.

12 George London made his professional debut in 1941 in Hollywood and by 1947 was touring with the tenor Mario Lanza. In 1949 he was engaged by the Vienna State Opera, in 1950 by Glyndebourne, and in 1951 by Bayreuth and the Metropolitan Opera. He was the first American singer invited to perform in Moscow, where he sang Boris Godunov, his favorite role. In 1968 he was appointed director of the Kennedy Center in Washington, DC. He was an impressive singing actor with a great command of vocal color, dramatic commitment, and an imposing personal magnetism.

13 José Rodriguez in *Script* magazine, May 12, 1938, retranslated from the German translation of the English original in the Hall ms., 21.

14 Isabel Morse Jones, *Los Angeles Times*, May 4, 1939.

15 Peter Yates wrote in a letter to Peyton Houston on January 18, 1940, that Ernst Toch and Edgard Varèse were present to hear Strelitzer conduct the Hindemith and Mozart works. Yates enthused: "Blessed land that can now sprout from cracks and crannies such perfecting intelligence!" Peter Yates Papers, Mandeville Special Collections Library, University of California, San Diego.

16 Hall ms., 30.

17 Jones, *Los Angeles Times*, June 7 and September 27, 1942.

18 Hall ms., 32–34, 45.

19 Strelitzer's assistant, Adolf Heller (from Prague) conducted the Zeisl opera, and Vladimir Rosing (a Russian, known for his work at the New York City Center Opera and at the Hollywood Bowl) staged the work. Heinz Blankenburg, who sang for many of the world's major opera companies, eventually returned to Southern California as a professor of music at UCLA and at the Music Academy of the West. He has also served as a stage director for universities and professional opera companies, both in the United States and abroad.

20 Foss had emigrated from Berlin by way of Paris and arrived in the United States in 1937 as a child prodigy of fifteen. After a meteoric career as a pianist and composer on the East Coast, he was appointed in February 1953 to Schoenberg's former position at UCLA. Through the influence of Elizabeth Sprague Coolidge, Milhaud had been teaching at Mills College in Oakland since his flight from occupied France in 1940. He had composed his only Hollywood film score, *The Private Affairs of Bel Ami*, in 1948.

21 Marilyn Hall became a member of the Essen opera company in Germany. Ella Lee studied in Friedelind Wagner's master classes at Bayreuth, was chosen by Walter Felsenstein for the Komische Oper in East Berlin, and was further engaged by the San Francisco Opera. Michael Davidson went to the Mannheim opera. Roderick Ristow sang in the Essen and Hanover companies. William Olvis sang in the Gelsenkirchen company. Catherine Gayer sang in Berlin's Deutsche Oper. Sam van Ducen went to the Bonn company. Brian Sullivan was in the original production of Kurt Weill's *Street Scene* on Broadway in 1947. Jean Fenn was a glamorous Manon in the 1950s. Maralin Niska also developed an international career and opened the inaugural year of the San Diego Opera in 1965 as Mimi in *La bohème*.

22 Hall ms., 44.

23 Elizabeth M. Surace, "Remembering Hugo," unpublished manuscript, courtesy of Ms. Surace.

24 Marni Nixon, interview with the author, November 12, 1997, Cambridge, MA. Nixon also remembered Strelitzer's lisp, which caused great mirth when he announced to an assembled chorus, "Velcome to Shitty College! Shopranos, shit down!" Nixon's gifts for modern music were being discovered at the time, and Strelitzer coached her in Webern songs (which she subsequently recorded under Robert Craft for Columbia Records) and in Berg's *Seven Early Songs*. Beside the works of Webern and Berg, she performed and recorded with musicianly ease much of the most difficult vocal music by Schoenberg, Stravinsky, Krenek, and Dallapiccola. From her girlhood she made a career dubbing songs for nonsinging actresses in many films. Among her most prominent assignments were for Deborah Kerr, Natalie Wood, and Audrey Hepburn in their respective roles in *The King and I, West Side Story,* and *My Fair Lady*. This occupation,

which earned Nixon the nickname "the Ghostess with the Mostess," testified to her keen ear, vocal flexibility, and art of mimicry.

25 Limonick, interview with the author.

26 Mansouri received a B.A. in psychology at UCLA in 1953.

27 Limonick, interview with the author.

28 Mildred Norton, *Los Angeles Daily News,* May 23, 1949.

29 Albert Goldberg, "The Sounding Board," *Los Angeles Times,* February 12, 1950.

30 Norton, *Los Angeles Daily News,* April 18, 1950.

31 Peter Ebert, *In This Theater of Man's Life: The Biography of Carl Ebert* (Sussex, England: Book Guild, 1999), 58–60.

32 Ebert's outstanding performance as the narrator in Stravinsky's ballet–chamber opera *Histoire du soldat* at the Kroll Opera under Klemperer in 1928 made such an impression on Marta Feuchtwanger that it supplanted even her experience of the recent premiere of Weill's *Threepenny Opera.* Marta Feuchtwanger, "An Émigré Life: Munich, Berlin, Sanary, Pacific Palisades," oral history transcript, UCLA Library Center for Oral History (1976), 1455. Feuchtwanger was interviewed in 1975 by Lawrence M. Weschler.

33 Carl Ebert, letter quoted in Peter Ebert, *In This Theatre,* 191–92.

34 Norton, *Los Angeles Daily News,* May 18, 1949. The following year Lucine Amara joined New York's Metropolitan Opera, where she was noted for the consummate ease of her singing. Her forty-one-year career at the Met encompassed fifty-six different roles in 882 performances, including five opening nights, nine new productions, and fifty-seven radio broadcasts. California-born Theodor Uppman had already sung opposite Maggie Teyte in a concert performance of Debussy's *Pelléas et Mélisande* with the San Francisco Symphony, and in 1951 he was chosen by Benjamin Britten to create the title role in *Billy Budd.* The success he enjoyed in that role led to his Metropolitan Opera debut in 1953. Uppman's vibrant, athletic stage presence and the beauty of his lyric baritone distinguished his portrayals of Mozart roles such as Papageno, Masetto, and Guglielmo. He created a number of roles in modern operas and later joined the faculty of Mannes College of Music in New York.

35 Nan Merriman (who also studied in California with Lotte Lehmann) had a distinguished career, particularly in Europe, beginning in the 1950s. She recorded several Verdi operas with Toscanini and Mozart operas with conductors Karajan, Cantelli, and Jochum; Bach's B-Minor Mass with Scherchen; and Beethoven's *Missa Solemnis* with Walter and Toscanini. She returned to Los Angeles in 1973.

36 Marilyn Horne (with Jane Scovell), *My Life* (New York: Atheneum, 1983), 70, 106. From the 1960s through the 1990s Horne's voice was considered one of the greatest in the world. She became an international star, and at the end of her performing career she created a foundation to encourage the work of young singers in the art of recitals. She returned to California as the director of the Voice Program at the Music Academy of the West.

37 Nixon, interview with the author.

38 Ebert, *In This Theatre,* 204.

39 Jan Popper, "Opera Potpourri," oral history transcript, UCLA Library Center for Oral History Research (1979), 61–62. Popper was interviewed in 1978–79 by Leslie K. Greer.

40 Mansouri was stage director at the Zurich and Geneva opera houses from 1960 to 1976; from 1976 to 1988 he was general director of the Canadian Opera in Toronto; and from 1988 to 2001 he was general director of the San Francisco Opera.

41 Popper, "Opera Potpourri," 145, 95, 71.

42 *Los Angeles Times,* 20 May 1936. In an interview at the age of 90, Lert dwelt on Beethoven: "I still discover Beethoven . . . I open a score again today, and the score speaks to me, and I am amazed—to tears, sometimes—about what's in a Beethoven symphony . . . I don't know many young conductors who know what this means." Lert interview, 13 January 1976, California State University, Long Beach, Oral History of the Arts Archive.

43 Subsequent conductors have been Daniel Lewis and Jorge Mester.

44 Jones, *Los Angeles Times,* August 6, 1939.

45 Limonick, interview with the author.

46 In his teens Lawrence Foster took on the Young Musicians Foundation Orchestra with great assurance. He introduced many new works at the "Monday Evening Concerts" in the 1960s; won the Koussevitzky conducting prize at Tanglewood in 1966; made his debut with the Los Angeles Philharmonic in 1967; and two years later was named permanent guest conductor of the Royal Philharmonic Orchestra of London. Foster's music directorships have included the Houston Symphony, the Aspen Music Festival, the Monte Carlo Philharmonic, the Jerusalem Symphony Orchestra, and the Barcelona Symphony. He is a prolific opera conductor who has performed with many of the world's most renowned opera companies.

47 Much of the material on Pia Gilbert comes from interviews with the author in New York, April 13, 1997; by telephone December 8, 2001; and from Gilbert, "Life in Several Keys," oral history transcript, UCLA Library Center for Oral History Research (1988). Gilbert was interviewed in 1985–86 by Richard C. Smith.

48 Pia Gilbert and Aileene Simpson Lockhart, *Music for the Modern Dance* (Dubuque, IA: William C. Brown, 1961).

49 After her retirement from UCLA, Gilbert moved back to New York to teach in the Juilliard School of Music's graduate division, codirecting a creative workshop for choreographers and composers. Gilbert's own composing for dance and theater, influenced by John Cage and encouraged by Stravinsky's admission to her that he composed at the piano, grew to encompass commissions for the Mark Taper Forum in the Los Angeles Music Center. In 1994 her opera *Dialects* was commissioned and premiered by the Bonn Opera.

50 Jura Soyfer wrote the words. The translation, by John Lemann, originally published under the pseudonym of Georg Anders, is included in Paul Cummins, *Dachau Song: The Twentieth-Century Odyssey of Herbert Zipper* (New York: Peter Lang, 1992), 267.

51 Ibid., 220.

52 In 1984 the Crossroads School won an award from the U.S. Department of Education as one of sixty exemplary private schools in America, with its arts programs given particular commendation. The school is now known as Crossroads School for Arts and Sciences.

53 Carolyn Doepke Bennet, quoted in Cummins, *Dachau Song,* 223.

54 Zipper, quoted in Ibid., 78.

CHAPTER 6 Arnold Schoenberg

Epigraph: Arnold Schoenberg, letter to Leonard Meyer, December 5, 1940, Arnold Schoenberg Collection, Music Division, Library of Congress.

1 Schoenberg, "Circular to My Friends on My Sixtieth Birthday," in Leonard Stein, ed., *Style and Idea: Selected Writings of Arnold Schoenberg,* trans. Leo Black (Berkeley: University of California Press, 1984), 28. The circular was written in November 1934.

2 Schoenberg, letters to Fritz Stiedry, September 12, 1934, and Anton Webern, November 3, 1934, in Nuria Schoenberg Nono [Nono-Schoenberg], ed., *Arnold Schoenberg, 1874–1951: Lebensgeschichte in Begegnungen* (Klagenfurt, Austria: Ritter Klagenfurt, 1992), 310, 311.

3 Leonard Stein, interview with Vivian Perlis, June 28, 1975, Los Angeles, Oral History, American Music, Yale University.

4 "Propaganda" occurs frequently in Schoenberg's correspondence with Engel. He even refers to "a Goebbels in your firm" who should be able to undertake "propaganda" for one of his projects. Schoenberg, letter to Carl Engel, October 19, 1943, Engel Correspondence, Arnold Schönberg Center, Vienna. Schoenberg's unpublished letters, diaries, and papers were consulted while the Schoenberg archive was housed at the Arnold Schoenberg Institute in Los Angeles.

5 Schoenberg, letter to Otto Klemperer, November 8, 1934, in Erwin Stein, ed., *Arnold Schoenberg Letters,* trans. Eithne Wilkins and Ernst Kaiser (Berkeley: University of California Press, 1987), 192.

6 Schoenberg, letter to Bessie Bartlett Fraenkl, November 26, 1935, in E. Stein, *Arnold Schoenberg Letters,* 195–96.

7 Miguel de Reul, *Los Angeles Daily News,* March 22, 1935.

8 Peter Yates, "Evenings on the Roof: 1939–1954," oral history transcript, UCLA Library Center for Oral History Research (1972), 66 (Yates was interviewed in 1967 by Adelaide Tusler); and Leonard Stein, "Schoenberg as Teacher" (panel, Bard Music Festival, "Schoenberg and His World," Annandale-on-Hudson, NY, August 22, 1999).

9 Schoenberg, *Los Angeles Herald Examiner,* April 15, 1936.

10 "As a conductor, Dr. [*sic*] Schoenberg is a first rate composer," wrote Richard Saunders in the *Hollywood Citizen News,* April 15, 1937, after a Federal Symphony Orchestra concert. Isabel Morse Jones, review of Emanuel Feuermann's performance with Klemperer conducting Schoenberg's Concerto for Cello and Orchestra after M. G. Monn, *Los Angeles Times,* March 2, 1936.

11 Schoenberg, letter to Engel, November 7, 1934, Schönberg Center, Vienna.

12 Leonard Stein, talk for the Schoenberg Seminars, Arnold Schoenberg Institute, Los Angeles, December 10, 1987.

13 Jones, *Los Angeles Times,* January 9, 1938.

14 Jones, *Los Angeles Times,* October 9, 1938. Schoenberg had compared himself to Einstein in Merle Armitage, ed., *Schoenberg* (New York: G. Schirmer, 1937), 249.

15 Armitage, *Schoenberg,* 144–55 and 249–57.

16 Schoenberg, letter to Roger Sessions, December 3, 1944, in E. Stein, *Arnold Schoenberg Letters,* 223.

17 Schoenberg was annoyed that in Los Angeles Klemperer performed only his tonal works: *Verklärte Nacht;* his Suite for String Orchestra; parts of *Gurrelieder;* his arrangement of Brahms's Quartet in G Minor (which Klemperer suggested to Schoenberg);

the String Quartet Concerto after Handel's Concerto grosso op. 6, no. 7; the Cello Concerto; and the 1939 version of his Chamber Symphony No. 2 (1906–16). Klemperer's choices were conditioned by the limitations of the Philharmonic audience. For New Yorkers Klemperer planned to conduct the Violin Concerto and *Pierrot lunaire* in 1940, but his illness prevented it. He admired the String Trio but found "no point of contact" with the Piano Concerto and the *Ode to Napoleon*. Otto Klemperer, *Minor Recollections,* trans. J. Maxwell Brownjohn (London: Dennis Dobson, 1964), 46.

18 Schoenberg conducted; it was the only work he recorded in America. He was persuaded by his friend Fritz Stiedry, a more experienced conductor, to take slower tempos than he thought right. Schoenberg, letter to Moses Smith, director of Columbia Masterworks, September 30, 1940, in Schoenberg Nono, *Arnold Schoenberg,* 370. The performers were Stiedry's wife, Erika Stiedry-Wagner (recitation), Rudolf Kolisch (violin and viola), Stefan Auber (cello), Eduard Steuermann (piano), Leonard Posella (flute and piccolo), and Kalman Bloch (clarinet and bass clarinet).

19 Time and place as recollected by L. Stein, "Schoenberg as Teacher." Stein remembered being asked to coach the rabbi for his entrances.

20 Schoenberg Nono, *Arnold Schoenberg,* 385.

21 Igor Stravinsky, letter to Hugo Winter (Associated Music Publishers), March 5, 1944, in Robert Craft, ed., *Stravinsky: Selected Correspondence,* vol. 3 (New York: Knopf, 1985), 291.

22 There were nine all-Schoenberg Roof programs between 1940 and 1954; several works were given their West Coast premieres, and one received its world premiere. See "Peter Yates and the Musical Modernists," in Dorothy Lamb Crawford, *Evenings On and Off the Roof: Pioneering Concerts in Los Angeles, 1939–1971* (Berkeley: University of California Press, 1995), 114–19; and Crawford, "Peter Yates and the Performance of Schoenberg Chamber Music at 'Evenings on the Roof,'" *Journal of the Arnold Schoenberg Institute* 12, no. 2 (1989): 175–201.

23 Peter Yates, letter to Peyton Houston, April 15, 1939, Peter Yates Papers, Mandeville Special Collections Library, University of California, San Diego.

24 Schoenberg, interview with José Rodriguez, in Armitage, *Schoenberg,* 149.

25 The radio performance (by Helen Swaby Rice and Frances Mullen) took place in early 1940, before Louis Krasner's world premiere of the concerto with Leopold Stokowski and the Philadelphia Orchestra. For a fuller account, see Crawford, "Peter Yates and the Performance of Schoenberg Chamber Music."

26 Stein found Schoenberg's pride in the case of Heifetz (and others) embarrassing; the refusal of Heifetz's help occurred in 1948–49. L. Stein, interviews with the author, July 7, 1988, Los Angeles, and with Perlis, June 28, 1975.

27 See Dika Newlin, *Schoenberg Remembered: Diaries and Recollections, 1938–76* (New York: Pendragon Press, 1980), 108.

28 Nuria Schoenberg Nono, interview with Vivian Perlis, Los Angeles, February 21, 1977, Oral History, American Music, Yale University.

29 Schoenberg's letter to Carl Engel of February 6, 1941, insulted Engel and claimed that the publisher believed in Schoenberg's future but had no concern for his "present." Engel Correspondence, Schönberg Center, Vienna. For other instances, see Dorothy Lamb Crawford, "Arnold Schoenberg in Los Angeles," *Musical Quarterly* 86, no. 1 (Spring 2002): 37n39.

30 Gerhard Albersheim, a German-born pianist with a doctorate in musicology from the University of Vienna, characterized Schoenberg in Los Angeles as an "unhappy, unharmonic, and frustrated personality." Albersheim, interview with Clare Rayner, Basel, Switzerland, August 5, 1975, Oral History of the Arts Archive, California State University, Long Beach. Paul Pisk, Schoenberg's student for twenty years, who taught at the nearby University of Redlands, California, from 1937 to 1951, saw little of his former mentor. Some of his (guarded) comments in an interview were: "Schoenberg had a tendency to be so . . . absolute. . . . In personal matters he wanted so much adoring. . . . [He] was very demanding. . . . I learned everything I know from him." Pisk, interview with Clare Rayner, Hollywood, January 23, 1975, Oral History of the Arts Archive, California State University, Long Beach.

31 Schoenberg, "A Text from the Third Millennium" (February 1948), reproduced in H. H. Stuckenschmidt, *Arnold Schoenberg: His Life, World and Work*, trans. Humphrey Searle (New York: Schirmer Books, 1978), 547–48. See also *Letters of Thomas Mann, 1889–1955*, trans. Richard and Clara Winston (Berkeley: University of California Press), 396, and Thomas Mann, *The Story of a Novel: The Genesis of Dr. Faustus*, trans. Richard Winston and Clara Winston (New York: Knopf, 1961). Mann also took every opportunity to consult other musical émigrés, such as Stravinsky, Krenek, Toch, Eisler, Klemperer, and his old friend Bruno Walter, on musical matters for his novel. Further sources are in Crawford, "Arnold Schoenberg in Los Angeles."

32 Marta Feuchtwanger, "An Émigré Life: Munich, Berlin, Sanary, Pacific Palisades," oral history transcript, UCLA Library Center for Oral History Research (1976), 1068. Feuchtwanger was interviewed in 1975 by Lawrence Weschler. Paul Pisk commented that Schoenberg was a puritan who could not understand such depravity. Pisk, interview with Rayner.

33 Mann, *Story of a Novel*, 103.

34 Schoenberg, memo dated December 1950, Arnold Schönberg Center, Vienna. See Jan Maegaard, "Schönberg hat Adorno nie leiden können," *Melos* 41 (October 1974): 262–64.

35 Schoenberg, letter to Josef Rufer, December 5, 1949, and codicil to will dated October 1, 1950, quoted in Stuckenschmidt, *Arnold Schoenberg*, 508 and 513.

36 Bertolt Brecht, *Journals*, ed. John Willett, trans. Hugo Rorrison (New York: Routledge, 1993), entry for April 27, 1942.

37 Schoenberg Nono, *Arnold Schoenberg*, 387. See also Brecht's entry for July 29, 1942, in his *Journals*; Eisler, interview with Hans Bunge, May 5, 1958, in David Blake, ed., *Hanns Eisler: A Miscellany* (Edinburgh: Harwood Academic, 1995), 413–15; and Eisler, "Bertolt Brecht and Music" (1957), in Manfred Grabs, ed., *Hanns Eisler: A Rebel in Music*, trans. Marjorie Meyer (Berlin: Seven Seas, 1978), 172–73.

38 Eisler, interview with Bunge, 414; Brecht, *Journals*, July 29, 1942.

39 Schoenberg, "A Dangerous Game," *Modern Music* 22, no. 1 (November–December 1944): 3–5. As early as 1934, Schoenberg spoke publicly about his wish to abstain from politics: "I did not come in [*sic*] this marvelous country to speak from terrors, but only to forget them," in "Driven into Paradise," his speech for a reception in Los Angeles, October 9, 1934, quoted in Sabine Feisst, "Schoenberg and America," in Walter Frisch, ed., *Schoenberg and His World* (Princeton, NJ: Princeton University Press, 1999), 297.

40 Schoenberg, letters to Rufer, December 18, 1947, and May 25, 1948, in E. Stein, *Arnold Schoenberg Letters*, 252, 255.

41 Eisler, lecture for the Second International Congress of Composers and Music Critics, Prague, May 1948, in Blake, *Hanns Eisler: A Miscellany*, 160–61.

42 From Eisler's notes for his opera, *Johann Faustus*, whose text he completed the day Schoenberg died, in Blake, *Hanns Eisler: A Miscellany*, 255.

43 Schoenberg, letter to Emil Hertzka, autumn 1913, in E. Stein, *Arnold Schoenberg Letters*, 43.

44 David Raksin, interview with the author, January 14, 1997, Van Nuys, CA.

45 Gerald Strang, interview with William Weber, July 22, 1975, Oral History of the Arts Archive, California State University, Long Beach.

46 Rose Heylbut, "The Odyssey of Oscar Levant," *Etude*, December 12, 1940, 316. In 1939 Levant facilitated Schoenberg's presentation for membership in the American Society of Composers, Authors, and Publishers (ASCAP), which gathers performance royalties for its members. Levant had come to Hollywood in 1929 to work sporadically for RKO as a songwriter, making frequent trips to New York for stage and concert engagements. His Nocturne was played on Schoenberg's program by the Works Progress Administration Orchestra in 1937 and published in Henry Cowell's *New Music* orchestra series.

47 Schoenberg's datebook notes a single hour-long meeting on that date with Gershwin at 3 p.m., between lessons for Levant and the songwriter Leo Robin. In 1933 Gershwin had contributed student scholarship funds for study with Schoenberg at the Malkin Conservatory in Boston. Schoenberg's datebooks are housed in the Arnold Schönberg Center, Vienna.

48 Quoted in Schoenberg Nono, *Arnold Schoenberg*, 340. In 1938 Schoenberg wrote another tribute in a memorial book for Gershwin: "An artist is to me like an apple tree: When his time comes, whether he wants it or not, he bursts into bloom and starts to produce apples. And as an apple tree neither knows nor asks about the value experts of the market will attribute to its product, so a real composer does not ask whether his products will please the experts of serious arts. He only feels he has to say something: and says it. . . . [Gershwin] expressed musical ideas; and they were new—as is the way in which he expressed them." Merle Armitage, ed., *George Gershwin* (London: Longman's, Green, 1938), 98.

49 David Raksin remembered that Gershwin paid the Kolisch Quartet for the recording session on a United Artists soundstage. Raksin, "Schoenberg in Hollywood" (panel, Bard Music Festival, "Schoenberg and His World," Annandale-on-Hudson, NY, August 22, 1999). The concertmaster of Newman's Fox orchestra at the time of the *Kol nidre* premiere was Schoenberg's friend the composer Joseph Achron.

50 Quoted in Frisch, *Schoenberg and His World*, 302.

51 Schoenberg's datebooks, Arnold Schönberg Center. Composer George Antheil, who had moved to Hollywood late in the summer of 1936 and was himself scoring a Cecil B. DeMille film at Paramount, wrote in "On the Hollywood Front," *Modern Music* 14, no. 2 (January–February 1937): 105–8, that "Schoenberg is engaged by Paramount to score *Souls at Sea*." The project never materialized.

52 Salka Viertel, *The Kindness of Strangers* (New York: Holt, Rinehart, and Winston, 1969), 207–8.

53 Gertrud Schoenberg, letter to Rudolf Kolisch, January 11, 1935 (a probable misdate for

1936), Rudolf Kolisch Papers, MS Mus 195, Houghton Library, Harvard University; Arnold Schoenberg, letter to Alma Mahler Werfel, January 23, 1936, in E. Stein, *Arnold Schoenberg Letters,* 197.

54 Italics Schoenberg's. Schoenberg suggested Klemperer as musical director, with himself as musical advisor for the project, but the film was not made. Schoenberg, letter to Charlotte Dieterle, July 30, 1936, in E. Stein, *Arnold Schoenberg Letters,* 198–99.

55 This essay is reprinted in L. Stein, *Style and Idea,* 153–60.

56 Letters from Arnold and Gertrud Schoenberg to Rudolf Kolisch, January 16, 1939, August 21, 1943, and June 2, 1950, Kolisch Papers.

57 Julius Korngold, quoted in Brendan G. Carroll, *The Last Prodigy: A Biography of Erich Wolfgang Korngold* (Portland, OR: Amadeus Press, 1997), 292.

58 Among them, Leonard Stein, Bard Music Festival symposium, Lincoln Center, New York, November 20, 1999, and Leon Kirchner, in various conversations with the author, Cambridge, MA.

59 Schoenberg remark appended to a letter from Alfred Leonard, president of the Los Angeles Music Guild, July 9, 1945, in which the guild promotes the objective that "composers might be encouraged," Arnold Schönberg Center, Vienna; "The Blessing of the Dressing" (1948), an essay on a similar theme in L. Stein, *Style and Idea,* 385–86. In another essay, "The Young and I" (1923), Schoenberg made similar remarks about his European teaching.

60 Strang, interview with Weber.

61 Jeff Goldberg, "John Cage Interviewed," *Transatlantic Review,* May 1970, 55–56, quoted in Richard Kostelanetz, ed., *Conversing with Cage* (New York: Limelight, 1988), 8–9.

62 Peter Yates, letter to Cage, August 8, 1953, John Cage Correspondence, Deering Music Library, Northwestern University.

63 Bernice Abrahms Geiringer, interview with Andrea Castillo-Herreshoff, Santa Monica, CA, November 29, 1993, Arnold Schönberg Center, Vienna. Geiringer became a concert pianist. Karl Geiringer, the Viennese-born musicologist whom she married in 1987, began study with Schoenberg, but they came to a parting of the ways.

64 Pauline Alderman, *We Build a School of Music* (Los Angeles: Alderman Book Committee, 1989), 84, 113, 125–33.

65 At the time, Schoenberg's royalties had shrunk to $13, according to Maurice Zam, "How Schoenberg Came to UCLA," *Journal of the Arnold Schoenberg Institute* 3, no. 2 (1979): 223. Schoenberg hoped to be able to earn a salary of around $10,000. His annual UCLA salary increased over the years to $5,400.

66 Pauline Alderman estimated a class of fifteen to twenty-five. She remembered the class analyzing string quartets, composing string quartet movements, and then assembling a composite class quartet, which was performed. Alderman, "I Remember Arnold Schoenberg," in *Facets* (USC newsletter, 1976), 49–58.

67 Strang, interview with Weber.

68 Schoenberg, letter to Engel, March 27, 1938, Schönberg Center, Vienna.

69 "Plan for the organization of a Music Department MD [doctorate] at UCLA," dated July 1, 1937, quoted in Schoenberg Nono, *Arnold Schoenberg,* 364.

70 Schoenberg, letter to Robert G. Sproul, October 2, 1937, in E. Stein, *Arnold Schoenberg Letters,* 202–3.

71 Memos and letters concerning UCLA, Arnold Schönberg Center, Vienna.

72 Among the performers he would have approved were the pianists Steuermann, Buhlig, and Olga Steeb, and the violinists Achron and Louis Kaufmann. Johanna Klemperer, the wife of Otto Klemperer, was among his choice of sopranos.

73 Schoenberg, memo, "Curriculum for Composers," Arnold Schönberg Center, Vienna.

74 Schoenberg, memo to Walter Rubsamen, March 5, 1941, discussing oral examinations in the UCLA music department, Arnold Schönberg Center, Vienna.

75 Schoenberg, memo on requirements for a master's degree at UCLA, Arnold Schönberg Center, Vienna.

76 Documents, including a letter from Schoenberg to UCLA faculty colleagues, March 14, 1940, in the Arnold Schönberg Center, Vienna. There are lists of faculty and departments, a "Prospectus for Conferences on Esthetics" [*sic*], and a memo outlining Schoenberg's purpose.

77 Strang, interview with Weber.

78 Schoenberg essays, "Why No Great American Music?" (June 28, 1934) and "Teaching and Modern Trends in Music" (June 30, 1938), in L. Stein, *Style and Idea,* 176, 376.

79 "I have realized that the greatest difficulty for the students is to find out how they could compose without being inspired. . . . It seems to me the only way to help is if one shows that there are many possibilities of solving problems." Schoenberg, letter to Douglas Moore, April 16, 1938, quoted by L. Stein, Bard Music Festival symposium, Lincoln Center, New York, November 20, 1999.

80 Leonard Stein, "Schoenberg's Pupils," foreword to *Journal of the Arnold Schoenberg Institute* 8, no. 1 (1984): 3; L. Stein, Bard Music Festival symposium.

81 L. Stein, interview with Perlis.

82 Schoenberg, "Eartraining through Composing" (1939), in L. Stein, *Style and Idea,* 379.

83 Schoenberg, "Encourage the Mediocre," in José Rodriguez, ed., *Music and Dance in California* (Hollywood, CA: Bureau of Musical Research, 1940), 9–13.

84 L. Stein, interview with the author, January 22, 1997, Hollywood.

85 Leon Kirchner, interview with the author, April 11, 1997, Cambridge, MA.

86 Leon Kirchner, Bard Music Festival symposium, Lincoln Center, New York, November 20, 1999.

87 Schoenberg, "Teaching and Modern Trends in Music," 377, and "Protest on Trademark," *New York Times,* January 15, 1950, reprinted in Frisch, *Schoenberg and His World,* 307–8.

88 Dika Newlin, "Schoenberg in America, 1933–1948," *Music Survey* 1, no. 5 (1949): 131. In her student diary on December 11, 1940, Newlin recorded Schoenberg's saying about himself "that he can't teach twelve-tone writing at all. . . . He writes it instinctively and not theoretically, and could not help himself if he made a mistake, let alone helping someone else." Newlin, *Schoenberg Remembered,* 290.

89 Schoenberg, letter to Ernst Krenek, December 1 and 12, 1939, in E. Stein, *Arnold Schoenberg Letters,* 210.

90 Peter Yates, papers on Lou Harrison, Peter Yates Papers.

91 Lou Harrison, interview with Vivian Perlis, March 24, 1970, Aptos, CA, Oral History, American Music, Yale University.

92 Diary entries for March 6 and December 2, 1940, in Newlin, *Schoenberg Remembered,* 193 and 286.

93 Strang, interview with Weber; L. Stein, Bard Music Festival symposium; Schoenberg,

Fundamentals of Musical Composition, rev. ed., ed. Gerald Strang and Leonard Stein (London: Faber & Faber, 1983), 95.

94 Alderman, *We Build a School of Music,* 49–58, and Gertrud S. Zeisl, "Eric Zeisl: His Life and Music," oral history transcript, UCLA Library Center for Oral History Research (1978), 356. Gertrud Zeisl was interviewed in 1975 by Malcolm S. Cole. Eric Zeisl wanted to study privately with Schoenberg in Los Angeles but felt he could not afford the fees. Zeisl's daughter, Barbara, later married Schoenberg's son Ronald.

95 Schoenberg, *Structural Functions of Harmony,* rev. ed., ed. Leonard Stein (New York: Norton, 1969), vii.

96 Schoenberg, "First California Broadcast, Fall 1934," quoted in Frisch, *Schoenberg and His World,* 299.

97 Schoenberg, letters to Rudolf Kolisch, April 12, 1949; to Henry Allen Moe, February 22, 1945; and to Oskar Kokoschka, July 3, 1946, in E. Stein, *Arnold Schoenberg Letters,* 233, 270, 242. Letter to William Schlamm ("If it is for the masses it is not art"), July 1, 1945, quoted in Stuckenschmidt, *Arnold Schoenberg,* 472.

98 Schoenberg, "Music and Morality," *The Composer's News-Record* 7–8 (Fall–Winter 1948–49), reprinted in Frisch, *Schoenberg and His World,* 306.

99 Schoenberg, letter to O. Partosh, accepting an appointment as honorary president of the Israel Academy of Music, April 26, 1951, quoted in Alexander L. Ringer, *Arnold Schoenberg: The Composer as Jew* (Oxford: Clarendon Press, 1990), 245.

100 Schoenberg Nono interview with Perlis.

101 Schoenberg, letter to Leopold Stokowski, July 2, 1945, quoted in Leonard Stein, "Stokowski and the *Gurrelieder* Fanfare: Further Correspondence," *Journal of the Arnold Schoenberg Institute* 3, no. 2 (1979): 220.

102 Schoenberg Nono interview with Perlis.

103 Schoenberg, recorded message to the National Institute of Arts and Letters, May 22, 1947, in E. Stein, *Arnold Schoenberg Letters,* 245.

104 Virgil Thomson, "Historic Remarks," *New York Herald Tribune,* June 1, 1947.

105 Lawrence Morton, letter to Virgil Thomson, June 15, 1947, Morton Collection, Charles E. Young Research Library Special Collections, University of California, Los Angeles.

106 Lawrence Morton, "Music," *Arts and Architecture,* January 1950.

107 Albert Goldberg, *Los Angeles Times,* September 20, 1949.

108 Schoenberg, letter, "Erst nach dem Tode anerkannt werden," September 16, 1949, Peter Yates Papers. On the back of the copy sent to Yates, Schoenberg expressed his appreciation for Yates's two "excellent" articles in the *New York Times* and *Arts and Architecture.*

109 Schoenberg, letter to Hans Rosbaud, May 12, 1947, in E. Stein, *Arnold Schoenberg Letters,* 243.

110 L. Stein, interview with the author, January 22, 1997.

111 Theodor Adorno, letter to Rudolf Kolisch, June 18, 1948, Kolisch Papers.

112 Albert Goldberg, "The Sounding Board," *Los Angeles Times,* April 24, 1949.

113 Milton Babbitt, "Celebrative Speech" (1974), in *Journal of the Arnold Schoenberg Institute* 1, no. 1 (October 1976): 10. Babbitt added, "I then did not know and still do not know whether she was admonishing me or ministering me." Bryan R. Simms writes that Babbitt "looks for an explanation of musical forms within the elements

and operations of the system itself, rather than within traditional music." Simms, "Schoenberg: The Analyst and the Analyzed," in Walter Bailey, ed., *The Arnold Schoenberg Companion* (Westport, CT: Greenwood Press, 1998), 244.

114 Schoenberg, "My Evolution" (his last public lecture, presented on November 29, 1949, at UCLA), in L. Stein, *Style and Idea,* 91–92. In Schoenberg's stead, Leibowitz taught the course on twelve-tone composition at Darmstadt, using Schoenberg's works.

115 Schoenberg, "On revient toujours" (1948), in L. Stein, *Style and Idea,* 109.

116 Schoenberg, letter to Rufer, May 25, 1948, in E. Stein, *Arnold Schoenberg Letters,* 255.

117 Schoenberg's text is a fervently personal prayer: "Who am I that I should believe my / Prayer a necessity? . . . Yet I pray because I do not want to lose / The sublime feeling of unity, / Of union with you. / Oh you, my Lord, your mercy has granted us / Our prayer, as a bond, / A sublime bond between us. As a / Bliss that gives us more than any fulfillment." Translation from liner notes for *Schönberg: Das Chorwerk,* Pierre Boulez, cond., with the BBC Orchestra, Singers, and Chorus (Sony Classical S2K44571). Although the text was completed, the music remained a fragment; Rudolf Kolisch transcribed it into full score. It ends as the chorus sings, "Yet I pray . . ."

118 Schoenberg, "My Evolution," 86.

119 Albert Goldberg, "The Transplanted Composer," *Los Angeles Times,* May 14, 1950.

CHAPTER 7 **Ernst Toch**

1 Peter Yates, in his "Music" column in *Arts and Architecture,* May 1949. Other prominent composition émigré teachers in the third category were Mario Castelnuovo-Tedesco and Eric Zeisl.

2 Nicolas Slonimsky remembered Toch telling him this in 1955. Slonimsky, interview with Lawrence Weschler, September 9, 1973, Los Angeles, Toch Archive, Music Department Special Collections, University of California, Los Angeles. Toch reiterated the comment in a letter to Karl P. Brauer at Associated Music Publishers, June 27, 1960, Toch Archive.

3 Nikolai Lopatnikoff, *Proceedings of the National Institute of Arts and Letters* 1964: 501, quoted in Diane Peacock Jezic, *The Musical Migration and Ernst Toch* (Ames: Iowa State University Press, 1989), 151.

4 "Acceptance Speech on Occasion of Germany Awarding Ernst Toch the Order of Merit of the German Government, 1957," Toch Archive.

5 "Well, it killed him. That's what my mother believed," said Ernst Toch's sister, Elsa Roman, to Lawrence Weschler, Toch's grandson. Weschler's unpublished lectures, "Talks on Toch," for Cowell College, University of California, Santa Cruz, February 1973. I am indebted to Lawrence Weschler for his generosity in providing me with numerous Toch family materials, as well as to his late mother, Franzi Toch Weschler, who provided important insights for this chapter. Much of the following biographical material is from Lilly Toch, "The Orchestration of a Composer's Life," oral history transcript, UCLA Library Center for Oral History Research (1978; she was interviewed in 1971–72 by Bernard Galm). Other sources include an interview with Ernst Toch by Robert Trotter, November 8, 1962, Toch Archive, and an article by Toch, "Toward New Sonorities," in José Rodriguez, ed., *Music and Dance in California* (Hollywood, CA: Bureau of Musical Research, 1940), 25–28.

6 Richard Lert, interview with Melinda Lowrey, January 13, 1976, Oral History of the Arts Archive, California State University, Long Beach. Orchestration of film scores was left to numerous arrangers.

7 This is reported by Hugo Friedhofer, at the time a freelance arranger, who was called in to assist Toch and immediately asked to study composition with him. Friedhofer continued studying with Toch for two and a half years. Hugo Friedhofer, interview with Irene Kahn Atkins, 1974, in Linda Danly, ed., *Hugo Friedhofer: The Best Years of His Life* (Lanham, MD, 1999), 99.

8 Toch, "Sound-film and Music Theatre," *Modern Music* 13, no. 2 (January 1936): 15.

9 L. Toch, "Orchestration of a Composer's Life," 342.

10 At Paramount Toch's first uncredited full score (1937) was for *The General Died at Dawn,* an adaptation by Clifford Odets of a story about an American who helps revolutionaries in China against a warlord. At the time, Group Theatre members had begun to defect from New York to Hollywood, and this was Odets's first film.

11 North had studied with Toch in New York. Charles Previn, music director for Universal, brought his grandnephew André as a child prodigy to consult with Toch. Moore was composing for films in the early 1940s but is best known for his operas *The Devil and Daniel Webster* and *The Ballad of Baby Doe.*

12 Slonimsky, interview with Weschler; Hugo Strelitzer, interview with Weschler, September 7, 1973, Toch Archive; and Franzi Toch Weschler, letter to her son, Lawrence Weschler, February 11, 1988, courtesy of Lawrence Weschler.

13 Lilly Toch, in "Ernst Toch: A Remembrance," a documentary produced by William Malloch for KCRW, National Public Radio, Santa Monica, CA, 1974.

14 F. Weschler, letter to L. Weschler.

15 David Raksin, interview with the author, January 14, 1997, Van Nuys, CA.

16 Barbara Barclay and Malcolm Cole, "The Toch and Zeisl Archives at UCLA," *Notes* [journal of the Music Library Association] 35, no. 3 (1979): 560.

17 Toch, letter to Elizabeth Sprague Coolidge, May 31, 1939, Toch Archive.

18 Isabel Morse Jones, *Los Angeles Times,* June 16, 1940.

19 Other scores for Columbia included two war films, *First Comes Courage* (1943) and *None Shall Escape* (1944). Matthew Doran, a student of Toch's at USC, learned that in that period Toch was paid $5,000 for a film score. Matthew Doran, interview with Lawrence Weschler, July 4, 1972, Toch Archive.

20 Toch, letter (in German) to "Meine Lieben," August 4, 1942, Toch Archive.

21 L. Toch, "Orchestration of a Composer's Life," 140–41. Toch dedicated his 1921 String Quartet on the Name "Bass," op. 28, to John Bass after receiving a generous check from him.

22 Toch, letter to Coolidge, January 16, 1944, Toch Archive.

23 Toch, memo, "Film Music," typescript in Toch Archive.

24 Toch, letter to Dorothy Lawton, International Society of Contemporary Music, August 11, 1936, Toch Archive.

25 The *Pinocchio* Overture, composed in California and based on the Carlo Collodi book given to his daughter, Franzi, was intended for youth orchestras. In the 1930s and 1940s it was performed by Frederick Stock with the Chicago Symphony, Arthur Fiedler with the Boston Pops Orchestra, Eugene Goossens with the Cincinnati Symphony, John Barbirolli with the New York Philharmonic, Fritz Reiner with the CBS Radio Orches-

tra, William Steinberg with the Chicago Symphony, and Serge Koussevitzky with the Boston Symphony.

26 Jones, *Los Angeles Times,* September 6, 1936.

27 Jones, *Los Angeles Times,* April 16, 1939; Bruno David Ussher, *Los Angeles Daily News,* April 16, 1939.

28 *Big Ben,* op. 62 (variations on the chimes of London's Westminster Palace), composed by Toch on the boat from England to New York and performed by the Boston Symphony soon after the family's arrival, was performed twice by the Los Angeles Philharmonic: in 1941 by John Barbirolli, and in 1963 by William Steinberg, a particular champion of Toch's work. *Pinocchio* received three performances: in 1943 by Alexander Smallens, in 1946 by Leopold Stokowski, and in 1947, Toch's sixtieth year, by Steinberg. Alfred Wallenstein conducted the overture to Toch's opera *Der Fächer* (The Fan) in 1950 and his Second Symphony in November 1952—after the Boston Symphony's premiere. In July 1955 André Kostelanetz conducted the Hollywood Bowl Orchestra in the 1953 *Circus* Overture.

29 Toch, "The Situation of the Composer in U.S.A.," *Ars Viva,* March 1, 1950 (translator unknown), Toch Archive.

30 L. Toch, "Orchestration of a Composer's Life," 388–89. The Villa Majestic was no longer useful after World War II brought gas rationing and blackouts to the coast. It eventually was swept out to sea. Elizabeth Sprague Coolidge had helped Toch financially during his difficult time in England and had met him soon after his arrival in New York in 1934.

31 Toch, letters to Coolidge, September 11, 1938, and December 28, 1940; Coolidge, letter to Toch, September 23, 1942, Toch Archive.

32 Gerald Strang, interview with William Weber, July 22, 1975, Oral History of the Arts Archive, California State University, Long Beach.

33 Letter of agreement from Toch to Rufus von KleinSmid, n.d. 1940; von KleinSmid, letter to Toch, August 14, 1940; and Toch correspondence with Warren Scott, head of the Department of Cinema, and von KleinSmid, August 17, 22, and 25, 1940, Toch Archive. Toch's part-time assignment was to teach six units each semester as the Alchin professor in the Department of Music and two units per semester in the Department of Cinema.

34 Neutra, who had emigrated from Berlin to the United States in 1923 to work with Frank Lloyd Wright and had practiced as an architect in Los Angeles since 1925, resented the fact that the Tochs did not ask him to design their house, and the relationship between the two couples cooled. L. Toch, "Orchestration of a Composer's Life," 468.

35 Eudice Shapiro, interview with the author, January 31, 1977, Studio City, Los Angeles.

36 Toch, letter to Aaron Copland, April 9, 1942, Toch Archive.

37 L. Toch, letter to Coolidge, September 16, 1942, and E. Toch, letter to Coolidge, May 10, 1944, Toch Archive.

38 The previous five quartets, offered to his first love, his Viennese piano teacher's daughter, vanished with their owner in the Holocaust.

39 Toch, letters to Coolidge, January 8, February 2, and February 21, 1943; and L. Toch, letter to Coolidge, September 8, 1943, Toch Archive. Lilly often did what Ernst would not: she implored Coolidge for more performances of his works.

40 Coolidge wrote to Koussevitzky, Goossens, and Stokowski. Correspondence between

Toch and Coolidge, March 29 and n.d. 1943. Schoenberg also tried to help Toch in his relations with G. Schirmer, through Schoenberg's son-in-law, Felix Greissle. Toch, letter to Greissle, August 8, 1945. All correspondence in Toch Archive.

41 Toch, quoted in Lawrence Weschler's introduction to the Dover reprint of Toch's *The Shaping Forces of Music: An Inquiry into the Nature of Harmony, Melody, Counterpoint, Form* (New York: Dover Publications, 1977), iii.

42 Toch, letter to Coolidge, January 19, 1942, Toch Archive.

43 Toch, quoted by Nicolas Slonimsky in liner notes for *The Music of Ernst Toch,* issued in the Discopaedia series Masters of the Bow: The Kaufman Legacy, vol. 6 (MB 1051).

44 Toch, *Shaping Forces of Music,* xxi.

45 Toch, "The Credo of a Composer," translated [by the composer?] from an article in *Deutsche Blaetter,* Santiago, Chile, April 1945. Toch Archive.

46 Toch's last film score was for *The Unseen* (1945), produced by John Houseman for Paramount, a mystery film on which Raymond Chandler collaborated.

47 Toch, letter to Coolidge, June 17, 1946, Toch Archive.

48 Toch, letters to Coolidge, July 17, 1945, June 17, 1946, and September 30, 1946, Toch Archive. Toch's Twelfth String Quartet was based on Eduard Mörike's poem, "Verborgenheit," the text of which mirrored his severe depression: "I do not know what it is I cry for—it is unknown sorrow; only through my tears can I see the beloved light of the sun."

49 L. Toch, "Orchestration of a Composer's Life," 450–51.

50 Drafts of letters to Max Krone by Toch, March 22, 1947, in Toch Archive; and by Coolidge, March 25, 1947, in Coolidge Collection, Library of Congress. Krone's reply to Toch, April 16, 1947, is in the Toch Archive, and a carbon copy is in the Coolidge Collection.

51 Toch, interview with Trotter.

52 L. Toch, "Orchestration of a Composer's Life," 438, 584.

53 Toch, letter to Douglas Moore, June 15, 1942, and Moore reply, July 17, 1942, Toch Archive.

54 Mantle Hood, quoted in Jezic, *The Musical Migration,* 105–6. Hood was a student at UCLA at the time.

55 Mel Powell, interview with Lawrence Weschler, January 11, 1973, Valencia, CA, in Toch Archive. Powell, widely known in his earlier life as a jazz pianist, recorded for Tom and Jerry cartoons in the 1940s. After his study with Hindemith, he taught at Mannes College of Music, at Queens College, and at Yale. He was the founding dean of the School of Music at the California Institute of the Arts in Valencia, where he taught composition until his death. He was awarded the Pulitzer Prize in 1990. Others of Toch's students during this period were German-born Peter Jona Korn, Aurelio de la Vega, and Matthew Doran.

56 Toch, letters to Harold Spivacke, March 22 and August 15, 1947; letters from Coolidge to Toch, August 24, 1947, and n.d.; and Toch to Coolidge, September 1947, Toch Archive.

57 See Dorothy Lamb Crawford, *Evenings On and Off the Roof: Pioneering Concerts in Los Angeles, 1939–1971* (Berkeley: University of California Press, 1995), 81, 90, 94, 206–7.

58 Shapiro, an accomplished graduate of the Curtis School of Music, was concertmaster of both the Paramount and RKO studio orchestras in the war years.

59 L. Toch, "Orchestration of a Composer's Life," 722; and Lawrence Morton, "Monday Evening Concerts," oral history transcript, UCLA Library Center for Oral History Research (1973), 388 (Morton was interviewed in 1966 by Adelaide Tusler). Also see Crawford, *Evenings On and Off the Roof*, 206–7.

60 L. Toch, "Orchestration of a Composer's Life," 724. Toch's recent *Sonatinetta*, op. 84 (for flute, clarinet, and bassoon), his early *Tanz-Suite*, op. 30 (a sextet for winds, strings, and percussion), and a repeat performance of his Piano Quintet alternated in the program with a Mozart piano trio and solo piano works by Mozart.

61 Toch, undated memo, and Zurich radio broadcast, 1964, Toch Archive.

62 This poignant piece was to serve as a farewell in memorial gatherings for Franzi's husband Irving Weschler (1962), Ernst (1964), Lilly (1972), and Franzi herself (1988). Franzi wrote in an autobiographical sketch that she had often felt peripheral in the family, for her parents had already been married twelve years when she was born, and during her childhood they were both consumed with Ernst's career. Franzi Weschler, letter to Lawrence Weschler, February 11, 1988, only months before her death in an automobile accident; courtesy of Lawrence Weschler.

63 Toch, letter to Coolidge, November 15, 1951, Toch Archive.

64 Toch, letter to Robert Trotter, February 19, 1950, Toch Archive.

65 "I am one of those composers who have little if anything to say [about a work] beyond what they try to express by their compositions themselves. . . . I felt guided by axioms of architectural and dramatic nature rather than by considerations of any set musical pattern, old or new." Toch, program notes for the Boston Symphony Orchestra premiere of the Second Symphony with Charles Munch, December 12 and 13, 1952, in Toch Archive.

66 Toch, program notes for the American premiere of the First Symphony by William Steinberg and the Pittsburgh Symphony Orchestra, January 1953, Toch Archive.

67 Schweitzer, then seventy-seven, had recently returned to his work in Africa from Europe. Toch did not know Schweitzer at the time, but his colleague at USC, the Austrian harpsichordist Alice Ehlers, had a long-standing friendship with Schweitzer, and provided the USC School of Music with information about his activities in Africa.

68 Toch told this to Robert Trotter and added, "He dictated [the symphony] to me. . . . I adored him for what he did." Toch, interview with Trotter.

69 Toch, program notes for the Boston Symphony premiere of the Second Symphony.

70 Toch, letter to Coolidge, November 22, 1952, Toch Archive.

71 Toch, letter to Richard F. French, Associated Music Publishers, May 27, 1954, Toch Archive (Toch's introduction was attached to the letter); Shapiro, interview with the author. The quartet, completed in 1953, was published in 1961 by Mills Music.

72 Albert Goldberg, "The Sounding Board," *Los Angeles Times*, January 24, 1954.

73 Among them were William Schuman, Peter Mennin, Virgil Thomson, Douglas Moore, Norman Dello Joio, Ernst Krenek, Geoffrey O'Hara, and John Vincent.

74 L. Toch, "Orchestration of a Composer's Life," 592.

75 Lawrence Weschler, "My Grandfather's Last Tale," *Atlantic Monthly*, December 1996, 14.

76 Lilly Toch felt this was "nearly an accusation," provoked by "a certain feeling of bitterness . . . of lonesomeness. . . . 'I am doing what I have to do, what has been given to me. Do you do more?'" L. Toch, "Orchestration of a Composer's Life," 571–72.

77 Toch, line notes for 1957 Capitol recording of the Third Symphony by the Pittsburgh

Symphony Orchestra, conducted by William Steinberg; and Toch on the Third Symphony, radio station RIAS, Berlin, December 7, 1962. Both excerpts quoted in Toch, *Placed as a Link in This Chain: A Medley of Observations,* ed. Mantle Hood (Los Angeles: Friends of the UCLA Library, 1971), 20, 27.

78 L. Toch, "Orchestration of a Composer's Life," 574–78.

79 Lawrence Weschler, in radio documentary, "Ernst Toch: A Remembrance," KCRW Santa Monica, CA, produced by William Malloch.

80 Toch, interview with Trotter.

81 Toch, note written at the MacDowell Colony, summer 1953; letter to Marian MacDowell, February 10, 1955, Marian Nevins MacDowell Collection, Music Division, Library of Congress.

82 This text was rejected by Antal Dorati, who premiered the work with the Minneapolis Symphony in November 1957. Los Angeles' first performance was by the USC student orchestra, conducted in October 1962 by Ingolf Dahl during USC's celebrations of Toch's seventy-fifth birthday.

83 Toch, letter to Arthur Cohn, April 25, 1959, Toch Archive. Mills Music (later Belwin Mills) published much of Toch's late-period music, including study scores of the symphonies, and agreed to extend advances to him.

84 Lengyel had developed as a playwright among a group of radical artists affiliated with the Thalia Theater, which initiated an extraordinary renaissance in the arts in Budapest in the first decade of the twentieth century. His scenario provided the basis for Béla Bartók's 1917 ballet *The Miraculous Mandarin.*

85 Toch, letter to Karl F. Bauer, Associated Music Publishers, July 11, 1960, Toch Archive; and Lawrence Weschler, liner notes for *Ernst Toch: Symphonies 5–7* by the Rundfunk Sinfonieorchester Berlin, Alun Francis, cond. (cpo 999 389-2).

86 Toch, letter to Cohn, July 18, 1962, Toch Archive.

87 Strelitzer also recalled the awe, respect, and admiration musicians in the city felt for Toch: "His ear for orchestral color was unbelievable. . . . He handled all the elements of music with amazing ease." Strelitzer, interview with Weschler.

88 In part because of flaws in the text, Toch's opera, retitled *Scheherazade,* was not premiered until November 1995 in Bautzen, Germany.

89 L. Toch, "Orchestration of a Composer's Life," 798. The diary entry was dated May 26, 1962.

90 Lion Feuchtwanger, *Jephta and His Daughter,* trans. Eithne Wilkins and Ernst Kaiser (London: Hutchinson, 1958), 266.

91 Weschler, liner notes for *Symphonies 5–7.* All seven of Toch's symphonies have been recorded for the cpo label by the Rundfunk Sinfonieorchester (Radio Symphony Orchestra) of Berlin, conducted by Alun Francis.

92 Toch's own daughter, Franzi, was a graceful gymnast, whom he often asked to perform for guests. Franzi Toch, conversation with the author, 1987, Santa Monica, CA. Her own tragic destiny was to fight multiple sclerosis with incredible success, only to be run over and killed by a car in 1988.

93 Doran, interview with Weschler.

94 Toch, letter to Nicolas Slonimsky, September 6, 1963, in Slonimsky Collection, Music Division, Library of Congress.

95 Toch, letter to Cohn, November 5, 1963, Toch Archive.

96 Toch, letter to Serge Koussevitzky, October 6, 1942, in Serge Koussevitzky Archive, Music Division, Library of Congress.

97 Toch, "Just What is Good Music?" address presented at the University of Minnesota, November 9, 1954, Marian Nevins MacDowell Collection, Music Division, Library of Congress. This address was developed from a statement Toch found and quoted from Thorton Wilder's novel, *The Bridge of San Luis Rey:* "The whole purport of literature is the human heart. Style is but the faintly contemptible vessel in which the bitter liquid is recommended to the world."

98 Strelitzer, interview with Weschler.

CHAPTER 8 European Composers in the "Picture Business"

1 Kurt Weill, "The Future of Opera in America," *Modern Music* 14, no. 4 (May–June 1937): 188.

2 Mario Castelnuovo-Tedesco, "Music and Movies" (February 29, 1940), trans. from the French by Blair Sullivan and edited by James J. Westby in the newsletter of the Society for the Preservation of Film Music, *Cue Sheet* 15, no. 1, January 1999.

3 Hanns Eisler, "A Musical Journey through America," quoted in Manfred Grabs, ed. *Hanns Eisler: A Rebel in Music,* trans. Marjorie Meyer (Berlin: Seven Seas, 1978), 90–91.

4 Igor Stravinsky, interview in *La Gazzetta del Popolo,* June 1, 1935, quoted in Vera Stravinsky and Robert Craft, *Stravinsky in Pictures and Documents* (New York: Simon and Schuster, 1978), 324.

5 Gottfried Reinhardt, "It Was No Paradise," in Carol Merrill-Mirsky, ed., *Exiles in Paradise,* Hollywood Bowl Museum, exh. cat. (Los Angeles: Los Angeles Philharmonic Association, 1991), 71–79.

6 Hans J. Salter, quoted in Tony Thomas, *Film Score: The Art and Craft of Movie Music* (Burbank, CA: Riverwood Press), 94, 168–69. Salter was a graduate of the Vienna Academy of Music who had held positions at the Vienna Volksoper and the Berlin State Opera. In Hollywood he was musical director or arranger for 150 scores, contributed uncredited stock music to some 416 others, and received four Academy Award nominations for his own scores.

7 Fred Karlin, *Listening to Movies: The Film Lover's Guide to Film Music* (New York: Schirmer Books, 1994), 183–84.

8 Hindemith wrote to his wife that he felt himself cured of the idea of working in Hollywood and that he certainly couldn't produce anything artistically worthwhile for such an ego as Disney's. Hindemith, letters to Gertrud Hindemith, March 1939, in *Paul Hindemith Briefe,* ed. Dieter Rexroth (Frankfurt: Fischer, 1982), 208–10, 220–21. Other composers taking refuge in America who found little satisfaction in their work in the film studios included Paul Dessau, Werner Heymann, Darius Milhaud, Karol Rathaus, Alexandre Tansman, and Eric Zeisl.

9 Alexandre Tansman, "Autobiography," trans. Jill Timmons and Sylvain Frémaux, *Polish Music Journal* 1, no. 1 (Summer 1998), http://www.usc.edu/dept/polish_music/PMJ/issue/1.1.98/contents.html.

10 "Among them were *Gaslight, Green Dolphin Street,* a lot of Lassie movies," said Raksin. David Raksin, interview with the author, January 14, 1997, Van Nuys, CA. A scherzo from Tansman's score for *Flesh and Fantasy* received a concert performance by the Janssen Orchestra in 1944; Isabel Morse Jones wrote, "It is a delightful fragment of ex-

ceptional delicacy and beauty and is one of the few screen excerpts worth a concert performance." Jones, *Los Angeles Times,* January 13, 1944.

11 Copland wrote, "I was an outsider to Hollywood, but I did not condescend to compose film music. . . . I was accepted. . . . But I was puzzled [in 1939] at why film composers were so isolated from the rest of the music world!" Aaron Copland and Vivian Perlis, *Copland: 1900 through 1942* (New York: St. Martin's/Marek, 1984), 300. Max Steiner and Alfred Newman, the most prolific film composers of the time, were not "concert composers."

12 Charlie Chaplin, Harold Lloyd, Claudette Colbert, Maurice Chevalier, Marlene Dietrich, Gary Cooper, Carole Lombard, Bette Davis, Ernest Hemingway, Ernst Lubitsch, Bing Crosby, Buster Keaton, Joan Crawford, and Jimmy Stewart signed his guest book. Friedrich Hollaender, *Vom Kopf bis Fuss: Mein Leben mit Text und Musik* (Munich: Kindler, 1965), 329.

13 Völker Kühn, *Spötterdämmerung: Vom langen Sterben des grossen kleinen Friedrich Hollaender* (Berlin: Parthas, 1997), 98.

14 Much of this biographical material is taken from Hollaender's memoir, *Vom Kopf bis Fuss.*

15 Here is Hollywood as it first appeared to Hollander, described in Hollander, *Those Torn from Earth* (New York: Liveright, 1941), 263–64: "Most obstinate little scrap of earth on this hemisphere and not to be catalogued. . . . Different from any conception a stranger might have of it. Different, too from the way those living there would like it to be. You can even say: it's different from the way it is. Today different from yesterday, tomorrow it'll be different again. Hellish heaven, delightfully depressing, artificially natural. Gossipy solitude, naive and perverted, all at the same time. Full of flower miracles, dirty tricks and kidnappings. Religious and stinko. Church-yards and metropolis. . . . Rain comes but once a year. Violent. Deluge following the downpour rapidly. Dropping as out of gigantic buckets. One quick wash-up. For the remaining ten months: sunshine; identical, every day. . . . Twelve o'clock noon, and hundreds of thousands of dark-lensed goggles flutter into sight: the city of the blind."

16 Hollaender, *Vom Kopf bis Fuss,* 337. Hollander's collaborators in Europe had included the expressionist writers Else Lasker-Schüler, Frank Wedekind, Ernst Toller, Walter Hasenclever, Fritz von Unruh, Erich Kästner, Lion Feuchtwanger, and Karl Kraus; the preeminent cabaret writers Kurt Tucholsky, Walter Mehring, Marcellus Schiffer, and Klabund; the screenwriter Billy Wilder; and the top cabaret performers Josephine Baker, Fritzi Massary, Carola Neher, Margo Lion, Ernst Busch, Rosa Valetti, Blandine Ebinger, and Hedi Schoop—the last two of whom became his first and second of five wives.

17 Ibid., 333–38.

18 Allen Weinstein and Alexander Vassiliev, "Double Agent/Hollywood Hustler: The Case of Boris Morros," in *The Haunted Wood: Soviet Espionage in America—The Stalin Era* (New York: Random House, 1999), 110–19. During his time at Paramount, Morros negotiated with Hindemith (who thought him full of hot air), Schoenberg, and Stravinsky, and conducted a work by Toch in its first performance. He left Paramount in 1939 for other musical ventures, became a double agent in 1945, and later wrote a book titled *My Ten Years as a Counterspy* (New York: Viking Press, 1959).

19 Hollaender, *Von Kopf bis Fuss,* 321.

20 Hollander's first American song was "Moonlight and Shadows," first sung by Dorothy

Lamour in *The Jungle Princess*. Sung by Bing Crosby on the radio, for many weeks it was number one on the Hit Parade. Crosby also sang "My Heart and I," from the film *Anything Goes*, on the Hit Parade. "You Leave Me Breathless" was another Hit Parade song. "Little Joe," and "See What the Boys in the Backroom Will Have," to lyrics by Frank Loesser, were Hit Parade songs from *Destry Rides Again* (Columbia, 1939), starring Marlene Dietrich and Jimmy Stewart.

21 Hollaender, *Von Kopf bis Fuss*, 330, 343–49.

22 Ibid., 339, 346, 350, 366–67, 373–77.

23 Arthur Morton, interview with Fred Karlin, in Karlin, *Listening to Movies*, 36.

24 Hollander's Academy Awards were for a 1942 score, *Talk of the Town* (Columbia), and a 1953 score, *The 5,000 Fingers of Dr. T* (Columbia). His Academy nominations were for a 1937 song, "Whispers in the Dark," in the Paramount film *Artists and Models*, and a 1948 song, "This Is the Moment," for the Twentieth Century-Fox film *Lady in Ermine*.

25 Kühn, Spötterdämmerung, 109.

26 John Waxman, interview with author, Westport, CT, April 14, 1997.

27 Hollander, letter to Mischa Spoliansky, March 25, 1955, in Kühn, *Spötterdämmerung*, 118–19.

28 Waxman interview.

29 Ibid.

30 The others were *Suspicion, Paradine Case,* and *Rear Window*.

31 These were for *The Young in Heart* (two nominations, 1938), Selznick; *Rebecca* (1940), Selznick; *Dr. Jekyll and Mr. Hyde* (1941), MGM; and *Suspicion* (1941), RKO.

32 Among his other war films were *Air Force* (1943), *Destination Tokyo* (1944), *God Is My Co-Pilot* (1945), and *Hotel Berlin* (1945).

33 The musical was called *Scampolo, ein Kind der Strasse* (Scampolo, a Child of the Streets).

34 Franz Waxman, interview, *Film Music Notes* 3, no. 8 (May 1944), and Waxman, "The New Music of Motion Pictures," *Film Music Notes* 5, no. 1 (September 1945). *Film Music Notes* was initiated in 1941 by the National Federation of Music Clubs to review film scores and to interview composers. It was a mimeographed periodical, chiefly for composers and orchestrators, produced by the musicians themselves, with news items, fan mail, biographies, reviews, interviews, and occasional articles (some of them reprints) by newspaper critics. By 1944 it was sponsored by the National Film Music Council.

35 Franz Waxman, letter to director Fred Zinnemann and producer Henry Blanke, 1958, in the Zinnemann Special Collection, Margaret Herrick Library, Academy of Motion Picture Arts and Sciences, Beverly Hills, CA, quoted in Karlin, *Listening to Movies*, 192.

36 *Newsweek*, June 20, 1955. Some of Waxman's other films include *To Have and Have Not*, 1945; *Humoresque* and *The Two Mrs. Carrolls*, 1947; *Come Back, Little Sheba*, 1952; *Prince Valiant* and *The Silver Chalice*, 1954; *Mr. Roberts*, 1955; *Crime in the Streets*, 1956; *Peyton Place*, 1957; *Sayonara*, 1958; and *Sunrise at Campobello* and *Cimarron*, 1960.

37 Waxman's chief objective was to build a forum for his conducting, which he felt was "a calling," according to his son, John Waxman. He tried to break out of film music, hiring Arthur Judson as his agent to develop a conducting career. As conducting positions in other states materialized, however, he realized that he did not want to drop his festival, which was filling a need in Los Angeles. His solution was to develop an international conducting career alongside his heavy load in the film studios and his intense

work for the festival. By 1962 he had conducted the Leningrad Philharmonic, as well as other major orchestras in Vienna, Hamburg, Paris, Zurich, Israel, Holland, Moscow, and Kiev. John Waxman, interview with author; and publicity for the Second International Los Angeles Music Festival, 1962, Franz Waxman Papers, Special Collections Research Center, Syracuse University Library.

38 He felt a particular affinity for these composers. Between 1950 and 1960 Waxman conducted the West Coast premiere of Mahler's Ninth and Third Symphonies, the American premiere of the Adagio from the Tenth Symphony, and—as a celebration of Mahler's centennial—the enormous Second ("Resurrection") Symphony. He gave Shostakovich's Second Piano Concerto its American premiere (with Oscar Levant as soloist) and also conducted Shostakovich's Eleventh and Fourth Symphonies.

39 In the 1961 festival Craft marked the tenth anniversary of Schoenberg's death by conducting the composer's arrangement of two Bach chorale preludes and the first West Coast performance of his *Die glückliche Hand*. On the same program Marilyn Horne sang the American premiere of four Schoenberg songs.

40 Both performed signature pieces: Lehmann sang Richard Strauss's *Four Last Songs* in one of her farewell programs, and Szigeti appeared as soloist in the Brahms Violin Concerto.

41 Andreas-Ludwig Priwin came to the United States in 1939 when he was ten. His granduncle, Charles Previn, was musical director for Universal Studios. André Previn was an orchestrator for MGM starting at the age of sixteen, and he composed for films beginning in 1949.

42 This work was originally composed for Warner Brothers' 1946 film *Humoresque*. It was frequently performed by Jascha Heifetz.

43 Compact discs of recordings of the Los Angeles festival concerts are being issued in a limited edition by Themes and Variations Records. *The Song of Terezin* has appeared on a compact disc in the *Entartete Musik* series issued in Germany (Decca 289 460 211-2).

44 David Raksin, interview with the author, January 14, 1997, Van Nuys, CA.

45 Jessica Duchen, *Erich Wolfgang Korngold* (London: Phaidon Press, 1996), 43, 155; Gottfried Reinhardt, *The Genius: A Memoir of Max Reinhardt by His Son* (New York: Knopf, 1979), 72–73.

46 Luzi Korngold, *Erich Wolfgang Korngold: Ein Lebensbild* (Vienna: Elisabeth Lafite, 1967), 22; interviews with Teddy Krise, September 5, 1980, Los Angeles, and with Eleanor Aller, August 30, 1975, Los Angeles, in Brendan G. Carroll, *The Last Prodigy: A Biography of Erich Wolfgang Korngold* (Portland, OR: Amadeus Press, 1997), 239, 287.

47 L. Korngold, *Korngold,* 70.

48 Linda Danly, ed., *Hugo Friedhofer: The Best Years of His Life* (Lanham, MD: Scarecrow Press, 1999), 46–47.

49 L. Korngold, *Korngold,* 72, 74.

50 Carroll, *Last Prodigy,* 275. Various sources give differing numbers for Korngold's total number of films. Brendan Carroll's list seems the most reliable; see *Last Prodigy,* 403–6.

51 Tony Thomas, *Music for the Movies* (New York: A. S. Barnes, 1973), 132. There is a full analysis of the score for *Anthony Adverse* in William Darby and Jack DuBois, *American Film Music: Major Composers, Techniques, Trends, 1915–1990* (Jefferson, NC: McFarland, 1990), 161–83.

52 Korngold's fan mail increased with *Juarez* (1939), the second of three film scores he

composed for director William Dieterle. Other popular scores included those for the swashbucklers *The Sea Hawk* (1940) and *The Sea Wolf* (1942); *Kings Row* (1941); and *The Constant Nymph* (1942), for which he wrote the tone poem *Tomorrow* (later published and recorded separately). "A Musician's Fan Mail," in *Film Music Notes* 4, no. 5 (February 1945).

53 Erich Wolfgang Korngold, letter to Hal Wallis and Henry Blanke, February 11, 1938, quoted in Karlin, *Listening to Movies,* 190.

54 Korngold supported not only his and his father's households but also his wife's family.

55 Reinhardt, *Genius,* 243; Duchen, *Korngold,* 194.

56 L. Korngold, *Korngold,* 79–80; Korngold, interview with Ross Parmenter, October 24, 1942, quoted in David Josephson, "The Exile of European Music: Documentation of Upheaval and Immigration in the *New York Times,*" in Reinhold Brinkmann and Christoph Wolff, eds., *Driven into Paradise: The Musical Migration from Nazi Germany to the United States* (Berkeley: University of California Press, 1999), 144n74.

57 Korngold, "Some Experiences in Film Music," in José Rodriguez, ed., *Music and Dance in California* (Hollywood, CA: Bureau of Musical Research, 1940), quoted in Carroll, *Last Prodigy,* 298–99; L. Korngold, *Korngold,* 79–80.

58 Korngold, letter to Mervyn LeRoy, July 1, 1941, Franz Waxman Papers (reprinted by permission of the Korngold Estate). Korngold, who was particularly respected and liked by his colleagues, sent copies of this letter to his fellow film composers. In answer to my query as to when the academy responded to this protest, reference librarian Lucia Schultz could give no precise year but noted that membership in the Music Branch, created in 1941, grew from nine in 1941 to fifty-five in 1942. E-mail reference request, August 8, 2007, Margaret Herrick Library, Academy of Motion Picture Arts and Sciences, Beverly Hills, CA.

59 Friedhofer's full statement about Korngold is quoted in Duchen, *Korngold,* 182–83.

60 Aller interview in Carroll, *Last Prodigy,* 287.

61 L. Korngold, *Korngold,* 85.

62 A facsimile score of String Quartet No. 3 in D Major, op. 34 (Mainz: Schott Music, 1978), ED 6822.

63 Korngold took the modal love song for the third movement from the film *The Sea Wolf* (1941). He used the second rondo theme in the fourth movement in the film *Devotion* (1943) about the Brontë sisters.

64 Carroll, *Last Prodigy,* 330.

65 Korngold died in Hollywood in 1957, six months after his sixtieth birthday. In the 1970s his son George Korngold, a producer for Victor Records, reissued a series of recordings of his father's film scores, and the Korngold revival began.

66 George Antheil, "On the Hollywood Front," *Modern Music* 14, no. 1 (November–December 1936): 47–48; 14, no. 2 (January–February 1937): 82–88; 15, no. 1 (November–December 1937): 48; and 15, no. 3 (March–April 1938): 187–88.

67 Kurt Weill, letters to Lotte Lenya, January 28–June 11, 1937, in Kurt Weill and Lotte Lenya, *Speak Low (When You Speak Love): The Letters of Kurt Weill and Lotte Lenya,* ed. and trans. Lys Symonette and Kim H. Kowalke (Berkeley: University of California Press, 1996), 196, 198, 200, 205, 209, 214, 231, 234, 236, 246, and 442. In 1937 the Group Theatre broke up its New York operations because of the Depression. Several members, including the director Harold Clurman, went to Hollywood at that time.

68 Weill, letter to Cheryl Crawford, 1937, in Weill and Lenya, *Speak Low,* 221n3. Weill earned $7,500 in 1937 for music (composed before shooting, and never used) intended for a film about the Spanish Civil War on a screenplay (which was also thrown out) by Clifford Odets, one of his friends from the Group Theatre. Weill was paid $10,000 for *You and Me* in 1938. In 1943 he won $283,000 from Paramount for film rights to his musical play *Lady in the Dark,* the highest sum paid for such rights to that date. In 1944 his salary from Twentieth Century-Fox for songs for *Where Do We Go From Here?* to Ira Gershwin's lyrics was $2,500 per week, and in 1945 he earned the same amount working for United Artists on another of his Broadway musicals, *One Touch of Venus.*

69 Weill, letters to Lenya, April–May 1938, in Weill and Lenya, *Speak Low,* 253, 258, 261, 268–69.

70 Ronald Taylor, *Kurt Weill: Composer in a Divided World* (Boston: Northeastern University Press, 1991), 285.

71 Film composer Bronislaw Kaper, quoted in Karlin, *Listening to Movies,* 190. Kaper explained Stothart's deity at MGM: "Because he was blond, had blue eyes, and in the eyes of the executives, he was a showman."

72 Clara Castelnuovo-Tedesco, "La sua fede," oral history transcript, UCLA Library Center for Oral History Research (1982), 26; Clara Castelnuovo-Tedesco was interviewed in 1981 by Rebecca Andrade. See also a translation by Harvey Sachs from Mario Castelnuovo-Tedesco's unpublished autobiography, "Una vita di musica," in *Grand Street* 9, no. 1 (Autumn 1989): 150–65; and Castelnuovo-Tedesco, program note, quoted in James J. Westby, "Castelnuovo-Tedesco in America: The Film Music" (Ph.D. diss., University of California, Los Angeles, 1994), 269n19.

73 Mario Castelnuovo-Tedesco, trans. Harvey Sachs, in Sachs, *Music in Fascist Italy* (New York: Norton, 1987), 185.

74 At MGM, Castelnuovo-Tedesco contributed to such films as *Gaslight,* several *Lassie* films, *The Yearling, The Picture of Dorian Gray, Above Suspicion, Bataan, Song of Russia,* and *A Journey for Margaret.*

75 Westby, "Castelnuovo-Tedesco in America," 268.

76 I am grateful to the late Lorenzo Tedesco for access to the original Italian version of "Hollywood," a section of the unpublished manuscript of his father's autobiography, "Una vita di musica," and for providing me with other materials as well as an interview in West Los Angeles on February 11, 1997. James J. Westby has guided me to his translation and edited version of "Hollywood," published in *Cue Sheet* 15, no. 1 (January 1999), from which I have quoted where necessary in the preceding passages.

77 Isabel Morse Jones, *Los Angeles Times,* February 22, 1946.

78 C. Castelnuovo-Tedesco, "La sua fede," 76. In all, Castelnuovo-Tedesco composed six operas. The first four were set to his own libretti: *La mandragola* (after Macchiavelli), op. 20 (1920–23); *Bacco in Toscana* (after Francesco Redi), op. 39 (1925–26); *The Merchant of Venice* (after Shakespeare), op. 181 (1956); and *All's Well That Ends Well* (after Shakespeare), op. 182 (unperf.).

79 Castelnuovo-Tedesco, "The Composer Speaks," in David Ewen, ed., *The Book of Modern Composers,* 2nd ed. (New York: Knopf, 1950), 392–93.

80 Castelnuovo-Tedesco was on the faculty of the Los Angeles Conservatory (which later became the California Institute of the Arts), yet he refused an opportunity to head the

conservatory of music in Florence. He spent summers there but valued most of all the security he had won for his family by becoming an American citizen.

81 Leslie T. Zador, *Eugene Zador: A Catalogue of His Works* (San Diego: Leslie T. Zador, 1978), 4. I am grateful to the composer's son, Les T. Zador, and to Mrs. Eugene Zador for providing me with helpful materials, including recordings of the composer's works, during an extensive interview at the late composer's home in Beverly Hills on June 3, 1997.

82 Clyde Allen, liner notes for a compact disc of Zador's music (Cambria CD 214501100, 1997). Reviews of *Christopher Columbus* from the *New York Post, New York Journal, Daily News,* and *Newsweek* are quoted in the liner notes.

83 Carl Hein, director of the New York College of Music, letter to Miklós Rózsa, August 21, 1940; Eugene Zador, letter to Jascha Heifetz, November 21, 1941, and Heifetz, response to Zador, December 10, 1941; Eugene Ormandy, letters to Rózsa, February 12 and 27, November 15, and December 28, 1943, in Miklós Rózsa Papers, Special Collections Research Center, Syracuse University Library, Syracuse, NY. Ormandy and the Philadelphia Orchestra performed Zador's *Pastorale and Tarantella* in 1942 and Rózsa's *Pastorale and Danza* in 1943.

84 For an example, Zador used a pseudonym for the original score he composed in collaboration with Bronislaw Kaper for the 1940 anti-Nazi war film *The Mortal Storm.* According to his son, Zador never felt particularly Jewish and tried to keep this aspect of his heritage hidden in the anti-Semitic climate of the times in the United States. Leslie Zador and Mrs. Eugene Zador, interview with the author, June 3, 1997, Los Angeles.

85 The operas written in America were *Christopher Columbus* (1939; first performed in New York), *The Virgin and the Fawn* (1965; Los Angeles), *The Magic Chair* (1965; Baton Rouge), *The Scarlet Mill* (1967; New York), and *Yehu, a Christmas Legend* (1974; Los Angeles). In addition, *The Inspector General* (1928) was performed in Los Angeles.

86 Thomas Mann, letter to Zador, n.d., quoted in biographical notes for L. Zador, *Eugene Zador,* 5. Mann's original four novels were published between 1933 and 1943, then published together under the title of the first novel. A recent edition is Mann, *Joseph and His Brothers,* trans. John E. Woods (New York: Knopf, 2005).

87 These works were Rhapsody for Cimbalom and Orchestra (1969), Concerto for Trombone and Orchestra (1966), *Fantasia Hungarica* for Contrabass and Orchestra (1970), and a Concerto for Accordion and String Orchestra with Percussion (1972).

88 Biographical notes in L. Zador, *Eugene Zador,* 6.

89 English translation by Elie Siegmeister of Eisler's 1935 speech, "Address to a Solidarity Concert," in Manfred Grabs, ed., *Hanns Eisler: A Rebel in Music,* trans. Marjorie Meyer (Berlin: Seven Seas, 1978), 70–71.

90 The score was conducted by Oscar Levant, who composed a song for it. This highly expensive and time-consuming project, *Pete Roleum and His Cousins,* with animation, puppets, stereoscopic technicolor, and stereophonic sound, excited wide attention. Berndt Heller, "Eislers Filmmusikalisches wirken im americanischen Exil, 1939 bis 1947" (unpublished ms., 1998), 2–3. I am indebted to Berndt Heller for sharing his work in this field with me.

91 These films included Joris Ivens's silent film *Rain* (1929); feature films on two John Steinbeck novels, *The Grapes of Wrath* (1940, originally scored by Alfred Newman) and

The Forgotten Village (1941); as well as *The Long Voyage Home* (1940), a war movie derived from stories by Eugene O'Neill and originally scored by Richard Hageman. Excerpts were also chosen from wartime newsreels, short nature films on icebergs and a snowstorm, and a short documentary on children, *A Child Went Forth,* directed and filmed for the project by Losey.

92 Eisler's criticism of his teacher had changed to that of "standing Schoenberg on his head somewhat, so that his feet are on the firm ground of our social links with the (historical) struggle of the masses for a new world." From Hanns Eisler, in *Musik und Politik: Schriften 1924–1948* (Leipzig: Deutscher Verlag für Musik, 1973; Munich: Rogner & Bernhard, 1973), 394; quoted in Albrecht Betz, *Hanns Eisler: Political Musician,* trans. Bill Hopkins (Cambridge: Cambridge University Press, 1982), 1.

93 Hanns Eisler and Theodor Adorno, *Composing for the Films* (repr., London: Athlone Press, 1994), 138.

94 Eisler's full quote on "vanishing" film music: "Cinema music should sparkle and glisten. It should attain the quick pace of the casual listening imposed by the picture, and not be left behind. . . . By displaying a tendency to vanish as soon as it appears, motion-picture music renounces its claim that it is *there,* which is today its cardinal sin." Eisler, *Composing for the Films,* 1st ed. (New York: Oxford University Press, 1947), 133. See also 4–5, 8–9, 13, 16, 32, 33, and 37.

95 Alfred Frankenstein, "Triumph of the 12-Tone System," *Film Music Notes* 4, no. 2 (November 1944).

96 Eisler's drinking created such tension for his wife, Lou, that she wanted to divorce him. Marta Feuchtwanger, "*An Émigré Life: Munich, Berlin, Sanary, Pacific Palisades,*" oral history transcript, UCLA Library Center for Oral History Research (1976), 1275–76, 1280. Feuchtwanger was interviewed in 1975 by Lawrence M. Weschler.

97 Eisler had composed for the Group Theatre in his New York period.

98 Bertolt Brecht, *Arbeitsjournal,* July 20, 1945, quoted in Hans-Michael Bock, "Paul Dessau, Komponist: Biographie," in *CineGraph Lexikon zum deutschsprachigen Film,* http://www.cinegraph.de/lexikon/Dessau_Paul/biografie.html (accessed December 15, 1998). Claudia Gorbman reports that "Eisler generally received two to three thousand dollars for a film score—on the lower end of the pay scale—plus about five dollars per score page of orchestration; so an Eisler job meant financial savings for the studio," in her article, "Hanns Eisler in Hollywood," *Screen* 32 no. 3 (Autumn 1991): 273. Dessau, born in Hamburg, worked under Klemperer and Walter as a conductor in Cologne and Berlin. He won the Schott Prize for composition in 1925 and conducted and composed film scores from 1926 to 1968. He fled to France in 1933. In the United States from 1939, he commuted from a New Jersey chicken farm to work as a music copyist in New York City. In 1942 Dessau moved to California to collaborate with Brecht. In 1948 he returned to Germany and settled in East Berlin.

99 Jean Renoir, in conversation with Albert Betz, September 1973, quoted in Heller, "Eislers Filmmusikalisches wirken," 15.

100 Eisler, letter to Clifford Odets, December 17, 1945, and Charlie Chaplin, remark to Eisler, quoted in Betz, *Hanns Eisler,* 195, 197.

101 The California fact-finding committee was chaired by State Senator John B. Tenney, who had been president of the Los Angeles branch of the American Federation of Musicians (Local 40). Tenney testified before HUAC in March 1947, goading HUAC's

chairman, John Rankin, into action, according to Neal Gabler in *An Empire of Their Own: How the Jews Invented Hollywood* (New York: Crown, 1988), 380–81.

102 *Investigation of Un-American Propaganda Activities in the United States: Louis F. Budenz,* Revised Hearings before the Committee on Un-American Activities, House of Representatives, 79th Cong., on House Res. 5, November 22, 1946 (Washington, DC: U.S. Government Printing Office, 1947). The correspondence and published writings of Ruth Fischer are in the Ruth Fischer Papers (MS Ger 204), Houghton Library, Harvard University. Gerhart Eisler had been a leading functionary in the German Communist Party and had held a position in the Soviet Comintern, for which he had carried out undercover missions in revolutionary Spain and China. As a member of the French Resistance, he had been imprisoned in France from 1939 until 1941, when he had emigrated to the United States, where he wrote articles for *The New Masses* and *The Daily Worker* under an assumed name.

103 Louise Eisler-Fischer, "Eisler in der Emigration" in *Ver Sacrum* 4 (1972), quoted in Manfred Grabs, ed., *Wer war Eisler* (Berlin: Europaeische Buch, 1983), 450.

104 *Los Angeles Examiner,* April 26, 1947.

105 Martha Gellhorn, "Cry Shame . . . !" *New Republic,* October 6, 1947, 20.

106 Hearings before the Committee on Un-American Activities: House of Representatives, 80th Congr., 1st session, September 25–27, 1947 (Washington, DC: U.S. Government Printing Office, 1947).

107 Thomas Mann, letter to Agnes Meyer, October 10, 1947, in Mann, *Letters, 1889–1955,* ed. and trans. Richard and Clara Winston (Berkeley: University of California Press, 1990), 390.

108 Betz, *Hanns Eisler,* 203.

109 Grabs, *Wer war Eisler,* 148–50.

CHAPTER 9 Issues of Identity: Ernst Krenek, Eric Zeisl, and Ingolf Dahl

1 Alfred Price Quinn, *B'nai B'rith Messenger,* May 29, 1942.

2 Ernst Krenek, letter to Dimitri Mitropoulos, January 10, 1948, at Ernst Krenek Institute, Vienna; formerly in the Ernst Krenek Archive, Mandeville Special Collections Library, University of California, San Diego. Krenek created the program of graduate studies in music at Hamline University.

3 Ernst Krenek, "The Past Once Was New," in Richard Drake Saunders, ed., *Music and Dance in California and the West* (Hollywood, CA: Bureau of Musical Research, 1948), 136. The school was sponsored by Captain G. Allan Hancock, a wealthy, eccentric, but generous marine biologist whose desire to play the cello had provided USC with a campus building in which were combined both studies in marine biology and a concert auditorium. At this time, Captain Hancock left Los Angeles to give his attention to a new flying school in Santa Maria, CA. Pauline Alderman, *We Build a School of Music* (Los Angeles: Alderman Book Committee, 1989), 232. Klaus Pringsheim (the twin brother of Thomas Mann's wife, Katia) had emigrated in 1931 to Japan, where he taught composition. He lived in Hollywood from 1946 to 1951, teaching and touring, then returned to Japan, where he taught again from 1951 to 1961 and died in 1972. As a conductor, Pringsheim had held distinguished positions at the Vienna Opera under Mahler, as well as in Prague and at Max Reinhardt's theater in Berlin.

4 Beverly Grigsby, interview with the author, February 1, 1997, Los Angeles.

5 Telephone interview by the author with Elizabeth Surace, one of Krenek's students, in February 1997.

6 Krenek, letter to Rudolph Kolisch, October 13, 1948, in Rudolf Kolisch Papers, MS Mus 195, Houghton Library, Harvard University.

7 Krenek, interview with Clare Rayner, February 11, 1975, Palm Springs, CA, Oral History of the Arts Archive, California State University, Long Beach; Krenek, interview with Vivian Perlis, March 22, 1975, Palm Springs, CA, Oral History, American Music, Yale University.

8 Krenek, quoted in Albert Goldberg, "The Transplanted Composer," *Los Angeles Times,* May 21, 1950.

9 Krenek, "Self-Analysis," *New Mexico Quarterly* 23, no. 1 (Spring 1953): 50.

10 Paul Fromm, an émigré from Germany to the United States in 1938, was a successful wine merchant and music lover who started the Fromm Music Foundation in 1952. In 1955 he commissioned Krenek's twelve-tone opera *The Bell Tower,* op. 153; in 1957 *Sestina,* op. 161; and in 1959 *Quaestio temporis,* op. 170. The latter two works were composed in the highly cerebral style of total serialism.

11 Krenek, "Self-Analysis," 33.

12 Krenek, letter to Kolisch, December 20, 1957, Kolisch Papers.

13 Albert Goldberg, *Los Angeles Times,* February 22, 1961; Burton L. Karson, *Los Angeles Daily News,* April 6, 1966; Walter Arlen, *Los Angeles Times,* November 29, 1967, and January 5, 1969; and Martin Bernheimer, *Los Angeles Times,* December 9, 1970, and January 13, 1971.

14 John L. Stewart, telephone interview with the author, February 12, 2001.

15 Krenek, *Spätlese* for voice and piano, op. 218 (1973), text by Krenek in program for *The Krenek Festival,* Santa Barbara, CA, April 8–15, 1979. Krenek's translation used the words "transitory" and "uncautiously" for the bracketed "transient" and "incautiously."

16 Krenek, "Looking Back on 75 Years as a Mainstream Misfit," *Los Angeles Times,* February 2, 1975; Krenek, interview with Andrew Porter, April 1979, at the University of California, Santa Barbara, in *Ernst Krenek Newsletter* 3, no. 1 (Fall 1992): 14–17.

17 Will Ogden, program notes, and excerpt from Krenek text, "The Dissembler," in *Entartete Musik: Banned by the Nazis* (Los Angeles: Los Angeles Philharmonic Association, 1991), 18. This booklet was published for the Philharmonic exhibits, concert, and symposium on "degenerate music."

18 Krenek's friend, originally interviewed by the author in 1997, later declined to be acknowledged as the source of the report of Krenek's confession. Gladys Krenek spoke with me by phone on the matter in 1997 and 2007. Krenek's statement on his memoirs is in "Self-Analysis," 5. The memoirs are available in the Music Division of the Library of Congress; restrictions may be in place.

19 Krenek, interview with Perlis.

20 John L. Stewart, *Ernst Krenek: The Man and His Music* (Berkeley: University of California Press, 1991), 273.

21 Krenek, "Self-Analysis," 7–8.

22 Goldberg, "Transplanted Composer," *Los Angeles Times,* May 28, 1950.

23 Gertrud S. Zeisl, "Eric Zeisl: His Life and Music," oral history transcript, UCLA Library Center for Oral History Research (1978), 43; Gertrud Zeisl was interviewed in 1975 by Malcolm S. Cole. Alma Mahler-Werfel was in Los Angeles from 1940 until 1952, when

she moved to New York City. Her third husband, the writer Franz Werfel, died of heart failure in 1945.

24 I am indebted to Barbara Zeisl Schoenberg for an interview with her, January 30, 1997, and for sharing materials from her father's archives with me.

25 Malcolm S. Cole and Barbara Barclay, *Armseelchen: The Life and Music of Eric Zeisl* (Westport, CT: Greenwood Press, 1984), 49.

26 Friml, a Czech composer, had been in the United States since 1906 and in Hollywood since 1925. His first operetta, *The Firefly* (1912), included the popular "Donkey Serenade," and his *Rose-Marie* (1924) contained the celebrated "Indian Love Call" duet. Later popular operettas included *The Vagabond King* (1925), and *The Three Musketeers* (1928). In her oral history, Gertrud Zeisl reports that Friml was so rich that he had become too lazy to write down his music. He composed on the piano, recorded, and brought the music to Eric to transcribe. Later Zeisl did orchestrations for Friml, for which he received regular union wages. G. Zeisl, "Eric Zeisl," 229, 232, 267.

27 Ibid., 4, 237.

28 Barbara Zeisl Schoenberg, interview with the author.

29 G. Zeisl, "Eric Zeisl," 260, 295.

30 Cole and Barclay, *Armseelchen*, 32.

31 Barbara Zeisl Schoenberg, interview with the author.

32 Gertrud Zeisl found Schoenberg "a good person . . . [who] gives without reservation from the treasure of his insight. . . . He burns with an electric fire, which makes him dart like a flame and which by its nature tends to give out shocks which only the stupid would resent." Gertrud Zeisl's diary, quoted in Cole and Barclay, *Armseelchen*, 51–52.

33 As there were few or no survivors from these death camps, the émigrés and their descendants could learn little about what happened there. It is thought that Eric's father, Siegmund Zeisl, was sent to Treblinka or Maly Trostinec (near Minsk). There is no trace of what happened to his wife, Malvine. Around 3,100 Austrian Jews were deported from Theresienstadt to Treblinka in early October 1942. In 1970 the commandant of Treblinka, Franz Stangl, was sentenced to life imprisonment in Düsseldorf. I am grateful to E. Randol Schoenberg, Eric Zeisl's grandson, for communicating this information to me.

34 Zeisl's *Requiem Ebraico*, conducted by Lawrence Foster with the Rundfunk-Sinfonieorchester Berlin for the *Entartete Musik* series of compact discs, was issued by Decca on London Classics 289460 211-1.

35 Critic Albert Goldberg found Zeisl's four songs "rather conventional in contrast to the Stravinsky, but [they] had interest as examples of fluent choral writing." *Los Angeles Times*, November 28, 1949.

36 G. Zeisl, "Eric Zeisl," 262–63.

37 Leon Levitch, "A Twentieth-Century Romantic Temperament," oral history transcript, UCLA Library Center for Oral History Research (1984), 84. Levitch was interviewed in 1980 by Thomas Bertonneau.

38 Eric Zeisl, letters to Lawrence Morton, April 26 and May 11, 1953, and October 4 and 14, 1956, in Lawrence Morton Collection, Charles E. Young Research Library Department of Special Collections, University of California, Los Angeles.

39 G. Zeisl, "Eric Zeisl," 336.

40 Ibid., 344–47. The problems with tenure may have resulted from new regulations man-

dating that courses be taken in order to be certified as a qualified teacher. According to Zeisl's biographer, Malcolm S. Cole, Krenek took over Zeisl's courses at Los Angeles City College.

41 Etta Linick's husband also befriended Ingolf in Zurich and agreed to aid Ingolf's visa application for citizenship by signing an affidavit guaranteeing his support, as did Etta's brother-in-law.

42 Michael Tilson Thomas, "A Tribute to Ingolf Dahl," *Los Angeles Times*, September 20, 1970. "Dahl was an inspiring teacher; over and above the subject matter, he showed his students about the practical application of humanism, that is, how to let humanistic concerns infuse your daily existence." Tilson Thomas, quoted in Deena and Bernard Rosenberg, *The Music Makers* (New York: Columbia University Press, 1979), 190.

43 Ingolf Dahl, "Tough Concerts in Los Angeles," *Modern Music* 20, no. 3 (March–April 1943): 191.

44 See Dorothy Lamb Crawford, *Evenings On and Off the Roof: Pioneering Concerts in Los Angeles, 1939–1971* (Berkeley: University of California Press, 1995), for many references to Dahl's activities with "Evenings on the Roof" and "Monday Evening Concerts."

45 Anthony Linick, *The Lives of Ingolf Dahl* (Bloomington, IN: AuthorHouse, 2008), 88. I am deeply grateful to Anthony Linick for generously providing me with the 1996 manuscript of this biography of his stepfather.

46 Dahl, diary note, October 13, 1940, in Linick, *Lives of Ingolf Dahl*, 101.

47 Dahl's letter was addressed to "Dear Friends," to be circulated in December 1942. Ibid.

48 Igor Stravinsky, *Poetics of Music in the Form of Six Lessons*, trans. Arthur Knodel and Ingolf Dahl (Cambridge: Harvard University Press, 1947). Dahl's work with Victor Borge in 1946 interfered with preparation of this translation, which Dahl then shared with Knodel, a French scholar completing his Ph.D. at USC at the time.

49 Isabel Morse Jones quoted excerpts from Dahl's article in the *Los Angeles Times*, February 6, 1943. The article appeared in *Script* magazine, with no date given by Jones.

50 Dahl's articles appeared in *Modern Music, Musical Digest*, and *Dance Index* in 1946–47. *Scènes de ballet* was a fifteen-minute work for which Stravinsky received a $5,000 commission from the Broadway entrepreneur Billy Rose. Dahl later told some of his students that he had orchestrated the resulting work. Leroy Southers, one of Dahl's students at the time, wrote to Anthony Linick that Ingolf reported that "He would go to Stravinsky's house every day or so, pick up the piano sketches, and take them home to orchestrate them." Linick, *Lives of Ingolf Dahl*, 49.

51 Ibid., 161.

52 Ibid., 104.

53 Ibid., 114.

54 Jones, *Los Angeles Times*, March 3, 1943. At the time, Copland was in Hollywood working on *The North Star*, an extravagant Samuel Goldwyn film about the 1941 Nazi invasion of the Soviet Ukraine, a film score assignment from which Stravinsky had withdrawn.

55 Anthony Linick, liner notes for *The Music of Ingolf Dahl* (Argo [Decca] CD 444459-2). This work, written at a time when there were few composers writing concert music for brass quintet, has been credited with reviving interest in the ensemble.

56 Linick, *Lives of Ingolf Dahl*, 108.

57 Ibid., 548–49.

58 Ibid., 106. The Marcus family had left Germany before the war and remained in Sweden. Dahl's *Variations on a Swedish Folktune* was published in 1946 by *New Music.*

59 Alderman, *We Build a School of Music,* 214. Dahl served with great effect on faculty committees, as director of an annual festival of contemporary music, and as musical director for the university's radio station, KUSC.

60 These included the chamber vocal work *Trois petites chansons,* sung by USC student Marilyn Horne in 1954; the West Coast premiere of *Perséphone* and the "Dumbarton Oaks" Concerto, both performed by the USC student orchestra for Stravinsky's seventy-fifth birthday in 1957; *Three Japanese Lyrics* in 1963; and *Symphonies of Wind Instruments* in 1970.

61 The Toccata was the last movement of Dahl's discarded 1943 Piano Suite. The Hymn was inspired by his new love for a Los Angeles art student.

62 Linick, *Lives of Ingolf Dahl,* 166.

63 Dahl, letters to Bill Colvig, February 28, 1960, and Gilbert Chase, July 27, 1963, quoted in Linick, *Lives of Ingolf Dahl,* 343–44 and 391.

64 He also received grants from the National Institute of Arts and Letters, several composing fellowships at the MacDowell Colony and the Huntington Hartford retreat, ASCAP awards, and two Guggenheim Fellowships. He received invitations to join other music faculties and in 1967 the USC Excellence in Teaching Award.

65 Albert Goldberg, *Los Angeles Times,* October 23, 1963 (after an October 12 performance by Dahl, Alexander Murray, and Laurence Lesser). Dahl, letter to Colvig, February 28, 1960, and diary, 1962, quoted in Linick, *Lives of Ingolf Dahl,* 343–44.

66 Michael Tilson Thomas, interview with the author, July 1, 1988, Laguna Beach.

67 Dated July 30, 1966, this comment appeared on a "Think Sheet" at the end of Dahl's journal. Linick, *Lives of Ingolf Dahl,* 621–22.

68 The *Elegy Concerto* for violin and chamber orchestra was published by Schott as completed by Donal Michalsky.

69 Linick, *Lives of Ingolf Dahl,* 448, 501.

70 Ibid., 498, 501, 613.

71 Lawrence Morton, letter to Peter Yates, October 10, 1971, Peter Yates Papers, Mandeville Special Collections Library, University of California, San Diego.

CHAPTER 10 Stravinsky in Hollywood

1 George Antheil, *Bad Boy of Music* (Garden City, NY: Doubleday, Doran, 1945), 30, 32.

2 Paul Rosenfeld quote, and Igor Stravinsky interview with Eugen Jolas for *The Tribune* [*sic*], in Vera Stravinsky and Robert Craft, *Stravinsky in Pictures and Documents* (New York: Simon and Schuster, 1978), 254, 256.

3 "Igor Stravinsky Arrives," *Los Angeles Examiner,* February 18, 1935. Alexis Kall (under the name Kahl) had obtained a doctorate in music from Leipzig ca. 1906–7 with a dissertation on "The Philosophy of Music According to Aristotle." In Los Angeles he had established himself as a piano teacher and musicologist.

4 Isabel Morse Jones, *Los Angeles Times,* February 28, 1935.

5 The interview was recorded and transcribed; see William H. Rosar, "Stravinsky at MGM," in Clifford McCarty, ed., *Film Music I* (Los Angeles: Film Music Society, 1998), 108, 109–22.

6 In early March telegrams from New York City, Dagmar Godowsky (the daughter of the

pianist Leopold Godowsky) recommended that Morros confer and close a contract with Stravinsky. The sum is erased but still visible in a copy of the contract, which, with copies of the accompanying correspondence, is in the Lawrence Morton Collection, Charles E. Young Research Library Department of Special Collections, University of California, Los Angeles.

7 George Antheil, "On the Hollywood Front," *Modern Music* 14, no. 1 (January–February 1937): 105–8, and 15, no. 1 (November–December 1937): 48–50.

8 Stravinsky's wife, Catherine, had been diagnosed with tuberculosis in 1925 and remained ill; his oldest daughter died of the disease in November 1938, his wife in March 1939. His mother died of pneumonia in June 1939.

9 Charles M. Joseph, *Stravinsky and Balanchine: A Journey of Invention* (New Haven, CT: Yale University Press, 2002), 161.

10 Robert Craft, letter to William H. Rosar, April 2, 1984, Lawrence Morton Collection.

11 Jones, *Los Angeles Times,* August 11, 1940.

12 Miklós Rózsa, *Double Life* (New York: Wynwood Press, 1982), 113; Alfred Frankenstein, "Stravinsky in Beverly Hills," *Modern Music* 19, no. 3 (March 1942): 178.

13 This music was intended for the hunting scene in which Rochester first meets Jane (Joan Fontaine). Bernard Herrmann ultimately composed the score for *Jane Eyre.*

14 Robert Craft states that sections of all three movements of this symphony were intended for films, as was part of Stravinsky's two-piano Sonata (1943–44), in V. Stravinsky and Craft, *Pictures and Documents,* 357. Twentieth Century-Fox's Alfred Newman won an Academy Award for his score for *The Song of Bernadette.*

15 From an interview with Stravinsky by Dahl in *Musical Digest,* September 1946, quoted in Charles M. Joseph, *Stravinsky Inside Out* (New Haven, CT: Yale University Press, 2001), 128. Film composer David Raksin refuted Stravinsky's statement in an article, "Hollywood Strikes Back," in the same periodical, January 1948.

16 Gerald Strang, "Schoenberg, Mahler and Others in Los Angeles," *Modern Music* 14, no. 4 (1937): 223–24.

17 This production was repeated by the Ballet Theatre (later the American Ballet Theatre) at the New York Metropolitan Opera House that year.

18 Jones, "Sharps and Flats," *Los Angeles Times,* September 2, 1939, and *Los Angeles Times,* August 8, 1940. Adolph Bolm and his wife were among the Stravinskys' closest friends in California.

19 Joseph, *Stravinsky and Balanchine,* 161.

20 Craft eliminated from his edition of Vera's diary her records of "a few thousand lunches and dinners at which they were hosts or guests" to the glitterati of Hollywood; when he settled in their household in 1949 he took it upon himself to "get rid of the movie people." Robert Craft, ed., *Dearest Bubushkin: The Correspondence of Vera and Igor Stravinsky, 1921–1954, with Excerpts from Vera Stravinsky's Diaries, 1922–1971,* trans. Lucia Davidova (New York: Thames & Hudson, 1985), 10; Craft, *An Improbable Life: Memoirs* (Nashville: Vanderbilt University Press, 2002), 114.

21 Joseph Szigeti, *With Strings Attached: Reminiscences and Reflections* (New York: Knopf, 1947), 126.

22 Artur Rubinstein, *My Many Years* (New York: Knopf, 1980), 498, 561. After Rachmaninoff's death the next year, Stravinsky's name appeared on the committee formed to honor the composer-pianist's memory through a fund for exceptional pianistic talent.

23 Diary entries for August 1, 1955, and July 14, 1958, in Christopher Isherwood, *Diaries,* vol. 1, *1939–60* (New York: HarperCollins, 1996), 516, 763.

24 Lawrence Morton, "Stravinsky in Los Angeles," in Orrin Howard, ed., *Festival of Music Made in Los Angeles* (Los Angeles: Los Angeles Philharmonic Association, 1981), 83. Several of the musicians interviewed for this chapter remembered being given their first experiences with alcohol of any sort by Igor when they arrived at the Stravinsky home for rehearsals with Craft. The effect erased their memories of rehearsing.

25 Babitz probably first met Stravinsky when, as a member of the violin section of Klemperer's Philharmonic, he had obtained an autographed photo of Stravinsky conducting the orchestra in 1935. See V. Stravinsky and Craft, *Pictures and Documents,* 325. Stravinsky wrote to his new American publishers that "an important" group of studio musicians place themselves "at the service of composers and conductors who wish to do readings of their scores," and would like to play his Violin Concerto. He subsequently conducted this group in several readings of new works. Stravinsky, letter to Ernest Voigt of Associated Music Publishers, September 30, 1940, in Robert Craft, ed., *Stravinsky: Selected Correspondence,* vol. 3 (New York: Knopf, 1985), 276.

26 In 1938 Dushkin, half American, had settled in New York, where he continued his interest in new literature for his instrument, commissioning Bohuslav Martinů's *Suite concertante* (1944) and William Schuman's Violin Concerto (1947–59).

27 Alfred Frankenstein, "Stravinsky in Beverly Hills," *Modern Music* 19, no. 3 (March 1942): 180.

28 Jones, *Los Angeles Times,* February 14, 1941.

29 The periods included September 1942, August–December 1943, October–December 1944, and January–June 1945. Correspondence on Nadia Boulanger's arrangements with the Longy School of Music in Cambridge, Massachusetts, can be found in the school library's Boulanger Collection. The correspondence with her former student Melville Smith, named director of the school in 1941 at her strong suggestion, is of particular interest. It was he who (along with a California doctor) provided excuses for her absences while maintaining her continuance in the school catalogue.

30 Bruno Monsaingeon, *Mademoiselle: Conversations with Nadia Boulanger,* trans. Robyn Marsack (Boston: Northeastern University Press, 1988), 40 and 88.

31 Jones, *Los Angeles Times,* December 5, 1943; Stravinsky, letter to Francis Poulenc, January 10, 1946, in Craft, *Stravinsky: Selected Correspondence,* vol. 2 (New York: Knopf, 1984), 212.

32 Ingolf Dahl, "Stravinsky in 1946," *Modern Music* 23, no. 3 (Summer 1946): 159–69.

33 Leon Kirchner, interview with Janet Baker-Carr, *Harvard Magazine* 77, no. 4 (November 1974): 47. After the Genesis Suite, Stravinsky probably did not see Schoenberg again until Franz Werfel's funeral in 1945. In 1951, at Alma Mahler Werfel's house, he was shown the composer's death mask soon after it was taken by her daughter, sculptor Anna Mahler.

34 Ernst Krenek, *Music Here and Now,* trans. Barthold Fles (New York: Norton, 1939), 85–87.

35 Leonard Stein, "Schoenberg and 'Kleine Modernsky,'" in Jann Pasler, ed., *Confronting Stravinsky: Man, Musician, and Modernist* (Berkeley: University of California Press, 1986), 310–24; Gerald Strang, interview with William Weber, July 22, 1975, Oral History of the Arts Archive, California State University, Long Beach; Mel Powell, interview

with Vincent Plush, May 13, 1983, Van Nuys, CA, Oral History, American Music, Yale University. Powell was a pianist and staff composer for MGM at the time.

36 Albert Goldberg, *Los Angeles Times*, October 28, 1949; Robert Craft, "Assisting Stravinsky," *Atlantic Monthly*, December 1982, 73. Byrns's orchestra premiered Stravinsky's Mass the following month with the Roger Wagner Chorale.

37 Stein, "Schoenberg and 'Kleine Modernsky,'" 315; Leonard Stein, interview with the author, January 22, 1997, Hollywood.

38 Notes from Dahl's conversations with Stravinsky, Ingolf Dahl Archive, Doheny Memorial Library, University of Southern California. This exchange was dated December 9, 1957; Dahl was conducting the USC student orchestra in Stravinsky's *Perséphone* and the "Dumbarton Oaks" Concerto. I am grateful for the help of Brian Harlan in finding this material.

39 Vera Stravinsky, letter to Eleanor Schreiber, August 19, 1940; Vera Stravinsky, diary excerpt, June 15, 1941, in Craft, *Dearest Bubushkin*.

40 Stephen Walsh, *Stravinsky: The Second Exile, France and America, 1934–1971* (New York: Knopf, 2006), 242.

41 Robert Craft, letter to Patricia Jean Craft, August 1, 1949, and Stravinsky, letters to Arthur Sachs, November 15 and December 2, 1949, quoted in Craft, *Improbable Life*, 103, 107, 110.

42 Stravinsky, letter to Boosey & Hawkes, October 23, 1953, in Craft, *Stravinsky: Selected Correspondence*, vol. 3, 378. The Roof program that inspired Stravinsky included a work by Giovanni Gabrieli, the Mendelssohn Octet for strings, and Monteverdi's *Combattimento di Tancredi e Clorinda*, conducted by Craft.

43 Craft, "Assisting Stravinsky," 71.

44 *The New Classicism* was performed by Craft on October 25, 1954; the translation was by Shibley Boyes.

45 Craft, "A Personal Preface," *The Score* 20 (June 1957): 7–13.

46 The union forbade "double stringing" in July 1960. Correspondence in 1960 between Morton in Paris and Stein, courtesy of Leonard Stein.

47 Stravinsky, letters to Boosey & Hawkes, July 7, 1954, and to Ralph Hawkes, August 4, 1948, in Craft, *Stravinsky: Selected Correspondence*, vol. 3, 380, 324.

48 Peter Yates, letter to Peyton Houston, February 3, 1954, in Peter Yates Papers, Mandeville Special Collections Library, University of California, San Diego.

49 Lawrence Morton, memo to Dahl, n.d. [1960?], courtesy of Anthony Linick.

50 Stravinsky, letter to Boosey & Hawkes, November 17, 1957, in Craft, *Stravinsky: Selected Correspondence*, vol. 3, 409. Morton, "Current Chronicle," *Musical Quarterly* 43, no. 4 (October 1957): 536.

51 Isherwood, *Diaries*, vol. 1, 704.

52 Dahl, diary note, February 7, 1957, in Linick, *Lives of Ingolf Dahl* (1996 ms.), 391–92.

53 Monsaingeon, *Mademoiselle*, 83.

54 Dahl, notes dated May 8, 1958; n.d.; June 28, 1958, "after Statler dinner"; 1963, "Dinner at Luau"; n.d., "talking about Haieff." All in Ingolf Dahl Archive.

55 Isherwood, June 18, 1960, *Diaries*, vol. 1, 866.

56 Dorothy Lamb Crawford, *Evenings On and Off the Roof: Pioneering Concerts in Los Angeles, 1939–1971* (Berkeley: University of California Press, 1995), 215. The date was April 6, 1964. The work was programmed at the last moment; the performers actually

rehearsed it backstage while the concert was in process, and Stravinsky made changes during the rehearsal.

57 Etta Dahl, letter to Lawrence Morton, June 12, 1960, in Morton Collection.

58 Donald Christlieb, "Remembrances of Lawrence Morton" (self-published ms. prepared for interview broadcast on KUSC, October 12, 1987): 13–16; courtesy of Donald Christlieb, quoted with permission of Anthony Christlieb.

59 Peter Yates, "Igor Stravinsky: The Final Maturity," *TriQuarterly Review* 28 (Fall 1973): 368.

60 Michael Tilson Thomas, interview with the author, July 1, 1988, Laguna Beach, CA; also quoted in Walsh, *Stravinsky: The Second Exile*, 525.

61 Peter Yates, letter to Peyton Houston, February 3, 1954, in Peter Yates Papers.

Epilogue

1 Peter Yates, "Music," *Arts and Architecture*, April 1952, quoted in Dorothy Lamb Crawford, *Evenings On and Off the Roof: Pioneering Concerts in Los Angeles, 1939–1971* (Berkeley: University of California Press, 1995), 13.

INDEX

Page references in italic type refer to photographs